KEY QUESTIONS ABOUT
CHRISTIAN FAITH

KEY QUESTIONS ABOUT CHRISTIAN FAITH

Old Testament Answers

JOHN GOLDINGAY

B
Baker Academic
a division of Baker Publishing Group
Grand Rapids, Michigan

Published by Baker Academic
a division of Baker Publishing Group
P.O. Box 6287, Grand Rapids, MI 49516-6287
www.bakeracademic.com

Printed in the United States of America

Library of Congress Cataloging-in-Publication Data

Goldingay, John.
   Key questions about Christian faith : Old Testament answers /
John Goldingay.
     p. cm.
   Includes indexes.
   ISBN 978-0-8010-3954-6
   1. Christianity—Miscellanea. 2. Bible. O.T.—Miscellanea. 3. Bible.
O.T.—Theology. I. Title.
   BR96.G65 2010
   230′.3—dc22
                                                          2010015702

10 11 12 13 14 15 16   7 6 5 4 3 2 1

green
press
INITIATIVE

TABLE OF CONTENTS

ACKNOWLEDGMENTS

The author thanks each of the various journals and publishers listed below for their kind permission to use previously published work.

Chapter 1: "Who Is God?" is a paper written for a meeting of the Doctrine Commission of the Church of England. Much of its material appears in revised form in the commission's report *We Believe in God* (London: Church House / Wilton, Conn.: Morehouse-Barlow, 1987). © Archbishop's Council. Copyright. copyright@c-of-e.org.uk. Reproduced by permission.

Chapter 4: "What Does It Mean to Be Human?" is taken from John Goldingay, "Being Human," in *Encounter with Mystery: Reflections on l'Arche and Living with Disability*, edited by Frances Young, published and copyright © 1997 by Darton Longman and Todd, Ltd, London, and used by permission of the publishers.

Chapter 5: "Can We Make Sense of Death and Suffering?" is taken from John Goldingay, "Wisdom on Death and Suffering," in *Understanding Wisdom*, edited by Warren S. Brown, published and copyright © 2000 by the Templeton Foundation, London, and used by permission of the publishers.

Chapter 7: "What Is the People of God? (A Narrative Answer)" is taken from John Goldingay, "A Contextual Study of the Theme of 'The People of God' in the Old Testament," in *Theological Diversity and the Authority of the Old Testament*, © 1986 by Wm. B. Eerdmans Publishing Company, Grand Rapids, Michigan. Reprinted by permission of the publisher, all rights reserved.

Chapter 8: "What Is the People of God? (An Answer in Images)". Reprinted by permission. "Images of Israel in the Writings," John Goldingay, in *Studies in Old Testament Theology*, edited by R. L. Hubbard et al., © 1992, Thomas Nelson Inc. Nashville, Tennessee. All rights reserved.

Chapter 9: "What Is a Covenant?" is taken from John Goldingay, "Covenant," in *The New Interpreter's Dictionary of the Bible*, edited by Katharine Doob Sakenfeld, © 2006 Abingdon Press Nashville, Tennessee. Adapted and used by permission.

Chapter 11: "Why Circumcision?" is taken from John Goldingay, "The Significance of Circumcision," in the *Journal for the Study of the Old Testament* 88 (2000): 3–18. Used by permission of SAGE Publications, Ltd, London.

Chapter 12: "Shall I Tithe Net or Gross?" is taken from John Goldingay, "Jubilee Tithe," in *Transformation* 19 (2002): 198–205. Used by permission of SAGE Publications, Ltd, London.

Chapter 13: "Was the Holy Spirit Active in First Testament Times?" is taken from John Goldingay, "The Holy Spirit in the Old Testament," in *Ex auditu* 12 (1996): 14–28. Used by permission of Wipf and Stock Publishers. www.wipfandstock.com.

Chapter 14: "How Does Prayer Work?" is taken from John Goldingay, "The Logic of Intercession," in *Theology* 99 (1998): 262–70. Used with permission of SPCK/Sheldon Press, London.

Chapter 15: "What Is Israel's Place in God's Purpose?" is taken from John Goldingay, "The Christian Church and Israel," in *Theological Renewal* 23 (1983): 4–19. Used with permission from *Theological Renewal*. And also from John Goldingay, "The Jews, the Land, and the Kingdom," in *Anvil* 4 (1987): 9–22. Used with permission from *Anvil*. And also from John Goldingay, "Modern Israel and Biblical Prophecy," in *Third Way* 6/4 (1983): 6–8; and "Palestine and the Prophets," in *Third Way* 2/7 (1978): 3–6. Used with permission from *Third Way*.

Chapter 16: "Is Election Fair?" is an excerpt from John Goldingay, "Justice and Salvation for Israel and Canaan," in *Reading the Hebrew Bible for a New Millennium*, Vol. 1, edited by Deborah Ellens, Michael Floyd, Wonil Kim, and Marvin Sweeney © 2000. Reprinted with the permission of the publisher, The Continuum International Publishing Group.

Chapter 17: "What Is the Relationship between Creation and Salvation?" is taken from John Goldingay, "A Unifying Approach to 'Creation' and 'Salvation' in the Old Testament," in *Theological Diversity and the Authority of the Old Testament*, © 1986 Wm. B. Eerdmans Publishing Company, Grand Rapids, Michigan. Reprinted by permission of the publisher, all rights reserved.

Chapter 18: "How Does the First Testament Look at Other Religions?" is taken from John Goldingay and Christopher J. H. Wright, "Yahweh Our God Yahweh One," in *One God, One Lord in a World of Religious Pluralism*, edited by Andrew D. Clarke and Bruce W. Winter © 1991 Tyndale House, Cambridge, 1991. Used with permission.

Chapter 20: "Is God in the City?" is taken from John Goldingay, "The Bible in the City," in *Theology* 92 (1989): 5–15. Used with permission of SPCK/Sheldon Press, London.

Chapter 21: "Does God Care about Animals?" is taken from John Goldingay, "Covenants and Nature," in *Covenant Theology,* edited by M. J. Cartledge and D. Mills, © 2001 Paternoster, Carlisle, UK. Used with permission of the publisher.

Chapter 23: Sections 1 and 3 of "What Does the Bible Say about Women and Men?" is taken from John Goldingay, "The Bible and Sexuality," in *Scottish Journal of Theology* 39 (1986): 175–88. Used with permission.

Chapter 24: "What Might the Song of Songs Do for People?" is taken from John Goldingay, "So What Might the Song of Songs Do to Them?" in *Reading From Right to Left,* edited by J. C. Exum and H. G. M. Williamson (Festschrift for David J. A. Clines) © 2003. Reproduced by kind permission of Continuum International Publishing Group Ltd.

PREFACE

Sometimes I write because there is a question that nags at me, sometimes because there is a question that nags at other people. This book is a collection of answers to questions of both kinds about the Old Testament and the way it interacts with Christian faith and life. Most of the chapters venture on into the New Testament, though the center of gravity lies in the Old Testament. Most have been published elsewhere, though I have lightly revised them all, and some appear here either in abbreviated or in expanded form; details concerning their original publication appear in the first footnote to each chapter.

After that opening paragraph, I use the expression "First Testament" throughout, instead of "Old Testament" (except when quoting from someone else). A student once told me that the Russian phrase equivalent to "Old Testament" could be rendered "Ramshackle Law." While another student told me this is not what the phrase would mean to a Russian speaker, it gives a good idea of what "Old Testament" often suggests to people.

The first three-quarters of the Bible is neither ramshackle nor law. In scholarly parlance it is the Hebrew Scriptures, though that phrase is slightly inaccurate (parts of Ezra and Daniel are in Aramaic), and "Hebrew Scriptures" does not offer any hint that for the church these scriptures are part of a larger whole. The Jewish term "Torah, Prophets, and Writings" with the Hebrew acronym Tanak is more precise, but it also presupposes that these books stand on their own. The expression "First Testament" implies that they relate to something else, the New Testament (I am not anal enough to insist on calling that the Second Testament). And it invites people to read these scriptures with new eyes, not as something old and legalistic but as something pristine and creative. As they are.

I am grateful to Maria Doerfler and Michael Crosby for digitizing some of the chapters. Biblical translations are my own, unless I indicate otherwise.

Abbreviations

ANET	James B. Pritchard, ed. *Ancient Near Eastern Texts Relating to the Old Testament.* 3d ed. Princeton: Princeton University Press, 1969.
BDB	Brown-Driver-Briggs
EVV	English versions
HBT	*Horizons in Biblical Theology*
HUCA	*Hebrew Union College Annual*
Int	*Interpretation*
JBL	*Journal of Biblical Literature*
JEcS	*Journal of Ecumenical Studies*
JETS	*Journal of the Evangelical Theological Society*
JSOT	*Journal for the Study of the Old Testament*
JSOTSup	Journal for the Study of the Old Testament Supplement
JSS	*Journal of Semitic Studies*
KJV	King James Version
NEB	New English Bible
NJPS	New Jewish Publication Society Translation
NRSV	New Revised Standard Version
OtSt	*Oudtestamentische Studiën*
RB	*Revue Biblique*
RelSRev	*Religious Studies Review*
RSV	Revised Standard Version
SJT	*Scottish Journal of Theology*
ThT	*Theology Today*
TNIV	Today's New International Version
TynB	*Tyndale Bulletin*
VT	*Vetus Testamentum*
VTSup	Vetus Testamentum Supplement
ZAW	*Zeitschrift für die alttestamentliche Wissenschaft*

Square brackets in Bible references such as 19:1 [2] indicate that the first reference applies to English Bibles, the second to printed Hebrew Bibles.

1

WHO IS GOD?

If we stand back and consider the impression the Bible as a whole gives of the character of God, what emerges?[1]

1. Personal God

The Christian Bible is dominated by a story or by a series of stories that belong to one overarching story extending ultimately from creation via Israel to Christ, and on via the church to the new Jerusalem. The story has a huge cast of major and minor figures, but its key participant is one who is not always present in the action at the front of the stage, yet who is involved from beginning to end, at least in the background to the drama, one who hovers there not only as the dramatist who dares not leave the play to the competence of the company but also as the central character and not merely the author of the story. The story concerns the achievement of the dramatist's purpose in the world.

The fact that the Bible is dominated by God's story points us to God's fundamental characteristic as a personal being. In the story, God establishes long-term objectives and immediate plans, makes decisions and implements them, enjoys successes and experiences frustration when other participants in the drama resist the dramatist's vision of how it should proceed, has changes of mind and formulates revised plans for reaching ultimate goals. All the way along God acts and lives in relation to other actors who sometimes fulfill roles manifestly written especially for them but who sometimes seem dangerously independent. The biblical God is not so much a moral force or an ethereal spirit as a person involved with people. When the story speaks of God out for a stroll in the cool of the evening or enjoying the whiff of food cooking, no doubt there were Israelites who understood this talk literalistically. The advantage of such anthropomorphism is its vivid testimony to the personal nature of the God of Israel, who can be described in our image in the conviction that we were made in God's image, so that God is sufficiently like us for us to take mutual understanding to be an exquisite possibility.

[1] A paper written for a meeting of the Doctrine Commission of the Church of England; much of its material appears in revised form in the commission's report *We Believe in God* (London: Church House / Wilton, Conn.: Morehouse-Barlow, 1987).

Speech is of the essence of personhood. Like other actors in the play, the biblical God often speaks, usually not directly to the audience but to other participants in the drama, though in such a way as we can overhear. While God's speaking is thus of importance in the biblical story, it comes into its own in the teaching of Torah and Prophets. "These are the words of Yahweh," say the prophets, using the personal name of Israel's God. They speak in the manner of the human messenger who declares, "These are the words of King so-and-so." They are uttered by the agent, but they come from the sovereign. Sometimes, it seems, the prophets believed that they heard with their own ears words God personally made audible. Sometimes they saw themselves as putting into their own words convictions felt within, which they knew came from God. Either way, they knew that God the actor in Israel's story was also God the communicator of personal feelings, desires, opinions, and intentions.

The content of Yahweh's speech also reflects a personal nature. Although capable of being likened to an animal such as a lion or an ox, or to an inanimate object such as a rock, most characteristically Yahweh is a king, a shepherd, a warrior, a guardian, a teacher, a judge, a potter, a builder, a farmer, a husband, a father (or a wife, or a mother). Yahweh has the feelings of a person: love, joy, satisfaction, sympathy, longing, frustration, regret, hurt, jealousy, anger. Yahweh is the dynamic, living God. The point is made concretely by the Torah's consistent prohibition on making an image of God as an aid to worship. The lively, energetic, moving, acting, speaking God of Israel could never be captured by an image; an image could not be an aid to worship of this God.

Being personal involves being in relationship with people, not only speaking but also being spoken to. Thus in the First Testament story, and in the address of Torah, Prophets, and Wisdom, speaking involves God in conversation. This being spoken to becomes a focus in the Psalms. "Spoken to," indeed, is too mild a term for the uninhibited expression of love, gratitude, honor, trust, and commitment, and of disappointment, grief, rage, hurt, and doubt that characterizes the Psalms. No doubt such self-expression would do the psalmist good whether or not God were a person able to hear, but the Psalms' presupposition is that the God of Israel is real enough and personal enough to appreciate the sharing of enthusiasm and wonder. God has not only ears to hear but also feelings to be aroused and energy to be activated. We have come full circle. The God of the First Testament is one who thinks and feels, who gives expression to thoughts and feelings in words and deeds, and who invites human beings into the shared speech of conversation and thus into a shared involvement in the world.

Developments in Judaism by Jesus' day have sometimes been thought to have rendered God a somewhat distant figure. Perhaps people could know God's presence and respond to God by keeping the Torah, but perhaps the Torah itself distanced God from them. Perhaps refraining from uttering the name Yahweh reminded them of God's reality, but perhaps removing that name from people's lips removed God as a living person. Perhaps the reports by visionaries of what they have seen and heard mediated God's reality to others, but perhaps they underlie God's apparent absence from the experience of ordinary people.

There are no such ambiguities about the relationship with God as a person which Jesus enjoys and which he shares with those who listen to him. It is summed up in the word "Father." At his baptism he hears God say, "You are my son, my beloved, I delight in you" (Mark 1:11). His baptism is a visionary experience like those other religious figures might have, yet it opens the door to an ongoing closeness of relationship with the one of whom he can henceforth say, "God is my father, God loves me, God chooses to fulfill a purpose through me." In reflecting on the strangely varying fruitfulness of his ministry, he recalls the Father's act of revelation, the Father's gracious will, the Father's giving of everything to him, the Father's knowledge of him and knowledge by him (Matt 11:25–27). At his transfiguration he finds the Father's words from his baptism being repeated (Mark 9:7). His anguished prayer in Gethsemane is "Abba, Father, all things are possible for you. Take this cup from me, yet not what I want but what you want" (Mark 14:36). These words, too, take up the themes of his baptismal commission. God is the Father who loves him, and therefore Jesus can bring to God his longings and his desire for relief. God is also the Father who has expectations of him, and therefore Jesus accepts that ultimately God's will is what counts. Fatherhood combines love and authority, and sonship thus combines trust and submission, and an attitude that is free to query the will of God even though (or because) it is committed finally to accepting it.

It is a fair inference that the "Abba, Father" with which the Gethsemane prayer begins also characterizes the frequent resorting to prayer that the Gospels note (e.g., Mark 1:35). In his prayer life Jesus speaks back as a son to a father. Admittedly his distraught prayer from the cross is, "My God, my God, why have you left me?" There is no "Abba Father" here (Mark 15:34; though see Luke 23:34, 46). Yet the exception proves the rule. As in Psalm 22, which Jesus here takes up, the fact that he prays at all, and the fact that he prays to "my God," indicates that the moment of abandonment is, paradoxically, one in which the personal relationship still holds.

While God was known and addressed as "Father" in Judaism, the image was not a prevalent one, and as far as we know the Aramaic expression "Abba" was not used in prayer in contemporary Judaism. It was the family word with which children addressed their "Daddy," but it should not be romanticized. It was also the word grown-up children used to address their father, and it suggests an attitude of humility, obedience, and reverence, as well as one of dependence, security, and confidence. To have God as Father, then, means to be able to take for granted not only the fact of God's personhood but also many aspects of God's nature. It implies that God is the kind of person who loves, cares, gives, listens, welcomes, seeks, accepts, guides, forgives, provides, who manifests interest, concern, and self-sacrifice, and the kind of person who has expectations and hopes, who exercises authority and power, who embodies discernment and wisdom, who has the right to criticize, to judge, and to determine.

Whatever the sense in which Jesus saw his own sonship as unique and God's fatherhood in relation to him as different from God's fatherhood in relation to others, he emphasized that God behaves like a father to all humanity and that all are invited to relate to God as children. Thus he encourages his disciples to pray "Father . . ." just as he does; Luke explicitly makes a connection between Jesus' praying and his teaching his disciples to pray like that (Luke 11:1–2). The Lord's Prayer, which Luke introduces at this point, parallels the Gethsemane prayer as it works out the implications of God's being Father in terms of authority and caring. For Jesus' disciples, as for him, praying to the Father involves a longing for God's name to be hallowed and God's reign to come, before it can imply expecting God to be concerned with our basic needs (hunger, guilt, the pressure of evil). God is, as Matthew emphasizes, a heavenly Father, a Father in heaven, one who commands all heaven's resources and power for the fulfilling of people's needs, but also one who must be reverenced as the Lord of heaven.

It is thus both a solemn and an encouraging fact that disciples live before God as their Father. It is solemn and comforting that nothing happens without the Father knowing (Luke 16:15; Matt 6:4, 6, 8, 18). Having God as Father provides no immediate explanation of the unpleasant and unpredictable aspects to human experience, but it does provide a way of coping with them in a confident, trusting submission to the Father's will.

In Matthew, the Lord's Prayer appears in the context of portraying the broader implications of God's fatherhood (Matt 6). Jesus notes that certain prayer habits implied the assumption that other people are the only ones who hear us praying, or that we have to win God's attention to our prayer, or that we can forget about other people when we pray. Such habits raise the question whether prayer is talking to yourself, whether God is really interested in us, or whether in prayer we can turn our backs on how we get on with others. Jesus affirms that praying to a Father implies praying to one who really listens, one who is aware of and concerned for our needs, and one who loves forgiving people and cares about my brother and sister as well as me. To this, Jesus later adds the "beggar's wisdom"[2] (or child's wisdom) of ask, seek, and knock, based on the logic that if a human father responds to children who ask for things they need, how much more will a heavenly one do so (Matt 7:7–11; cf. Luke 11:5–13). And Paul adds that in the Spirit through Christ believers in general join Jesus in calling on God as "Abba, Father" (Rom 8:15; cf. Gal 4:6).

2. Involved God

The God of the First Testament is involved in the world. God is independent of the world and far too significant a figure to be in any way confined to it or captured in it. Yet for reasons the First Testament hardly goes into (does the play ask the playwright, "Why did you write me?"), God did create the world and does direct its story. Our terms "creation" and "history" may suggest two separate enterprises; in the First Testament, however, creation is the opening of that ongoing drama that stretches from beginning to end. God is involved in it throughout, though in varying ways, sometimes intervening with sovereign initiatives, sometimes applying

---

[2] Joachim Jeremias, *The Parables of Jesus* (reissued ed.; New York: Scribner's, 1963), 159; he refers to K. H. Rengstorf, "Geben ist seliger denn Nehmen," in *Die Leibhaftigkeit des Wortes* (ed. Michel Otto; A. Köberle Festschrift; Hamburg: Furche, 1958), 29.

a mid-course adjustment to a trajectory that seems to have gone severely wrong, sometimes apparently leaving the story to develop on its own because it is doing all right or because it has to be allowed to get worse before it can be helped to get better, sometimes arranging behind the scenes for the right person to appear or the right event to take place at the right moment.

Partly because God's involvement is so varied in its dynamic, that involvement is often difficult to identify. Belief in it removes little of history's ambiguity, at least as people live through history, unless God offers some interpretation of events before they take place, or in their midst, or after them. The First Testament pictures the ambiguity of history being substantially reduced over several centuries through the activity of prophets who could interpret the meaning of current events as well as the present significance of events of the past and of events still to come. The prophets' concern was not merely to announce or explain these events but to bring home the demand and the promise bound up in them. They declare that God is involved now in the destiny of Israel and of the nations, and that this involvement looks for a response.

God's involvement in the world is not confined to the macro-history of national and international affairs set in the context of ultimate beginning and final end. Nor is the world that God invented a machine with an inbuilt energy source to keep it working on its own until God's purpose for it is finished. The God who gave stability and life to the world at the beginning continues to be the source of its stability and life. It is God's life breath that animals breathe; plants drink the water God makes rain down. God is involved in the affairs of individual human beings as lifegiver, provider, liberator, healer, companion, counselor. The conversation between humanity and God that the Psalms transcribe presupposes the awareness of that involvement in Israel's life over the centuries, the experience of it in ongoing provision and crisis intervention on the part of each generation and within the life of individuals, and the prospect of that involvement in God's once again turning back and acting on behalf of the needy when they seem to have been abandoned. It is this same involvement that is presupposed by Proverbs, missed by Ecclesiastes, and agonized over by Job.

The messianic expectations of Judaism presupposed that God's activity was not evident in the present in Israel's history. The reign of God is something Israel awaits rather than experiences. When Jesus begins to preach, he asserts that the moment has now come when the King is asserting kingship (Mark 1:14, 15). This new assertion of God's royal authority is the best news the needy could hear. It means blessing for the poor, the grieving, the meek, the just, the merciful, the pure, the peaceable, the persecuted. They are to be given recompense, recognition, revelation, mercy, justice, property, comfort, and the "reign of heaven" (Matt 5:3–12).

The fact that God reigns is not a mere theological theory, statement of faith, or hope for some future day but a living awareness both based in and creative of the experience of witnessing God's involvement as King in the world. God the King is at hand. God's time is now; God's reign dawns. Jesus' ministry means people can witness the blind receiving renewed sight, the disabled walking, people with diseases that cut them off from the rest of society being cleansed, the deaf enabled to hear, the poor having good news preached to them (11:4–5). A new age dawns in joy, a reign of God where Jesus and his people will drink a cup of wine anew instead of a cup of suffering and join with Abraham, Isaac and Jacob in a heavenly banquet (8:11; 26:29).

The implementation of God's reign turns upside down the expectations encouraged by human experience and rubber-stamped by religious tradition. The blessings of God's reign are given, not earned, so that they come to all no matter how long they have worked for them. Indeed, God's mercy naturally finds a home more readily with those who clearly need it than with those who have found ways of living independently of it. The prodigal son finds an unexpected welcome from a prodigally loving father, the child is the model for the receptivity that embraces God's reign, and God's heart fills with joy when one sinner repents (Matt 20:1–16; Mark 10:15; Luke 15; 18:9–14).

God's activity in the world as King is a reassertion of an ongoing involvement in the world that underlies it. God is the original creator as well as the Lord of the End (Mark 13:19). God made humanity male and female and joins together each couple in marriage (10:6–9). In the generosity of power God blesses all, just and unjust, with rain and sun (Matt 5:45–48). It is God that Jesus thanks for bread and fish (Mark 6:41; 8:6–7). God feeds the wild birds and clothes the wild flowers and sees that food and clothing are provided for those who seek God's just reign (Matt 6:25–33). God decides when to take back the life that God originally gave, and thus it can safely be entrusted to God on one's deathbed, or one's cross (Luke 12:20; 23; 46). It is also God's power that renews life on resurrection day; God is not Lord of the dead but of the living (Mark 12:24–27). The notions of God as Creator, Father, and King intersect in connections such as these. When Jesus handles topics we might see as belonging to God's activity in creation and providence, he himself commonly speaks in terms of God's fatherly provision for those who acknowledge God's kingship.

Paul works out the implications of the way involvement in the world cost God an acceptance of a share in humanity's suffering. It was not only Abraham who was willing not to spare his own son; God did so, being willing to give him up for us all (Rom 8:32). He also works out the way God continues the involvement that came to a climax in incarnation, by God's Spirit's dwelling among God's people (1 Cor 3:16–17; cf. Rom 8:11, 16).

3. Holy God

The First Testament God is involved in our world as a being with personal characteristics like ours. Yet God is not one of us; God is not a human person writ large. The First Testament's fundamental way of referring to God's distinctiveness is by speaking of God as the holy one. "Holiness" denotes the mysterious Godness of God, distinctive, set apart, belonging to the heavenly realm, and therefore deserving the awed worship of those who belong to the created order. It points to the supercharged power, the self-assertive freedom, and the jealous wrath of the sometimes inexplicable God of Israel's story. God is not a person to be trifled with. Holiness denotes the majesty and glory of the one whom prophets were sometimes confronted by, a majesty and glory that are acknowledged for more everyday purposes by religious institutions such as the temple with its rituals.

In itself, holiness is not an ethical term. From where, then, do its ethical connotations come? Holiness means divinity, and it derives its further content from the nature of the God to whom holiness is ascribed. The God of the First Testament is righteous and just, and loving and merciful. It is by acting in righteousness and love that God reveals the essential content of holiness or divinity.

Isaiah, whose vision of Yahweh as the holy one expresses something of the notion of holiness summarized above (see Isa 6), also sums up in a convenient phrase the connection between holiness and justice: "the Lord of Hosts is exalted in justice, and the holy God shows himself holy in righteousness" (Isa 5:16). "Justice" denotes acting decisively in the cause of what is right ("judgment" in the older translations brings out more of the word's concrete, active meaning, and its connection with the judges of the book of Judges). "Righteousness" or "rightness" indicates the moral and relational quality of this activity: it suggests doing right by the people with whom one is in relationship. In Isaiah's context, the holiness of God issues in just judgment on those who ignore the God-ness of God and the rights of other people.

The link between holiness and love or faithfulness or mercy is captured in a phrase from Isaiah's northern contemporary, Hosea. Hosea's understanding of God's personal involvement with Israel is expressed in terms of the mixed feelings of a parent for the child who does not respond to a parent's loving care. Yahweh is tempted, as it were, to cast off Israel, as such a parent might be tempted to cast off an unresponsive child. But parents cannot really do that, and neither can Yahweh. Motherly love triumphs over hurt anger: "for I am God and not a man, the Holy One in your midst" (Hos 11:9). The holiness of God that expresses itself in just judgment also expresses itself in mercy and grace.

A key First Testament expression for this aspect of God's character is the word *khesed*, often translated "steadfast love." It suggests the loyalty and faithfulness that always keeps a commitment that has been made to someone. Thus when Israel is unjustly oppressed, it can appeal to Yahweh to act "for the sake of your steadfast love"—that is, in order to be faithful to undertakings you have given. Yet Israel can also appeal to this steadfast love when it is quite justly oppressed, for the love it denotes is also one that goes beyond mutually binding commitments into the realm of grace, mercy, and forgiveness. Even when acting in mercy and forgiveness, Yahweh retains the sovereign freedom of God, choosing when to show grace and mercy; but even at the moment of wrath, one can plead with God to remember mercy (Exod 33:11; Hab 3:2).

There is a close relationship between the love and justice that give expression to God's holiness, though there is also a tension between them. When God acts in justice on people's behalf, God is acting in love for them. In this sense, love and justice are two ways of speaking of the same reality. The tension arises from the difference between having God act in love or justice for you or against you. Hosea's prophecies express that tension particularly sharply, but it runs through the First

Testament story from Gen 3–11 onwards. Whether one is reading of the experience of humanity as a whole, or of that of Israel in particular, one is reading of God's attempt to relate to people as the loving giver, and of God's willingness, in light of the response they make, to relate to them as the righteous judge. Key symbols of God's relationship with Israel such as King, Father, and Judge can express both aspects of that relationship.

In the New Testament, the close relationship between God's love and God's justice, in the sense of God's doing right by a relationship of commitment to people, is illustrated by the way the former is the great emphasis in one of the classic theological expositions of the gospel (John 3:16) and the latter in another (Rom 3).

The first three Gospels follow Jesus' baptism with his ordeal in the isolation of the Judean desert. The challenge Jesus faces here is whether he will let the holy one be the holy one, let God be God, acknowledged as sovereign over his living and dying, trusted for protection without first being proved, worshiped and served to the exclusion of other claims (see Matt 4:1–10).

Humble submission before this God includes turning one's back on sin. Jesus had accepted John's baptism of repentance for the forgiveness of sins, even though it is he to whom John's ministry points. Jesus' preaching of good news then includes the demand for this turning from sin that John had also made. The assertion of God's rule in the world that Jesus heralds and embodies means good news for the needy but danger for the sinner, and it often transpires that the needy are those who have been designated sinners, and the sinners are those who did the designating. Jesus talks much about judgment and about God as judge, and he continues to do so to those who have become disciples, who remain in danger of God's judgment if in their relationships with others they prefer a judging or a begrudging attitude to the forgiving attitude the judge has shown to them (Matt 7:1–5; 18:21–35).

The coming of God thus puts an urgent challenge before people. Jesus announces an imminent confrontation with God in all the holiness, purity, goodness, mercy, and love of God's being. God cannot be placated by pointing to one's religious status or religious observance, for God's demands extend far beyond the outward righteousness for which these commonly stand. God manifests little sympathy with people committed to political action in order to bring about a reversal of political order, because this loses significance in light of the imminent utter collapse of the kingdoms of this age. Indeed, he comes to earn the enmity of both the politico-religious establishment and the politico-religious revolutionaries. They cooperate in order to ensure his death, a death in which, as later theology came to reflect, God was involved and which was the means of God's rule being established at the expense of all other kingdoms.

It is on the basis of his own "But I say to you . . ." that Jesus urges forgiveness and reconciliation, marital faithfulness in thought and act, straightness in speech, submission and generosity, love and acceptance toward enemies as well as friends. God is rarely directly associated with such teaching, though God's fatherhood underlies the stance that is to be taken. It is to reflect God's style and bring glory to God (Matt 5:16, 45, 48).

Jesus himself has to let God be God over the fruits of his ministry. The rule of God is a mystery he comes to unveil, but there is a continuing mystery over whose eyes God opens to perceive what is unveiled and about the process whereby God gives more to those who have and takes away from those who have nothing (Mark 4:10, 12, 24–25; 11:25–26). There is an awesome authority about the God of Jesus, one who requires the death of people for speaking evil of their parents, who roots up what others have planted, who expects Jesus to pick up his cross and walk to execution, who threatens a fiery hell for someone who leads others into sin, who can be likened to a vineyard owner who puts to death his son's murderers (Matt 15:5, 13; 16:21–23; 18:1–9; 21:33–43). Only God knows the day or hour when the Son of Man will come (Mark 13:32). But it is precisely the Father of whom Jesus says this. As with the fact that nothing happens without God knowing about it, the awesome God-ness of God can be lived with because God is a Father who can be trusted.

4. One God

It has often been tempting for Christians to assume that the God of justice and the God of love are two different gods or to infer from the complexity of human experience (which embraces both blessings and trouble, both encouragement and temptation) that good and evil powers exercise approximately similar degrees of influence in the world. The First Testament emerged from contexts that did acknowledge many gods, or gods and demons, or balanced powers of light and darkness, yet it affirmed "Yahweh our God Yahweh one" (Deut 6:4). This central confession of Jewish faith is as difficult to interpret as it looks. It makes clear enough that God is one, but it is not simply a statement about monotheism. It is an affirmation that Yahweh has the exclusive allegiance of First Testament faith; there can be no worshiping of Yahweh and some other power. It also suggests a contrast between the oneness of Yahweh and the multiplicity of the supernatural powers acknowledged by the Canaanites, the Babylonians, the Persians and other powers Israel lived among.

It was once customary to portray the history of First Testament faith as a development from animism (the worship of spirits of nature) via polytheism (the worship of many gods) and henotheism (the worship of one god among many) to monotheism (the recognition that there is only one God). The whole scheme has to be read into the First Testament; it is not there. From the beginning of its story, Israel was laid hold of by one whose evident authority and might knew no rivals. Not that Israel therefore assumed that only one being dwelt in heaven. The diversity of earthly reality is at least matched by a diversity of heavenly reality. But none of the "sons of God" or "angels" has inherent divine power. One will rules in heaven.

Such a statement is made only by faith. Other peoples did assume that the complexity of human experience suggested that the decision-making processes of heaven were as fraught and haphazard as those of earth. And in the context of modernity, there has been no more pressing philosophical question for the person who wishes to believe in God than that posed by the way suffering is distributed in the world, which makes it difficult to maintain that God is both powerful and fair.

Invited to qualify either their commitment to God's power or to God's love, Christians generally prefer to yield the former, thinking that humanity itself and supernatural powers other than God have significant responsibility for evil in the world. The First Testament is hesitant about this move. It does refer three times to a heavenly adversary (a "satan") concerned to trouble humanity, but it generally seeks to emphasize the conviction that one will ultimately rules on earth and in heaven. It prefers to believe in a God who is in control, but who thus has to be held responsible for some very mysterious events, than in a God whose heart is in the right place but who is not very efficient. The prophet who declares most unequivocally that Yahweh alone is God is also the one who has God affirming the status of creator of both light and darkness, blessing and trouble (Isa 45:7).

If reality knows only one supreme locus of power and authority, and that is Yahweh, this raises questions about Yahweh's relationship with the rest of the world outside Israel. It is not surprising that in the way Israel tells its story, it expresses the conviction that God has been involved with Israel itself. It is more surprising that it sets its own story in the context of the world's story, acknowledging that God's involvement with it is secondary to God's involvement with the world as a whole. It is a means of reversing the curse that seemed to come on world history and of replacing this curse by the blessing God intended from the beginning.

In the bulk of the First Testament, the conviction that God's concern for the world lies behind an involvement with Israel is expressed only intermittently. That is nevertheless the context in which the opening chapters set Israel's story, and it remains part of Israel's background awareness that finds expression from time to time in the Torah, the Prophets, wisdom, and psalmody. Israel recognizes that though the religion of Canaan is deeply perverse and the religion of Babylon dangerously beguiling, foreign peoples are within the control of Yahweh and are not without some true apprehension of God. The God Most High of Melchizedek and Nebuchadnezzar (Gen 14; Dan 3) is not wholly other than the God Most High of Abraham and Daniel, whose ultimate purpose is to bring all the nations to know God fully.

Israel also acknowledges that largely because of its own recalcitrance its own story has not led to the degree of blessing suggested by the way the story opened. When it paints its most explicit future scenarios, it does so out of a feeling of being in exile, cut off from the place of blessing, still looking for that decisive intervention of God that will set world history right. It is this unfinishedness of the First Testament story that leaves it open to having the story of Jesus linked onto it.

Jesus will have believed that the awesome Father whose reign he came to proclaim and implement was the one God who is Lord of the nations as well as of Israel (cf. Mark 12:29). Yet this perspective has little prominence in his life and teaching, at least before his resurrection. Similarly he does not picture the God of Israel involved in world history. By implication, fatherhood is God's attitude to all peoples; by implication, the benevolent reign of God will extend over all peoples. But these themes are not very explicit. Jesus comes to Israel; it will be only on the basis of its renewal that the nations will be won. Jesus focuses on the former task and resists being drawn into meeting the needs of people outside Israel (cf. Mark 7:24–30).

Ultimately, however, he is destined to rule the whole world. The story of his initial testing presupposes this (Matt 4:8). It also indicates that at the beginning of his ministry the confession of one Lord is made in the context of the pressure to bow down to another. A disciple, too, has to choose between God and Mammon (Matt 6:24).

Like the creative figures of First Testament faith, Jesus ministers in a context whose thinking might be described as demon-ridden, and he distances himself somewhat from it. Whereas the First Testament normally distances itself by declining to speak of such forces of evil, Jesus does so by seeing such forces centered in one entity, Satan, the enemy who exercises hostile power in the name of an alternative kingship. Apparently from the beginning Jesus experienced evil as focused in this form. He lived in real conflict with it but experienced clear victory: Satan is no threat to him or to his disciples (Luke 10:18–19).

Like his contemporaries, Jesus takes for granted aspects of their First Testament inheritance that qualify an affirmation of the oneness of God by speaking of God's wisdom or God's spirit as nascently distinguishable from God's person or by picturing God's will being executed and God's care being exercised by means of God's supernatural aides. The significant development of such insight into plurality within the one Godhead, however, takes place after Easter. The disciples come to affirm that Jesus is Lord, thereby describing Jesus by a term with the resonances of the actual name for God in the First Testament. The implications of this are present in a passage such as Rom 10:9–13, where the statement that confessing Jesus as Lord is key to salvation is buttressed by a quotation that originally referred to the Lord Yahweh. These implications become more explicit as Jesus is seen as the unique embodiment of the divine wisdom (Col 1) and the divine word (John 1). The person who has seen Jesus has seen the Father (John 14:9). Further, in light of the church's experience of the personal activity of God's Spirit in its own midst, it sees that spirit as simultaneously personal and distinguishable from the Father and Jesus (John 14–16). Affirmation of the oneness of God, never too important a concern (see 1 Cor 8:5–6), is well on the way to the qualifying that belongs to the postscriptural period.

2

How Do God's Love and God's Wrath Relate to Each Other?

The Bible portrays God as having both a soft side and a tough side. The soft, positive, generous, creative, life-giving, merciful, faithful side of God expresses itself in creating the world, having mercy on it despite humanity's rebelliousness, and acting to restore it to what it was designed to be. The tough, angry, negative side expresses itself in killing people for falsifying their pledges, pouring bowls of wrath over them, and sending them to hell.[1]

How do we relate these two sides to God—or rather, how does God relate them? Christians commonly think that the God of wrath is the First Testament God while the God of love is the New Testament God, and this has been supported by scholarly emphasis on Yahweh's inexplicably rough and tough acts.[2] But apart from making one wonder why the New Testament thinks the First Testament is inspired scripture, as an analysis this answer does not work: in that first paragraph I have illustrated God's soft side from the First Testament and God's tough side from the New. One could take that point further. In general, the First Testament does not describe the world as under God's wrath, though God does from time to time get angry at particular peoples and more often gets angry with the people of God in particular. Only in the New Testament does the whole world sit under God's wrath (e.g., Eph 2:3).[3] In the First Testament, God's temper stays under control for long periods, boils over for a moment, and then subsides again (e.g., Isa 54:7–8). In the New, God is not explosive but is coolly negative and resentful, at the same time as loving. It is not self-evident that this is preferable to an occasional explosiveness.

---

[1] Not previously published.

[2] See, e.g., David Penchansky, *What Rough Beast* (Louisville: Westminster John Knox, 1999); David Penchansky and Paul L. Redditt, eds., *Shall Not the Judge of All the Earth Do What Is Right?* (J. L. Crenshaw Festschrift; Winona Lake, Ind.: Eisenbrauns, 2000).

[3] Admittedly, Genesis's talk about a curse on the world does parallel some New Testament talk of God's anger. When Paul speaks of God's anger being revealed against wickedness, and of this issuing in God's giving people up to the consequences of their deeds (Rom 1:18–32), it is his way of describing the same reality that is described in terms of curse in Genesis. In the First Testament, God's curse, like God's blessing, is more rational and longer lasting than God's anger, and it more characteristically works via ordinary processes of cause and effect, and thus works like God's wrath in Paul. See further chapter 6 below.

I was brought up to see the soft and the tough sides as equally balanced within God. One could apparently support that by texts such as ones that describe God as "a just God and a Savior" (Isa 45:21). There was a tension within God that the cross then resolved, because it both expressed God's love and satisfied God's justice. The First Testament's way of seeing the matter is rather different, as I think is the New's. Tough and soft are not equal within God, and God was not first tough in the First Testament then merciful in the New. The soft is God's dominant side and was so in the First Testament, but God also has a tough side in both Testaments and can give expression to it from time to time. It is important not to ignore the tough side, not least the sometimes inexplicable toughness, but neither to be overwhelmed by it.

1. Exodus 34

At Sinai, Yahweh offers a self-description outlining the First Testament's systematic theology or doctrine of God. That we might so regard it is suggested by its being Yahweh's self-description at Sinai and by the way the First Testament often refers to this classic statement (e.g., Num 14:18). It has already been partially anticipated in the Decalogue, in the prohibition on making images (Exod 20:5–6), which referred to God's short-lived punishment and long-lived love. In Exod 34:6–7 it follows on Yahweh's threat to abandon Israel because of its rebellion. Yahweh then claims to be "a God compassionate and gracious, long-tempered and big in commitment and steadfastness, extending commitment to thousands [of generations], carrying wrongdoing, rebellion, and failure, certainly not acquitting, attending to the wrongdoing of parents on children and grandchildren, on those of the third and fourth [generation]."

The positive and tough sides to Yahweh come into clear focus here, as does the dominance of the former. The positive side comes first; but then, something has to come first. Beyond this, it is more fulsomely expressed, with an accumulation of adjectives and nouns with encouraging resonances. And it declares that whereas Yahweh's commitment extends for thousands of generations, Yahweh's punishing extends only to three or four, the number that live together. Yahweh works through the way the senior members of a household influence the family as a whole, and this has an effect both for good and for ill, but Yahweh's positive commitment goes far beyond this in its effects.

The expression "carrying wrongdoing" is especially significant. It is usually translated "forgiving wrongdoing," but this obscures its point. The only Hebrew term for "to forgive" is *salakh*,[4] the word Moses uses soon afterwards in an appeal to Yahweh (Exod 34:9). But in this self-description Yahweh uses *nasa'*, the much more common verb meaning lift and thus carry.[5] Yahweh is taking up the word Moses

---

[4] J. J. Stamm, in *Theological Lexicon of the Old Testament* (ed. Ernst Jenni and Claus Westermann; Peabody, Mass.: Hendrickson, 1997), 798.

[5] See H.-J. Fabry et al., in *Theological Dictionary of the Old Testament* (ed. G. Johannes Botterweck, Helmer Ringgren, and Heinz-Josef Fabry; 15 vols.; Grand Rapids: Eerdmans, 1999), 10:24–40.

used previously in appealing to Yahweh to carry the people's sin (Exod 32:32; cf. earlier Gen 50:17; Exod 10:17; and later, e.g., Ps 32:1, 5). Ordinarily, people have to carry their own wrongdoing in the sense of accepting responsibility for it, accepting the burden of it, and accepting the consequences of it (e.g., Gen 4:13; Lev 5:1, 17; 24:15; Num 14:33–34). Yahweh's self-description goes on to affirm that people who persist in their wrongdoing indeed do not have their guilt cleared but pay for it (cf. Josh 24:19–20). But first comes the emphatic statement of intent, that paradoxically Yahweh is the one who intends to carry people's wrongdoing.

Exodus does not explain the relationship between these two statements. It does not, for instance, say that people must first repent and then Yahweh will carry their sin, and Exod 32–34 includes no account of the people's repenting. Indeed, at Sinai Yahweh's undertaking to carry the people's sin does not exclude also punishing them. But Israel's ongoing story will presuppose that carrying the people's wrongdoing is not conditional on their first having repented. If anything, the logic works the other way round: "I am carrying your wrongdoing: Now are you prepared to turn back to me?" This is explicit when Yahweh declares, "I am wiping away your acts of rebellion like thick cloud, your failings like thunder cloud. Now turn to me, because I am delivering you" (Isa 44:22).[6] Forgiveness is the basis for repentance, not the other way round. Admittedly one cannot universalize that principle. When Nineveh gains Yahweh's forgiveness in what Jonah knows is a fulfillment of this Sinai revelation, it is the city's repentance that opens the way to this forgiveness. A relationship with Yahweh is a personal one, like that of parents and children or husbands and wives, not a contractual one. Yahweh's self-description is not a legal statement that provides a basis for calculating how to make it work to one's advantage or discovering what one can get away with. Both Yahweh's carrying people's responsibility and people's carrying their responsibility feature in the relationship, but there are varying ways in which that may work out.

We might say that in carrying the people's wrongdoing, Yahweh takes the wrongdoing away, though the nature of this taking away needs clarifying. The Greek verb for forgiveness, *aphiemi*, means to send away, and the First Testament can talk in terms of Yahweh sending away sin (e.g., Mic 7:19). But *nasa'* does not mean take away in this sense. It denotes taking something away with you, not disposing of something (see, e.g., 1 Sam 17:34; 1 Kgs 15:22). Yahweh does take away sin but does so by taking it and keeping it. Yahweh takes up and carries Israel's wrongdoing—carries responsibility for it and carries the burden of it.

Such acceptance of responsibility does not imply declaring that one was responsible for what happened. It implies taking responsibility for the consequences of what happened, not for its causes. Normally, when we wrong someone, this imperils our relationship with that person. Yahweh declines to be bound by this inevitability. Israel's wrongdoing will not be allowed to destroy its relationship with Yahweh.

---

[6] I understand the qatal verbs as instantaneous, though they might be understood (e.g.) as aorist (and referring to God's longstanding forgiveness), or as perfect (referring to an act God has just undertaken), or as performative ("I hereby wipe away…"). Whichever understanding is right, the act of forgiveness precedes the challenge to repentance.

If Yahweh had not explicitly declared that intention, we might have been compelled to infer it from the history of Israel. Like the history of the church, the history of Israel was as much a history of faithlessness as one of faithfulness. How then did it continue for so many centuries, and how has the church's history so continued? The question is already raised by Israel's faithlessness at Sinai, which presages how the history of Israel and of the church will be. Yahweh's self-description as one who carries the people's wrongdoing explains in advance how it can possibly continue.

At Sinai, Israel has not accepted responsibility for its wrongdoing. The only person who has repented at Sinai is Yahweh (Exod 32:14). Although Yahweh punished some of the people for their rebellion, this punishment fell far short of the dimensions of the rebellion. Yahweh has already started carrying the people's sin. Israel will not change its mind or relent or repent, so Yahweh has to do so. Over subsequent millennia, it will be the exception rather than the rule for Israel or the church to repent and accept responsibility for its faithlessness. Yahweh is better at keeping the promise to carry the people's wrongdoing than at keeping the threat not to clear the guilty.

The God who became incarnate in Jesus and died for us is the God who had been carrying Israel's sin through First Testament times. The incarnation and the cross are the logical climax to the story that has run through the First Testament. The fact that people such as pastors and theologians in Jesus' day could not see it that way illustrates the point.

We customarily think of the cross in sacrificial terms, in judicial terms, or in military terms, or we combine these (Christ's self-offering constitutes his paying the penalty for sin and thus he wins the victory over the devil). But thinking in terms of sacrifice requires Western people to learn another metaphorical language, the judicial metaphor gives the impression of a legal rather than a personal relationship between God and us, and talking in terms of Christ winning the victory over evil undergirds the impression that violence is at the heart of reality. We would do better for ourselves and for the preaching of the gospel to go behind the sacrificial, legal, and military language to the relational dynamics implicit in Yahweh's speech about carrying wrongdoing. On the cross God went to the omega point of letting humanity do its worst. There is nothing worse you can do to someone than kill him, especially God, or no further that you can go in submitting to people than to let them kill you. If that does not also destroy the relationship, nothing can. On resurrection day God once again stands with arms open, showing that God has even carried murder.

2. Genesis

Not surprisingly, Yahweh's self-description at Sinai coheres with the picture of Yahweh conveyed by Genesis in several ways.

At the beginning, God blessed the sea creatures, the human beings, and the seventh day of the week. The implication of the first two is that these creatures will be fruitful, and perhaps this is also the implication of the last.[7] Following on Adam and Eve's act of disobedience, Yahweh God declares that the snake is cursed, and so is the land itself. Henceforth blessing and curse will struggle for dominance in the story.

Blessing and curse are thus correlative, but they are not expressed as exact antonyms. God actively blesses creation but does not actively curse the snake and the ground; Yahweh only declares that they are cursed.

At one level the distinction is a purely syntactical one. If we ask, "Who does the cursing?" presumably the answer must be God. God is the subject of the verb that spells out the implications of the curse on the snake, "I will put enmity. . . ." And Noah's father, at least, sees the subsequent curse on the ground as God's act (Gen 5:29). Further, saying something "is cursed" is not merely a statement of fact but a statement of intent and commitment (cf. Gen 9:25; 49:7; Deut 27:15–26).[8] Presumably the intent and commitment are God's. Yet not having God say "I curse you" is significant. Noah's father assumes like a structural linguist that a passive verb can be turned into an active one without changing the meaning. The logic parallels that of theologians who infer that if God predestines to salvation, God must also predestine to damnation, even if scripture does not say so. Scripture's implications are more subtle and less rationalist. To describe God as blessing but not directly cursing suggests that blessing is Yahweh's natural activity, while cursing is less so.

Next, there is the interesting fact that the only emotion attributed to Yahweh in Genesis is pain. Pain was to characterize a woman's relationship with her children and a man's relationship with his work (Gen 3:16–17)—a woman's relationship with her work and a man's with his children, no doubt, too. It now emerges that pain (*'asab* hitpael) characterizes God's experience, too (Gen 6:6). The curse also lands on God. Whereas God had originally looked at the earth and enjoyed the sight, now God is grieved at the frustrating of the creation aim of achieving something good. It will not be the last time God experiences such pain. The forming of Israel as a people, too, will soon bring pain to Yahweh's holy spirit, because that forming is followed by rebellion (Isa 63:10). The story will repeat itself. So God regrets making humanity (Gen 6:6, 7). Like the English word "regret," *nakham* (piel) denotes sorrow at something and a change of mind that issues in a change of plan. These two are related, and the word thus commonly denotes both, though it can focus more on the one or the other. Both ideas belong here. The further reference to emotion adds more explicit testimony to Yahweh's nature. Possessing emotions is one of the respects in which God and humanity are fundamentally alike. God is not without passions, as Christian doctrine has sometimes thought. As the First Testament will go on to show, God has all the emotions human beings have, and has them in spades. Indeed, the fact that human beings are passionate creatures (does that distinguish us from animals?), creatures characterized by compassion and anger, reflects our being made in God's image. The reference to pain and regret

---

[7] So Claus Westermann, *Genesis 1–11* (Minneapolis: Augsburg / London: SPCK, 1984), 172.

[8] Num 22:6 uses a passive form of the finite verb to make the statement of fact.

before there is any reference to anger again suggests that such soft emotions are more intrinsic to God's nature than hard emotions such as anger. Presumably the same is true of the beings made in God's image.

Admittedly Yahweh's reaction is then to decide to destroy the world, but Noah found favor in Yahweh's eyes (Gen 6:8). Yahweh acts in linear sequence. Excepting someone from the destruction was not part of the intention formulated in Gen 6:5–7, the emotional response of a grieved spirit. God made a decision and then modified it in the direction of mercy. That fits a pattern that will recur in the story of Sodom, of Israel at Sinai, and elsewhere, often because an intercessor prevails on Yahweh to modify a tough decision. Here there is no intercessor, but having punishment as second rather than first nature makes Yahweh capable of modifying tough decisions without necessarily requiring pressure from outside. The fact that Yahweh responds to such pressure constitutes an encouragement to intercession, but the fact that Yahweh can generate such modifications without being urged to do so constitutes an encouragement not to feel constrained by possible limitations within Yahweh's own character, as if Yahweh might be hard to persuade.

Genesis 12 also implies that blessing is Yahweh's natural activity, while cursing is less so. We might translate Yahweh's opening words to Abram, "Go from your land . . . to the land which I will show you, that I may make you a great nation, and bless you, and make your name great that you may effect blessing, and that I may bless the ones blessing you—and should there be one who regards you with contempt I will curse him. So, then, all the families of the earth can gain a blessing in you."[9] The last of the first-person verbs, "I will curse him," takes a different form from the four preceding ones. Those all state the purpose of the commission to "go."[10] The last first-person verb, "I will curse," is simply a declaration of intent, not a declaration of purpose.[11] Yahweh commands Abraham to go out to receive blessing and convey blessing, not to bring a curse, though Yahweh grants that the latter may happen in the process. The declaration about the curse is not part of Yahweh's direct intention but part of the undertaking to Abraham that promises him protection from people who oppose Yahweh's purpose to bless. Indeed, paradoxically, the curse is thus uttered for the sake of the world's blessing, to ensure that Yahweh's purpose to bless the world is not derailed.

The same point emerges from several aspects of Abraham's intercession for Sodom. First, that intercession is an outworking of Yahweh's commitment to bless the world, which leads Yahweh to determine to tell Abraham about the imminent fate of Sodom (Gen 18:18). Abraham does not take long to work out several implications of this revelation. As Yahweh waits with him (waiting for him to speak?), Abraham immediately begins to talk to Yahweh about Sodom and to challenge Yahweh about the propriety of destroying the city in a way that brings death to the

---

[9]In this paragraph I follow Patrick D. Miller, *Israelite Religion and Biblical Theology* (JSOTSup 267; Sheffield: Sheffield Academic Press, 2000), esp. 495.

[10]They are imperfect or cohortative, all preceded by simple *waw* indicating purpose. This construction is resumed in the subsequent clause that closes the quotation.

[11]The word order is varied so that the linking *waw* ("and") does not attach to the verb, as happens in a purpose clause.

faithless as well as the faithful. Yahweh agrees not to do that. Abraham's conversation with Yahweh anticipates Moses' conversation with Yahweh in Exod 32 (though Abraham is more deferential) and anticipates some other acts of intercession in the First Testament.[12] One of their recurrent features is that intercession is commonly designed to get Yahweh not to implement an intention to bring punishment and death. Their presupposition is the one explicitly and delightfully disparaged by Jonah when he fails to fulfill a prophet's vocation to pray for Yahweh not to implement the intention to punish. Jonah had said to himself back in Israel that Yahweh could not be relied on to carry out a threat to punish Nineveh, and this had been his reason for attempting to get out of being the means of providing Yahweh with the excuse for failing to do so. "I knew that you are a gracious and compassionate God, long-tempered and big in commitment, and relenting about calamity" (Jonah 4:2, with a reference to Exod 34).

Prayers for Yahweh to abandon the idea of bringing calamity may not always work, but being tough is not Yahweh's first nature, and therefore Yahweh is often a pushover when urged not to act in punishment. So Abraham can imagine the possibility that Yahweh might get angry with him (Gen 18:30, 32), and he knows Yahweh can curse, but he also knows that this is not Yahweh's first nature. In Yahweh's nature blessing has priority over cursing, love over anger, mercy over retribution.

3. The Intention to Punish in Hosea and Isaiah

Hosea 11 is the classic passage in the Prophets where Yahweh gives testimony to a tension between anger and compassion and to the victory of the latter. Yahweh speaks as a mother or father who has lovingly cared and provided for a child but found the child declining to acknowledge its parent. Yahweh therefore determines to thrash Israel. It will end up like other cities such as Admah and Zeboiim that Yahweh "overturned in his hot anger" (Deut 29:22).

But "how can I give you up, Ephraim? How surrender you, Israel? My heart has overturned upon me" (Hos 11:8). "Overturn" (*hapak*, here niphal) now describes something of which Yahweh is victim rather than subject. Yahweh's heart will not allow the implementing of the inclination to destroy. Yahweh had indeed acted on those other cities in "angry blazing" (cf. Deut 29:23), but here Yahweh says, "I will not act on my angry blazing" toward Ephraim (Hos 11:9). The reason is that "all my sorrow has heated up" (Hos 11:8). On the other occasions when something heats up, it is compassion (*rakhamim*; Gen 43:30; 1 Kgs 3:26), and compassion has had some prominence earlier in this book (Hos 1:6, 7, 8; 2:1, 4, 21, 23 [3, 6, 23, 25]; also 14:3 [4]). One might thus have expected compassion to feature in Hos 11, especially as *rakhamim* is a motherly virtue and this testimony may reflect a mother's experience. Talk instead of sorrow (*nikhumim*), a word similar in sound and overlapping in meaning, introduces a suggestive ambiguity. This word occurs only twice elsewhere (Isa 57:13; Zech 1:13), where it suggests pity or comfort

---

[12]See further chapter 14 below.

and thus has similar implications to compassion. But we have noted that the verb *nakham* can also suggest sorrow at having done something (e.g., 1 Sam 15:35) or second thoughts at the idea of doing something (e.g., Amos 7:3, 6). Either or both implications would be appropriate here (NRSV has "compassion," NEB "remorse"). Yahweh could be pulled back from overturning Ephraim either by pity at the idea of it or by a capacity for relenting in connection with a proposed act of punishment. Either way, Hos 11 acknowledges that within Yahweh two fires burn, the fire of anger and the fire of sorrow, but these are not fires of equal strength. The fire of sorrow is stronger than the fire of anger.

That is so because Yahweh is God and not a man (Hos 11:9). Again, Yahweh perhaps makes the most of the ambiguity in a word. From NRSV's "mortal" or TNIV's "human being" we might have inferred that the word for man is *'adam*, but it is *'ish*, which commonly suggests a man over against a woman (*'ishshah*). It can refer to an individual person without drawing attention to gender, like traditional English "a man," but it would be an odd word to use thus in this context, especially when Hosea has made much use of *'ish* to denote a male, and specifically a husband (Hos 2:2, 7, 10, 16 [4, 9, 12, 18]; 3:3).[13] Hosea's statement is that Yahweh is not a man but someone in Ephraim's midst as holy one (Hos 11:9). There is a sense in which Yahweh wants Israel to look at Yahweh as her *'ish*, as opposed to her *ba'al* (Hos 2:16 [18]). Yahweh wants to be her man, not her lord and master. Patriarchal marriage is not Yahweh's ideal. But any form of marriage might be a frightening prospect when we have seen in Hos 1–3 how Hosea and Yahweh treat their women. Hosea 11 implies that the abusive husbands of Hos 1–3 are not the book's sole model for the way Yahweh wants to relate to Ephraim. Yahweh there threatened to behave like a man but here withdraws the threat. Yahweh has threatened to withdraw from Ephraim (Hos 5:6, 15) but has not done so, like a woman who said she was going to abandon her children but in the end could not let herself do so. Yahweh is not a man but is the holy one, still in the people's midst.[14] Yahweh's testimony has indicated that the essence of Yahweh's holiness lies in being vulnerable to the overcoming of fierce anger by sorrow, pity, and the inclination to relent about punishing people.

The closing sections of the book show that we cannot read the move from the story in Hos 1–3 to the testimony in Hos 11 as a once-for-all linear sequence; there are more threats to come. Indeed, Yahweh will declare that "sorrow hides from my eyes" (Hos 13:14).[15] And the broader context of Hosea in the prophets also suggests that the tension between anger and compassion abides.

Isaiah 28:21 implies the same tension and comes to the opposite conclusion to Hos 11. Yahweh is to bring death on Judah. "As at Mount Perizim Yahweh will arise, as at the Valley of Gibeon will thunder, to do his deed (strange his deed) and to work his work (alien his work)." Isaiah looks back to battles when Yahweh spectacularly

---

[13] See further John Goldingay and Gillian Cooper, "Hosea and Gomer Visit the Marriage Counselor," in *First Person: Essays in Biblical Autobiography* (ed. Philip R. Davies; London / New York: Sheffield Academic Press, 2002), 119–36 (see 135–36).

[14] Cf. Graham I. Davies, *Hosea* (Grand Rapids: Eerdmans, 1992), 264.

[15] "Sorrow" is *nokham*, a variant for *nikhumim* occurring only here.

defeated the Philistines before David (see 1 Sam 5; 1 Chr 14) and declares that Yahweh is again to arise and thunder thus.[16] But this time the deed that emerges from that arising and thundering will be strange and alien.

The statement that Yahweh will act in a strange way is allusive. It surely means more than that this is a strange experience for Judah.[17] Perhaps the prophet speaks elliptically and describes bringing calamity to Judah as the act of a stranger, the kind of thing one might expect of another god or another people. It is strange and alien to Yahweh's relationship with Judah. The natural way for Yahweh to exercise the capacity to bring death is to do that to the people's enemies. For Yahweh to act thus toward Judah is to turn things upside down. Indeed, Yahweh is thus acting in a way that is strange and alien to who Yahweh is. It is not natural to Yahweh to bring calamity, but Yahweh is going to be resolute about acting thus, alien though it is.

In practice in Isaiah's day, Yahweh's resolution fails at the last minute. Yahweh can bring foes to the gates of Jerusalem but is not steadfast enough to let the city fall (e.g., Isa 29:1–8). In the end, the implication is similar to that of the testimony in Hos 11.

4. After Punishing: Lamentations, Jeremiah, Isaiah 40–55

But Yahweh does become tired of sorrow (Jer 15:6), raises the resolve to punish, overcomes the instincts of the heart, and lets blazing anger express itself on Ephraim and later on Judah.

After that, Lamentations nevertheless restates the point about the relationship between anger and Yahweh's heart with particular succinctness. At the center of Lamentations comes the affirmation, "The Lord does not reject forever, but hurts and [then] has compassion, in accordance with the magnitude of his acts of commitment, because he does not afflict and hurt human beings from his heart" (Lam 3:32–33). It is the phrase "not . . . from his heart" that is especially striking. English translations paraphrase the expression by speaking of Yahweh not "willingly" afflicting people. This translation makes the point in a vivid way, in offering the picture of Yahweh acting unwillingly. And the expression "from my heart" can indeed imply "of my own will": Moses and Balaam use it to refer to something that does not come from their own will but from Yahweh's (Num 16:28; 24:13). But if Yahweh's act emerged from some other will, whose will was that? And if Yahweh's act emerged from some other will, how would that support the idea that Yahweh does not reject forever?

More likely the heart here suggests not the will but the deepest springs of the person. Action undertaken from the heart is action that corresponds to the inner being and is thus undertaken with enthusiasm. It expresses who the person truly

---

[16]RSV translates *ragaz* "be wroth," and it would suit my argument to give the verb this meaning, but it is doubtful if it ever has that precise connotation; it refers to a physical stirring of oneself, in other contexts often caused by fear.

[17]Cf. L. A. Snijders, "The Meaning of *zār* in the First Testament," *OtSt* 10 (1954): 1–154 (see 38). He later sees the word as suggesting something harmful and hostile (see 55).

is (e.g., Isa 59:13). Lamentations is then implying that the reason Yahweh's punishment does not last forever is that, as we might put it, Yahweh's heart is not in it.

After the fall of Jerusalem and the assassination of the Babylonian governor, during the period when the traditional critical view assumes Lamentations was being written and used, Judeans somewhat belatedly ask Jeremiah what they should do now. The answer is consistent with Jeremiah's previous words and actions. If they submit to the Babylonian yoke and stay in Judah, Yahweh says, "then I will build you and not demolish, plant you and not uproot, because I regret the disaster I caused to you. Do not be afraid of the king of Babylon . . . because I am with you to deliver you and rescue you from his power. I will grant you compassion, and he will have compassion on you and restore you to your land" (Jer 42:10–12).

Yahweh here uses the verb "feel sorry/regret" (*nakham* niphal) related to the word "sorrow" in Hos 11, with the two possible meanings we have noted. There are contexts where Yahweh's regret implies that a knowledge of how things would turn out would have made Yahweh act differently. The implication is that while having the capacity to foresee how things will turn out, Yahweh often refrains from doing so and lives through events in linear sequence with people.[18] It could then be that seeing how things are going from bad to worse makes Yahweh here express regret at letting Jerusalem fall to Babylon. Or, regret can also mean being sorry that one has to act in a certain way but accepting that one has to do so. It then does not mean one would act differently next time. The context suggests that here Yahweh is indeed thus regretting the necessity to take the action that had to be taken. Yahweh is prepared to do the tough thing, if necessary, and will do it again. But Yahweh does it with regret.

Against the background of the exile, Yahweh elsewhere declares, "Shaper of light and creator of dark, maker of well-being and creator of adversity, I am Yahweh, maker of all these" (Isa 45:7). As is often the case, dark is an image for disaster and light for deliverance and blessing in the midst of disaster (e.g., Isa 8:22 [9:1]; Pss 27:1; 36:9 [10]). The same significance attaches to the introduction of light in Gen 1, the creation story that suggests the context of exile. When God says, "There is to be light," Gen 1 doubtless does refer to physical light illumining literal darkness. But following on the talk of formless void, darkness over the deep, and mighty wind, "light" also carries those other resonances, suggesting safety where otherwise there would be threat, meaning where otherwise there would be a void, order where otherwise uncontrollable tumult could develop. God can act as creator of darkness as well as shaper of light, but at the beginning it was not so. Genesis does not tell us "God said, 'There shall be darkness and light,' and there were darkness and light, and God saw that both darkness and light were good." It presupposes darkness and has God introducing light.[19] At the beginning it was the background for God's insisting that these realities should be succeeded by light. That indicates God's purpose for Israel.

Declaring that disaster as well as blessing comes from Yahweh reassures readers that there is no other power than Yahweh's at work in the world. The disaster

---

[18] See further chapter 3, which follows.

[19] Jon D. Levenson, *Creation and the Persistence of Evil* (reissued ed.; Princeton, N.J.: Princeton University Press, 1994), xxiv.

that has come on the community is within Yahweh's sovereignty. But such disasters are no more God's first word than God's last. All that God did at the beginning looked good. The world was founded as something good. When it went bad, it went against its nature. Further, the founding of the world involved the streaming of light into darkness. While darkness and light are equally within God's sovereignty, they are not equally God's purpose or aim (Gen 1:3–4). God's drive is toward light, not darkness, and in founding the world God asserted that priority.

A further feature of Isa 40–55 is significant here. These chapters promise that Yahweh will restore the Judean community in exile in Babylon. Yahweh will do that as an expression of *sedeq* (e.g., Isa 45:13; 51:1, 5, 7) or of *sedaqah* (e.g., Isa 46:12, 13; 51:6, 8). They will be the acts of one who is *saddiq* (e.g., Isa 45:21). Elsewhere these words are routinely translated by English words such as "justice" or "righteousness," and we have noted the familiar idea that God is "a just God and a savior." But in a number of the above passages this does not work, and NRSV, for instance, thus renders the nouns "deliverance." Yahweh's act of restoration is an act of *sedeq*. But it would be weird to describe it as an act of justice, as if the Judeans deserved to be delivered. The prophet rather implies that it is an act of grace. It is indeed an act of *sedeq* in the sense that it means Yahweh is doing the right thing by the community. But Yahweh is doing the right thing by them in the sense that this is the act that emerges from Yahweh's character and from Yahweh's commitment to this people. It is not an act of justice, but it is an act of *sedeq*. The notion of justice presupposes that people are treated in a fair way and that everyone is treated in the same way. There are contexts in which the First Testament believes in such justice, but it is not the essence of the idea of *sedeq*. That is a relational word that denotes acting in a way that is proper to one's relationship with people. Thus *saddiq* often means something like "faithful."

After people have been freed to return to Judah and some have done so, Ezra prays a prayer of confession in which he declares, "Yahweh, God of Israel, you are *saddiq*, because we have survived as a remnant" (Ezra 9:15). His argument is not merely that Yahweh was in the right in reducing them to a remnant. It is that Yahweh's true nature as *saddiq* has also been reflected in not letting them cease to exist altogether. The Levites later comment that in giving the land of Canaan to their ancestors, "You kept your word, because you are *saddiq*" (Neh 9:8). In our terms, giving the land to the Israelites may seem an act of injustice to the Canaanites. This prayer sees it as an act of *sedaqah* toward Israel. Such an understanding of Yahweh's being in the right corresponds to the meaning of the idea in Isa 40–55. What Isa 45:21 declares is that "Yahweh is a faithful God and a deliverer." The people continue in being because Yahweh continues to treat them as a special people who have rights emerging from Yahweh's having made a commitment to them.

5. Yahweh's Asymmetry

It is a commonplace of human experience that people have dominant aspects to their personality and secondary aspects. They may, for instance, be more inclined to action or reflection, to idealism or realism, to planning or the serendipity, to firmness or flexibility, to orientation on the present or on the future. Both elements in each pair are good. We might be inclined to think that it would be ideal to have each of these in balance within the individual, though people are rarely like that. Perhaps God prefers to achieve that balance by having within the human body and within the body of Christ people who are more inclined to one or the other, because this encourages us to live together rather than being self-sufficient.

Whatever are our dominant characteristics as individuals, however, we have some capacity to summon up the correlative characteristics when we require these. Our dominant side is complemented by a secondary side.

The First Testament picture implies that in this regard God is like a human being; once again, it links with our being made in God's image. It may be that God has some personality aspects in balance. God holds together idealism and realism, which often startles Bible readers who expect God to be wholly visionary and are surprised at the condescension to practicalities and waywardness expressed in Moses' Teaching. God holds together firmness and flexibility, so that Moses' Teaching lays down the law in detail, yet does so in ways that reflect changes in the way God guided people over the centuries and sometimes explicitly testifies to the way God can be flexible (e.g., Num 27; cf. 2 Chr 30:18–20).

At other points there are dominant aspects to God's character and secondary aspects. For instance, while Gen 1 and Gen 2 indicate that God combines a capacity for planning and for the serendipity, the biblical story as a whole suggests that God is more inclined to serendipity. Again, this surprises Bible readers who have inferred from references to God's planning and to God's sovereignty that God had a detailed plan for world history from the beginning, and for their own lives, but find that the Bible does not suggest that.

The First Testament also makes clear that toughness and softness or justice and mercy do not have an equal place in Yahweh's moral character. Yahweh can summon up the capacity to act tough from time to time, but this does not issue from the heart. Yahweh's dominant side is to be loving and merciful.

First Testament study has difficulty in accepting that there is both a compassionate and a tough side to Yahweh. For the most part, First Testament study emphasizes the positive side to Yahweh, leaving it to a minority from time to time to draw attention to the acts of Yahweh the rough beast. We do not see how to bring these two together. In this we resemble ourselves as children in our attitude to our parents, and in our attitude to ourselves. As small children our instinct is to see our parents either as all good or as all bad; either they do what we want, and they are all good, or they fail to do what we want and act in ways that seem inexplicable, and they are all bad. Good and bad are thus not moral categories but relational ones that point to what seems good or bad from the perspective of our desires and perceptions. Growing toward maturity involves coming to see that our parents are neither all good nor all bad, in that sense and in other senses. They are people in their own right with their own agendas and concerns, which include matters that are priorities to us but which extend beyond those in ways we may not be able to understand. They are not all good or all bad in the way they approach our agenda, but a mixture.

Growing toward maturity involves coming to a related realization about ourselves, though here good and bad have more moral connotations. To see oneself as wholly good or wholly bad is a sign of immaturity or delusion. We, too, are not all bad or all good, but a mixture. Maturity involves coming to own that ambivalence in ourselves.

Christians often expect God to be all good. In a moral sense that is presumably true, but our perspective on God's goodness is often that of children in relation to their parents' goodness. A major theme in Yahweh's confrontation of Job is that Yahweh's agenda and concern for the world are much broader than involving merely what is good for Job or even for humanity as a whole. As far as we are concerned, God does good and bad things, and often we cannot see how the things that feel bad and look bad (the acts of the rough beast) can be the acts of one who is good. Living by trust in God involves coming to believe that they may be so. As with our parents (if we are lucky), the evidence is the fact that many of God's acts do look good. We then trust God for the others. The First Testament shows us that this need by no means exclude protesting about them or owning them by telling stories about them that do not at all pretend to explain them. If we have been able to come to recognize our parents as people who combine good and bad in the first sense, and ourselves as people who combine good and bad in the second sense, we may have an easier time accepting that God combines good and bad in the first sense. And we may have an easier time accepting that the appearance of bad in the second sense may indeed be only an appearance, even though we cannot see how that is so.

There are acts of grace and roughness that are inexplicable as there are acts of blessing and toughness that are explicable, though many, many more of the former than of the latter. Whether acting explicably or inexplicably, Yahweh's dominant side is to be loving and merciful.

3

DOES GOD HAVE SURPRISES?

Over the past twenty or thirty years there has been a lively debate about the omniscience of God.[1] It is in large part a revisiting of the older debate about predestination and free will, or a subset of that debate, and many people on one side of the debate do not mind being called Calvinists, while many on the other side do not mind being called Arminians. Much of the practical energy of the debate issues from a concern that belief in God's sovereignty and omniscience is hard to reconcile with belief in human freedom and responsibility.[2] The question then is how we can hold onto both beliefs or whether we need to qualify one of them. The debate has been largely carried on by philosophers and theologians, though they have also sought to pay serious attention to scripture.[3] In this chapter, I come at the question as an exegete, albeit one who has been described as a theologian who only presents himself as an exegete and who doesn't mind that description, in order to look at the material in scripture that relates to the nature and extent of God's knowledge. My suspicion has been that the biblical material partly supports and partly contrasts with both open theism and classical theism, but also that in the way it does so it suggests a different framework for considering the question. Convictions and questions that we bring to scripture commonly enable us to see things there that we might otherwise miss but also need to have their own perspective reframed, and that is true about classical theism and open theism, as of other things that end in "-ism" (Calvinism, Arminianism, evangelicalism, fundamentalism, feminism, postcolonialism, pietism, pacifism . . .). These –isms overlap with scripture, but they combine scripture with traditions or thinking from elsewhere. Classical theism then involves scripture by pointing to texts that might

---

[1] Not previously published.

[2] See, e.g., Paul Helm, *Eternal God* (Oxford / New York: Oxford University Press, 1988), xiii; Steven C. Roy, *How Much Does God Foreknow?* (Downers Grove, Ill. / Nottingham, UK: InterVarsity Press, 2006), 13.

[3] For instance, Richard Rice, the originator of the debate on open theism in *The Openness of God* (Nashville: Review and Herald, 1980) and the author of the chapter "Biblical Support for a New Perspective" in Clark Pinnock et al., *The Openness of God* (Downers Grove, Ill.: InterVarsity Press, 1994), 11–58, is a professor of theology and philosophy of religion. Steven Roy, the author of *How Much Does God Foreknow?* is a professor of pastoral theology. But Terence Fretheim, who writes on divine foreknowledge in *The Suffering of God* (Philadelphia: Fortress, 1984), 45–59, is an Old Testament professor.

seem to support the theological convictions it affirms. Open theism likewise looks for biblical support for the perspective that it advocates on the basis of different theological convictions.[4] But both sets of convictions emerge from cultures (one more ancient Greek, one more postmodern). My study will also reflect who I am, a renegade English Episcopalian professor of Old Testament. But that may enable me to see some other things.

1. God's Knowledge of the Future

In the debate about the extent of God's knowledge, the major difference concerns God's knowledge of the future. Classical and open theists agree that God knows everything. Their disagreement concerns the extent of this "everything." Classical theism affirms that it embraces past, present, and future. Augustine, an ancient classical theist, declares, "One who is not foreknowing of all future things is certainly not God."[5] Omniscience is part of the definition of the word "God." By contrast, open theism notes that the future does not exist and therefore logically cannot be known; the "everything" that exists and that God knows is confined to past and present. John Sanders, a contemporary open theist, declares, "God knows all the past and present but there is no exhaustively definite future for God to know."[6]

While I want to try to look at the way scripture talks about God's knowledge without letting that way of setting up the question determine the way scripture has to provide its answers, I begin with the question whether God knows everything about the future, because of this disagreement.

a. When God Knows How Things Will Turn Out

God often does know ahead of time things that are going to happen. One reason for this is that God has decided that they will happen; and when God decides things, they come about. An Egyptian king has a dream about fat cows and thin cows, and Joseph tells him what it means and prefaces this explanation by declaring, "God has announced to Pharaoh what he is doing" (Gen 41:25; cf. 28). Joseph's words concern not merely what God foresees. God intends to bring about seven years of plenty and seven years of famine. "The matter has been fixed by God, and God is ready to do it" (Gen 41:32). God can speak of such events in the future because God has decided to make them happen.

The book called Isaiah emphasizes this perspective more systematically than any other book in the Bible. Near its beginning, Isaiah declares that many nations are going to come to Jerusalem and that God will sort out their conflicts so that they can enjoy a huge peace dividend (Isa 2:2–4). More solemnly, God declares

---

[4] See the title of the chapter by Rice just noted.

[5] Augustine, *City of God* 5.9.

[6] John Sanders, *The God Who Risks* (Downers Grove, Ill.: InterVarsity Press, 1998), 129.

that before then, Assyria, the superpower of the day, is going to invade Judah and attack Jerusalem (e.g., Isa 5:26–30). God is going to make these things happen. Later in the book, being able to declare what is going to happen and then make it happen is one of the reasons why people should recognize that Yahweh alone is God. Assyria is put down by Babylon, and Babylon is put down by Persia to make it possible for Judean exiles in Babylon to go home. Who made that happen? Yahweh made it happen. And the evidence of this is that Yahweh had said it was going to happen. Yahweh or Yahweh's prophets are not like someone telling you after 9/11 what it meant and why it happened. Yahweh tells people before things happen and is then in a position afterwards to say, "You see? I said it would happen, and it has happened. *Now* will you acknowledge that the Babylonian gods are not worth paying attention to?" (Isa 41:21–29). In the New Testament, Peter similarly argues that Jesus' betrayal happened "by the fixed plan and foreknowledge of God" (Acts 2:23). In this connection, it is inappropriate to think of God predicting things; you do not predict things if you are the person who makes them happen. At the beginning of a class, if a student tells a visitor, "He will lecture for thirty minutes, and then we will have twenty minutes' discussion," this is a prediction. But if the professor says, "I will lecture for thirty minutes, and then we will have twenty minutes' discussion," this is not a prediction but a declaration of intent.

There are other events that God knows about ahead of time without being the one who makes them happen, at least not in that direct and purposeful way presupposed by Genesis and Isaiah. God knows that Abraham's descendants will live as serfs in a foreign country and will be ill-treated for four hundred years (Gen 15:13). God's aide is able to say what kind of person Ishmael will turn out to be (Gen 16:12). God knows Pharaoh will not let Israel go unless he is forced to (Exod 3:19). Sometimes it is not clear whether God knows something because of having supernatural knowledge or whether God is declaring an intent; this is the case when God declares the consequences that will follow from Adam and Eve's disobedience and from Cain's fratricide and declares how Esau and Jacob's personalities will emerge (e.g., Gen 3:14–19; 4:10–15; 25:23). In the New Testament, NRSV sees the readers of 1 Pet 1:2 as "chosen and destined by God . . . to be obedient to Jesus Christ," but TNIV describes them more literally as "chosen according to the foreknowledge of God," which could imply that God chose on the basis of foreknowing their own decision. On other occasions God may know what is going to happen because it is possible to infer it from facts about the present, especially for one who is very knowledgeable about the present.

Now God is not timeless in the sense of outside time,[7] but God is involved in all time. God is omni-temporal. Might that be why God can know the future, because all time is simultaneously present to God? This would be a rather paradoxical concept, though it might be none the worse for that. Yet being involved in all time need not imply that all time is simultaneously present to God. I have been involved in and present to the whole of the last sixty-six years, but not all at once.

---

[7] But Helm defends this traditional view in *Eternal God*, whose subtitle is *A Study of God without Time*.

Scripture's narrative account of God would suggest that God's involvement in all time is a linear one. There is a before and after for God. For God, there is such a thing as remembering and anticipating. But that does open up the possibility for God of moving from present to past and future, as in a limited way human beings can. And thus God can make it possible for a prophet to see something and speak of it as past when it is still future.

Further, God is not the only person who can know things about the future, and prophets who speak in Yahweh's name are not the only human beings who do so. While scripture sometimes portrays diviners, astrologists, and "false prophets" as charlatans, it sometimes assumes that such people do have true knowledge about the future. Deuteronomy 13 envisages a prophet or diviner wishing to get Israel to worship another god and announcing a sign that then does come about, though it probably implies that it is God who makes this false prophet able to do this. The serpent speaks more accurately than God of the consequences that will follow from eating the fruit of the knowledge tree (Gen 3:5). In the New Testament, prophets such as Agabus can announce things about the future (Acts 11:28); the New Testament sees prophecy as a gift that would be exercised in the church, and Christian history has seen much exercise of that gift. One of the stories about Agabus also indicates the assumption that knowing about the future makes it possible to change it (Acts 21:10–12), which is also a presupposition of divination and astrology.

And if human beings can sometimes know the future without all time being present to them, we can perhaps surrender to Ockham's razor the problematic idea of all time being simultaneously present to God.

b. When God Does Not Know How Things Will Turn Out

So there are many occasions when God knows about what is to happen in the future, either on the basis of being the one who decides it, or by supernatural insight, or by inference from the present. But there are other occasions when this is not so. For instance, there are occasions when God has not yet decided what to do. When the people make the golden calf at Sinai, God says, "Remove your finery, and I will know what I shall do with you" (Exod 33:5). In light of this comment, God's exasperated question, "What am I to do with you, Ephraim?" (Hos 6:4) may not be purely rhetorical. God's decision-making takes place in time.

There are other aspects of the future that God does not know. I begin from the fact that God sometimes uses the word "perhaps." God sends Jeremiah to address the worshipers in the temple. "Perhaps they will listen and turn, each one, from his wrong way, so that I may relent of the trouble that I am planning to cause to them" (Jer 26:3; cf. 36:3). God sends Ezekiel to dramatize before his people the exile that threatens those same worshipers, and God comments, "Perhaps they will see" (Ezek 12:3). It is an open question whether this will happen, an open question for God as for anyone else. God has hopes that it might happen but waits on events to discover whether it will be so. Not all the future is present to God.

This had been so from the beginning, as appears from passages that do not use the word "perhaps." God brings the animals to Adam "to see what he would call them" (Gen 2:19); it is perhaps implied that only in light of doing this does God decide to make Adam a dedicated partner (Gen 2:20–22). When God bids Moses lead the Israelites out of Egypt, Moses asks what to do if they will not listen. God gives Moses a sign to perform before them, then another sign, and adds, "If they do not believe you or pay heed to the first sign, they may believe the second,"[8] and after this adds further that "if they do not believe even these two signs and pay heed to your voice," Moses is to perform a third sign (Exod 4:1–9). God seems not to know at what point the people may come to believe.[9]

c. When Things Turn Out Differently from God's Expectations

Further, God experiences disappointment. It is possible to experience disappointment only if one hoped for something and had not foreseen that it would not happen. About the year 740, the prophet Isaiah became a singer-songwriter. "I am going to sing for my dear friend a love song about his vineyard," he declared (Isa 5:1). To us the notion of a love song about a vineyard would be odd, but this would not be the case for Isaiah's friend; he would be familiar with the metaphor of vinedresser and vineyard as a way of speaking about a man and the woman he loved. The metaphor recurs in the Song of Songs (e.g., 1:6; 2:15; 7:8 [9]; 8:11–12). Isaiah was composing a song that his friend could sing for his girl, or that Isaiah could sing to her on his behalf. The song comes to an unexpected conclusion. The vinedresser expected the vineyard to produce good grapes, but it produced sour grapes. The song turns out to be more like a blues, a song about a love affair that did not work out, which is what singer-songwriters usually sing about. But Isaiah's actual audience is his usual one, the people who gather in the temple courts in Jerusalem. In case they cannot work out the significance of his sad song, he spells it out. The vinedresser assumed grapes would grow, but they did not. The lover hoped love would grow, and it did not. God expected *mishpat and tsedaqah* to grow, and they did not.[10]

In what sense had God expected *mishpat* and *tsedaqah* to grow? Might God have expected it only in the sense of requiring it?[11] On the eve of the Battle of

---

[8] Or "they *will* believe the second" (NJPS); but God's adding a possible third sign suggests the matter is not fixed.

[9] But Berel Dov Lerner, for whose critique of this chapter I am grateful, suggests that this is a kind of *argumentum ad hominem*: God is trying to calm Moses down by saying, "If the first sign does not convince them, don't worry, the second one will, or the third one will."

[10] We do not have words in English that correspond very well to *mishpat* and *tsedaqah*; translations use words such as "justice" and "righteousness," but these come rather short of giving the right impression. The words suggest something like "the faithful exercise of authority."

[11] So David Hunt, "A Simple-Foreknowledge Response," in *Divine Foreknowledge: Four Views* (ed. James K. Beilby and Paul R. Eddy; Downers Grove, Ill.: InterVarsity Press, 2001), 48–54 (50–51).

Trafalgar in 1805 Lord Nelson signaled to his fleet, "England expects that every man will do his duty." He could have meant that he anticipates that they will, or that he is laying an obligation on them. But this ambiguity about the English word "expect" does not extend to the Hebrew verb *qawah* (piel). That verb means expect in the sense of "hope" (NJPS). God, like some vinedressers and some lovers, expected but had a surprise, and it was an unpleasant one, as was usually the case in God's experience; God gets few nice surprises, though that is partly because God is always hoping for the best of us, as hope springs eternal in the divine breast. God had not foreseen the result of tending the vineyard.

Isaiah's love song is not unique in implying that God had hopes that were disappointed. Jeremiah, too, speaks of Israel's attitude to God as surprising and disheartening. Israel had been unfaithful to God. "And I said [to myself],"[12] God tells us, "after doing all these things, she will turn to me; but she did not turn" (Jer 3:6–7). Later, God puts it another way, recalling having resolved to adopt Israel as a member of the family, "and I said [to myself], you will call to me as 'my Father,' and in future you will not turn [away]";[13] but Israel had been faithless, had turned away elsewhere (Jer 3:19–20). Zephaniah likewise underlines the depth of God's disappointed conviction about Jerusalem: "I said [to myself], 'She will definitely revere me, receive discipline.' . . . On the contrary, they could not wait to practice corruption in all their deeds" (Zeph 3:7).[14] Isaiah 63:8–10 reports that "God said [to himself], 'They are indeed my people, children who will not play false.' . . . But those people rebelled and grieved his holy spirit." Things turn out differently from God's expectations.

Deuteronomy 32 speaks in very different terms from Isa 63 and Jeremiah.[15] It is a song Moses recites to Israel as part of his dying farewell to the people. Like Exod 15:1–17, it first speaks of events in Moses' day, then of events to follow after Israel enters the land, but Moses continues to describe these in the past tense. In Deut 32, rhetorically Moses stands at a point after Yahweh has abandoned Israel because of its faithlessness but when Yahweh is promising that this will not be the end. In this respect it differs from the chapters that precede (Deut 28–31), which speak about the obedience and disobedience that Israel may show after Moses' day and the consequences that will follow. It is logically possible that Moses composed the song in this form, but the rest of Deuteronomy was composed not by Moses but by anonymous theologians long after Moses' day, and it makes sense to assume that the same is true of Deut 32. Why, then, was the song put onto his lips?

The phenomenon parallels the visions in Dan 7–12. God gave these not to Daniel in the sixth century but to anonymous visionaries in the second century, though humanly speaking, those visions are in some sense inspired by the vision in Dan 2. A further parallel is the way the prophecies in Isa 40–55 were in part inspired by prophecies in Isa 1–39, and the prophecies in Isa 56–66 were in part inspired by

---

[12] "I said to myself" is a common implication of the ordinary Hebrew verb "I said."

[13] Again, this is a common implication of the ordinary word for "turn."

[14] "They could not wait" translates the verb *shakam*, which etymologically suggests that they got up early in the morning to practice this corruption.

[15] I am grateful to Joe Henderson for suggesting I consider this chapter.

prophecies in Isa 1–55. Likewise, the song in Deut 32 was perhaps in part inspired by Moses. Its theology coheres with his; it projects that theology forward, showing how it works out in the centuries that followed.

Through the visions in Dan 7–12, God assures the people of Jerusalem that events since Daniel's day have been under divine control. It is as if God had laid them out ahead of time in their meaninglessness and tragedy. If they were under divine control, people have a basis for believing that God is in control of the Antiochene crisis as it unfolds and that God will deliver the community. This indeed happened and showed that these pseudonymous visions did come from God. Deuteronomy 32 does something parallel for its audience, though its message is different, and it presents it in a slightly different way. Instead of putting onto Daniel's lips future-tense predictions of events that are past from the perspective of their authors and audience, it puts onto Moses' lips a past-tense report of events that are future from Moses' perspective but past from the perspective of its authors and their audience. Like Deuteronomy as a whole, it thereby puts them into the position of the generation standing before Moses. It challenges them to see themselves there and to come to repentance in light of the history that (as it were) Moses knows all about. It promises them that God's abandonment is not the end of their story. If we assume that the rhetorical position that Deut 32 takes, after Israel's abandonment and before its restoration, is the time when it was composed, this could imply a time between Jeremiah and Isa 63. As God did not foretell the events in Daniel's visions but could have done so, so God did not foretell the events in Deut 32 but could have done so.

Reading the chapter in its own rhetorical context has another implication. Deuteronomy 31:14–29 has worked with that placing of Moses and the people on the edge of the land, with Moses gloomily convinced that the people will turn from the way he has taught them when they are in the land. The Torah book will thus sit there beside the covenant chest "as a testimony against you." But God has already prescribed that like the Torah, the song in Deut 32 "is to be written, taught, and put in the mouths of the people (v. 19)," and thus "like the law, it will be not only a testimony after the fact but a warning beforehand."[16] The implication then is that Moses' song has not predetermined what must happen. Like the predictions in Deut 31, it is a prophecy that Israel has the chance to refute. And Yahweh will be hoping that Israel does so.

d. When Things Turn Out Differently from God's Announcements

This leads into a consideration of other passages where things indeed turn out differently from God's announcement. While scripture often states or assumes

---

[16] Patrick D. Miller, *Deuteronomy* (Louisville: John Knox, 1990), 225. He goes on to quote Harold Fisch, who speaks of it acting as a mnemonic, "because during the intervening period it will have lived unforgotten in the mouth of the reader or hearer, ready to come to mind when the troubles arrive. Poetry is thus a kind of time bomb," waiting its time to explode (*Poetry with a Purpose* [Bloomington: Indiana University Press, 1988], 51).

that events happen as God declared they would, a number of accounts of God making such declarations are followed by accounts of how events did not turn out as God said. Micah's prophecy that Jerusalem would be destroyed (Mic 3:12) was not fulfilled, because the king submitted himself to God and begged mercy (Jer 26:17–19). God commissioned Jonah to proclaim that in forty days Nineveh would be destroyed, but it was not (Jonah 3:4, 10). In such situations, the declaration of intent presupposed an "unless" clause, "unless you repent"; the "unless" clause is elaborated in Jer 18:1–12. That is, God's declarations of intent presuppose that people will carry on behaving as they are behaving at the moment, for good or ill. But if they do not, what God says will happen, will not happen.

A different form of "unless" clause is presupposed by the story of David's escape from Keilah (1 Sam 23:7–13). David is being pursued by Saul. He asks God whether Saul will follow him to this town where he has taken refuge and whether its people will surrender him to Saul. God says the answer to both questions is yes: Saul will follow him, and the people will surrender him. So David flees, and neither declaration comes true. God's statements about the future can be dependent on certain assumptions, but it is open to the people involved to change the suppositions.

God said Nebuchadnezzar would capture Tyre but later refers to the fact that Nebuchadnezzar did not, and God therefore promised him Egypt instead (Ezek 26:1–21; 29:17–20). Here in yet another way, human responses have caused God's declaration not to come true; God notes that Tyre resisted Nebuchadnezzar too hard. Now presumably God could have made it possible to overwhelm Tyre's resistance, as happened when God deprived Sennacherib of the satisfaction of taking Jerusalem (1 Kgs 19). But God did not do so. The First Testament makes no further comment on this phenomenon and seems untroubled by it.[17] We might compare other stories of God being overcome by human strength. When Moses is on his way back to Egypt, "God met him and sought to kill him." But God did not succeed. Zipporah took action, circumcising her son, "and God let him [Moses] alone" (Exod 4:24–26). God sought to kill Moses, but Moses or Zipporah would not cooperate. The story recalls an earlier occasion when someone wrestled all night with Jacob and in the morning declared, "You have striven with God and with humanity and won." Jacob's naming of the place Peniel suggests the conviction that "I saw God face to face and my life was preserved" (Gen 32:25–31).

God had said that on the day Adam ate of the knowledge tree, he would definitely die (Gen 2:17); he did not do so, though on that day he did lose the possibility of immortality. There is no indication of a change of heart on Adam's part that leads God to have a change of heart. There are other accounts of God having a change of heart or relenting (*nakham* niphal) because of considerations that come from inside God rather than as a result of human response to God's word (e.g., Exod 32:11–14; Num 14:13–20; Amos 7:1–6). God can make a decision on the basis of the need to punish wrongdoing but then change it on the basis of the need to be merciful.

---

[17] For further examples in Jer 22; 34; 36, see John Goldingay, *Old Testament Theology Volume Two: Israel's Faith* (Downers Grove, Ill.: InterVarsity Press / Carlisle: Paternoster, 2006), 83–84.

When things turn out differently from God's announcements, this does not mean God is fallible. There are implicit if not explicit conditions attached both to declarations of intent and to declarations of what must follow as an outworking of the present. God's declarations imply "unless I find reason to change my mind" or "unless circumstances change or people change." In either case, God having a change of mind will happen only within the context of consistency and commitment to achieving the goals that God had determined.

Similar considerations apply to occasions when things turn out differently from Jesus' announcements.[18] Jesus said that some people standing in his presence would not taste death until they saw God's reign come with power (Mark 9:1). While his transfiguration, his death, his resurrection, the giving of the Spirit, the spread of the gospel, and the fall of Jerusalem all count in different ways as such a coming of God's reign with power, none has the finality of consummation that his words suggest. His prophecy in Mark 13 likewise gives the impression that all the events he speaks of will come in the lifetime of the disciples to whom he is speaking. In some words that appear only in the Matthean version of part of his prophecy (Matt 9:23), he promises the disciples that when they flee from persecution, they will not have exhausted all possible refuges "before the Son of Man comes." Even though he emphasizes that only God knows the day or hour when everything will be fulfilled (Mark 13:32–33), he does imply that this will come in the disciples' lifetime; it is they who need to be alert. He does not give the impression that he expects or that God intends world history to go on roughly as it always has for two more millennia. How things work out would need to interact with the way the disciples and the Jewish community and the Romans acted. This is then confirmed by the extraordinary statement in 2 Pet 3:12 that it is possible for the readers of the letter to "hasten the coming of the day of God."[19] It is illustrated on a smaller scale by the difference between the declaration that Agabus gives, which he says comes from the Holy Spirit and which the community accept as such, and the events as they turn out (Acts 21:10–12, 27–36).

To summarize so far, then, God sometimes knows how things will turn out on the basis of making the decisions about them or because of possessing in spades the kind of great insight a human being can possess in extrapolating into the future. Open theism stresses both these aspects of God's capacity to know the future.[20] But attempting to explain all examples of foreknowledge in these ways seems to be forced. It is a theory driven by the philosophical conviction of open theism that by its nature the future cannot be known until it happens. As scripture sees it, God sometimes knows how things will turn out, simply on the basis of some supernatural capacity to do so. Precisely how it is possible to know the future when it has not happened, I do not know, but there is too strong scriptural testimony to this for it to be appropriate to try to explain away the idea.

---

[18] I am grateful to Bruce Fisk for suggesting I think about these parallels.

[19] The verb is *speudo*, whose regular meaning is "hasten," though it can mean "be zealous for" (cf. NRSV and TNIV margins).

[20] See Rice, "Biblical Support for a New Perspective," 51.

Sometimes God does not know how the future will turn out, and God sometimes has expectations about the future that are not fulfilled. God has surprises. Neither God nor the scriptures think that this has troublesome implications. Here, it is classical theism that seeks to explain away scripture's statements. But here, too, there is too strong scriptural testimony concerning this for it to be appropriate to try to explain it away. God does not know everything about the future.

2. God's Knowledge of the Present and the Past

God also has extraordinary, supernatural knowledge of the present and the past; God knows things about present and past that ordinary human knowledge would not cover. God knows that when King Abimelech added Sarah to his harem, the king was not aware that she was married, so that in this sense he had acted with integrity of heart (Gen 20:5). "I know their plan that they are making today, before I bring them into the land," God says (Deut 31:20–21); God's capacity to extrapolate what Israel will do in the future issues from God's present knowledge of what is in Israel's heart.

a. Innate and Empirical Knowledge

How does God possess such knowledge? Well, how do human beings possess knowledge? There is a longstanding philosophical argument concerning whether we are born with no knowledge, so that all our knowledge is empirically derived, or whether we are hardwired with some knowledge in areas such as mathematics, logic, morality, and God. It would suit me to presuppose that humanity's knowledge indeed involves both hardwiring and discovery, because I could then suggest that in this respect as in others the scriptures presupposes that we are made in God's image, though my colleague in philosophical theology and theology of science Nancey Murphy warns me not to do so. Whether or not this is true of human beings, scripture does imply that God is hardwired with some knowledge but gains other knowledge empirically.

Amusingly, the first witness to God's having innate knowledge is the snake, who knows that God knows that eating from the knowledge tree will lead to discernment of the difference between good and bad (Gen 3:5). I take it that God's self-description in Exod 34:6–7 in terms of being compassionate, gracious, and so on, reflects innate knowledge of what it means to be God.

But scripture makes clear that God's knowledge is empirical as well as innate. "God—from heaven he has looked down at human beings to see if there is someone discerning, someone having recourse to God" (Ps 14:1 [2]). To discover things about the present, God looks, God discovers things empirically. Human hearts lie open before God (Prov 15:11): that is, God does not automatically know what is in them but can look in and discover what is there. It is on the basis of being able to see the mind and heart that God tests the faithful (Jer 20:12).

In the New Testament, Heb 4:13 notes how no one can hide from God; "all are naked and bare to the eyes of the one to whom we must render account." Other passages similarly affirm God's capacity to look into people's minds: "God searches every mind and understands every plan and thought" (1 Chr 28:9). The fact that God "knows the secrets of the heart" is linked to the fact that God "searches out" what people do (Ps 44:21 [22]). God has the capacity to find things out. "'If a person hides in a hiding place, can I myself not see him?'" (Jer 23:24). You can run, but you cannot hide (cf. Job 34:21–22).

God acts to discover things about the past as well as about the present. After Abraham and Sarah serve a meal to three mysterious visitors and two of them have set off for Sodom and Gomorrah, God says, "I will go down to see: have they acted entirely in accordance with the outcry about it that comes to me? If not, I will know [it]" (Gen 18:21). God's form of speech is very similar to the words Abraham's servant uses when he is wondering if he has found the right wife for Isaac and to the words Moses uses when he is wondering if his birth family are still alive (Gen 24:21; Exod 4:18). God knows about the past as about the present on the basis of empirical investigation as well as innate knowledge; God can discover anything in this way.

A further indication that God gains knowledge empirically is that God asks questions. Admittedly some of God's questions may be taken as rhetorical and thus as not indicating that God lacks knowledge on a matter. As their use by the prophets show, rhetorical questions are a means of communication that involves the audience, who have to provide the obvious reply (which the speaker knows) or because—paradoxically—formulating the statements as questions strengthens the assertions they imply. In passages such as Jer 2:31–32; 5:7, 9, 29; 23:23–24, God knows the answer, and the question can be turned into a statement without changing the content of the words. In passages such as Jer 4:14; 8:5, the question is a protest, not a request for information that the questioner lacks, like the protests in the Psalms. Other passages might seem to indicate limitations on God's knowledge, but they do not seem to me to do so. Jeremiah 19:5; 7:31; and 32:35 speak of things that never came into God's mind, but this indicates that God did not think about requiring something, not that God was unaware that people might act in such a way. When God confronts Adam and Eve and Cain, some of God's questions might be taken as rhetorical (Gen 3:13; 4:6), but some look literal (Gen 3:11). Some could be understood either way (Gen 3:9; 4:9–10; the same applies in Gen 16:8).

Further, there are many occasions when God tests people, and the object of a test is to find out something one would not otherwise know. God can be engaged in such testing when the verb "test" does not appear, not least in Gen 2–3 and in Job 1–2, but I focus here on passages that use the verb "test." God first tests (*nasah* piel) Abraham by bidding him sacrifice his son. When Abraham has demonstrated his willingness to do so, God declares, "Now I know[21] that you revere God" (Gen 22:12).[22] After the exodus, God declares the intention to provide the manna "so that

---

[21] Or "I have come to know" (the verb is *qatal*) or "I acknowledge."

[22] Roy's survey of alternative suggested but implausible approaches to this passage (*How Much Does God Foreknow?* 177–82) gives eloquent testimony to its difficulty for the view that God has total knowledge.

I may test them: will they walk by my teaching or not?" (Exod 16:4). Subsequently, if a prophet appears and urges Israel to follow another god, "God your God is testing you so as to know if you are committed[23] to loving Yahweh your God with all your heart and soul" (Deut 13:3 [4]). A principle behind God's causing Israel to travel through the wilderness for forty years was "so as by afflicting you and testing you, to come to know what was in your heart: will you keep his commands or not?" (Deut 8:2; cf. v. 16). In the land, one reason for God's not expelling the former inhabitants of Canaan is "so as to test Israel by means of them: are they keeping the way of God . . . or not?" (Judg 2:22; cf. 3:1). For God, these peoples thus "became a means of testing Israel so as to know: will they obey God's commands?" (Judg 3:4). When God abandoned Hezekiah to the invading Assyrians, it was "to test him, to know everything in his mind" (2 Chr 32:31). Psalm 139 concludes, "Examine me, God, and know my mind; probe me (*bakhan*) and know my concerns. See if there is an idolatrous way in me, and lead me in the ancient way." Psalm 26:2 urges, "probe me, God, test me, try my mind and heart" (lit., "my heart and kidneys"). A number of other passages refer to God's trying the mind and heart, with the implication that God is thereby discovering whether there is an inner attitude of trust in God and commitment to God that corresponds to the outward profession (e.g., Ps 7:9 [10]; 17:3; 26:2; cf. 1 Chr 29:17; Jer 11:20; 12:3; 17:10; 20:12). Other brief references to God's testing (Exod 15:25; 20:20 [17]; Job 23:10; Pss 66:10; 81:7 [8]; 105:19; Prov 17:3; Isa 48:10; Jer 9:7 [6]; Zech 13:9) mostly look at the testing from the angle of the people being tested and focus on its refining effect on them rather than its significance for God's knowledge.

God does not have innate knowledge of what is in people's hearts but does have the capacity to get to know this, and sometimes uses that capacity, yet does not always do so. Like God's capacity to know the future, God's distinctive capacity to know what is in someone's heart is paralleled by occasional human capacity to have the same insight.

b. Omniscience

So scripture suggests that God is not omniscient about the past or present any more than about the future but that God can discover anything God wants to know about past, present, or future.

A prominent open theist, Clark H. Pinnock, declares, "God must know all things that can be known and know them truly."[24] Alongside this sentence in our library copy of this book, someone has written, "Very speculative!" It was wicked to write in a library book, but it was a perceptive observation. The declaration about God's omniscience is one that open theism shares with classical theism; to be omniscient is part of what the word "God" means. But this conviction shared by classical theism and open theism is not one derived from scripture or present in scripture.

---

[23] The verb is again *shakam*: see the comment on Zeph 3:7.

[24] "Systematic Theology," in Clark Pinnock et al., *The Openness of God* (Downers Grove, Ill.: InterVarsity Press, 1994), 101–25 (121).

So where did it come from? When Christian theology differs from scripture, the usual rule is, "When in doubt, blame the Greeks," and open theists do that.[25] But where did the Greeks get their views from? Theologically, the answer is that they come from what we might call innate knowledge, or natural revelation, or human culture, or human speculation; I will refer to this as natural theology, things about God and us that we know or think we know but that do not come from the Bible. There are many such convictions that come from natural theology, and they can be true; but we bring them to scripture to see how and where scripture confirms or refines them. Commonly scripture does that by drawing our attention to what God did in Israel and in Christ, which provides clues to the nature of God and of everything else that could not emerge from natural theology. These clues reframe the insights of natural theology, often in radical ways

The problem is that natural theology, convictions about God that seem obviously true, becomes embedded in Christian theology. The role that scripture then plays is to provide the justification for the positions of Christian theology, whether these positions were intrinsically scriptural or not. The theologians engaged in this task are people committed to the authority of scripture who think that their positions must be compatible with scripture or required by scripture. And, of course, one can prove anything from scripture if one tries hard enough. So the way –isms proceed is by noting scriptural texts that support their position, in order to demonstrate that a position that did not necessarily emerge from scripture is scriptural. The rude term for this is proof texting, but there is nothing wrong with it in principle. One question is, Does the text support the position in question? Another question is, What place does it have in scriptural thinking as a whole?

In connection with the present subject, it is striking that when the First Testament offers descriptions of God (e.g., Exod 15:1–11; 34:6–7), it does not major on God's knowledge, though it does refer to God's wisdom. Similarly, when Paul refers to the innate knowledge of God that everyone has, he speaks of God's power and deity, not specifically of God's knowledge (Rom 1:20). Indeed, it is hard to find scriptural affirmations of divine omniscience; the affirmations that are quoted in connection with the present debate are inclined to dissolve on examination. Psalm 147:5 often appears in lists of significant texts: "Our Lord is great and mighty in power; of his insight there is no reckoning." But this does not imply omniscience. Isaiah 40:13–14 appears in such lists; but it concerns the fact that God knew all about the way to go about creating the world (Paul quotes that passage in Rom 11:33–34 in connection with the way God has been at work in the destiny of Israel and the world). Elihu describes God as "perfect in knowledge" (Job 37:16); the phrase is puzzling in the context, but in any case Elihu has made the same claim for himself (Job 36:4), so it does not prove very much.[26] First John 3:20 is the nearest to a proof text for divine omniscience; it declares that God "knows everything" and

---

[25] Though classical theists note the problems in this ploy: for instance, which Greeks? See, e.g., Roy, *How Much Does God Foreknow?* 195–211.

[26] For further passages, see, e.g., Bruce Ware, "An Evangelical Reformulation of the Doctrine of the Immutability of God," *JETS* 29 (1986): 431–46 (442); Roy, *How Much Does God Foreknow?* 11.

therefore knows our hearts. But a commentator sees the point in this statement as lying in that inference about knowing our hearts: "God . . . unlike our fallible scruples, knows everything necessary to render a valid judgment." He compares John 21:17, where in a similar context Peter affirms to Jesus, "You know all things."[27] It is a telling comparison because this cannot be understood in a hard sense, for even the Son does not know about "that day or hour" (Mark 13:32). Jesus tells us he does not know all things. And it is surely unrealistic to think that Jesus already knows the answer to every one of the many questions he asks in the Gospels, even though he, too, is fond of rhetorical questions.

Within the First Testament, Ps 139 is especially commonly appealed to as implying divine omniscience, but, even apart from the fact that it speaks only about God's relationship with one individual, it is at best ambiguous in this connection. Many lines acknowledge God's extraordinary knowledge of the supplicant. "Before a word is on my tongue you know it completely, LORD" (Ps 139:4 TNIV). But the psalmist's confession is more literally, "There is not a word on my tongue but that You, O LORD, know it well" (NJPS). In other words, God hears every word I say. Further, the psalm's statements about God's knowledge are all set in the context of a significant opening declaration, "You have searched me, LORD, and you know me" (Ps 139:1 TNIV) or "O LORD, you have searched me and known me" (NRSV). In other words, God indeed has extraordinary knowledge of the psalmist but has that knowledge as a result of doing research. It is not something that God simply possesses by nature. Once again, God gains knowledge in the same way as anyone does. The difference between God and anyone else is God's monumental research capacity. "You perceive my thoughts from afar" (Ps 139:2 TNIV). It has been inferred from v. 16 that "all the days of David's life were ordained by God before any one of them came to be" so that "God knew them all in advance" and "knew David thoroughly and exhaustively before any divine searching took place."[28] But this is to read rather a lot into an enigmatic line, which NJPS translates "my unformed limbs . . . were all recorded in your book; in due time they were formed." Like other First and New Testament passages already noted, the psalm affirms that God can find out anything, even our inner thoughts, but not that God knows everything without looking.

c. Speaking in Human Terms

A classical theist declares, "The debate . . . is not about individual texts but about which texts are to be given hermeneutical priority in formulating a doctrine of God."[29] This comment articulates an important principle. A good illustration is

---

[27] See C. Clifton Black, "The First, Second, and Third Letters of John," in *The New Interpreter's Bible* (Nashville: Abingdon, 1998), 12:363–469 (422). John's Gospel has already emphasized Jesus' extraordinary knowledge in the course of his ministry (e.g., John 2:24–25), which makes the Samaritan woman see him as a prophet (John 4:17–18).

[28] So Roy, *How Much Does God Foreknow?* 29.

[29] Paul Helm, "An Augustinian-Calvinist Response [to the open theism view]," in *Four Views* (ed. James K. Beilby and Paul R. Eddy; Downers Grove, Ill.: InterVarsity Press, 2001), 61–64 (62).

passages that speak of God having a change of mind, or not doing that. Classical theism gives priority to passages declaring that God does not have a change of mind over passages declaring that God does have a change of mind. This works by suggesting that the former are literal statements, the latter are figurative; specifically, they are anthropomorphic. God is described as if God were a human being, and human beings do find things out by discovering them. Further, those statements are phenomenological; God is described in light of the way God's acts are experienced by human beings, and from a human perspective, it seems that God has a change of mind.[30]

This process of interpretation raises several questions. One is that asserting hermeneutical priority has become a process whereby some texts silence others. Asserting hermeneutical priority does not need to be that. When Jesus declares the principle that everything in the Torah and the Prophets is an exposition of love of God and love of one's neighbor (Matt 22:40), this can, for instance, help us perceive possibilities and adjudicate conflicts in the interpretation of passages in the Torah and the Prophets and thus enable them to speak to us. But applied to talk of God's having as opposed to not having a change of mind, or knowing everything as opposed to discovering things, the assertion of hermeneutical priority seems simply to silence the second set of texts. They have nothing to say.

Second, there is that troublesome fact that, as it is hard to find declarations of God's omniscience but easy to find descriptions of God's discovering things, only two passages declare that God does not have a change of mind (Num 23:19; 1 Sam 15:29), whereas a score of passages speak of God doing so (e.g., Exod 32:14; 1 Chr 21:15; Jer 18:4–10; 26:2–3, 17–19; Joel 2:12–13; Jonah 3:10; 4:2).[31] And one of the passages that speaks of God having a change of mind (Jer 18:4–10) is the most systematic discussion of the entire question. Why do the first two passages have the hermeneutical priority?

People appeal to anthropomorphism when statements about God do not fit with what they can believe about God. They make this appeal when scripture describes God as having strong feelings such as jealousy or as experiencing pain. The definition of God might seem to exclude God's having such feelings or experiences. Once again we can blame the Greeks for this assumption.[32] But it is simply an assumption, not an aspect of the way God is described in scripture. It is natural theology that tells us to read scripture this way.

Then it is questionable whether statements about God having a change of mind or discovering things are more anthropomorphic or phenomenological than many other scriptural statements. Nearly all God's actions are described as if God were a

---

[30] See, e.g., Roy, *How Much Does God Foreknow?* 159–76.

[31] In addition, on one hand Mal 3:6 simply declares that God does not change (cf. Jas 1:17), while conversely, many passages in effect describe God having a change of mind without using this verb (e.g., 2 Kgs 20:1–6).

[32] John Sanders, "Historical Considerations," in Clark Pinnock et al., *The Openness of God* (Downers Grove, Ill.: InterVarsity Press, 1994), 59–100, seeks to demonstrate that the appeal to language being merely anthropomorphic and phenomenological comes from Greek philosophy via Philo into Clement and Origen.

human being and in light of the way God's acts are experienced by human beings. Theologically this is not worrisome because human beings are made in God's image, so in principle using human models to understand God is illuminating. We speak of God loving, making decisions, seeing, hearing, showing mercy, acting, and so on; all these are characteristic of human beings, but we can take them as also divine characteristics. While we need to be wary of making God wholly human-like, to say God loves or acts (or discovers things or has a change of mind) is to speak anthropomorphically, in the sense of analogically, but truly.

We also speak of God having eyes, ears, hands, and feet, and we usually assume that this is anthropomorphic in another sense. Whereas reference to God loving or acting is analogical language, reference to God's body parts gives concrete, metaphorical expression to the analogical language. God acts, sees, and hears; it is *as if* God has hands, eyes, and ears. The metaphor serves the literal, and we can then give a less metaphorical account of the subject: for instance, we can speak of God's power instead of God's hand. It is not clear that there is a basis for describing talk of God discovering things or having a change of mind as anthropomorphic in this metaphorical sense, or it is not clear what it is a metaphor for.

Indeed,

> If ever there was a miserable anthropomorphism, it is the hallucination of a divine immutability which rules out the possibility that God can let Himself be conditioned in this or that way by His creature. God is certainly immutable. But He is immutable as the living God and in the mercy in which He espouses the cause of the creature. . . . He can give to this creature a place in His will.[33]

The Zohar notes Solomon's testimony that "not one word has failed of every good word that he spoke by means of his servant Moses" (1 Kgs 8:56) and comments that if this said simply that "not one word of every *word*" has failed, as opposed to "not one word of every *good* word," it would have been better if the world had never been created. But fortunately (it goes on), an argument does go on within God,[34] God's words about calamity do not always come true.

It would be more appropriate to ask what distinctive affirmation each sort of statement is making and to seek to combine these. Of the two declarations that God does not have a change of mind, the context of the first, in Num 23:19, indicates its point, that God will not go back on a commitment to bless Israel. The situation with 1 Sam 15:29 is the more paradoxical, because on either side of this verse the chapter itself declares that God has had a change of mind about making Saul king (1 Sam 15:11, 35).[35] Perhaps the emphasis lies on God's not having a change of mind like a human being; God is not arbitrary in having changes of mind, as human beings can be. Further, Samuel's statement may be concrete, not general, as is the case in other passages that refer to God not having a change of mind in a particular con-

---

[33] Karl Barth, *Church Dogmatics* III/4 (repr., Edinburgh: Clark, 1969), 109.

[34] See the selections in *Zohar: The Book of Enlightenment* (New York: Paulist, 1983), 137; cf. Mark E. Biddle, *Deuteronomy* (Macon, Ga.: Smith and Helwys, 2003), 160.

[35] At least, it has made God the subject of the verb *nakham* niphal, though some translations vary in the way they render the verb.

crete connection (e.g., Ps 110:4; Jer 4:28). God will not have a change of mind about deposing Saul. There are occasions when God has a change of mind, and there are occasions when God does not. It is quite possible to let all the passages have their say without giving any the hermeneutical priority. Some passages assure us that God is not arbitrary; others assure us that God is not inflexible.

3. Conclusion

To conclude: Scripture implies that God has some innate knowledge and also has access to all knowledge about everything past, present, and future. I infer that God sometimes chooses to exercise that access but sometimes chooses not to do so. One might hypothesize that it is natural to God as for us to live in linear time and thus not usually to know the future, and that this makes for more real relations with other beings such as ourselves if God does not continually utilize the capacity to look into our minds or our futures. But this is guesswork, human theorizing, like the human theorizing that underlies both classical theism and open theism.

No doubt we will all be glad that God may often choose not to know what we are thinking. But we would be unwise to make too much of this; we still cannot conceal things from God when God wants to know them. You can run, but you cannot hide. We may alternatively be apprehensive about the idea that God does not know how the future will turn out. But this same God is one characterized by infinite self-giving and infinite power. People who want to hide may never experience God like that. People who are afraid that God may get caught out can be sure that God will be up to coping with whatever happens. God has surprises. But God is not afraid of surprises.

4

WHAT DOES IT MEAN TO BE HUMAN?

Christian theology emerges from our interacting with the gospel, with scripture, with the church's doctrinal tradition, with the thinking of our age, and with our own experience. That is not so much a statement of what ought to be the case but of what is inevitably the case, whether we like it or not and whether we acknowledge it or not. Sometimes Christian theologians may wish to interact only with the gospel and scripture and to avoid the influence of tradition, contemporary thinking, and personal experience, but whether they like and are aware of it or not, they will also reflect those other influences, as is apparent when one considers examples of the attempt to avoid it. On the other flank, theologians can avoid interaction with the gospel or scripture, but by definition their work will not then be Christian theology; and arguably that would also be the case with theology that avoided interaction with the church's doctrinal tradition.[1]

It is as well, then, to try to be reflective about the way this inevitable process will take place. I write as someone involved professionally and existentially with the First Testament scriptures. I write in the context of some interesting developments in doctrinal thinking over recent decades concerning what it means to be human, and that not least in the context of developments in thinking over what it means to be God. I write in the context of more secular thinking about the person and of feminism. And I write in the context of being married to someone who has become physically disabled, who in her own being is a different person from the woman I married, and who as I write has just asked me what day it is.

When people meet the disabled, the way they sometimes instinctively treat them suggests that they subconsciously regard them as not quite the same sort of beings as the rest of us. This applies to the physically disabled, but especially to those who are in some way disabled in spirit or mind. As an alternative starting point, I presuppose the conviction and the experience that when as an ordinary person I meet someone who is disabled, I meet a person who is different from me in an important way but who is a genuinely human being. There are analogies with what can happen when I meet someone of a different race. I meet someone else made in God's image. Their different-ness contributes to my understanding of what it means to be human and what it means to be God.

---

[1]First published as "Being Human," in *Encounter with Mystery: Reflections on l'Arche and Living with Disability* (ed. Frances Young; London: DLT, 1997), 133–51, 183–84.

It is an aspect of the glory and the challenge of humanity that we are different from each other. If the diversity within humanity reflects our being made in God's image, it reflects the diversity within God, epitomized in God's being Father, Son, and Holy Spirit. Disabled people contribute to that diversity of humanity, modeling other ways of being human than the way of the abled. It is thus when abled and disabled live, work, and worship together that humanity is represented in its fullness and God imaged.

The statement that human beings were created in God's image has had a prominent place in discussion of what it means to be human,[2] but it has functioned more as a vehicle upon which to project convictions or as a stimulus to reflection than as a concrete indicator of what it means to be human. Over the centuries, the statement has thus rung a series of different bells. In ages that wanted to stress rationality or morality or humanity's spiritual nature, reason or morality or humanity's spiritual nature became that in which the image of God lay. Our age is inclined to stress creativity as well as control, relationship as well as inner being, body as well as spirit. Theological attention has thus been attracted to the fact that the image in which humanity was created is the image of a creator, that the beings created in God's image are physical beings, and that Genesis goes on to tell us that "God created humanity in his image, created it in the image of God, created it male and female" (Gen 1:27), though the observation that God created humanity male and female is more likely a separate statement than a spelling out of the implications of being in God's image.

Like much of Gen 1–3, the notion of being in God's image has been able to stimulate or reflect so much theological thinking because it is a symbolic statement. As such it constitutes not a proposition with fixed content but a stimulus to thought, an invitation to reflection whose content is not predetermined by the person who presents us with the symbol. In this it resembles the cross or the breaking of bread. And it is a "tensive symbol" rather than a "steno-symbol."[3] A red traffic light is a steno-symbol; it needs to denote something explicit and straightforward, in the United States as much as in Britain; we can cope with driving on a different side of the road, but we would have more difficulty with green meaning "Stop." The fact that the expression "image of God" is a tensive symbol is in keeping with its lack of explicitness in its context. By its nature it opens up fields for thought rather than circumscribing thought. In principle it thus legitimates the insights regarding what it means to be human that have been expressed when people have stressed the importance of rationality or morality or spirituality or control or creativity or bodiliness or relationship, though it will be important to see the dangers in using texts as mirrors that confirm what we think rather than windows that enable us to see something new. Describing us as made in God's image invites us to keep chewing over the question, What does it mean that we are like God? My concern here is to consider the implications of counting disabled people among the "we."

---

[2] On its meaning, see J. Richard Middleton, *The Liberating Image* (Grand Rapids: Brazos, 2005).

[3] So also G. McFarlane, "Strange News from Another Star," in *Persons, Divine and Human* (ed. Christoph Schwöbel and Colin E. Gunton; Edinburgh: Clark, 1991), 98–119.

It would be a suspicious situation if we thought we knew what it means to be like God; it would seem to imply we knew what God is like. This leads into a second sense in which we should not necessarily resist thick understandings of the divine image, understandings that go beyond what may be justified by a historical exegesis of Gen 1:26–27. What that statement means is spelled out over many pages that follow in the Bible. When we meet with God at the beginning of the Bible story we meet with all of God, as we meet with all of a human being when we first meet someone. Yet the more we hear a person's story the more we understand the person, as the story fills out the initial impression. No doubt occasionally that process means the impression gets corrected, but more predominantly it gets deepened. So it is with the story of God. In considering the way the scriptural story has this effect, I group my thoughts around the notions of task, of journey, of relationship, and of body.

1. Task

If the idea of being in God's image is spelled out in Gen 1, this most likely comes in the declaration of God's intent in so creating us: "Let us make humanity in our image, after our likeness; and let them have dominion. . . ." Being like God means being commissioned to control the world on God's behalf; this is the task for which God created humanity.[4]

As the First Testament story unfolds, this insight has little overt prominence, despite its being a key point in Gen 1. On the usual view, Gen 1 was composed among people transported from Israel to Babylon, within a refugee community whose world had collapsed and who had no control of their lives or their destinies. This creation story is told in such a way as to proclaim a gospel to them. One aspect of that preaching is the declaration that against all appearances God intends them to share in the control of the world and of life that God intended for all humanity. The fact that they are deprived of control of their lives and are controlled by others is not the last word, because it belies the creator's vision for humanity, in which an integral place is taken by the exercise of responsibility and stewardship, and thus of authority and power.

Now presumably all that is true of disabled people, with at least two implications. First, it implies that the abled accept an obligation to seek to share with the disabled the task of making the world and the responsibility to exercise control and authority in the world. One aspect of this is that it is our vocation to seek to free the disabled to be in control of their own lives as we are, to be free, rather than to run their lives for them. In the context of modernity, the notion of sovereignty or control recalls that of self-transcendence, the idea that humanity makes the world and even makes itself. The idea that humanity makes the world resonates naturally

---

[4]Cf. Hans Walter Wolff, *Anthropology of the Old Testament* (London: SCM / Philadelphia: Fortress, 1975), 159–65, 226–27; Ian Hart, "Genesis 1:1–2:3 as a Prologue to the Book of Genesis," *TynB* 46 (1995): 315–36.

enough with Gen 1, for if there is one evident characteristic of the God in whose image we are created, it is that this God is creator, so it is natural for us to see creativity, world making, as a characteristic of humanity, and a characteristic in which disabled people thus share.

Second, the presence of the disabled among those who are in God's image implies that the abled learn from the disabled how to go about creativity, world making, control, exercising authority, as well as vice versa. It has become a commonplace to blame Gen 1:26 for the spoiling of the world by a humanity that believed it had the right to do what it liked with it. The text has implications that work in another direction. If humanity is commissioned to rule the world on God's behalf and as God-like, its ruling will reflect God's activity and nature. The story has already shown this activity and nature to be of a generous and liberating rather than a grasping and oppressive character.

Beyond that, the disabled have the capacity to reveal to humanity a facet of being human from which the abled can often hide: our weakness, vulnerability, and dependence. It is only modernity that has exploited the earth on the gargantuan scale that threatens the earth's survival, which implies that the key factor was something other than the text of Genesis written twenty-five hundred years ago. This key factor is more likely modernity's re-visioning man as omnipotent, in the image of God who had already been re-visioned as having omnipotence as his key attribute (the gender-specific "man" and "his" are appropriate).[5] If the disabled are characterized by vulnerability and the capacity to call forth love, they embody aspects of humanity that reflect aspects of the being of God, Father, Son, and Holy Spirit, aspects of the nature of God that humanity is called to image in its controlling of the earth. They embody the fact that there is sometimes a mysterious power in poverty, vulnerability, and weakness, a power to move and transform.

The people who are called to rule, as people who are God-like, are people who are insufficient for the demands that life places upon us and who need to own this if we are to rule in a way that is not ruined by it. We need to prove that it is not only being Christian that depends upon trust (that is, we are justified by faith). Being human itself depends upon trust. We live by faith, by depending on something outside ourselves, on God or an idol.[6] The disabled embody that fact about being human. We cannot be self-sufficient in relation to other human beings or in relation to God.

The disabled also draw our attention to the fact that the attempt to exercise control, the activity of creation, occupies six days but not seven. Further, it does not constitute the ultimate climax of creation's story. That climax lies in a rest from activity, such as the disabled may be constrained to accept. But then they give us the opportunity to prove that "only those who live slowly get more out life."[7] They invite us to a patient, listening attentiveness that replaces decisiveness and

---

[5] Jürgen Moltmann, "Destruction and Liberation of Nature," a lecture at St. John's Theological College, Nottingham, U.K., October 1995.

[6] Wolfhart Pannenberg, *Anthropology in Theological Perspective* (Philadelphia: Fortress, 1975), 71.

[7] Jürgen Moltmann, "On Grief and Consolation in Modern Society," a lecture at St. John's Theological College, Nottingham, U.K., October 1995.

competitiveness and offers us transformation.[8] They invite us to the play, spontaneity, and impulse that are part of being human.

On the sixth day, then, humanity is created in the image of God the worker, the creator. On the seventh day God stops and suggests another aspect of deity that this image will reflect. If disabled people need to be freed to take a share in the stewardship of the world that is involved in creativity in the image of God the worker, the converse is that they can already model for us the possibility of being human and God-like by inactivity and not only by activity. Many disabled people are people seeking to live ordinary lives in unconventional bodies.[9] Perhaps they refuse to accept the fact that they are different. But others are people who live nonstandard lives in their nonstandard bodies, lives that are less active and more like a sabbath without a week's work.

2. Journey

In the filling out of the identity of the God is in whose image we are made, a key point is God's appearing to Moses, when Moses asks who God is and is told "I am who I am" and that God's actual name is Yahweh (Exod 3:14–15). When we call someone by name, we indicate that we recognize him or her as a person; the name encapsulates the mysterious treasured individuality of the person.

Perhaps it is no coincidence that the statement "I am who I am" is as disputed and as enigmatic as the phrase "in God's image." One insight to which it points is the fact that God is who God is as I am who I am, a unique individual who cannot be summed up by a list of characteristics. God is prepared to provide such a list (classically, that God is merciful, gracious, patient, committed, faithful, forgiving, though prepared to be tough: for instance, Exod 34:6–7).[10] But the list does not capture the person.

As a human being I can be described by means of a list of characteristics such as enthusiastic, imaginative, colorful, physical, and unassuming (to repeat some of the more repeatable ones that my friends have suggested). Yet such lists do not satisfactorily sum up the person. In a strange sense the fact that I am John Goldingay says more about me than an inventory of adjectives does. While in Western cultures names do not usually have the significance they commonly have in some traditional cultures (they do not express someone's destiny or God's promise to them), they have just as much reference. My name refers distinctively to that unique configuration of characteristics, both attractive and quirky, that comprises me. When someone who knows me addresses me as "John" it can be a reminder of all that, and thus, it is a precious experience when someone who loves me addresses me by name. I am acknowledged as who I am, even if neither speaker nor addressee knows all of what that is. As a human being I am a person called by name, by God, and by another human being.

---

[8] Jean Vanier, untitled talk at Cliff College, Calver, U.K., June 1995.

[9] Nancy L. Eiesland, *The Disabled God* (Nashville: Abingdon, 1994), 23.

[10] See chapters 1 and 2 above.

In addressing disabled people by name, we affirm to them *that* they are and *who* they are. We affirm our love for them, which operates despite or because neither we nor they may yet know much of who they are. Naming reflects knowing and loving, but at least as much it expresses loving and thus facilitates knowing. This has implications for people such as those with Alzheimer's disease who may be so profoundly mentally disabled that we may wonder what their knowing of themselves can mean. "They may no longer 'know' who they are, but the church knows who they are."[11] Oftentimes it may be apparent that addressing them by name is received as an affirmation of love that meets with a response of love and trust. The one who names thus receives in return the gift of being loved and trusted and is built up.

So in Exod 3:15 it is suggestive that as well as saying "I am who I am," God offers Moses the name Yahweh. There is a hint that this name recalls the "I am who I am," but it is at least as significant that Yahweh has a name and shares it. God's having a name at all draws attention to a unique individuality, an aspect of the one whom humanity images. And if there is a mystery about the unique individuality of each human person, how much more is there a mystery about the unique individuality of God?

God's "I am who I am" points to the freedom of God that makes it possible for God to be whatever God wishes or needs to be. It makes God also the origin of and the model for the freedom of humanity made in that image. Freedom, "creative freedom," is the "conscious, rational, discriminating, unifying, purposeful element in the human being that leads us in one direction rather than another."[12]

In that context it also hints at a key feature of the way in which this freedom is exercised. God's being "I am . . ." is a promise to Moses, a promise about God's being one who will always be always there, there when needed, there when a crisis comes. It is not a statement about abstract being, as the Greek equivalent *ego eimi* probably is, but a statement about a consistent yet changing presence. Who God is emerges in contexts where God is needed, contexts where other persons are in need and God becomes something new or gives expression to something new from the depths of that inexhaustibly resourced mystery and freedom, in a way called forth by the context and by the other person. For God and for human beings the realm of freedom consists of possibilities not yet realized, so that our humanity is actualized only contextually.

Freedom and the reality of possibilities not yet actualized is thus another aspect of being in God's image that the disabled may have spectacular opportunity to enter into. The point may emerge in its own way from the story of Adam and Eve in Gen 2. They are surely created with maturity as their destiny rather than as being already perfect. Further, as human beings we are strangely capable of reflecting on who we are and thus of changing who we are and how we act.[13]

---

[11] Stanley Hauerwas, "What Could It Mean for the Church to Be Christ's Body?" *SJT* 48 (1995): 1–21 (see 10).

[12] John Macquarrie, *In Search of Humanity* (London: SCM / New York: Crossroad, 1983), 15, 38.

[13] Cf. John Macquarrie, "A Theology of Personal Being," in *Persons and Personality* (ed. Arthur Peacocke and Grant Gillett; Oxford / New York: Blackwell, 1987), 172–79 (see 172–75).

Yet one fact that the subsequent Bible story certainly reflects is that God-like is one thing humanity is not, however we understand the term. God-likeness is humanity's destiny, the goal of its journey; indeed, becoming human is the goal of our journey. Paradoxically, one of the things that is then constitutive of being human now is our being on the way to this goal that is at the moment unreached.[14]

When I was twenty or twenty-five I subconsciously assumed, I think, that now I was grown up, nothing else much would happen to me; I was shaped, and the rest of my life would be more of the same. One of my slightly astonished reflections when I passed fifty was that nothing could have been further from the truth; and one of my excitements was to realize that there was no reason why a process of change and growth should not continue for another twenty-five years (unless death intervened, but then that is but a paradigm shift of change and growth). I was sad to read recently a novelist observing that he has to do more research for his novels now he is sixty because he does not have so much new experience to treat as a resource. I was then encouraged to hear a theologian incidentally reveal that in his sixties he has carried on having all manner of new experiences that become a resource for his theological reflection. The disabled both point to this in themselves and enable it in others.

Our lives are journeys. This may not mean they are progressing toward some definable goal, as if ideally we could reach that goal and then be ready to die. They may be more like individual equivalents to history itself: history manifests no progress, except in the trivial technological sense, but it constitutes humanity's journey, in which achievements and insights come and go, sometimes becoming platforms for new insights and achievements, sometimes giving way to failures and blindnesses.

The story of Israel's ancestors on their journey is a parable of the fact that all humanity is on a journey. The journey motif does not reappear in stories such as those of Saul and David, but they continue to embody or to stimulate reflection on the mystery of what it means to be human. Both these two kings are of chief interest not because they were kings but because this leads to the telling of their human lives, both of which ironically were characterized as much by constraint as by freedom, constraints from outside in the case of Saul (pulled this way and that by the Yahweh who cannot be understood) and constraints from inside in the case of David (pulled this way and that by the inner personality that cannot be understood).

If our lives are journeys, our reflection on them will naturally take such narrative form. That is true for disabled people. The difficulty is that they may have difficulty telling their story. Jean Vanier describes one of the first disabled people he lived with, a man who had not been told that his mother had died. Jean Vanier in due course took him to her grave, upon which the man cast himself in sobbing anguish. No doubt that reflected the pain of losing his mother such as anyone might feel, and the pain of not being told.[15] I wonder whether another significance of the sobbing anguish is the fact that his mother represented his story, his past,

---

[14]Cf. Pannenberg, *Anthropology*, 50, 60, with his references to Johann Gottfried Herder.
[15]So Vanier, untitled talk.

his journey. He was now cut off from it and unable to articulate it. He had lost his history, his story, his "memory." He became in this respect a non-person. There is no doubt that disabled people live narrative lives, that their lives are journeys, but these lives' narrative significance may not become a reality for people themselves until they have the opportunity to articulate their story.

The lives of disabled people are manifestly journeys. They illustrate how part of the mystery of human individuality is that it is not static and unchanging. When a disabled person who has been neglected or institutionalized comes to be befriended and known, that person can change and grow. When a person becomes disabled, that takes him or her onto another journey that can look (and probably is) more painful but can also involve breathtaking transformation. The former may be led from bondage to freedom. The latter may look as if they are on the way from freedom to bondage, but they may be able to take control of or own their changing humanity in such a way as to make it a new form of freedom.

Because the abled are the statistical norm, we may think we define real normality, and we may thus assume that we represent full humanity and creativity. Disabled people minister to us by making more obvious a truth that applies to us all: we have not arrived. Full humanity lies ahead of us, in the resurrection of the body which transforms the whole person so as to make us fully human, and in the little experiences we have now, the little steps that we take, toward full humanity, as the Holy Spirit has God's way with us and brings about some anticipation of resurrection fullness. The disabled draw our attention to the fact that all of us are on the way to full humanity.

Insofar as the journey is a corporate one, the disabled are part of humanity's journey, the church's journey, their family's journey, my journey. They not only take part in that journey but also form a resource for others on it; for the question whether we are becoming human, growing toward imaging God, is in part a question about whether disabled and abled are journeying more and more closely together.

3. Relationship

Disabled people thus draw our attention to the fact that human beings are designed to live in relationship. They may sometimes draw attention to this negatively, by their unhappiness and frustration at not being in relationship. They certainly do it positively, by their uninhibited joy in relationships, by their lack of self-sufficiency, which makes them more evidently need to be in relationship in order to live at all, and by their capacity to draw others into relationship.

Genesis draws attention to the fact that human beings are created male and female. At least three possible implications of this fact are worth noting.

First, in the context God goes on to commission them to procreate, to fill the world, and this has been thought to be the point of their being male and female. Yet on the previous day other creatures were commissioned to procreate and fill the world without such reference to their sexual differentiation (v. 22), and this makes it unlikely that procreation is the main or only point of the reference to human sexual differentiation. In many cultures, having children is felt to be a mark of being fully human, both for men and women. For many disabled people, having children may be an impossibility. They help us handle the question whether full humanness depends on that experience. Humanity as a whole has, in any case, well kept the commission to fill the world and may have to resist the temptation any more to overfill it. Disabled people may be compelled to discover and to evidence for the rest of humanity that there are other forms of fecundity, of "capacity to touch hearts and to give life."[16]

Second, sexual differentiation epitomizes the differentiation and diversity among human beings. It is the glory and the challenge of humanity that we are different from each other, and the sexual difference is the most elemental difference. When men and women live, work, and worship together, humanity is represented in its essential diversity, and God is imaged. When abled and disabled live, work, and worship together, humanity is represented in another form of its essential diversity, and God is imaged.

Third, in the context of that differentiation we are indeed made to be in relationship. That is so for human beings made in God's image because it is true for God in the relationship between Father, Son, and Spirit. "It is communion which makes things 'be.'"[17] God is love in the sense that the Father is love and reveals the fact by realizing the threefold divine being. God thus issues in Son and Spirit, each of the three unique but realizing their uniqueness in relationship rather than in egocentrism. Our divinization (our realizing the goal of becoming like God and thus being human) thus consists in our participating in God's existence, having the same kind of personal life as God does. Our salvation consists in the survival of that personal life of love in relationship despite all the pressures that assail it, including death. "A particular being is 'itself'—and not another one—because of its *uniqueness* which is established in *communion* and which renders a particular being unrepeatable as it forms part of a relational existence in which it is indispensable and irreplaceable," so that we come into being in communion and love.[18] While will, reason, self-understanding, and moral instinct are important aspects of what it means to be human, it is now a commonplace to note that these emphases of the Western tradition overemphasize the inner working of the individual. I know I exist not because I think but because I am loved and I love. Conversely, fear threatens existence; indeed, if my reaching out to someone else meets rebuff, my existence is threatened in an absolute fashion.[19]

A further implication of God's having a name that symbolizes God's unique individuality is that we should not try to identify the uniqueness of Father, Son, and

---

[16] Jean Vanier, *Man and Woman He Made Them* (London: DLT, 1985), 141.

[17] J. Zizioulas, *Being as Communion* (New York: St. Vladimir's Seminary / London: DLT, 1985), 17.

[18] J. Zizioulas, "Human Capacity and Human Incapacity," *SJT* 28 (1975): 401–48 (see 410).

[19] Cf. John Aves, "Persons in Relation," in *Persons, Divine and Human* (ed. Christoph Schwöbel and Colin E. Gunton; Edinburgh: Clark, 1991), 120–37 (see 125).

Holy Spirit any more than that of the individual human being, because that can only tell us what the person is, not who that person is; it is to destroy the person's uniqueness and make him or her a classifiable entity. The person's real identity is recognized only in relationship.[20] As Yahweh's exchange with Moses suggests, this being is intrinsically a "being with." It is of the essence of the triune God that it is metaphysically impossible to be without being in relationship, and the same is true of human beings in God's image. It is not that we first exist and then relate.[21] Our humanity and our freedom are actualized contextually not merely by means of individualistic acts of choice but only in encounter with other people in acts of love and trust set in the context of relationships of understanding and shared life.[22] Who God is emerges in relationships.

This is hinted in God's "I will be with you"; it is nearer to being explicit in God's chosen repeated self-description according to which, as well as being "I am" and "Yahweh," God is "God of Abraham, Isaac, and Jacob" (Exod 3:15). They are words Jesus later cast at some smart-aleck theologians who produced rationalist arguments for questioning the possibility of resurrection (Mark 12:26–27). He added the gloss "God is not God of the dead but of the living," with the implication that when God enters into relationship with someone, that infuses the person with a life that cannot simply expire. The relationship cannot have died if it was real. Jesus' gloss is in keeping with Exodus. God's being is identified by relationships, involvements, and commitments to Abraham, Isaac, and Jacob. The being of those made in God's image is identified in relationships, involvements, and commitments.

Disabled people and our relationships with them draw our attention to this fact. They themselves enter into a fuller humanity in relationships, and they call us to the same destiny in our relationships with them.

The reality to which we are here referring needs to be expressed in terms of living in community as well as in terms of living in relationship, for the two are not the same. I live in relationship as an individual; being-in-community takes the matter further. Living in community with disabled people gives both the abled and the disabled the possibility of realizing their humanity by being drawn out of their closed individual worlds (which the abled, at least, may see as the means of safeguarding their humanity) into a shared life in a network of relationships. This network transcends exclusiveness and both embraces and is embraced by other people who are different from us. That makes us alive, personal, human. Disabled people have a strange power to call forth love and thus both to call forth humanity and to reveal the nature of divine love. When a culture like that of the West is characterized by interrelated individualism, isolation, alienation, and homelessness, alternative communities such as those of the abled and the disabled offer an alternative culture to the collapsing one, an alternative culture that can establish an alternative order.

---

[20] So J. Zizioulas, "On Being a Person," in *Persons, Divine and Human* (ed. Christoph Schwöbel and Colin E. Gunton; Edinburgh: Clark, 1991), 33–46 (see 45–46).

[21] Zizioulas, "Human Capacity and Human Incapacity," 415.

[22] Wolfhart Pannenberg, "Speaking about God in the Face of Atheist Criticism," in *Basic Questions in Theology* (vol. 3; London: SCM, 1973) = *The Idea of God and Human Freedom* (Philadelphia: Fortress, 1973), 99–115 (see 111, 113).

It has naturally been customary to find differentiation in relationship expressed in marriage, but disabled people are less likely to marry and are among the groups of human beings who draw our attention to the fact that marriage is but one illustration of humanity's destiny to live in relationship. If the assumption that people will have children is one tyranny that hangs over humanity, another is the assumption that people will marry, and even more that the relationship between husband and wife will fulfill virtually all a couple's need of or capacity for relationship. A couple have the capacity and the need for other forms of love and friendship, and the disabled remind us and illustrate for us the capacity and the need for such relationships of love and friendship. More specifically, if they are not involved in full sexual relationships, they help to relativize the importance of sexual relationships for us. There are other forms of loving friendship.

On a gloomy day I am inclined to reflect that in some Western cultures, at least, it seems that men do not want to be in relationship and women want to be in relationship only with other women. There are reasons for both phenomena. The disabled remind us of the point that Gen 1 hints at, that some of the most fruitful relationships involve differentiation. It can seem easier for men to relate to other men, or at least for women to relate to other women, for like to relate to like, for abled to relate to abled and avoid disabled, and in some ways perhaps for disabled to relate to disabled; when Ann went for a while to a disabled day center, I was struck by the sense of community and relationship there based in part on what people have in common. The "differently abled" political correctness at least invites us to see that abled and disabled are human beings who need to be in relationship with each other in order to realize more of their full humanity in differentiation.

4. Body

Being human is an intrinsically bodily matter. Disabled people draw attention to this, paradoxically, because they have to battle with being bodily in ways that others do not, and this continually reminds them and us of their bodiliness.[23]

We have noted that discussion of the image of God has often focused on human characteristics such as rationality or morality or spirituality. If this discussion referred to bodiliness, it did so to affirm that likeness to God did not lie here, because God is spirit. Yet an image is usually a physical thing, and a natural way to understand humanity's being in God's image is to see it as signifying that we are the appropriate physical beings to represent God in the physical world. The commission to rule the world draws our attention to an ongoing feature of the story of humanity and of the people of God, that it is lived in the world, in the way bodiliness makes possible.

The statement that human beings are made in God's image stands at the beginning of the story told through the First and New Testaments, and it both interprets this story and is interpreted by it. It is as if during the Bible story we are invited to

---

23 Eiesland, *Disabled God*, 31.

keep reflecting, "Now you need to remember that this is so because they are made in God's image." The incarnation is a key point at which this invitation is issued. God had no logical difficulty about becoming a human being because human beings were created in the beginning as just the kind of physical beings that God would be if God were a physical being. Indeed, God's becoming a human being makes more plausible the idea that God's image lies precisely in humanity's embodiedness and not in a spiritual nature divorced from the body.

As well as providing something of the explanation of what happens as the story unfolds, the fact that humanity is made in God's image is itself explained and given content by that story. At the end of the Bible story we are thus invited to conclude "So *that* is what it means to be made in God's image," and the incarnation will again illumine what that signifies.

Human freedom has been described as not the ability to make a decision but the capacity to embrace incapacity, the capacity to turn weakness into strength by realizing power in weakness.[24] Disabled people have forced upon them the opportunity to find the freedom that comes from embracing incapacity, and insofar as they do so, they embody for the rest of humanity that aspect of being human which we may not have forced upon us and may avoid. In denying capacity we too may find freedom and capacity. We may again consider an insight from the moment when God appears to Moses and asserts a commitment to Israel. The Israelites are a weak people, bound and frustrated, groaning and crying in bondage. Initially God does nothing to alleviate their weakness, except tell them to go and confront Pharaoh. Perhaps that is the way they are to find freedom and thus realize the image of God before they leave Egypt, embracing their weakness and thus turning it into strength. In turn the incarnation leads to the cross and the disabling of God, which shows the way to a distinctive kind of perfection or maturity that is more explicitly related to vulnerability and weakness.

At the beginning of the scriptural story, once humanity is outside the garden in Eden there is more reference to sex, parenthood, and work (Gen 4:1–2); then one of the first things Adam and Eve's children do is pray (Gen 4:3–4). The understanding of the divine image that sees it as lying in our spiritual nature, our capacity to relate to God, has not misconceived the Bible's assumptions about what it means to be human. Prayer is an intrinsic part of that, even when people have transgressed God's limits and found themselves cast out of God's garden. Disabled people may remind us that worship and prayer are not spiritual in such a way as not to be physical, bodily. Worship and prayer are not necessarily or solely refined matters of brain and rationality.

Within the Bible's own book of prayers, the first actual prayer is a wail (Ps 3), and as such it reflects the character of human speech in its elemental nature, before it becomes a cooler matter of brain and reason (as we fantasize, at least). But "all our early speech is an inarticulate eloquence that gets us what we need to survive: food, warmth, comfort, love. We need help. We need another. We are not furnished, as the lower animals are, with instincts that get us through the life cycle with minimal help

---

[24] Zizioulas, "Human Capacity and Human Incapacity," 428.

from others. We are unfinished creatures requiring complex and extensive assistance in every part of our being, and language is the means for getting it."[25] Disabled adults are real adults, but they draw attention to an intrinsic feature of humanity that in adulthood we can evade as we cannot in childhood: we are not designed to be self-sufficient. We begin in frailty and dependence and end there; the disabled remind us of our ongoing frailty, which maturity enables us to hide from.[26] They may unself-consciously draw attention to hopes and fears and longings that belong to all humanity, to the loss of the past and to fears of nothingness and longings for completeness, to agonizings and yearnings, to alienation from oneself, specifically from our bodies, from other people, from society, from the world, and from God, to frustration, deprivation, and loss. They may also draw attention to trustings and self-loves that can be relaxed and confident and laid-back in spite of the insecurity of the present, which they are less free to evade by striving for false securities (for instance, in activism or do-gooding or entertainment) than the abled are.

The mention of language might at first seem further to disable the disabled, who may lack language. By virtue of not lacking bodies—indeed, by being more focused on bodies—the disabled do not generally lack body language. They may indeed lack much informative and performative language, but not that elemental bodily language of relationship such as all human beings use before they have words, the language of plea, protest, love, hope, gratitude, and recognition, which adults surrender to their own loss. The disabled enable us to lament and to praise. As the gift of speaking in tongues enables the tongues of speechless people to find expression, as also happens in the primal scream,[27] so in their scream the severely disabled voice the scream of humanity. (A decade after first writing this chapter, I must note that Ann is now virtually lacking in any means of consciously signifying anything, by words or body language; I do not know for sure whether even the occasional raising of an eyebrow is simply involuntary. Yet that also draws attention to a contrasting fact, that somehow in her total incapacity she communicates something to which people respond.)

Disabled people draw our attention to human beings' ambivalent relationship to their bodies. Our bodies are neither merely the shell within which the true person is found nor the precise embodiment of the person. There is something miraculous about the way in human beings freedom, transcendence, and rationality are conjoined with a material organism. Disabled people help us avoid the universal tendency to take too grand a view of humanity by so exaggerating spirituality and rationality that we forget the material substrate; it is through the body that we experience sensation, emotion, desire, and relationships.[28] They teach us to laugh and to cry, which are boundary reactions, expressive rather than linguistic.[29] When we

---

[25] Eugene H. Peterson, *Answering God* (San Francisco: Harper, 1989), 35.

[26] Jean Vanier, *Community and Growth* (London: DLT, 1979), 64–65.

[27] Cf. Jürgen Moltmann, "The Charismatic Variety of Life," lecture at St. John's Theological College, Nottingham, U.K., October 1995.

[28] Macquarrie, *In Search of Humanity*, 47–58.

[29] See Helmuth Plessner, *Laughing and Crying* (Evanston, Ill.: Northwestern University Press), 1970.

laugh, cry, make love, or give birth we have to surrender to our bodies, to surrender control of our selves to them.[30] Disabled people illustrate sharply this aspect of normal human experience that we may fear and avoid, and thereby reduce ourselves to less than human. Our ambivalent relationship with our bodies as human beings means we need to let them have their way if we are to be fully human.

The lack of spoken language is a terrible deprivation, one of the most terrible of deprivations, and one that may more threaten the humanity of the disabled person than any physical handicap. This is not only because it so inhibits communication but also because it inhibits thought and reflection, for the possession of language plays a key role in making thought possible. The lack of language thus inhibits self-awareness and identity. In the narrow sense that might be only an intellectual's perspective, but we also live in the context of broader contemporary awareness that "if you haven't told the story you haven't really had the experience."[31] So disabled people, like women whose story has not been told, may not have had the experience.

Alongside the possibility that disabled people may lack that developed capacity for reasoning which is so important to intellectuals, we must then put the fact that nevertheless one does not experience disabled, even speechless, people as subhuman, certainly no more so than (schizoid) intellectuals. Perhaps human nature and the image of God should be viewed in the light of Ludwig Wittgenstein's notion of family resemblances.[32] There are a number of features that recur throughout the human family, but most human beings will manifest some and not others, and the possession or lack of one or another does not make or prevent someone belonging to the family.

Disabled people also thus remind us again that being human, being in God's image, is a corporate affair. To the corporateness of humanity's being in God's image they bring some gifts, as intellectuals bring others, and none is to be despised. The points Paul makes about the church as the body of Christ apply also to the body of humanity. The unity of humanity lies not in identity but in shared and complementary diversity. The disabled contribute their gift(s) to this body, even if we have no right to insist that they themselves view their disability as a gift to them. We and they nevertheless recall that whatever parts we are inclined to view as weak- and foolish-looking therefore possess particular glory and dignity (1 Cor 12:22–24). Thus communities without disabled people are disabled communities, so that the world needs the awakening of the community of the abled and the disabled if it is to be human.[33] It is important for the sake of the disabled themselves that we are wary of talk of "common human experience" which excludes their uncommon human experience.[34] But in addition, when the church or the world marginalizes disabled people, it disables and dehumanizes itself.

---

[30] Pannenberg, *Anthropology*, 82.

[31] Cf. Heather Walton and Susan Durber, eds., *Silence in Heaven* (London: SCM, 1994), 153.

[32] See *Philosophical Investigations-Philosophische Untersuchungen* (Oxford: Blackwell / New York: Macmillan, 1953), 65–67.

[33] Moltmann, "The Charismatic Variety of Life."

[34] Eiesland, *Disabled God*, 21.

5

CAN WE MAKE SENSE OF
DEATH AND SUFFERING?

"Where shall wisdom be found?" (Job 28:12).[1] David Allan Hubbard, the distinguished former president of Fuller Theological Seminary, once gave a paper on Wisdom in the First Testament in which he summarized its diverse perspectives in these terms: "Proverbs seems to say, 'These are the rules for life; try them and find that they will work.' Job and Ecclesiastes say, 'We did and they don't.'"[2] I have often made the quotation the basis of an examination question that required students to discuss its truth and significance.

What Proverbs affirms, then, Job and Ecclesiastes agonize over. One should not draw the distinction too sharply: Proverbs does acknowledge the complexity of human experience even while looking for generalizations, and in different ways both Job and Ecclesiastes affirm Proverbs' generalizations. But the mood is different. That of Proverbs is confidence; that of Job and Ecclesiastes is questioning. And the key expression of that questioning is their concern with death and with suffering, for these are two key human experiences that threaten to subvert the confidence of wisdom. If wisdom cannot embrace these realities, if it cannot speak to them, then it subverts its own capacity to speak to anything else. Death and suffering are universal human experiences of which wisdom must take account.

It is because the two books are preoccupied with these realities that they speak particularly effectively in our own context. There are some interesting overlaps between the way death and suffering feature in the First Testament and in the Western world. On one hand, we often note that the Western world avoids talk of death (belying what we say by the frequency with which we make the point). In an oddly parallel way the First Testament in general talks about death relatively little, though the reason may be different. But Ecclesiastes is the great exception, for here the reality of death stands on or between the lines of every page.

On the other hand, the Western world is very aware of suffering. It is one of *the* questions in the philosophy of religion, one of *the* questions that ordinary people

---

[1] First published as "Wisdom on Death and Suffering," in *Understanding Wisdom* (ed. Warren S. Brown; Philadelphia / London: Templeton Foundation, 2000), 121–34.

[2] David Allan Hubbard, "The Wisdom Movement and Israel's Covenant Faith," *TynB* 17 (1966): 3–34 (6).

raise in discussing the credibility of Christian faith, one of *the* questions that agonizes Christians, and one of *the* issues that sells books ("Why do bad things happen to good people?"). It is also one of the issues that run through the First Testament, whether in telling stories about it, or showing how to pray in the midst of it, or promising that God will do something about it, or urging you to do what you can do to reduce it. It thus features throughout the First Testament, but Job is the First Testament's great repository of reflective thought on the subject.

One of the striking features of the position of suffering in our world is that it seems if anything to be felt as more of a problem in our well-fed, well-doctored, and well-counselored societies than it is in societies where people have nothing. Among seminary students there is hardly an aspect of the First Testament that engages people more personally than the study of the psalms of lament. They prize the discovery of the freedom such psalms give them to voice their hurt and anger to God. Now these are a collection of bright and suntanned young people who enjoy the benefits of living in a country that has more of the world's resources than any other. Yet they are not happy. And what is true of them is true of the rest of our lonely, driven, anxious modern societies. To put it another way, they prove the truth expounded in Ecclesiastes, that it is possible to have everything but to have nothing.

1. Ecclesiastes

Ecclesiastes is a Greek word meaning "member of the church" that attempts to provide an equivalent to the Hebrew title Qohelet. The book goes through the motions of pretending to be written by King Solomon. I say "goes through the motions" because it never quite says that it represents the voice of Solomon (only the voice of an anonymous son of David), because it does not try to talk in Solomon's way (the Hebrew is the Hebrew of a much later period, as presumably author and audience would be able to tell, just as we know we do not speak Shakespeare's English), and because it drops its guard from time to time (for instance, talking about relating to kings in a way that Solomon presumably would not). What it does is invite its audience to an act of imagination, to picture Solomon speaking in its own day: Solomon who is the great First Testament symbol of wisdom as Moses is the symbol of Torah and David the symbol of psalmody.

But Solomon is more than the great symbol of wisdom. He is the great temple builder, the great achiever, the great politician, the great city planner, the great activist, the great businessman, the great entertainer, and the great womanizer. Indeed, he is the great Californian.

What happens when you look with the eyes of wisdom at these activities and achievements? They all look like "emptiness and a shepherding of wind" (e.g., Eccles 1:14; 2:11, 17, 26). "Emptiness" is *hebel*, literally a "breath": these things are as insubstantial and evanescent as a breath. Outside the Wisdom books *hebel* came to be applied especially to aspects of other religions, which Israelites saw as particularly pointless and empty. Preeminent among these was the making of images, which could look impressive but could never adequately represent any being who deserved to be called God. These were pointless and empty but also deceptive and dangerous.

The notion of shepherding wind in turn suggests the attempt to capture something that cannot be captured and may destroy you in the attempt. The striving for success, the drive to achieve, the addiction to activism, the quest for entertainment: they are all hollow and dangerous.

In the end, the same judgment applies to wisdom itself. It is also ultimately pointless and empty. Ecclesiastes does not mean that wisdom is useless. It is absolutely useless, but it is relatively useful. Wisdom excels folly as light excels darkness (2:13), which is a very marked degree of excelling, even an absolute one. Wisdom is important because it enables us to face the fact that success, achievement, activism, sex, and entertainment are ultimately futile. It enables us to face these facts and think about what we do with them and about what stance to take to life in light of them. Yet wisdom is absolutely useless because it is itself relativized by the fact of death, which comes to us all, we know not when (2:14–15). Wisdom cannot give us any control over that.

I have noted the possibility that people in First Testament times generally avoided thinking about death the same way as we do. At one level they may have been more accepting of it than we are. They did not rail against death, at least not when it came at the end of your threescore years and ten. They recognized that death then is the natural end to life. Life is like a symphony or a song or a film: it has a beginning, a middle, and an end. By its nature it does not go on forever. The time comes when you go to be with your ancestors. People accepted this. Yet they did not talk about it a great deal.

Ecclesiastes attempts to force them to talk about death, because it thinks that the fact of death makes a radical difference to the way we need to look at life. There are, no doubt, psychologists who would say that the relentless commitment to activism, achievement, sex, entertainment, and success, which characterizes our own culture and the one Ecclesiastes contemplates, is but a relentless striving to avoid the fact that we are going to die or a striving to find ways of living on. Ecclesiastes does not offer such a diagnosis, though its analysis is compatible with that depiction. It concerns itself with getting people to face the facts about the future and then to live in the present in light of these facts.

In the Middle East, people knew as we do that dying does not mean you cease to exist. They could see the body of a dead person, and they knew that the body represented at least fifty percent of the person, so the person has not ceased to exist. Its problem is that there is no longer any life in it. It cannot move, or act, or speak, or worship, because these are all activities that involve the body. The person still exists, but in an inert state. This inert person then goes to join other inert persons in a family burial place or a community burial place. People depart to be with their ancestors in a quite literal sense. They transfer from one community to another, from a living community to a dead one.

Israel portrayed what happens to the invisible person, the personality, the self, the soul, in an analogous way. I imagine that they reasoned by analogy from what they could see to what they could not see. The self, like the body, does not cease to exist, but it becomes lifeless. It, too, moves from a living community to a dead community, called Sheol, the Hebrew equivalent of hades. This is not a place of punishment or suffering, except in the sense of being a place of loss. It is a place of negation.

Ecclesiastes gives a particularly systematic account of this. Its most concentrated collection of negations comes in Eccl 9. Death is indiscriminate, Ecclesiastes points out: it comes to the just and the unjust, the good and the bad, the clean and the polluted, the religious and the irreligious, the honest and the dishonest. It constitutes a great contrast with life. Everyone rushes madly around the freeways of life, says Ecclesiastes, till the earthquake finally happens and they have driven off the freeway edge. Death is the place where there is no hope: "a living dog is better than a dead lion," says one of the book's more memorable aphorisms (9:4). Death is the place where there is no knowledge: there sounds a threat for a sage, a philosopher, a theologian. The living know at least that they will die; the dead know nothing. The living enjoy rewards for what they do, not least other people's recognition. The dead become the forgotten. "Both their love and their hate and their passion have already perished; they will never again have a share in anything that happens under the sun" (9:6). "There is no action or thought or knowledge or wisdom in Sheol, where you are going" (9:10).

When the New Testament documents were written, some centuries after Ecclesiastes, the facts about death were again looked in the face, but in the context of something else having happened. They were written in light of Jesus' having come back from the dead, not merely resuscitated but risen to a transformed, heavenly kind of life, which gives empirical evidence for the possibility of such a transformation after death. The First Testament is resolutely empirical. It knows that in its day there is no evidence of life after death, apart from that feeble existence in the grave. It is not the case that human thinking or divine revelation has not yet progressed as far as envisaging life after death. The Egyptians knew the idea well enough; that is the reason for the pyramids. But Israelite faith is resolutely life-affirming and empirical; it does not go in for religion as the opiate of the people. Only at one point does its resolve seriously falter, in a vision in Dan 12. There it finally gives in to the theological pressure of the fact that many people do not live their threescore years and ten, and it imagines some of them brought back to life to do that. But in general the First Testament sticks resolutely by the empirical convictions that Ecclesiastes propounds most directly.

Just before the end of the book Ecclesiastes offers an unexpectedly poetic picture of death's reality. Death is the moment when "the silver cord snaps, and the golden bowl shatters, and the pitcher breaks at the fountain, and the wheel shatters at the cistern, and the dirt returns to the earth as it was, and the spirit returns to God who gave it" (12:6–7). The description leads into the conclusion of the main body of the book, which was also its starting point: "Utter emptiness. . . . All is emptiness" (12:8; cf. 1:2).

So what are we supposed to do? Or rather, how does wisdom help us look at life in the face of death? Ecclesiastes' most significant suggestion is that we need to see life as God-given. It repeats this observation several times. It appears in that poetic picture of death, for this is the moment when our life returns to the one who "gave it" (12:7). "Here is what I myself have seen to be good," Ecclesiastes says (the perspective is indeed empiricist): "eating and drinking and seeing what is good in all the toil with which one toils under the sun the few days of the life God gives one. . . . All those to whom God has given wealth and possessions and whom he permits to enjoy them, and to accept their lot and rejoice in their toil: this is the gift of God. For they will not think much about the days of their lives, because God occupies them with the rejoicing of their hearts" (5:18–20 [17–19]).

To Western intellectuals this may not seem empiricist because it assumes that God is part of the reality in light of which we seek to make sense of life. That has, of course, been the assumption of most cultures; we ourselves happen to belong to a strange blip in the history of civilization, which came to believe that one needs to prove the existence of God, though usually it is oddly content not to have to prove one's own existence or to prove the reality of other elusive realities such as love or justice. Ecclesiastes assumes that God is part of the picture. It then reminds us that the experience of anything depends on the stance you take in relation to it, on how you look at it.

In our house we have a number of things that are simultaneously worthless and precious. They are worthless in the sense that they will cause no stir on the *Antiques Roadshow* when our effects are disposed of, but they are precious because they were given to us by people who loved us. Ecclesiastes' wisdom then is, "The relentless pursuit of success, fame, achievement, pleasure, or amusement is folly. So is the relentless pursuit of wisdom, if you think it will give you ultimate answers or tell you the meaning of life. Death relativizes all that, either at your threescore years and ten, or earlier if you fail to live that long. Instead, accept the life, the happiness, the fame, the success, the achievements, and the pleasures that come, accept and treasure these as God's gifts. And stop hurtling up and down the freeway and in and out of the transit lounges." It is an important piece of wisdom for the seminary and the church, and for the university and the world if we could only embody it.

> Death is the touchstone of our attitude to life. People who are afraid of death are afraid of life. It is impossible not to be afraid of life with all its complexity and dangers if one is afraid of death. This means that to solve the problem of death is not a luxury. If we are afraid of death we will never be prepared to take ultimate risks; we will spend our life in a cowardly, careful and timid manner. It is only if we can face death, make sense of it, determine its place and our place in regard to it, that we will be able to live in a fearless way and to the fullness of our ability. Too often we wait until the end of our life to face death, whereas we would have lived quite differently if only we had faced death at the outset.
>
> Most of the time we live as though we were writing a draft for the life which we will live later. We live, not in a definitive way, but provisionally, as though preparing for the day when we really will begin to live. We are like people who write a rough draft with the intention of making a fair copy later. But the final version never gets written. Death comes before we have had the time or even generated the desire to make a definitive formulation.
>
> The injunction "be mindful of death" is not a call to live with a sense of terror in the constant awareness that death is to overtake us. It means rather: "Be aware of the fact

that what you are saying now, doing now, hearing, enduring or receiving now may be the last event or experience of your present life." In which case it must be a crowning, not a defeat; a summit, not a trough. If only we realized whenever confronted with a person that this might be the last moment either of his life or of ours, we would be much more intense, much more attentive to the words we speak and the things we do.

Only awareness of death will give life this immediacy and depth, will bring life to life, will make it so intense that its totality is summed up in the present moment. All life is at every moment an ultimate act.[3]

2. Job

In this chapter, I deliberately deal with death and suffering in the opposite order to the one we are used to; we naturally think in terms of suffering and death, aware that the former may lead to the latter. Ecclesiastes and Job remind us that they are separate subjects. Ecclesiastes presses the question of death on us, for the most part independently of the question of suffering. Job presses the question of suffering, independently of the question of death.

Job tells the story of a man whose life falls apart as a result of the ancient equivalent to a visit to the physician that leads to your being told you have cancer or AIDS. Job is a man of faith and commitment to the community, so his experience more than anyone's raises the question whether there is any link between one's relationship with God and one's health and happiness. The book comprises a discussion of possible understandings of the nature of that link, a discussion that takes the form of a drama.

The *LA Weekly* commented on the Merchant-Ivory movie *A Soldier's Daughter Never Cries* that "one senses James Ivory's heartfelt attachment to his characters, but the question that hangs over the movie is, What's the question?" There is no doubt that there is a question in the book of Job, indeed several. What are we to make of the way calamity can destroy a life? What does it say about the nature of our relationship with God? How are we supposed to handle the experience and help someone else handle it?

A Soldier's Daughter Never Cries is apparently an autobiographical novel; perhaps its problem is then that it is more autobiography than novel, and that facts get in the way of there being a question. Fiction is so much easier a medium with which to handle a question, unconstrained by facts. Perhaps that is why God inspired so many wonderful fictional stories in the Bible: Ruth, Esther, Jonah, Jesus' parables; and Job. I guess that like many pieces of historical fiction, Job is quite likely based on something that happened, but this has become the vehicle for a work of the theological imagination in which a dramatist walks round a question and analyzes it from various angles and has the characters embody a variety of stances to it. The

---

[3] Metropolitan Anthony of Sourozh (Anthony Bloom), "Preparation for Death," in *Seasons of the Spirit* (ed. George Every et al.; London: SPCK, 1984), 42; reprinted from *Sobornost* 1/2 (1979).

book notes that suffering is something that tests us, for instance; it reveals who we are as maybe nothing else does. The book invites us to let suffering contribute to our formation as people. It implies that we must face the possibility that our suffering issues from our own acts, though it also urges us not to be pressured into assuming that this must be so.

The bulk of the book is a dialogue between Job and three friends, Eliphaz, Bildad, and Zophar. But "dialogue" is for more than one reason quite the wrong word. Argument, quarrel, confrontation, dispute, altercation, or struggle might be better ones. It is also not a dialogue because that implies that people respond to each other, the way they do in a tennis match. Job and his friends resemble tennis players serving a continuous stream of balls, which their opponents decline to return, except sometimes in the next rally but one, or tennis players serving on two different courts (and perhaps in the end they are both serving on the same side of the net).

This is so because Job's experience, or rather—as his friends see it—Job's interpretation of his experience, his willful resistance to facing the implications of his experience, scandalizes his friends. They represent a hard-line version of the belief that what happens to us is the fruit of our own acts, that you make your own good luck, that people can succeed if they work hard, if they follow the right rules, if they live by wisdom. "These are the rules for life; try them, and you will find that they work." Job has tried them, has believed them, has proved them for some years, but then has found that they fail to work. The rules say, "If you live a holy and just life you will find that your life works out well." As a prophet has God once putting it to a failed priest, "Those who honor me, I will honor" (1 Sam 2:30). On Job's account of his experience, this is not true. It may often be true, but it is not always true, and therefore perhaps it ceases to be true at all.

In claiming this, Job is an affront to his friends' world, to the basis upon which they live their own lives. By implication, there is nothing about their devotion to God or their lives that makes them inferior to Job; they are also committed to God and committed to justice. That is precisely the problem. They can see themselves mirrored in him. If what he says is true, their own world collapses.

It is an uncomfortable experience when your world collapses. A piece of current conventional wisdom says that we therefore do not let this happen until we have an alternative world to put in its place; we prefer an inadequate world to no world at all. So scientific hypotheses sometimes continue to reign long after they have ceased to be convincing, because there is nothing to put in their place. Job and his friends have nothing to put in the place of their old theory about how life works. Like them, Job might nevertheless have continued to hold to the old theory long after it had been discredited; people do sometimes deny the reality of what has happened to them in this way. But Job does not. And his friends cannot handle it.

Perhaps one reason why Job can handle it is that he spends as much of his time confronting God with his questions as he does confronting his friends. Like the 1990s tennis player, John McEnroe, he serves at the referee and not merely across the net. One of the possibilities I suggest to students for their papers is that they write a letter to God about the issues the course has raised for them, and one of the freedoms this gives them is that they do not have to have the answers to all the questions they raise. That is the nature of asking questions. Life's worthwhile questions tend not to have answers; otherwise they would not be worthwhile questions. If I can persuade students of this, I may be able to reconcile them to the fact that seminary turns out to be a place that adds to their questions at least as much as answering them.

There is a psalm that paradoxically begins, "My God, my God, why have you forsaken me?" (Ps 22). How can you ask a question like that if you believe the person to whom you are addressing the question has gone? Yet somehow the process works, not merely because the enterprise the psalmist or Job is involved in is mostly one whose point is to get things off their chest, but because it presupposes that there must be more to the situation than meets the eye. It presupposes the reality of God and the faithfulness of God, and in Job's case the conviction that God is a moral God and that this is a moral world, even when the experience of the person praying is that this is not so.

I have hinted that Job's story implicitly suggests how we may handle the experience of our lives falling apart and how we may help someone else handle it (or rather, mostly, it suggests how not to help them, except perhaps for the week at the beginning when the friends sit silent with Job, until they are unable to cope with his questions). One of the book's chief contributions to what we call the problem of suffering is to invite us into an extraordinary freedom to say the most outrageous things to God in the midst of suffering. Pain is allowed to talk; it does not have to come out indirectly in the way Job treats his wife. Job's solution to the problem of suffering is thus a practical one. The book no more claims to be able to solve the theoretical problem of suffering or the problem of evil than Ecclesiastes does.

It witnesses to this in at least three ways. First and most explicitly, when God appears to Job at the climax of the book, it is essentially to say, "I'm not going to tell you the answer." Again, I sometimes have the impression that students think that I know more answers to the tricky theological questions than is the case. Students in the United States love to call their teachers Professor and Doctor, and perhaps their teachers like this, too. In Britain I was just John, and that is a parable of the fact that before life's big unanswerable questions the ground is level. Job no more knows the answer to the question about suffering than his friends do; and the author of the book of Job no more knows the answer than Job does. Perhaps God knows the answer, but if so, God is not letting on.

What God does do in an extraordinary speech at the climax of the book is rub Job's nose in two points. First, the world is much bigger than Job, and he has to accept his place as rather a small cog in a big wheel. He has been talking as if the world revolved around him and as if it could therefore be arranged to make sure that his needs are met. It does not and will not. God's second point is that if Job is capable of doing a better job of running the world than God is doing, he is welcome to have a go, but he had better look first at the dimensions of the task (and incidentally at the evidence that God does not do so feeble a job of it). With delicious irony, God then goes on to tell Job's friends what a great person Job is for the way he has been telling the truth about God in all those protests and questions, as they have not when they have been parroting their theological orthodoxies (Job 42:8). The freedom to say the most outrageous things to God is affirmed.

Such, I think, are implications of God's speech. But when we study Job in courses, I regularly get students to take part in a dramatized reading of the book, and whenever I myself take part in this reading, I feel like tearing up my lecture notes, as I imagine a teacher of English must do after taking students to a Shakespearean play. My one-sentence summaries of the points made in the book's various sections now seem so trivial. Indeed, I now realize, instead of talking about Job and Ecclesiastes, I should just have been getting you, my reader, to read them. You might think about doing so.

The second way the book witnesses to its inability to solve its problem is that God's refusal to tell Job the answer has as a paradoxical part of its background the fact that there is an answer to the question why calamity came to Job, but Job is never told it.

The book opens with a scene in heaven, a meeting of the presidential cabinet. God comments on what a great person Job is, but one of God's presidential aides whose task is to sniff out people who might be other than what they seem suggests that Job's piety may be only a front. Perhaps Job is religious only because it pays. God doubts whether this is so; we usually think that we can tell if our best friends are the real thing. But God cannot prove it. So God agrees that this accuser can put some screws on Job to see whether it is so. And the entire story develops from there. There is a perfectly good reason for Job's suffering: it is designed to vindicate the seriousness of his commitment to God.

Now you may think that this is far from being a perfectly good reason for Job's children to be killed and Job's wife to be put on the rack, let alone for Job to go through what he does. When Job pressed to be told the reason for what had happened to him and his family, let us suppose that God had simply appeared and told Job the answer to this question. I do not imagine he would have responded, "Oh, well, that's okay then." The explanation would only have provoked more questions, as it does for us. But at this point there may be consolation in the fact that this is after all a piece of fiction, particularly in the opening chapters. (Even if the rest of the story issued from something the author had witnessed, the opening did not.) The point about the beginning of the story is to illustrate the possibility of a logic behind calamity. It sets the scene for what follows by establishing the fact that there *is* an answer to Job's question "Why in hell are you making me go through all this?" There is an answer that is at least logical even if it raises some other problems.

The point still is, Job is never given this answer. That means he has to go through his experience of calamity the same way as everyone else does. The introduction illustrates the possibility of imagining reasons for one's suffering but still leaves us having to go through it without knowing what the reason is.

A third way the book witnesses to its inability to solve its problem is the fact that after God appears and confronts Job, Job's life is restored to what it had been before, and everyone lives happily ever after. The story thus reasserts the truth of the assumptions about the question that much of the book is devoted to denying. It affirms that Proverbs is right. The book starts from the Wisdom conviction with which we all approach life, the conviction that ultimately life is fair. It is the conviction that we all want to be true even though we recognize the evidence to the contrary. The book makes us look in the eye the fact that life is not fair. But then, lo and behold, in the last scene it turns topsy-turvy and says, "Well, it is really." The man of that supreme commitment to God and to other human beings is fine in the end. This is so because in the end, perhaps the End with a big E, this conviction must be true, otherwise we could not live with the consequences. If life is random, if there is no cosmic morality, how could we live at all? What would life mean? Job declares that we must not view our experience of suffering as the end of the story.

Israelite faith worked by betting on the conviction that in the end there is cosmic morality. This was not merely a matter of whistling in the dark. Israelites knew that they had empirical evidence for their conviction. It is empirical evidence analogous to that empirical evidence that would give some later Israelites such as Paul grounds for their conviction that death is not the end. It is not empirical evidence of the scientifically repeatable kind but of the historical kind.

Israelites knew that their lives stemmed from an extraordinary act of their God. They had immigrated into Egypt and become a privileged minority group as Europeans did in Africa, but they had lost their privileged position and become more like African Americans in the south two centuries ago. Then their God intervened and forced the imperial authorities to let them leave so as to start a new life with this God somewhere else.

Israelites took this experience as a key to understanding the world and life and God. They bet on the conviction that this experience showed that this is a moral universe. And they looked at creation and saw evidence of the same dynamic. They saw that creation evidenced the restraining hand of God holding back the terrifying forces that might overwhelm us. And it is on this basis, the evidence of God's activity in creation, that Job argues. God's speech points to that arena. Indeed, these books, which the world of scholarship calls the Wisdom Books, do not refer to the exodus at all.

Admittedly it may be that by being books about Yahweh, the God revealed to Israel in Egypt, they do presuppose that other arena. Certainly they are set in its context by virtue of being within the scriptures that tell of that deliverance from Egypt near their beginning. Perhaps Job itself also implies it in the way it handles that question with which I began. "Where shall wisdom be found?" it asks in a poem that follows on the argument between Job and his three friends (28:12). By human endeavor you can find many things, it says, but you can never find wisdom. To use Ecclesiastes' terms, the quest is futile. There are no answers. The only person who knows the way to wisdom is God. And God is not giving you wisdom in the form of answers to your philosophical questions; they will remain questions.

However, "reverence for the Lord, that is wisdom; turning from evil, that is understanding" (28:28). Since the time when the First Testament was translated into Greek, that statement has been rendered as if it meant that "the fear of the Lord" is wisdom. Recent English translations recognize that this gives a false impression of the significance of the Hebrew word. It can mean fear, but it also covers awe and worship, and the First Testament does not regularly assume that God is someone to be afraid of. So there is no basis for introducing the idea here. "Reverence for the Lord, that is wisdom."

6

WHAT IS SIN?

"Your iniquities have made a separation between you and your God" (Isa 59:2 RSV). In what sense is this so? What is the nature of sin?[1]

1. The Symbolism of Sin

Scripture has a telling range of terms for sin: to list the most common, sin means failure, rebellion, transgression, trespass, turning from the right road, stain, infidelity. Each of these terms is a symbolic expression, one that takes some deeply significant human experience and utilizes it to illumine aspects of our relationship with God. This illumination is not just one-way traffic. Being aware of such features in our relationship with God also helps us understand our ordinary human experiences and relationships, as the notions of fatherhood and family start with God and move from there to humanity rather than vice versa (see Eph 3:14–15). But we do go about conceptualizing and articulating our relationship with God in light of our deep and significant human experiences. These provide us with our symbols for thinking and communicating. And as is often the case with symbols, any individual expression opens a window on a broader symbolism or on a story of which it freezes a single frame. Each symbol belongs to a comprehensive picture of relations with God.

We are familiar, for instance, with the experience of living under the political authority of an imperial power. A postcolonial context is aware of the oppressive aspect to that, but the First Testament is also aware of the benefits of security and order such a position can bring to a little people like Israel. The treaty relationship places a people under the obligation of allegiance to the superior power and limits its freedom in relation to other powers, both great imperial powers to whom it might submit and other powers of equivalent status to its own with which it might ally for mutual benefit. To transfer its allegiance to some other authority or to ally with other states independently of its relationship with that supreme authority or to adopt some other policy unapproved by the imperial power counts as rebellion (e.g., 2 Kgs 1:1; 18:7). It is likely to attract the imperial power's attention and provoke

---

[1]First published as "Your Iniquities Have Made a Separation between You and Your God," in *Atonement Today* (ed. John Goldingay; London: SPCK, 1995), 39–53.

that power to "pay it a visit," as the delightfully mafia-like Hebrew expression puts it (it is the verb *paqad*, usually translated "punish" in this connection in modern translations), to bring it back into line. Such redress may possibly be averted if it terminates the rebellion and pledges renewed allegiance; the imperial power may then be willing to grant pardon. God, then, is like an imperial power (God is Lord), our covenant relationship with God involves allegiance to God to the exclusion of other allegiances, sin is like the rebellion that breaks such a covenant relationship (e.g., Hos 8:1) and puts us in danger of God paying us a visit to put us in our place, but repentance can open up the possibility of pardon. The two Hebrew terms for rebellion are *pesha'* (often translated "transgression" in English Bibles) and *mered*. The word "rebellion" appears strangely rarely in the English New Testament, where it translates the Greek word *parapikrasmos*, but it seems likely that the more common word translated "sin," *hamartia*, also has this connotation (in the Septuagint *hamartia* often translates *pesha'*).

In this example, as in the ones that follow, in various ways I schematize for the sake of clarity. The First Testament speaks of "rebellion" in the context of parent-child relationships, for instance (see Isa 1:2), as well as those of political relationships. No doubt the word for rebellion gained a theological life of its own; people who used it were not immediately aware of the whole story I have just summarized. Christians often use expressions such as "Christ's redemption" without being consciously aware that we are speaking in terms of someone anointed by God who buys back a slave from bondage. Yet these are not merely dead metaphors but symbols that still carry freight, as we can see from their usage in other contexts.

The example also points to the limitations as well as the potential in all such symbols. Talk in terms of political authority-allegiance-rebellion-pardon illumines some aspects of our relationship with God but obscures others, as critique of the "monarchic metaphor" notes.[2] Any one family of symbols needs to be set in the context of the others so that we can avoid being led astray by some features of it. There are limitations to a comparison of God and the mafia godfather.

Alongside the symbolism of rebellion is thus that of infidelity (Hebrew *meshubah*, literally "turning" [to someone else]; Greek *apistia*). So the relationship between God and humanity is like a marriage: "I belong to my lover and my lover belongs to me" has as its equivalent "I belong to you as your God and you belong to me as my people." One basic requirement of this relationship is a committed faithfulness that excludes other partners. Sin is then like the infidelity that involves men or women behaving as if they have the same rights over themselves as they had before they married, as if they are still free to give themselves to someone else. The imagery is used especially powerfully in Jer 3. Such action probably indicates that there was already some breakdown in the relationship; when uncovered, the breakdown is deepened and is on the way to becoming separation and divorce. Reversing that process requires a desire to heal the relationship, a willingness to resume that exclusive mutual commitment, and a forgiveness on the part of the wronged party.

---

[2] Cf. Brian Wren, *Faith Looking Forward* (Oxford / New York: Oxford University Press, 1983).

Or sin is like some equivalent act of disloyalty that wrongs a friendship (e.g., Jer 5:11; the Hebrew noun is *beged*, the Greek adjective *asunthetos*). So God is a friend who shares the mutual love of friendship with us. While friendship does not require exclusive loyalty in the manner of marriage, it presupposes a form of mutual commitment. Speaking ill of a friend, or taking advantage of the friendship, or acting in a way calculated to bring loss to the friend imperils the friendship. It risks replacing friendship by the anger, conflict, and enmity that are so often the other side of hurt when a friend treats us in a way that suggests the relationship means nothing to that person. Restoring the friendship requires mutual reconciliation. Our friendship with God is likewise imperiled by our behaving in a way that suggests the relationship means nothing to us, provoking that anger that is the other side of hurt. Its restoring depends on mutual reconciliation.

Or sin is like the ungrateful forgetfulness of a child. Hosea 11 relates the classic pained testimony of a mother or father who has given all the attention required of a parent in bringing up a child and met with no response. Paul strikingly includes ingratitude as a damning feature of the attitude to God shown by humanity as a whole, which leads to its standing under God's wrath (Rom 1:21).

Or sin is like getting dirty (Isa 6:5; Lam 1:9). In the First Testament, this symbol is linked with the holiness of God. This holiness that suggests God's majesty, heavenliness, and glory is the characteristic that marks God off from human beings. It is originally not a moral category but a metaphysical one; it suggests supernatural transcendence, the distinctiveness that differentiates creator from creature.[3] It requires a parallel distinctiveness on the part of people who associate themselves with God. Such distinctiveness is imperiled through contact with the realm of blood and death, which stains people and renders them taboo. The stain (in Hebrew *tum'ah*) or impurity (in Greek *akatharsia*) spoils the relationship and requires cleansing.

Or sin is like wandering out of the way (the Hebrew term is '*awon*, a common expression usually rendered "iniquity"; the less common equivalent Greek term is *plane*). So God is a guide who points out the right way to go if we wish to reach a certain destination. The relationship of travelers to their guide is that they take care to follow the way the guide points. But distractions or alternative advice or inattention may lead to their accidentally losing their way or deliberately turning out of the right way (cf. Isa 53:6; Jer 3:21). Instead of being straight their journey becomes tortuous, twisting, and twisted. They err and go the wrong way rather than the right way and as a result get lost or find themselves in exile. By its nature, being lost or exiled makes it difficult or impossible to get back to the right road or to return to one's home; we need the guide to follow us and restore us.

Or sin is like trespassing on someone's property or rights or honor (e.g., Josh 22:16–31; Rom 4:5; 5:6). A human being may possess home, land, and rights such as honor, freedom, and privacy; God, too, is one who has rights that require respect. God's own person deserves honor. Sin involves trespassing on God's rights (in Hebrew *ma'al*), refusing to recognize God's majesty (in Greek *asebeia*), and

---

[3] See chapter 1 above.

putting oneself into God's debt (the expression that comes in the Lord's Prayer). The question is whether we can make up for such neglect or offer God satisfactory compensation for such loss. Some debts can be repaid, but others cannot; we can only rely on the creditor's willingness to remit the debt so that it no longer stands between the two parties.

Or sin is like the transgression of law (the Hebrew verb is *'abar*, the Greek noun *parabasis*). God, then, is like a human monarch in his or her capacity as lawmaker or legal authority. This aspect of the monarch's role had great importance in the Middle Eastern world: there the monarch had responsibility for the making of laws that preserve order in society and safeguard people's rights, especially the rights of the less secure and powerless. Subjects had responsibility for obedience to those laws to that same end. Refusal to obey them counts as "transgression," the crossing of bounds set by the law; it puts us in the wrong in relation to the law. It makes us guilty and renders us liable to the judgment of the courts and to the penalty they have authority and power to exact, not least as a way of dissociating monarch and nation from the values expressed in the acts of lawlessness. Normally there is no way to escape that punishment, though in special circumstances the monarch may exercise power of reprieve that restores guilty persons without their undergoing punishment. Similarly God is the lawmaker and legal authority in the world. As is ideally the case with the state's laws, God's laws reflect the concerns of justice and reflect and buttress the very structure of reality itself. To live by God's laws is to live in obedience to God and in accordance with justice. To decline to acknowledge the just requirements of God's law (for instance, by violence toward one's neighbor or by trampling on the rights of the powerless) is to decline to acknowledge God or to know God (see, e.g., Hos 4:1–6). It is to become a transgressor: "Sin is lawlessness" (1 John 3:4). It makes us guilty before God and renders us liable to God's judgment and to the punishment that God has power and authority to exact, which dissociates God from our injustice and lawlessness as well as doing something to restore justice to the violated. In considering reprieve with regard to such penalty, God would have to consider what this said about the unimportance of flouting just laws.

Or sin is like failure to achieve something (Hebrew *hatta't*, Greek *hamartia*). In secular usage, the term suggests missing a target or missing the way (Judg 20:16; Prov 19:2). The most familiar allusion to sin in the entire Bible may be Paul's assertion that "all have sinned and fall short of the glory of God" (Rom 3:23). It well illustrates how the term "sin" itself can in Greek as in Hebrew suggest the idea of failure, though we have noted that its regular usage points to some more active wrongdoing. The story to which this symbol belongs envisages God as like a parent who lays a possible destiny before a child, a possible role for the child to fulfill, a possible calling, and who has the insight and experience to be able to indicate ways for the child to realize this destiny. The implication need not be that the child is merely doing what mother says; children have the opportunity to develop their own insight, make their own decisions, and make that calling their own. They are challenged to take up this calling and fulfill their destiny in a way that will bring glory to them and glory to their parent. Sin is like neglect to make that destiny one's own, willful and stupid failure to realize it. This willfulness indeed indicates that we are speaking of more than accidental failure. If the New Testament does use the word *hamartia* with some of the flavor of the First Testament word for "rebellion," that reflects how sin involves active resistance to the destiny God sets before us. Its result is disappointment and futility: life has become pointless and meaningless, and the relationship between parent and child is spoiled by sadness, regret, frustration, letdown, and discomfiture. The question for the future is whether parent and child can find a new beginning to the path toward that destiny that the one has in mind for the other. Discipline (God's and the human parent's) will be of importance in encouraging this process.

2. The Extent of Sin

Both Testaments use this wide range of symbols to express the nature of sin. How prevalent a problem is it?

In our own parlance we have two ways of speaking of this matter. We can think of humanity as divided into the good, the bad, and the ordinary. The good are the especially generous, open, forgiving people. The bad are the abusers, the oppressors, the deceivers. We locate ourselves and most other people in between these two categories: neither especially good nor especially bad, as we are neither especially wise or rich, foolish or poor. At the same time we recognize that whatever may be true of the bad, strangely the good do not see themselves as good (as the wise and rich fail to see themselves as wise or rich). Indeed, paradoxically we would doubt their goodness if they did. They are characteristically aware of a meanness, a self-centeredness, and a resentfulness, even a capacity to abuse, oppress, and deceive, which they share with the so-called ordinary and bad.

Both Testaments also have these two ways of looking at goodness and badness. On the one hand, they can imply the division into the good, the bad, and the ordinary. Asked what one should do to inherit eternal life, Jesus reminds a questioner of the contents of the commandments about human relationships (Mark 10:19). When his questioner says he has kept these, Jesus declares that this achievement entitles him to an attempt at a higher hurdle. Neither directly nor indirectly does he express doubt about the man's claim; after all, the commandments were never intended to be some impossibly idealistic standard (see Deut 30:11–14). God gave them to be fulfilled as the condition of staying in a right relationship. In line with that, First Testament believers can declare that they have indeed fulfilled them, so that, for instance, God has no moral reason for letting them be in the trouble they are in. Psalm 18:20–27 [21–28] invites the worshiper to declare an astonishing innocence of sin, while the premise of the debate in Job is that there is such a thing as a person wholly committed to walking in God's way. Israel has its remarkably good people, and it has its remarkably bad people: that devastating declaration "your iniquities have made a separation between you and your God" is not a general statement about human sinfulness but a pointed critique of a particular group of people in a specific context.

The First Testament also includes indications of the other attitude that assumes the universality of sin. In Christian tradition we have been used to associating it with the opening chapters of Genesis; while this is a distinctively Christian understanding, not paralleled in Jewish interpretation, it is not foreign to the chapters. One aspect of their opening emphases is that there was nothing wrong with the world as God created it. The story is expressed in such a way as to set it off over against the way other Middle Eastern peoples told the story of the world's beginnings, where the world came about as a result of fear and violent argument among the gods and humanity itself was formed by the recycling of the corpse of the losing side's champion in this conflict. Conflict and violence antedate creation and permeate the raw material of creation. In Genesis, the world and humanity were created good, even if it is odd that the serpent tempter is there in the garden of Eden. Things go wrong because of human covetous stupidity inside the garden and human jealous resentment east of Eden. The inclination to invade the divine sphere and the inclination to violence in the human sphere lead God to the gloomy conclusion that "the wickedness of humanity was great in the earth, and every inclination of the intentions of its heart was only evil continually" (Gen 6:5), though in Gen 6:1–4 as in Gen 2–3 humanity might feel itself a tragic victim of alien pressures as much as a willful violator of divine love.

Of course that statement of humanity's universal corruption and violence (cf. Gen 6:11–12) might be seen as another contextual statement about a particular generation. Its apparent universalism is in any case compromised by the recognition that Noah does not conform to the rule of sin. Noah, indeed, is a man of justice and integrity, a man whom God likes to take out for company: in effect, the story virtually implies he is without sin. Yet Noah subsequently manages to prove himself fallible like the rest, unable to contain his drink or control his children, though there is again an element of tragedy as well as of humored pathos in the account (Gen 9:20–27). So he is no complete exception to the further gloomy acknowledgment, the other side of the flood, that in general "the inclination of the human heart is evil from its youth" (Gen 8:21; cf. Jer 17:9). When a psalm invites us to recognize that we were sinners when our mothers conceived us (Ps 51:5 [7]) it is only taking that conviction to its logical conclusion. We are sinners from our earliest beginnings. There is no one who does not sin (1 Kgs 8:46).

This second side to the First Testament's convictions about sin also reappears in the attitude of Jesus. He reacted negatively to being called "good"; is the term appropriate to any human being (Mark 10:18)? In truth he was the exception to this rule, but his questioner hardly implied such an awareness. Jesus identifies with the rest of humanity in affirming that in the absolute sense the word does not apply to him. Given that he rejected this description for himself, it is not surprising that when faced by people who were committed to a life of goodness or other people who were inclined to be impressed (or depressed) by them, he attempted to shake the former into a recognition that they had to face questions about what was going on in their inner selves and not be taken in by the outward symbolism of their goodness (Mark 7). These are the people who set the benchmark for goodness and commitment, so Jesus tells his own followers that he expects of them a more spectacular standard of right living (Matt 5:20). Not that he is romantic about those followers, as if poverty or ordinariness can be equated with goodness. They themselves are "evil" rather than good (Matt 7:11).

Paul's talk of sin also has those two strands to it. He can (semi-humorously?) mull over the question whether a person might be willing to sacrifice his or her life for a righteous person or, more plausibly, for a good person (Rom 5:7). But even that hypothesizing is set in the context of a declaration that in the case of the self-sacrifice of Jesus the beneficiaries were ungodly, sinners, enemies of God, a characterization not of a wicked group within humanity but of humanity as a whole.

Paul's thinking is indeed dominated by the second of the strands. That most systematic exposition of his gospel in Romans begins by setting forth his understanding of the nature and prevalence of sin, for this is the necessary backcloth to his understanding of the gospel. Its prominence reflects the fact that we are now this side of Jesus' death and resurrection. Paradoxically (or perhaps not), sin becomes a problem when it has been dealt with.

Before being confronted by Christ on the Golan Heights, Paul took the view Jesus encouraged, that his responsibility as a member of the covenant people was to see to his obedience to the commandments and live a life of commitment to God's ways. He recalls the moral and spiritual achievements of that life when he gives us his testimony in Phil 3. There is no indication that he felt any conscious dissatisfaction with it as he drew near Damascus that day. Then he is overturned by the risen Christ and has to rethink his entire scale of values. Now he has to view Christ's resurrection as fact and to discover the positive theological significance of Christ's death. Attempting to think through convictions inherent in the account of the gospel he received (1 Cor 15:3), he comes to expound Christ's death as in some way designed to deal with human sin, but this means that the problem of human sin and the nature of real goodness must be more profound than he had realized. It gives him access to that second strand in First Testament thinking expressed in Genesis, the Psalms, and Isaiah, which he expounds in Rom 1–5.

He sees that by nature we are not merely occasional lawbreakers but habitual ones, like teenage joyriders breaking the law for kicks (but no doubt indicating our inner need as we do so), living a life not merely marked by individual transgressions but characterized by inherent lawlessness (*anomia*); against our own better judgment we ignore what the law expects and what we ourselves want (Rom 7). We prefer our own vision of our destiny and our own insight on how to achieve it, "earthly wisdom" rather than the divine grace expressed in the folly of the message of the cross (2 Cor 1:12), and we thus inevitably fail and fall short of the glory of God because that is not the destiny at which we are aiming (Rom 3:23). We are constitutionally rather than periodically rebellious; far from living as in a realm in which God exercises authority, we live under the authority of sin, in a sense by choice, but now unable to declare independence from its power, at least until God acts to take us from that realm into the realm of God's rule (Rom 5:21; 6:12–18). Having once wandered off from that path toward the provision of grass and water along which the shepherd guides the sheep, we are lost and incapable of finding the way again (Luke 15:3–7). Far from being inclined to reverence God's claim on our lives and our worship, we are characterized by irreverence, impiety, and ungodliness. Our lives are not so much generally clean and pure even if needing cleansing from the occasional dirt that inevitably comes to attach to them, as hopelessly and deeply stained in a way that affect their every layer, quite spoils them, and shames us into hiding from the purity of God. Our infidelity to God as lover, our disloyalty to God as friend, and our ignoring of God as generous father has placed a barrier of conflict, anger, and enmity between us that we as the people in the wrong can hardly begin to attempt to overcome.

It is these realities that are analyzed theologically as original sin and total depravity. As the Church of England Articles put it, "Original sin standeth not in the following of Adam": it is not that we all start afresh and fall for ourselves. We are born into a humanity characterized by realities such as rebellion, lawlessness, and failure, living in a world in which sin has been allowed to exercise some authority. There is a certain inevitability about our being the same sort of people as those among whom we are born, grow, and live; we are bound up in the web of life with them in a way that links us in sin (as well as in other aspects of our humanity) with humanity, as it goes back to humanity's first turning away from God. And even our best deeds are affected by sin ("have the nature of sin": Article 13) because of the context in which they are set in our lives and the stain it gives them.

3. The Consequences of Sin

We have already begun to consider what are the consequences of sin. A prominent theme in theological discussion of this matter is God's anger.

One can perceive two ways in which scripture envisages humanity under God's anger. They correspond to the two ways of seeing the problem of sinfulness that we have considered. In the First Testament in general, anger is God's response to particular wrong deeds rather than a characteristic attitude for God to take to human beings. The First Testament repeatedly affirms how slow God is to get angry (e.g., Exod 34:6), sometimes to the despair of God's servants who wish God would be a little quicker (Jonah 4:2). In considering the Bible's symbols for sin we have referred to anger in connection with the friendship-disloyalty-reconciliation family of words. Sometimes a friend or relative or someone else of whom we have expectations because of their relationship with us lets us down or deceives us or attacks us or imposes unreasonable expectations on us. It is then that we find we get angry (cf. Gen 27:45; 30:2; 31:36; 34:7; 39:19; 44:18). Anger is a strong feeling associated with jealousy, pain, and grief in the context of a personal relationship.

God's anger thus emerges from a close personal relationship with Israel. Israel is not permanently subject to God's anger, but is so from time to time as a consequence of its unreasonable attitudes that are parallel to the ones we have noted in connection with human relationships (e.g., Num 11:1; 12:9; 22:22; 25:3; 32:10). The motif of Yahweh's anger exercised on Israel from time to time (and on other nations) becomes a prominent one in the prophets (e.g., Isa 10:4, 5, 25).

In contrast to the way systematic theology has sometimes seen things, anger is noticeably less prominent when the First Testament talks about atonement and where one might have expected talk of the propitiation of God's anger. The language of atonement-propitiation-expiation and of anger do not come together. The problem with sin in Leviticus is not that sin makes God angry but that sin pollutes, stains, and spoils and thus makes people or things incompatible with who God is and incapable of coming into God's presence because of the clash between what they are and what God is. The problem that sacrifice then deals with is not anger but revulsion or abhorrence, a pollution of which human beings are as aware as God is. By means of sacrifice God makes it possible for humanity's stain to be dealt with. In this connection sacrifice "is not something human beings do to God (propitiation) but something which God does for humankind (expiation)."[4] Sacrifice does not directly relate to anger.

A number of psalms appeal to God to turn from wrath when no reason for the exercise of wrath is indicated. Christian instinct is to assume that such psalms implicitly acknowledge that this wrath is a response to human sin; thus Ps 6 is one of the Christian penitential psalms despite its offering no expression of penitence. More likely the talk of wrath in such psalms has a different background. It presupposes an experience of illness, defeat, or other calamity, and it assumes that God is responsible for what happens in the world and is thus responsible for this experience. The event is the kind of thing that happens when someone is angry with you, so it is described as an expression of God's anger even though the psalmist does not know what might have caused this anger and is not aware of having done something to offend God in a way that would properly have provoked it. There is an even more impersonal expression of this way of thinking when the First Testament refers to wrath coming on someone (see notably 2 Kgs 3:27). Once again, here anger is particular, not general.

The Pauline notion of anger as a standing attitude to humanity corresponds to the second of the Bible's strands of attitude to the extent of sin. It sees the whole world as lying under God's wrath. This is not a First Testament way of speaking, though there is a First Testament equivalent to it. The First Testament's way of expressing the reality to which Paul is drawing attention is to speak in terms of curse, not in terms of anger. As a result of events related in the opening chapters of Genesis, the ground comes to be under God's curse, and so does humanity. The curse works itself out in the way the ground produces its fruit only at the cost of excessive toil. The idea of such a curse at work is paralleled by the way Paul speaks of God in wrath giving up humanity to the grievous consequences of its own rejection of God, in Rom 1. Both indicate awareness of the fact that there is something grievously wrong with human life as we experience it, as a result of decisions made by God to allow (even to encourage) the consequences of human sin to work themselves out in human experience in the world. They do not imply that God's characteristic attitude to humanity is one of glowering anger. They do indicate awareness of the

---

4 Paul S. Fiddes, *Past Event and Present Salvation* (London: DLT / Philadelphia: Westminster Press, 1989), 71.

alienation and estrangement that may be the secularized form taken by separation from God in the modern age, not least as reflected in the work of writers such as Hegel, Marx, Freud, Camus, and Sartre.[5]

In both the senses in which scripture sees humanity as under God's anger (as an occasional and as an ongoing reality), it is something that hangs over us as well as something we experience. The wrath that is to come threatens to be more fearful than the wrath that has yet fallen upon us or yet worked out its way in our lives.

God's act of self-sacrifice in Christ was designed to deal with the deep and incurable sinfulness of humanity that expresses itself in rebellion against God's authority, infidelity that issues in breakdown of the relationship, disloyalty that has interrupted a friendship, ingratitude that has imperiled love, stain that has rendered humanity repulsive, perversity that has landed us in exile, offensiveness that has put us in debt, lawlessness that has made us guilty, and failure that leaves us far short of our destiny.

---

[5] Cf. F. W. Dillistone, *The Christian Understanding of Atonement* (London: Nisbet / Philadelphia: Westminster Press, 1968), 2–16, 399–404; Fiddes, *Past Event and Present Salvation*, 6–12.

7

WHAT IS THE PEOPLE OF GOD?
(A NARRATIVE ANSWER)

The people of God is one of the most prominent themes in the Bible. This need not have been so: a religion could give theological significance only to people in general or to the relationship between God and individuals. It has not always been acknowledged to be so: while Jewish theology has naturally recognized and wrestled with the theme, Christianity has found it easier to be predominantly in-dividualistic, and biblical theology has not always given appropriate centrality to the theme of the community.[1]

So what does it mean to be the people of God? Different contexts in First Testa-ment times suggest different answers to this question. What it means to be God's people is bound up with history, in that it is worked out in concrete and changing human situations; we find ourselves examining the changing face of the people of God. And what it means to be God's people is bound up with history in the sense of socially significant, public events. God's people is a clearly identifiable social entity; for a significant period it is an actual nation. It has a culture of its own, and it is involved in changing mutual relationships with other cultures. Its life has to be lived in this context; its changing social structure interacts with its faith, and its social and historical experience affects what being God's people means.

Its story, as Israel tells it, divides itself by major events that herald new develop-ments: Abraham's leaving his homeland, the Israelites' departure from Egypt and occupation of Canaan, the institution of the monarchy, the exile, and the partial return of exiles to Judah. These epochs may be seen as a history of its covenant with Yahweh: the Abrahamic covenant, the Sinai covenant, the Davidic covenant, the covenant broken (with the exile) and renewed (with the return to Judah). Each epoch brings a change in the mode of being of God's people. It begins as a family (*mishpakhah*), one of the families of the sons of Shem (Gen 10:31–32). The fulfill-ment of God's promise makes it more than a family, a people (*'am*; e.g., Exod 1:9; 3:7), and indeed a nation (*goy*) alongside other nations, a political entity (e.g., Gen 12:2; Judg 2:20). The monarchy turns it into a state, a kingdom (*mamlakah* and re-

---

[1] First published as "A Contextual Study of the Theme of 'The People of God in the Old Testament,'" in *Theological Diversity and the Authority of the Old Testament* (Grand Rapids: Eerdmans / Carlisle: Paternoster, 1986), 59–96.

lated words; e.g., 1 Sam 24:20; 1 Chr 28:5). The exile reduces it to a remnant (*she'erit* and other expressions; e.g., Jer 42:2; Ezek 5:10). It is restored, to its land and to its relationship with Yahweh, as something more like a religious community (*qahal*; e.g., Ezra 2:64; Neh 13:1).

1. The Wandering Family

Strictly, the history of Israel begins only in Egypt or in Canaan; as the Torah sees it, however, the story of God's people goes back to the family of Abraham (compare, e.g., Neh 9:7; Matt 1:1–18) if not that of Seth (Gen 4:25–26). God's people is thus portrayed as a genetic unit, and in a sense it always remains that. The name Israel marks it as the seed of one person. It is a family (e.g., Amos 3:2; Mic 2:3), a brotherhood (e.g., Deut 15), a clan (e.g., Jer 10:16), a household (e.g., Exod 16:31; 2 Sam 1:12), a people (*'am*, too, suggests a kinship relationship; unlike the English word "people," it is rarely used to mean merely persons in general).[2]

Nothing outward distinguishes Abraham from many other second-millennium figures. It is God's particular purpose that marks out from other emigrations his departure from Ur. Genesis calls it Ur of the Chaldeans; the designation suggests the Neo-Babylonian period and points to the might and pomp, as well as the arrogance and superstition, associated with the Chaldeans from the seventh century.[3] Abraham leaves such a background in "the first Exodus by which the imperial civilizations of the Near East in general receive their stigma as environments of lesser meaning."[4] It is a calling out of the world.

Yet Abraham is called out of the world for the world's sake. God's purpose is that he should experience such blessing that the world will pray to be blessed as he is blessed (Gen 12:3 NEB). Out of its context, such a promise might seem good news only for Abraham; it does not say that this prayer will be answered. Following on Gen 1–11, however, it affirms that seeking blessing from Abraham's God is the way that a world under the curse can experience the fulfillment of God's original purpose of blessing. Specific stories, such as Abraham's prayer for Sodom, offer illustrations of the international and open stance of the stories in Gen 12–50.

The stress on genetic relationship would give the impression that individuals have no choice whether or not they belong to God's people. They have to be born into it; if they are born into it, this settles the matter. No prior confession of faith or acceptance of obligation is a necessary, or even a possible, condition of belonging to this people; this indicates that it is God's sovereignty, not human initiative,

---

[2]G. E. Mendenhall believes that these kinship terms are only expressions for social links produced by some other cause, ethnic feeling being a postexilic phenomenon (*The Tenth Generation* [Baltimore: Johns Hopkins University Press, 1973], 5, 27, 155, 171, 174, 220; cf. Norman K. Gottwald, *The Tribes of Yahweh* [Maryknoll, N.Y.: Orbis, 1979 / London: SCM, 1980], 235–341). But the expressions are so pervasive and their implications are worked out so systematically that this seems implausible. See further sections 5 and 9 below.

[3]N. M. Sarna, *Understanding Genesis* (repr., New York: Schocken, 1970), 98.

[4]E. Voegelin, *Israel and Revelation* (Baton Rouge: Louisiana State University, 1956), 140.

which brings it into existence. It is not a merely natural entity. A special act of God creates it. The notion of election is key to understanding the notion of Israel. It is not even that God turns an already existent people into a personal possession; God brings a people into being. It exists as a people only because of an act of God.[5] More specifically, a special act of a specific God creates it. What is distinctive about Israel is not that it sees itself as God's people (most peoples would make that claim) but that it sees itself as Yahweh's people, and it is this latter phrase that the First Testament nearly always uses.[6]

In Genesis, the divine initiative takes the characteristic form of a summons to the particular family of Abraham and a promise to them of blessing, a special relationship, and concretely of land and increase. Thus Israel is constituted the people of the promise, a people brought into existence by God's word.[7] The populousness that is intrinsic to being a people will come about not by natural growth but by a divine gift that ignores ordinary human expectation, let alone the particular inability of Abraham and Sarah. The land that is also intrinsic to being a people will come to be theirs not by natural inheritance or natural right or by human achievement but by divine gift that is also of a magnitude to belie both ordinary human expectation and the particular obstacles to its fulfillment that confront Abraham in the land. Thus faith is required of God's people, trust in the promise of its God. Obedience is also required of it, though not a life of obedience to a system of ethical, cultic, and social regulations such as Israel later received, but a commitment to Yahweh's calling that follows where Yahweh directs on a particular pilgrimage toward a goal known only to Yahweh.[8]

Abraham's call out of the world also involves an exodus from politics; Abraham's family stands outside the power structures of the land it comes to live in. Perhaps the description of them as *'ibrim* places them among the many *'apiru* people outside the social structure of second-millennium Canaan. Yet they are not the freebooting mercenaries of the Amarna letters. Military and political involvement comes to Abraham exceptionally and accidentally, and even then Abraham undertakes only a limited rescue operation, by which he refuses to be personally profited (Gen 14). Such an attitude puts Abraham in an exposed position in a ruthless world. But Yahweh will see that he and his descendants are enriched (the term *rekush* appears in Gen 14:21; 15:14). Yahweh will be his protector (the root *mgn*

---

[5]Cf. G. C. Macholz, "Das Verständnis des Gottesvolkes im Alten Testament," in *Jüdisches Volk—gelobtes Land* (ed. W. P. Eckert et al.; Munich: Kaiser, 1970), 169–87 (172–77).

[6]Cf. N. Lohfink, "Beobachtungen zur Geschichte des Ausdrucks עַם יהוה," in *Probleme biblischer Theologie* (ed. Hans Walter Wolff; Gerhard von Rad Festschrift; Munich: Kaiser, 1971), 275–305. Theological interest in the people of God thus tends to ignore the particularity of the usual First Testament phrase: cf. J.-M. Leonard, "Invitation à la prudence dans l'emploi de l'expression 'Peuple de Dieu,' *Communio viatorum* 19 (1976): 35–60. Like the term "covenant," "people of God" has come to be a theological technical term of broader meaning than it has in the First Testament.

[7]Cf. H.-J. Kraus, *The People of God in the Old Testament* (London: Lutterworth / New York: Association, 1958), 14.

[8]Cf. J. D. W. Watts, *Basic Patterns in Old Testament Religion* (New York: Vantage, 1971), 45.

appears as a verb in Gen 14:20 and as a noun in 15:1). Yahweh, not a human ally, will be his covenant Lord (the term *berit* appears in Gen 14:13; 15:18).[9]

Political involvement with the cities of the Arabah brought also religious involvement. The priest-king of Salem attributes Abraham's victory over the Mesopotamian kings to "El Elyon, owner of heaven and earth" (Gen 14:18–19). Abraham neither rejects Melchizedek's blessing nor accepts it without qualification: "Yahweh El Elyon" is his Lord. He can accept that the Canaanite high god is God, and he can express his faith in Canaanite terms, as the ancestors elsewhere happily worship at Canaanite shrines, accept Canaanite observances such as the sacred tree, and acknowledge the Canaanite high god by names such as El Roi and El Olam, though they do not seem to identify with Canaanite Baal worship.

Yet this is not the whole of the ancestors' faith, nor its distinctive characteristic. The personal name of their God, according to passages such as Gen 14:22, was Yahweh, though if the name was known before Moses' time, its significance was to be revealed later. The distinctive designation of the ancestors' God is as the God of the fathers, the God of Abraham, the God of Isaac, and the God of Jacob. Such phrases identify God by drawing attention to a link with a human individual and with the family he leads, wherever they may be. The distinctive faith of the people of God in the ancestors' times was thus one suited to their way of life. As they moved about, they needed God to guide them, provide for them, and be accessible to them as they traveled, and not to be limited to particular places. As a small landless group their concerns were with progeny and land, and these were their God's promise. It was such needs that the God of the fathers met; this God could be identified with El or with Yahweh, but that way of conceiving of God would not match their needs in the same way.

2. The Theocratic Nation

Moses is both the last representative of the ancestors' religion and the first adherent of the new faith of Israel that he mediates. God appears to him as the God of his father (Exod 3:6), and he keeps the ancestral leader's close relationship with the guiding and providing God. Sinai itself is like a manifestation to one of the ancestors writ large,[10] and Yahweh relates to Israel as one who chooses to attach himself to a group and then sets before them expectations of them, a promise to bless them, and an undertaking to accompany them in the vicissitudes of life in the everyday world. Yahweh, Israel, and the relationship between them are thus congruent with what we have seen before. Yet the people of God is now in a new situation. The family has become a people, and one to be reckoned with (Exod 1:7,

---

[9]On this movement from Gen 14 to Gen 15 see Sarna, *Understanding Genesis*, 121–22; Voegelin, *Israel and Revelation*, 192–95. Voegelin (194) comments on *berit* in 14:13 and 15:18, "the symbol of bondage has become the symbol of freedom."

[10]So G. Fohrer, *History of Israelite Religion* (Nashville: Abingdon, 1972 / London: SPCK, 1973), 81.

9, 20). Expressions such as "Yahweh's people," "your people," and "my people" occur for the first time (Exod 3:7; 15:16; Num 11:29).

This increase is an evidence of Yahweh's blessing, yet Israel is a people in bondage. They have lost the freedom of the family in Genesis and become an oppressed minority enslaved in a foreign country. By rescuing them from this bondage, Yahweh makes them not only an *'am* but also an independent nation in their own right, a *goy*. The people of God becomes something not merely different in size but different in nature. Israel is now a political entity with a place in the history books.[11] A further aspect of God's promise becomes reality (Gen 12:2; Exod 19:6; 33:13), and a further stage in the fulfillment of God's purpose is reached.

Yahweh thus enters a new sphere of activity as the God of the family becomes the God of history and the God of politics, battling with the Egyptian pharaoh and defeating him. Yahweh meets the people's needs in a new mode of life, though this now involves Yahweh in taking one nation's side against another in a way that is novel. Yahweh also gains new stature as the lord of nature at whose bidding seas part and come together again, as the warrior whose fury brings a shiver even to the hearts of those who are its beneficiaries, as the master of the elements whose coming makes Sinai tremble (Exod 14; 15; 19–20). While being Israel's God, then, Yahweh "is not a national god *simpliciter*. . . . Yahweh is too much himself, too free of Israel, for that."[12]

While the First Testament excludes war from its ideal picture of beginning and end and implies that Yahweh is not essentially warlike, it accepts wholeheartedly the warring activity of Yahweh in Israel's history (on their behalf and against them) which is a corollary of being involved with them as a nation at all. To be the God of all of life, Yahweh must be a God of war. Even this area is embraced by Israel's calling "to have the entirety of its life constructed out of its relation to the divine" so that "the separation of religion and politics that stretches through history is here overcome."[13]

This notion is summed up by the picture of Israel as Yahweh's kingdom (Exod 19:6); Israel's song of praise after the exodus comes to a climax with the assertion that Yahweh will reign as king over it forever (Exod 15:18; cf. Num 23:21). Israel is a theocracy,[14] Yahweh's personal property (*nakhalah, segullah, kheleq*: Exod 19:5; Deut 4:20), Yahweh's priesthood (Exod 19:6). Its human leaders do not reign by right, as kings; they serve under and by the appointment of Yahweh and only for as long as Yahweh wills, and Yahweh is capable of directing Israel without using a human intermediary (Exod 13:21–22; 23:20–21).[15] Its priestly clan cannot claim a position that goes back to the beginning (the ancestors had no priest except the

---

[11]Cf. the mention on Pharaoh Mer-ne-ptah's victory stela (see *ANET*, 378).

[12]T. C. Vriezen, *The Religion of Israel* (London: Lutterworth / Philadelphia: Westminster Press, 1967), 132.

[13]Martin Buber, *Kingship of God* (New York: Harper / London: George Allen, 1967), 118, 119, cf. 145.

[14]Josephus, *Against Apion* 2.16–17 [171–75].

[15]Judges 1–12 with its anti-monarchic attitude shows how the will toward actualizing Yahweh's kingship over Israel still lived (cf. Buber, *Kingship of God*, 59–84, 164–69).

head of the household) or one that will last at the end (see Isa 61:6). They are a peculiar kind of nation with a peculiar kind of religion.

Israel has to be available to Yahweh to treat as a personal possession. Its status is its calling.[16] This calling is itemized at Sinai: the obligation of the people of God now includes a detailed obedience in the ethical, social, and cultic spheres. The covenant shape of Deuteronomy makes the point especially clear. Like a human overlord laying down the law in a treaty, Yahweh the divine overlord lays down the law to this covenant people. Middle Eastern law is the point of departure for Israel's law, indeed, so that the most important distinctive feature of the Israelite version is not so much its origin or actual content but its context in this covenant, in "the framework of relationship which breaks through that which is merely moral."[17] This context, however, does decisively influence the content of Israel's ethic, to the extent that it establishes the notion of the people of God as an ethical principle. In their behavior the people of God are bound to one another. Yahweh being their overlord, they have no human overlords. Theocracy and socio-political equality (radical theology and radical sociology) go together.[18]

By stressing the declaring and accepting of Yahweh's will, the covenant motif emphasizes that it is not mere natural kinship that makes Israel a people. It is Yahweh's act and laying down of the law, and their submission to Yahweh as their covenant Lord, that make Israel Yahweh's people and make them one people.[19] Indeed, being born into the right family is not only insufficient but apparently unnecessary to give someone a place among Yahweh's people. A rather mixed company leaves Egypt with the Israelites (Exod 12:38; Num 11:4), Moses marries a Cushite (Num 12:1), only a Kenizzite matches the faith of Joshua (Num 13–14), and Yahweh's greatness is acknowledged by a Midianite priest, a Jericho prostitute, and the frightened inhabitants of Gibeon (Exod 18:11–12; Josh 2:1–11; 6:25; 9:9–10).

Most important may be the scene at Shechem, where Joshua challenges his audience to be Yahweh's people rather than worshipers of Mesopotamian, Egyptian, or Canaanite gods (Josh 24). At this town whose conquest has not been recorded and which apparently accepted Joshua and his God without resistance, perhaps a

---

[16] Cf. N. A. Dahl, *Das Volk Gottes* (repr., Darmstadt: Wissenschaftliche, 1963), 4, 12.

[17] J. J. Stamm and M. E. Andrew, *The Ten Commandments in Recent Research* (London: SCM / Naperville, Ill.: Allenson, 1967), 74–75.

[18] Cf. Mendenhall, *The Tenth Generation*, 16, 19–31. Gottwald sees theocracy or mono-Yahwism as "the function of sociopolitical equality" (*The Tribes of Yahweh*, 611; cf. 622–49). He thus "demythologizes" the First Testament into sociology (692) as Rudolf Bultmann demythologizes the New Testament into anthropology in the sense of an understanding of the real possibilities of the individual's human existence (see, e.g., *Jesus Christ and Mythology* [New York: Scribner's, 1958 / London: SCM, 1960], 52–54). As Gottwald sees it, we are therefore not required to appropriate the First Testament's symbol system by believing what ancient Israelites believed but to follow them into freedom and the mastery of our social circumstances, developing such transcendent images as will help us fulfill that task (703–9). One can indeed read theology in light of sociology and vice versa, but this does not establish that only one level of understanding is valid.

[19] See Walther Eichrodt, *Theology of the Old Testament* (2 vols.; London: SCM / Philadelphia: Westminster Press, 1961), 1:39.

very mixed multitude, including many who had not taken part in the exodus, the covenant making, or the victories under Joshua, now accepts the united worship of Yahweh. Even if this theory reads too much into Josh 24, the general point nevertheless holds that the covenant's stress on human response makes possible a greater openness to admitting foreigners into Yahweh's people. Israel is still understood in kinship terms and in effect new members are seen as adopted into the Israelite family and given a genealogy in keeping with their adoption; there is thus no one who does not belong to one of the clans. But the qualification for membership is not birth but willingness to commit oneself.

The biblical text itself suggests another reason for seeing Josh 24 as marking an important point in the story of the people of God. It marks the end of the major stage in Israel's occupation of the promised land, the land itself having now been distributed among the clans. The final aspect of the ancestral promise is fulfilled. The land becomes "the land of Israel," the holy land, Yahweh becomes the God of this particular country, Israel becomes the people of the land. Land, people, and faith are henceforth bound together.[20]

This line of thinking is a dangerous one. It threatens to reduce Yahweh's stature; it also obscures the fact that Israel had become Yahweh's people before the settlement, which might mean that actual possession of land was not intrinsic to the meaning of "Israel." Nor can Israel presume assured possession of the land, for this depends on continuing obedience to Yahweh. Its historians show how incomplete, precarious, and temporary was its lordship over it, while the fact that the land that had been named after the Canaanites was subsequently named after the Philistines is a parable of the uncertain, ambiguous nature of the relationship between "the land of Israel" and "the people of Israel."[21]

The choice that Joshua presses on the people gathered at Shechem contrasts with the ancestors' easy acceptance of Canaanite El religion. The difference in attitude may reflect the abhorrent nature of the religion of Baal, or the more exclusivist claims of the God of Moses, the jealous God, or Israel's vulnerability to the religion of the more sophisticated Canaanites (a danger whether Israel absorbs them or they absorb Israel), or the specific attractiveness of a religion geared to agricultural life, a realm in which Yahweh had not yet proved to be competent. Allowing Baal practices within Yahwism will lead to disaster; "saying 'No' to the Canaanite cult" becomes the mark of whether the church stands or falls.[22]

The danger that Israel and its distinctive faith would disappear after the occupation of Canaan was the more real as Israel entered a period when the clans were divided from each other by Canaanites and Philistines and when relations between them were rather loose. Yet their inclination to turn their back on Yahweh goes back into the wilderness period. Indeed, their complaints and their attempts to go back on their election calling begin when they are hardly out of Egypt (Exod 14–17). At Sinai, Moses only delays a while on the mountain and Israel has hastened into a

---

[20] Cf. Dahl, *Das Volk Gottes*, 17.
[21] Ibid., 19. See further chapter 15 below.
[22] Gerhard von Rad, *Old Testament Theology* (2 vols.; New York: Harper, 1962), 1:25.

well-meaning but guilty assimilation to heathen religion, while in the tabernacle story no sooner is the priesthood consecrated than alien fire is offered on Yahweh's altar (Exod 32; Lev 10). "Embedded at the heart of the sacred tradition lies Israel's disobedience and rebellion";[23] the First Testament acknowledges the original sin of the people of God, a rebelliousness that goes back to their beginnings (cf. Ezek 16).

Yet Israel cannot get away from Yahweh. Formally they have opportunities to refuse the covenant relationship (Exod 24:3; Josh 24), but in reality it is too late for that, and these are only occasions for public plighting of troth. Israel cannot go back to Egypt. They can attempt to ignore Yahweh, but they will find that Yahweh will not let them alone.

3. The Institutional State

The judges period establishes that Israel cannot exist in Canaan as a Yahwistic nation. Social, moral, religious, and political pressures threaten to demolish both their inner and outer life. Although God's promises have been fulfilled and Israel lives in Yahweh's land as Yahweh's people, its subsequent experience is an unhappy one. It returns to a life not so different from the one it had once known in Egypt.

Although the rule of the individual leaders of this period was occasional and limited, it showed that with strong leadership, crises can be overcome, and the latter part of Judges adds to its lament "everyone did what was right in their own eyes" the explanation "there was no king in Israel" (e.g., Judg 21:35). There was thus a historical inevitability about the transition from nominally theocratic nation to monarchic state. The alternative to such a development was to cease to exist. Thus this transition takes Israel from fragmentation to the peak of its historical achievement in the time of David and Solomon.

Twentieth-century scholarship was inclined to associate both the writing of connected history and the development of Wisdom with the development of the monarchy, which thus reflected how the monarchy opened people's eyes to the regularities and interconnections of human life. The monarchy also brought developments in Israel's worship as Canaanite forms were allowed to influence the worship of the Jerusalem temple and the worship of El was once more appropriated by the worshipers of Yahweh. Like the development of Wisdom, this is a matter of inner beliefs as well as outward form. Yahweh becomes more explicitly the universal sovereign and creator who rules the world through a Davidic viceroy in Yahweh's chosen city (see Pss 2; 46–48; 93; 96–99; Isa 2:2–4). The story of the acts of God continues in the covenant with David and the building of the temple, and even the failure of the kings generally leads not to disillusion with kingship but to the hope of a future king who will fulfill the kingship ideal. Human kingship can be a means of Yahweh's kingship receiving more effective concrete expression in the encouraging of justice, peace, and true religion.

---

[23] Brevard S. Childs, *Exodus* (London: SCM, 1974) = *The Book of Exodus* (Philadelphia: Westminster Press, 1974), 579.

Von Rad thus portrays the "Canaanisation of Jahwism" as an enriching of Israelite faith that enables its own inherent dynamic to emerge more clearly.[24] But
this "paganization" of Israel can be evaluated much more negatively.[25] It includes
the narrowing of Yahwism to a matter of piety and worship and a divorcing of
Yahwism from politics, justice, and fertility, and of these from each other. The
monarchy encourages the replacement of a clan system by a class system, with
its inequalities, unfairnesses, and excesses (cf. 1 Sam 8:10–18; 1 Kgs 21). Like the
transition from family to people or nation, becoming an institutional state turned
Israel into a different entity, and one with the same structure as other contemporary
states: there was no other model to follow. The "liberation theology" of the exodus
tradition no longer began where a national state found itself, even if in reality the
monarchy meant that "Israel had reversed the Exodus and re-entered the Sheol of
civilizations."[26] Further, the request for a king implies the rejection of Yahweh as
king (1 Sam 8:7). Theocracy is incompatible with any humanly devised form of
settled government; earthly leaders must be those Yahweh appoints, and they have
authority only until Yahweh removes them.

Although Yahweh allows the introduction of institutional leadership, henceforth there is always the possibility of a clash between the institution Yahweh once
established and the person without strictly institutional authority who nevertheless
declares "thus says Yahweh" and who may be right. Indeed, Yahweh's real activity is
now more clearly seen confronting the institutions of Israel (not necessarily from
outside, since prophets had a place in cult or court) because they have not taken the
rule of Yahweh seriously and held together faith, fertility, politics, and social order.
The prophets take up the key question of the relationship between the sovereignty
of the human king and that of the divine king, the question of "the politics of God
and the politics of man."[27]

The tension between prophecy and kingship is paralleled by tensions between
prophecy and priesthood and prophecy and Wisdom. Priesthood can encourage
stability in a vital religion by the use of sacred forms, application of that religion
to life by means of teaching and counseling, costly self-offering to God in response
to God's self-giving, safeguarding of the true faith, and personal encounter with
God; it can also encourage people to replace divine lordship by human authoritari-
anism, divine nearness by divine inaccessibility, ethical commitment by outward
observances, and openness to God by attempts to manipulate God and human
beings. The wise can enable the affairs of state and family life (as these are lived
together before Yahweh) to be conducted in accordance with the nature of the
world as Yahweh makes it function, or they can enable people to organize their
lives in such a way as to eliminate Yahweh from them. The verdict of the prophets
whose work is preserved in the First Testament is that the ambiguity of kingship,

---

[24] So von Rad, *Old Testament Theology*, 1:19–30.

[25] So G. E. Mendenhall, "The Monarchy," *Int* 29 (1975): 155–70.

[26] Voegelin, *Israel and Revelation*, 142.

[27] Cf. Jacques Ellul, *The Politics of God and the Politics of Man* (Grand Rapids: Eerdmans, 1972).

priesthood, and wisdom is generally resolved by the latter sets of tendencies coming to predominate.

The account of the monarchy's origin (1 Sam 8–12) illustrates the First Testament's ambivalence about kingship, which reflects the ambiguity of this institution itself. "Without the monarchy, the Israel of the confederacy might have disappeared without leaving much of a trace in history; with the monarchy, it survived but betrayed the Mosaic institutions."[28] Apparently Israel could develop only in this way. It could not ask whether it was better to be charismatic or institutional; it could ask only how it was to be what historical forces compelled it to be. It had discovered what being a Yahwistic theocracy meant, though it had not succeeded in realizing the ideal. Now it was challenged to discover what being a Yahwistic institution meant.[29]

It failed here, too, and ultimately the institutional state is put under the judgment of Yahweh that the prophets declared. Yet this "no" to Israel as it exists is not a casting off of Yahweh's elect people. The "no" is, indeed, designed to elicit a response from it.[30]

4. The Afflicted Remnant

Prophecy thus demands a reversal of the paganization of Israel; the alternative is a judgment that would decimate the people.

Although the picture of Israel surviving judgment as a mere remnant begins as a negative idea, the fact that a remnant will survive becomes a basis for hope. The felled tree can produce new growth; the decimated nation can increase again. Beyond judgment there will be deliverance, because it is still true that Yahweh has taken hold of Israel and will not let it go.

In some sense the remnant preexists the exile; it goes back at least to Elijah and the seven thousand who refused to acknowledge Baal, and it persists in Jeremiah, Baruch, and those associated with them. When a remnant survives judgment, however, it does so not because of its righteousness; its survival is of grace. The call to the remnant to be righteous is made on the basis of the fact that it has been preserved. It is exhorted to give Yahweh the response that should characterize the whole people; it is after being a warning and a promise, the remnant idea becomes a challenge (Isa 10:20–21; Ezek 18).

Thus, when God abandons the people as a whole, it is not to turn to the individual.[31] Perhaps one can say that the origin of the idea of the church lies in the

---

[28] Voegelin, *Israel and Revelation*, 180. Thus alongside the negative view expressed in parts of 1 Sam 8–12, the appointment of a *nagid* is the gift of Yahweh's saving initiative (1 Sam 9:16), and Saul is made king before Yahweh (1 Sam 11:15). Judges, too, combines a negative attitude (Judg 8–9) with a positive one (Judg 17:6; 21:25).

[29] There is a strand of idealism in the enthusiasm of Gottwald and Mendenhall for the Mosaic period, which has not faced up to the failure of the theocratic order.

[30] Cf. Dahl, *Das Volk Gottes*, 32.

[31] Cf. T. C. Vriezen, *An Outline of Old Testament Theology* (rev. ed.; Oxford: Blackwell / Newton, Mass.: Branford, 1970), 358.

idea of the remnant;[32] if so, the remnant idea does not signify the abandoning of the idea of a people of God. It is rather a means of its continuance.

The end of the northern kingdom comes soon after the emergence of the writing prophets; Judah's political, moral, social, and spiritual disorder also portends its judgment. Before the axe falls on the tree, Josiah makes a final attempt to preserve it whole by providing the turning back that Torah and prophets demand, seeking to implement Deuteronomy's vision of a holy nation and insisting that the whole (surviving) people commit itself to living in light of its election as the people of God in every aspect of its life (inner attitude, cultic practice, social life, religious commitment, moral standard).[33] But even if the inadequacy of Josiah's reforms was not apparent in his lifetime, they died with him. His sons' reigns see religious, social, and ethical degeneration. The Josianic reform comes to a "miscarriage" that reflects the story of Genesis–Kings as a whole.[34] There is a more profound problem about Israel's human nature than can be solved by a book of teaching. A new kind of circumcision, a new kind of relationship to this teaching, and a new kind of covenant are needed (Deut 30:6; Jer 31:31–34). The idea of Israel being the people of God becomes future prospect, not present reality (Jer 31:1; Ezek 11:20; cf. Hos 1:9–2:3, 25 [2:1, 23]).

As with the transition from theocratic nation to institutional state, there is a certain logic about the failure of the institution that turns it into a remnant. To the extent that the people of God is where the kingship of God is a reality (a notion given outward form by the theocratic nation), it forms a microcosm of what the whole world is called to be. But in that this kingship is in practice rejected, this people becomes instead a microcosm of what the world itself also is. If the state's importance and sovereignty compete with those of God, it has to be judged.[35] The people of God is not a means of God's revelation but a threat to it; for the sake of that revelation, the Israel of the day therefore has to be cast off. The people of God has no security independent of its obedience. It is not indispensable; rather, God will be revealed through it by judging, if not by blessing. It thus represents in microcosm the judgment of all those who go against God.

Although the exile makes into a reality the nightmare that Israel will be reduced to a mere remnant, its religion absorbs the experience of exile rather than being absorbed by it. The survivors take up anew the challenge to keep Yahweh's instruction, meditate anew on the lessons to be learned from their history as a people, and ask anew whether there might be some future for them. It is, however, a demoralized remnant that hears a second Isaiah proclaiming that they *are* God's people, that they are not finished, that they are Yahweh's servant and have not been abandoned by Yahweh. In Isa 40–55, the description of Israel as Yahweh's servant is the key motif

---

[32] So Otto Eissfeldt, "Geschichtliches und Übergeschichtliches im Alten Testament," *Theologische Studien und Kritiken* 109/2 (1947): 9–23 (10, 13).

[33] Cf. ibid., 15.

[34] Cf. Rudolf Bultmann, "Prophecy and Fulfillment," in *Essays on Old Testament Hermeneutics* (ed. Claus Westermann; Richmond: John Knox, 1963) = *Essays on Old Testament Interpretation* (London: SCM, 1063), 50–75 (72–75).

[35] Cf. Mendenhall, *The Tenth Generation*, 100.

to designate Israel as the people of God. Their servanthood is the guarantee of God's concern for them (41:8–10). It also implies their responsibility to God (42:1–4, 5–9). The trouble is that they are too deaf and blind to meet this responsibility, and in need of enlightenment themselves (42:18–20). God first promises to restore them to the land, though the anointed king through whom God will do this is not a son of David such as Jehoiachin or Zerubbabel but the Persian Cyrus (45:1). They need to be "on the way," however, in another sense, on the way from sin to new creation,[36] and the prophet hears Yahweh's summons to minister to these inner needs, to be the servant to them, and to accept the affliction this will bring (49:1–6; 50:4–9).

The last major servant passage (52:13–53:12) develops the motif of the servant's affliction, which has been gaining increasing prominence through Isa 40–55. The portrait of Yahweh's arm revealed in this servant's humiliation suggests that it is through the servant's acceptance of affliction and suffering, not through the exercise of triumphant power, that humanity's personal needs find their fulfillment. It would be an oversimplification to say that Israel is this servant (earlier chapters have made it clear that Israel needs to receive such a ministry) or that the prophet is the servant. Yet to the extent that Israel is God's servant at all, this is its calling, and both the nation's experience of exile (which for some Israelites was undeserved, though Isa 40–55 does not explicitly refer to this point) and the prophet's experience of opposition contribute to the insight expressed in this portrait. The calling of the people of God is the calling of the servant; the calling of the servant is a call to die. That is the exile's deepest insight on what it means to be the people of God.

5. The Community of the Promise

In later times, the notion of exile or dispersion deeply influenced both Jewish and Christian thinking about the people of God.[37] The same is true of the servant idea, which both Jews and Christians can see as a (if not the) high point of the First Testament. Yet the idea all but disappears from the First Testament after the exile, except for enigmatic passages such as Zech 12:10–13:1 and Dan 11:32–12:3. It seems to have exercised little influence on ideas of what it means to be God's people in the Second Temple period. Not unnaturally, the glorious promises of restoration were what caught people's enthusiasm.

In the event, the restoration fell far short of the glory of these promises, as Haggai, Zechariah, and Ezra 1–6 make clear. It is no triumphant return winning all the nations' acknowledgment of Yahweh. Though the exiles are free to return to their land, Judah remains a subject people. In a way history does repeat itself; the situation in Ezra 4 resembles that of the judges period. The question now is how such a subject people can live faithfully as the people of Yahweh.[38]

---

[36] Yves Congar, "The Church," *Concilium* (London) 1/1:7–19 (15).

[37] For the latter, see, e.g., 1 Pet 1:1.

[38] Cf. P. R. Ackroyd, *The Chronicler in His Age* (JSOTSup 101; Sheffield: Sheffield Academic Press, 1991), 13.

Israel threw off statehood along with monarchy with remarkable ease; "the state as such was somewhat of a borrowed garment for Israel."[39] They had been the people of Yahweh before and could be after. They had been the Israelite *qahal*, the assembled community, before, and they could be again. Becoming a community does not mean becoming a church in the sense of a body with no awareness of itself as a people; the *qahal* bears a people's traditions and hopes.[40] Yet as a people they are in a different position because they have been through nationhood, the experience of Yahweh acting in their political history, and the receiving of Yahweh's promise to do so again. They are now the community of promise. The failure of the promise to live up to expectations forces Israel to find ways of living with God's promises; it leads to the emergence of at least four models of what it must mean to be the people of God now.

First, the First Testament's postexilic narrative presentation of Israel's story portrays it as a *worshiping* community. This understanding presupposes that God's promises have been fulfilled in the restoration: God is still present and active with Israel. The "branch" may have disappeared, but the high priest has not:[41] Yahweh's activity is seen in political events (the Persian authorities serve Yahweh), though more significantly in Israel's religious life, which Yahweh established in the first place and where the promises of the prophets are fulfilled. Yahweh calls the Israelite *qahal* to be also the *'edah*, the community gathered for worship. It is this that Ezra established[42] and that Chronicles provides with its ideological base, still, significantly, in the form of narrative history. Of course Israel had been a worshiping community from the beginning, and Ezekiel's prophecies had this at the center of their vision. Indeed, "a theology that saw Israel's existence in the eyes of Jahweh as so strongly conditioned by praise" could hardly have "strayed so very far from the proper road."[43]

In theory, at least, the community welcomes all who are willing to join God's people in Jerusalem to worship with it; yet there is an unresolved tension in its attitude to outsiders. It is still a people, organized by clan and family, as Chronicles especially emphasizes. Indeed, community leaders such as Ezra and Nehemiah perceive a need to close the ranks against alien influence if Israel is to survive as a distinct entity in the pressures of their time. They are less tolerant of the "mixed multitude" than Moses had been (Neh 13:1–3). Such a protectionism may have enabled Judaism to survive, even if it could not enable it to triumph.[44]

Second, other Judeans approached exilic prophecy in a different way and saw God's people as called to be a *waiting* community. If God could not be seen as presently active in history, faith's response was not to narrow God's sphere of activity to a worship focus but to look to God's future. While one should not despise the day of small things, one should not be satisfied with it either. The time will come when God brings to an end this God-forsaken order of history in judgment and deliverance.

[39] Von Rad, *Old Testament Theology*, 1:90.
[40] Cf. Dahl, *Das Volk Gottes*, 36.
[41] Cf. Vriezen, *An Outline of Old Testament Theology*, 360.
[42] So K. Koch, "Ezra and the Origins of Judaism," *JSS* 19 (1974): 173–97.
[43] Von Rad's comment on Chronicles, *Old Testament Theology*, 1:354.
[44] Cf. J. H. Chamberlayne, *Man in Society* (London: Epworth, 1966), 176.

Some of the tensions between the vision of the worshiping community and that of the waiting community perhaps reflect the respective positions of different groups in the power structure of the postexilic community as a whole. Yet they are also intelligible as alternative responses to a real problem of faith. Nor should the tensions between those who hold these viewpoints be exaggerated. Visionaries such as Ezekiel, Haggai, and Zechariah have a temple-focused faith, and works such as Ezra-Nehemiah that focus on the reestablishment of temple, community, and city still look to the future for God to bring about a more satisfactory restoration of the people's fortunes than the one they experience in the present. Both perspectives are concerned for purity over against outside influence; they stand together over against the views of the Jews of Elephantine and of those who were prepared to accept or to take up arms against the Hellenizing pressures of the Maccabean crisis. A concern for purity over against outside influence thus involves a concern for purity within the people of God, and this, too, both perspectives share. The division between righteous and wicked is one not only between Israel and the world but also within Israel.

Third, others emphasize *obeying* the Torah. In the context of the covenant the instructions in the Torah function as an expression of God's grace that provide people with the framework for a response to God's acts. After the exile, the instructions seem to function more independently of the covenant and gain a central place in their own right as a means of people relating to God. The Torah is the direct object of the believer's meditation, delight, hope, longing, trust, and love (e.g., Ps 19:8–15 [7–14]; 119:14–16, 40–49).

In Mendenhall's view, postexilic Israel becomes for the first time ethnocentric, not least in connection with its observance of the Torah (see Neh 13).[45] But it is implausible either to remove the ethnic base from early Israel or to remove the confessional base from the postexilic community. The idea of conversion to Judaism, of becoming a Jew by taking on the demands of the Torah, begins in postexilic Judaism.[46] It is the postexilic community's focusing on the Torah that encourages the idea that any who respond to it, whatever their race, can belong to Yahweh's people—the idea illustrated by Ruth and Jonah. Yet this same focusing on the Torah issues in the more exclusive attitudes of Ezra and Nehemiah.

There are other possible drawbacks about an emphasis on the Torah. Turning Israel's faith into a religion of a book could release the community from having to listen for the living word and from the tension of living with God in history.[47] It may imply that the relationship between God and people depends on people rather than on God and may turn the religion that had been Israel's freedom at the beginning of their story into their bondage at the end of their story.[48] Yet

---

[45] *The Tenth Generation*, 5.

[46] Cf. Jacob Milgrom, "Religious Conversion and the Revolt Model for the Formation of Israel," *JBL* 101 (1982): 169–76.

[47] So Voegelin, *Israel and Revelation*, 374.

[48] Cf. G. E. Mendenhall, "The Hebrew Conquest of Palestine," *Biblical Archaeology* 25 (1962): 66–87 (86–87). Julius Wellhausen saw individual commitment to the Torah as the essence of postexilic religion and evaluated it negatively (*Prolegomena to the History of Ancient Israel* [repr., Gloucester, Mass.: Peter Smith, 1973], e.g., 424–25).

with this faith, Jews can live without national existence, staying on in Babylon and Egypt. They can find a unity based on commitment to the Torah,[49] a commitment that embodies Deuteronomy's demand for a response of love, trust, and fear and brings a fulfillment of the vision of people's hearts being circumcised and of the Torah being written on them (Deut 30:6; Jer 31:33). Here is the birth of a confessing church.

The fourth model is *questioning*; even more than the third, it appeals as much to the individual as to the community as such. The postexilic community is usually thought to be the home of the First Testament's most serious wrestling with doubt and uncertainty, in Job and Ecclesiastes. Here the exceptions to the confident affirmations that characterize Proverbs are felt more keenly than are the affirmations themselves. The fact that the affirmations do not always work will have been apparent before the exile, and doubt and uncertainty about basic affirmations of the faith find periodic expression throughout First Testament times. The exceptions can be accommodated as long as people retain a living conviction that the world does make sense, a conviction reinforced in Israel by the experience of God's great acts of redemption in their history. But the exodus is now ancient history, and it is a demanding venture of faith to recognize the restoration as a genuine new exodus. Disappointment with historical experience seems likely to have contributed to doubt becoming so articulate in Job and Ecclesiastes. In their circles within the postexilic community, it feels impossible to make the ancient faith very meaningful. They recognize that there is nowhere else to look for answers; the situation can be faced only by discovering new bases for believing in Yahweh. But they find it is easier to pose questions than to reach satisfying answers.

6. The Continuing Story in Judaism and Christianity

We have reached the end of the story of the people of God as the First Testament reflects it, yet that story has not come to a proper conclusion. "Colonial dependence" in the Persian and early Greek periods is followed by "wars of independence; controlled independence; and then a last revolt leading to annihilation."[50] From either a rabbinic or a primitive Christian perspective this postcanonical history of the people of God involves a repoliticization that is discredited by its results.[51]

Rabbinic Judaism sees itself as taking up where the First Testament leaves off. The ghetto comes to stand not only for the Jewish people's continuing calling to a distinctive obedience but also for its continuing election to the suffering of the

---

[49] Cf. Koch, "Ezra and the Origins of Judaism," 197.

[50] A. Dumas, *Political Theology and the Life of the Church* (London: SCM / Philadelphia: Westminster Press, 1978), 118.

[51] So Mendenhall, *The Tenth Generation*, 101; H. J. Schoeps, "Faith and the Jewish Law Today," in *The Church and the Jewish People* (ed. G. Hedenquist; London: Edinburgh House, 1954), 63–76 (65).

servant, in which once again its God is revealed.[52] Zionism preserved the vision of being "a model for the redemption of the entire human race."[53] Understandably tired of being treated as the afflicted remnant, however, it has once again repoliticized its life and sought to be a nation like the other nations, guided as much by Joshua, the Maccabees, and Bar Kochba as by Moses, and experiencing the same effectiveness as it once enjoyed under David and Solomon, with the same risks.

A Christian perspective is more impressed by the lines that lead from the First Testament to Jesus than by those that lead to Rabbinic Judaism; it finds the continuing existence of the Jewish people a theological puzzle.[54] Among the streams of thought represented in the late First Testament period, Jesus has obvious affinities with the community waiting for the coming of the Day of Yahweh, but it is to representatives of the worshiping community that the coming of this Day is first announced (Luke 1:5–25), while Jesus thinks that the community concerned with obeying the Torah ought also to find itself drawn to him (John 5:39), and the new revelation and new events he brings offer some response to the doubt and questioning of those for whom the traditional faith no longer carries conviction. Thus Jesus addresses himself to Israel and forms around him the nucleus of a responsive remnant of Israel: not a replacement people of God but a group through whom Israel as a whole will be reached.

In fact, Israel as a whole does not recognize him. As there were lines that could lead from the First Testament to Jesus, there were others that could lead to Rabbinic Judaism, to his rejection, and to the First Testament's own miscarriage. Not that the church can then dispense with Israel; to attempt to do so is "perilously like playing Hamlet without the Prince of Denmark,"[55] and Israel still belongs to the God and Father of our Lord Jesus Christ.

Meanwhile it is the remnant that receives the Holy Spirit, the distinctive foretaste of the end with its blessings, which makes it the community that both lives by and looks for the end of all things. It becomes the church, the gathered community; Christian faith is no less corporate, no more individualistic, than First Testament faith was. Far from settling down as a remnant, it is expected to take an essentially outward-looking, open stance, expectant of growing into not only the fullness of Israel but the fullness of the Gentiles, who are fellow heirs with the saints in a body that sees itself as the same old people of God yet at the same time as a new entity in which ethnic distinctions cease to count. All become one in Christ Jesus, for the people of God now focuses on a person, on shared relationships with him, and on a shared acknowledgment of him as Lord. It is called to preach and to embody his calling as the crucified one, relying on the cross, accepting the cross, and preaching the cross.

---

[52] Cf. K. H. Rengstorf, "The Jewish Problem and the Church's Understanding of Its Own Mission," in *The Church and the Jewish People* (ed. G. Hedenquist; London: Edinburgh House, 1954), 27–46 (34–35).

[53] David Ben Gurion, quoted by A. Elon and S. Hassan, *Between Enemies* (New York: Random House, 1974), 12.

[54] See chapter 15 below.

[55] G. S. Sloyan, "Who Are the People of God?" in *Standing before God* (ed. A. Finkel and L. Frizzel; J. M. Oesterreicher Festschrift; New York: Ktav, 1981), 103–14 (113).

On the way to the cross, Jesus had gone through stages in his ministry that in part parallel Israel's experience.[56] He had the power to be the mighty one of Mal 3, exercised the ministry of liberator and deliverer described in Isa 35 and Isa 61, had the opportunity to become the messianic king of Israel but found his true calling in the role of the afflicted servant of Isa 40–55.

The church's own story also manifests parallels to Israel's. Perhaps the patterns and recurring developments can be accounted for in sociological terms: the turning of theocracy into state and of church into institution are examples of developments one can perceive in culture and history, while any beleaguered remnant may well cope with and survive its minority situation by turning in on itself.[57] Thus, like Israel, the church begins as a family and starts to spread through the known world under God's direct leadership. It begins to need ordered leadership and to institutionalize the Spirit's lordship. With Constantine, it comes to be accepted by the world and to operate in the world like the world, often on the basis of the world's agenda. With the Enlightenment and the Industrial Revolution, in Europe it becomes an exiled remnant, though in some ways thus finds itself. Like postexilic Israel, it then lives with a tension between the way scripture describes the church's significance and the insignificance of its place in the world, often coping with this experience by means of similar devices to Israel's: the agnostic faith of the theological community, or individualistic piety, or a concentration on the church's internal affairs and life of worship, or an escape into hope and striving for a coming kingdom that contrasts with the present one.

7. Permanent Insights

These models of what it means to be the people of God are all part of the canonical history; all thus contain material open for our appropriation. How do they help us in later contexts to perceive what it means to be the people of God?

It is not enough that we should simply feel free to choose from the First Testament story those insights that we find immediately helpful. The way the tradition develops reflects the conviction that the insights of earlier periods must be brought to bear on later ones; what it meant to be the people of God in Abraham's time does not cease to be relevant when Israel is no longer a homeless family. J and P, for instance, speak to the institutional state and the afflicted remnant by retelling the stories of the family, with their radical implications for each. Arguably the different traditions become more, not less, important when they offer insights that derive from a quite different social and historical experience.

Conversely, the subsequent history of particular First Testament traditions or motifs is relevant to our interpretation of the significance of these traditions as

---

[56] For what follows, see J. A. T. Robinson, *The Human Face of God* (London: SCM / Philadelphia: Westminster Press, 1973), 80–83.

[57] So Peter L. Berger, *A Rumour of Angels* (repr., Harmondsworth, U.K.: Penguin, 1971), 31–34.

they appear earlier. This later history may allow hidden tensions to be revealed or visible tensions to be resolved, intrinsic difficulties to emerge or open questions to be faced, confident affirmations to be qualified or situational overemphases to be set in a broader context. Even if we find it instinctively easy to identify with one model of being the people of God, we must see this model in the context of the others to which it is historically linked. Precisely because the various modes of being the people of God were linked historically and developed from each other, they may be expected to convey insights of permanent significance.

First, being a wandering family speaks of closeness of relationship, in the present and through the generations. It speaks of mutual love and concern, of the people of God as a brotherhood and sisterhood in which conflict is overcome by reconciliation and to which all belong as equal partners.[58] Here "the whole of existence is defined by the communal form of the family, a pre- and a-political form of existence."[59] It speaks of being a people on the way, between promise and fulfillment, and dependent on the God whose will brought it into existence (it did not come into existence by the initiative of human beings individually or corporately) to take it to its destiny by whatever route God chooses, willing to sacrifice all securities, even God-given ones, in order to keep receiving the good things of this world anew as the gifts of the God of this world.[60] It must not mean a group turned in on itself, which rests on the mere fact of genetic relationship rather than acknowledging the importance of historical choice, and which may even become settled in an unsettled way of life.

Second, being a theocratic nation speaks of the evident blessing of God demonstrated in the increase God gives, of the experience of God keeping promises, of God's direct leading and God's people following, of human leadership not allowed to obscure God's kingship and of the priesthood of the whole people not annulled by the existence of a priestly clan. It speaks of living in the world and of learning from it, but of standing over against the world and its religion, though being willing to welcome others to the same commitment to Yahweh as King and Lord that the people themselves must make. It must not mean a confidence in God that produces a false confidence in themselves, in their position and their response to God; the theocratic nation especially has to recognize that it is the rebellious nation that cannot exist in the world as the theocracy because of its sin.

Third, being an institutional state means that God starts with the people where they are; if they cannot cope with God's highest way, God carves out a lower one. When they do not respond to the spirit of Yahweh or when all sorts of spirits lead them into anarchy, Yahweh provides them with the institutional safeguard of earthly rulers. It speaks of an openness to learn from the world, to let the world

---

[58] Cf. Dumas, *Political Theology and the Life of the Church*, 24–42; M. C. Lind, *Yahweh Is a Warrior* (Scottdale, Pa.: Herald, 1980), 39–42.

[59] Claus Westermann, *What Does the Old Testament Say about God?* (London: SPCK / Atlanta: John Knox, 1979), 83.

[60] Cf. A. H. J. Gunneweg, *Understanding the Old Testament* (Philadelphia: Westminster Press, 1978), 170; John Macquarrie, *The Faith of the People of God* (London: SCM / New York: Scribner's, 1972), 21–22.

provide the vehicles for expressing the faith, and to attract the world to that faith. It must not mean that the people of God assimilates to the nations, or that the institution quenches the Spirit and its rulers replace God, or that the gifts of God come to be viewed as inalienable possessions or as rights that God has to defend.[61]

Fourth, being an afflicted remnant means recognizing that the final purpose of God cannot be effected in the regular course of human history, because of the waywardness both of God's people and of other nations. It means that God's people are subject to judgment but that all is not lost when God cuts them down to size. It means reaching one's furthest influence on the world not by exercising the world's power or by sharing the world's faith and attitudes but by accepting the affliction that comes from confronting the world, in the awareness that the call of the servant is a call to die. It must not mean trusting in being those who have escaped judgment (for this came about by God's grace), or settling down to being the remnant in a ghetto, or courting martyrdom.

Fifth, being a community of promise suggests being a people that faces up to facts yet recognizes that even when history ceases to be the sphere in which God's ultimate purpose is fulfilled through them, it does not cease to be the sphere in which they have to live; that is honest about what they can believe yet pledged to making sense of the old faith; that is committed to personal discipleship if the corporate seems to lapse; that lives as a people dedicated to praise for what Yahweh has done yet to hope for what Yahweh is yet to do.[62]

Sixth, being God's people means being especially God's, especially responsible to God, and especially likely to reject the Messiah.

Seventh, being God's people means being grasped by the Holy Spirit without being susceptible to the influence of other spirits, being taken out of the world without becoming isolated from the world, accepting the lordship of Christ, the mission of Christ, but also the cross of Christ.[63] It means recognizing that the church remains sinful and that even the New Testament embraces a concern with law (Matthew), with institutional ministry (the Pastorals), with individualism (John), and with the visionary future (Revelation).

These insights suggested by what it means in different periods to be the people of God may be set up thus as antitheses: they should be this, they should not be that. But the tragic paradox of the people of God is that they are both at once. They are "my people" but "not my people"; a means of God's purpose being effected and the biggest obstacle to that end; the agent of God's being revealed and the means of God's being obscured; a microcosm of what the world is called to be and a microcosm of what the world already is; set apart and sanctified but also rebellious and indistinguishable from the world; separated from the nations and a mixed multitude; the event by which God gives expression to the divine will and the anti-event by which God's will is frustrated.

---

[61] Cf. Gunneweg, *Understanding the Old Testament*, 169.

[62] Thus the "not yet" must not be allowed to take all the truth from the "is now" (Congar, "The Church," 16)—or vice versa.

[63] See further Ernst Käsemann, *New Testament Questions of Today* (London: SCM / Philadelphia: Fortress, 1969), 257–59.

8. Recurring Questions

Such generalizations lead from a diachronic approach that looks at what it means to be God's people in different ages to a synchronic approach that asks what issues recur throughout this material. There are certain constants about the First Testament's underlying understanding of the people of God, family resemblances that generally appear. God's people is that entity brought into existence by God's historical choice, which lives by God's promise and is the heir of God's blessing. It is that entity where God's kingship is to be made a reality corporately, in a body and not merely in individuals; that entity that accepts God's lordship and follows God's leading. It is a visible body; even where there is a distinction drawn between so-called Israel and real Israel, that is not a distinction between a visible church and an invisible one. And it lives in the world and in history in order that it may model there the calling of a people of God, which it is the destiny of all peoples to share.

Such constants that underlie the changing form of the people of God may, however, be less striking and less illuminating than the series of questions that recur throughout the material.

First, what is the relationship between life in the Spirit and life in the world? In Abraham's time, God's people ignore the world and live before God but eventually find themselves under the world in Egypt. With Moses begins the glorious experiment in which the tension between religion and politics is overcome. But eventually Israel finds itself in a state of religious and moral anarchy—one indeed presaged from the start by the rebellions of Israel—and of political subjection. The monarchy triumphs in the world (at first) but on the whole fails in the realm of the Spirit. The exile again brings earthly humiliation, but new insights to some, though one should not assume a responsiveness on the part of the exiles as a whole. These insights include the belief that outward affliction may be the means of (others') growth in the Spirit (the servant), though the prophets and preachers of the exile do not abandon the parallel vision of political triumph. The restoration sees only a partial realization of either vision, and the First Testament thus leaves us with a vision unfulfilled. Israel's story suggests that the relationship between life in the Spirit and life in the world is insoluble. The people of God cannot live as a political theocracy ruling the world in Yahweh's name, but neither can it take the way of separation that evades life in the world.[64] Nor is there any way of living in obedience to God and being organized for existence in history.[65] History, politics, and statehood, though inevitable, make it difficult to live as the people of God. The New Testament has little to add to this First Testament picture, and church history confirms it.

Second, what is the relationship under God between divine rule and human leadership, and between institutional order and individual freedom and responsibility? The ancestral leader is taken hold of and guided by God, and there is no question of others deciding for themselves where and how they will live their lives; the leader is father, king, and priest. The theocracy emphasizes Yahweh's lordship,

---

[64] Cf. H. W. Hertzberg, *Werdende Kirche im Alten Testament* (Munich: Kaiser, 1950), 23.
[65] Cf. Voegelin, *Israel and Revelation*, 183.

but the people are slow to follow, and both kingship and priesthood fulfill a need for institutional leadership, though not without compromising Yahweh's own position, as the rise of the prophets as an alternative order witnesses. The New Testament sees the Spirit given to the whole community or perhaps vice versa, but still the community can be led astray by individuals, and the New Testament begins to develop the features of an institution for similar reasons to the First Testament's.

Third, what is the relationship between triumph and affliction? The story of the ancestors is arguably one that takes them from glory to humiliation (in precise contradiction to what had been promised to Abraham), and for no apparent purpose. In the exodus and conquest Israel experiences triumph, but this is followed by humiliation again in the judges period; the pattern repeats itself in the monarchy and exile. Here, however, while political restoration is promised, a new vision appears. It may not be the case that only triumph can win people for God: affliction may do so too. Though the notion of Israel's call to suffering is not further developed in the First Testament, it has become significant in later Jewish theology. Israel's very election seems to be one to suffering. In the New Testament, suffering is seen as both preceding glory and as itself a peculiar form of glory, both for Jesus and for the church.

Fourth, what is the relationship between "Yahweh the God of Israel" and "Yahweh the lord of the world"? Israel's story is set on the broadest canvas, the creation of the whole cosmos and the forming of the first human pair by Yahweh Elohim, Yahweh who *is* God, who is worshiped as such from the beginning. The experiences of the ancestors and of Israel were to be only a paradigm of what God purposed for the whole world. Yet Yahweh's concern with the rest of the world for its own sake is not prominent in the First Testament. The world is as often seen as the locus of sin before God and enmity toward Israel (and therefore to be punished) as it is seen as living in ignorance and need (and therefore to be saved). Jesus' ministry is concerned only with Israel, and despite the Great Commission, there is an air of afterthought about the New Testament's suggestion that the purpose behind the delay in the consummation is that this provides an opportunity for the gathering in of the Gentiles.

Fifth, what is the relationship between faith in Yahweh and the cultures of other peoples? When the world's concerns are marginal to Israel's and the world's beliefs are less misguided than they might be, God's people are not afraid to identify with it. When they are confronting the world and the world is more degenerate, they resist and attack its beliefs; they thus give expression to their calling to be the people of *Yahweh*. When Israel is itself a power in the world, it allows the nations to influence it, though not without a price being paid. When Israel is being reduced to a remnant and is dominated by the world, it again resists the world's beliefs and emphasizes practices that distinguish it. When Israel is lord of its own domain but still under the world's higher overlordship, it is wary still of alien influence and increasingly longing for people to make their individual commitment to Yahweh's way. When Israel ventures confidently with the gospel into the Gentile world it is not afraid to reconceptualize that gospel in the terms of Hellenism/Gnosticism. Israel's willingness to be influenced by other cultures is part of its own theologizing; it is also a chief way in which Israel falls into sin and fails to maintain a distinctive faith in Yahweh. The tension between the positive and the negative aspects to this willingness cannot be resolved.

Sixth, what is the relationship between the people of God as a vision and the people of God in reality? The theological statements made about Israel are characteristically larger than life; in that they never correspond to visible reality, they are always open to the explicit forward-looking reinterpretation that they eventually receive. The designation of Israel as God's people is not merely a descriptive statement; it is promissory and also prescriptive. There is a danger inherent in the descriptive interpretation (cf. Jer 7:10; Matt 3:9). The image may be absolutized and turned into an idol.[66] If it is not taken prescriptively it is not true at all and becomes only a hope for the future (Hos 1:9–2:1 [1:9–10]; Jer 31:1, 33).[67] The tension between vision and reality is not to be resolved by abandoning the visible people. Throughout the First Testament the people of God is visibly organized yet based on faith, and has to be viewed in this-worldly terms yet also be viewed theologically.[68] The New Testament people of God, too, lives with this tension; it both asserts that Christ's community ignores all ethnic boundaries and believes in the continuing significance of the actual people Israel (see esp. Rom 9–11).

9. What, Then, Does It Mean to Be the People of God?

It is an encouragement to find within scripture the people of God coping with different modes of being, with the ambiguities we ourselves experience. God has said yes to each of these. The monarchy was part of God's will, even though it had its earthly origin in an act of human rebellion. The community has to find ways of living with the experience of God's promises not being fulfilled, and the First Testament as a whole includes responses such as the development of a focus on the end and of the Chronicler's realized eschatology; while worship can have a low place on God's list of priorities for Israel, Chronicles' emphasis on God's presence in its worship helps to sustain it and keep it alive when it is in danger of disillusion and loss of identity. How it understands itself and lives out its calling has to vary with circumstances; the mode appropriate before may be inappropriate now. The Rechabites' anachronistic way of life was their calling even in the time of Jeremiah, but it was not that of the majority.

The danger is that our choice of a perspective from the varied ones the First Testament offers may be arbitrary. A predetermined understanding of what it means to be God's people may be bolstered exegetically by appeal to biblical warrants that support a stance chosen before coming to the Bible. Even the appeal to context may provide only a rationalization for using the First Testament to justify a predetermined stance without examining the possibility that the First Testament points in other directions. In other words, it may function ideologically.

---

[66] Cf. J. H. Marks, "God's Holy People," *ThT* 29 (1972–73): 22–33 (26).
[67] Cf. Dahl, *Das Volk Gottes*, 38.
[68] Cf. Hertzberg, *Werdende Kirche im Alten Testament*, 10, 25.

It needs to take account, for instance, of the fact that some of these modes of being are of more lasting significance than others. Contrary to common popular assumption, Israel was not always a nation; still less was Israel always an institutional state. However, Israel always remained a collection of families, a people, and Israel was from the beginning a *qahal* that gathered together for worship, judgment, and war (e.g., Exod 32:1, the verb; Judg 20:1–2; 1 Sam 17:47). Israel's history cannot be portrayed as a simple development from family to state to religious community, nor in the reverse direction from a community with a distinctive ideology via a state to a society that now emphasized kinship bonds. Israel was always a community of faith, though always also an ethnic one.

Further, while various contexts enable certain aspects of what it means to be the people of God to find expression, they also impose limits on what can find expression there. Living with the tension between vision and reality is both the strength of the postexilic community and its limitation. Historical practicalities determine what aspects of being the people of God emerge in this context.

Indeed, this is true of any context. Israel finds itself at different points a family, a nation, an institutional state, a defeated remnant. Each of these experiences has corollaries for what it means to live as the people of God: being unsettled, involving oneself in politics and war making, taking on the structures of statehood, beginning to be scattered over the known world. It cannot be assumed that any of these are intrinsic to being the people of God; they may be the chance results of historical particularities, part of the context in which Israel has to discover what it means to be the people of God, and not part of the meaning itself. We need to look not only at the historical accidents of the form of the people of God, the ways in which they could not help following the drift of history, but also at the way they modified the trajectory.

By implication, then, the people of God cannot take for granted that each of these models of what it means to be the people of God is equally available for appropriation. Although God says yes to each of them, at each point God's activity with and through the people necessarily means God is involved with them where they are; this does not imply thereby designating that place as an ideal one. Although God then takes them some way along a road, this does not mean they have thereby arrived. God's purpose and vision for them has to interact with the intransigent realities of the situation and the flaws in the raw material God has to deal with. God's yes to war, kingship, urbanization, worship, a focus on the end, and early catholicism may thus be a qualified yes. God's grace in the story of the people manifests itself not least in staying with them out of a willingness to adapt to historical and human realities, yet without abandoning the ultimate will and vision.

So "when is Israel really Israel?"[69] Hardly at the beginning of the story, in the period of the ancestors, despite the far-reaching significance of both the emphasis on kinship and that on promise. The First Testament itself recognizes this period as prehistory, as the time of the ancestors; Israel in the strict sense is not yet even present.

John Macquarrie suggests that the trajectory reaches its high point at the end. On his view, the postexilic community's self-understanding is the noblest and clear-

---

[69] Gunneweg, *Understanding the Old Testament*, 172.

est, recognizing as it does that peoplehood is based on faith and is not bound to any natural community, nation, or political institution.[70] But this perspective oversimplifies the postexilic community's self-understanding, under the influence of a churchly perspective that prefers to regard nationhood and land as accidental rather than intrinsic to the being of the people of God. Whether or not this view does justice to the New Testament, it makes an inadequate starting point for the dynamic of the First Testament's own perspective on when is Israel really Israel.

Nor is Israel really Israel at the center of the story, in the period of the monarchy, for the story makes quite explicit that the trappings of state are at best ambivalent in significance, that the dynamic of God's dealings with Israel during this period resides in the prophets, not in the official institutions of state, and that the exile constitutes an eventual negative judgment on the period of being a state like other states.

The modern state of Israel may seem to have found its model and support for its self-understanding and stance in political affairs in the exodus from bondage among the nations and the confident aggressiveness of the conquest of the promised land.[71] For liberation theology, too, the exodus was the paradigm experience of Israel that the church sought to experience for itself.[72] It will hardly do, however, to reassert the triumphalism of the theocracy as if it had not collapsed into the disorder of the judges period and, via the monarchy, into exile. If we will not learn from history, we are condemned to repeating it. A central question for modern Judaism has to be the relationship of the desolation of the Holocaust and the triumphs of the state.

Precisely because being cut down to size by exile was God's act of judgment, Israel is not really Israel when it is the afflicted remnant. Increase, not decimation, was its destiny. Yet in certain respects God's people found themselves in exile, and the vision of the afflicted servant has often provided Israel with the model that has most meaningfully enabled it to interpret its position in the world, even if after Auschwitz the Jewish people have shown signs of declaring that enough is enough.

Similarly, Latin American Christians cannot be expected to accept that humiliation and oppression are their lot forever. Yet they, too, need a theology of exile. In light of the experience and the achievement of Jesus, the vision of the afflicted servant has often seemed to Christians the point of deepest insight and moment in the First Testament. Whether or not the question of the relationship between humiliation and triumph is raised for the church by its experience in a particular context, it is raised by the church's origins: both the experience of Jesus and that of his apostle to the Gentiles (see esp. 2 Cor 4) open up the question of the relationship between suffering and death on one hand, resurrection and gift of the Spirit on the other. Either a Jew or a Christian might be in danger of imposing this question

---

[70] *The Faith of the People of God*, 25.

[71] Cf. L. Grollenberg, *Palestine Comes First* (London: SCM, 1980), 130–31.

[72] The exodus is "the original principle on which the whole biblical concept of God and faith is based" (H. Assmann, *Practical Theology of Liberation* [London: Search, 1975] = *Theology for a Nomad Church* [Maryknoll, N.Y.: Orbis, 1976], 35).

on the First Testament if it were not there; but it is there, in the issue raised by the relationship of Israel's two paradigm experiences, exodus and exile.

So the trajectory traced by the motif of the people of God reaches its first high point with the theocratic nation, but (to allegorize) blows a fuse at this point that ultimately requires a massive midcourse correction with the afflicted servant.

While it will not do to ricochet back from the exile to the exodus as if intervening history had not taken place, neither can we regard exile as the people of God's ultimate destiny. The midcourse correction does not go back on the fundamental insight of the theocratic nation; this is reasserted in the exile. It does, however, suggest a radical reformulation of what is involved in being the theocratic nation. We discover what it really means to be Israel when the vision of the theocratic nation and the vision of the afflicted servant come together in the exile.

The two do so, in particular, in Isa 40–55, though not in such a way as to make the relationship between them completely clear. Indeed, as these chapters unfold, both visions come into increasingly sharp focus, but the relationship between them becomes less and less clear. Yahweh's arm is made bare before the nations in the triumphant restoration of the suffering exiles and in the suffering and triumphant restoration of Yahweh's servant (Isa 52:10; 53:1), but these two very different manifestations of Yahweh's might are juxtaposed without being brought into relationship. It is when the two come together, however, that Israel is really Israel. It is from this vantage point that the First Testament material on the people of God can most satisfactorily be perceived as a whole. What precedes, leads here; what follows, leads from here without exactly taking us further, until (if we see the continuation of the story of Israel in the New Testament) Jesus brings glory and humiliation together in his own person and passes on this vision to his followers.

The people of God, then, are called to follow God's lead wherever it takes them, expectant of being led into their inheritance, yet also obliged to accept that their calling takes them via affliction and death. The church is the community led by the Holy Spirit in the way of the crucified one. Neither aspect of this calling comes naturally, and neither has the church found easy to accept; *a fortiori*, to hold them together is more difficult. Often the church, like Israel, has been able to fulfill only some less demanding calling, but God's way of relating to Israel shows that, even so, God will not abandon them. If in a particular context the church's situation most resembles that of the postexilic community and the church can only subsist as (for instance) a worshiping community, the acceptance of the worshiping community in First Testament times and the presence of Chronicles in the canon indicate that God will not cast it off. It may not fulfill God's highest will, and triumph, but it may at least survive. Nevertheless, theocracy tempered by the call of the servant remains the calling.

8

WHAT IS THE PEOPLE OF GOD?
(AN ANSWER IN IMAGES)

Chapter 7 considered the way unfolding circumstances kept changing what it meant to be the people of God. It was a diachronic or historical study. This chapter looks at the question more synchronically or canonically and asks what impression the third section of the Hebrew Bible, the Writings, conveys of what it means to be the people of God.[1]

1. One People, a Worshiping Congregation

Israelite worship moves between the triad of prayer and teaching in the family or in other small groups, the priestly round of sacramental worship in the temple, and the whole people's celebration of great pilgrim festivals, Passover, Pentecost, and Sukkot. In the Writings, the individual lament psalms likely presuppose family or small-group worship as the context in which people prayed for healing or restoration. The regular round of temple worship is a focus in the narrative of Chronicles: for instance, Hezekiah's restoration of the temple and its worship (2 Chr 29; 31). The festivals are celebrated by the whole people together (e.g., 2 Chr 30; Neh 8:13–18), partly to safeguard the orthodoxy of their observance. The community worship offered at local sanctuaries is deprecated, perhaps mainly because of its syncretistic associations (e.g., 2 Chr 31:1–3).

The worship of the Psalms has commonly been thought to have three facets.[2] It involves praise in response to who God is and how God works, lament and plea in the context of God's not being and acting in the way Israel would expect, and public testimony when God turns back and once more acts in faithfulness and power. It is in such worship that Israel thus discovers, expresses, and grows in its faith.

The praise of the Psalms belongs especially "in the congregation of the committed [*khasidim*]" (Ps 149:1), and perhaps specifically in the context of the great

---

[1] First published as "Images of Israel in the Writings," in *Studies in Old Testament Theology* (ed. R. L. Hubbard et al.; David Hubbard Festschrift; Dallas: Word, 1992), 205–21.

[2] See, e.g., Walter Brueggemann, *The Message of the Psalms* (Minneapolis: Augsburg, 1984).

pilgrim festivals. These recall different acts of God on Israel's behalf; they also celebrate God's kingship and grace as creator and rejoice in the gifts of creation. This praise involves both unrestrained exuberant honoring of Yahweh as king and bowed prostration before the creator who deigns to be "our God" (see Ps 95). Ritual form, orthodox belief, awed reverence, and joyful hope appear together in Israel's worship as essential features of its relationship with God, without any sense of tension (e.g., 1 Chr 15:25–28; 2 Chr 30:13–27; Ezra 3; Pss 22; 147:11).

Such worship is world-creating. Against the perceptible world it sets one characterized by justice, truth, and meaning, because it belongs to Yahweh. It declares this world more real and powerful than the perceptible world and invites its participants to live in it as the more real of the two worlds, and thereby to make it so.[3]

The lament of the Psalms belongs in the context of gatherings for prayer on the part of the community as a whole during crises such as famine and defeat, and gatherings of smaller groups to pray with individuals in their personal crises.[4] Lamentations also models the communal prayer that lays hold on Yahweh in the experience of disaster; acknowledgment of sin is sometimes a feature of it (cf. Ezra 9; Neh 1; 9; Dan 9). The temple is especially a place of prayer. As a place where Yahweh dwells, it is also a place toward which people pray, particularly when their failure in relation to God has brought them defeat, deprivation, loss, and exile; in such contexts, self-humbling, prayer, seeking of God's face, and turning from wrong ways will meet with a response from the God who will hear, forgive, vindicate, and heal (2 Chr 6:18–40; 7:12–16; also the intercession of 2 Chr 30:18–20; Dan 6:10–11).

The Psalms' testimony issues from the acts of deliverance that bring such crises to an end. The normal pattern of Israel's life with Yahweh comprises calling on Yahweh, experiencing Yahweh's deliverance, and glorifying Yahweh as its deliverer in fulfilling the promises made in the midst of its prayer (Pss 50:14–15; cf. 65:1–3 [2–4]). The deliverance of the individual also draws the congregation as a whole into the grateful confession that glorifies Yahweh (22:22–27 [23–28]). Thus one makes one's confession "in the company of the upright, in the assembly" (111:1). Material offerings accompany and give costly support to praise, plea, and testimony. Joyful communal feasting is a natural concomitant when people make offerings of animals and crops to Yahweh. One of the joys of the powerless when restored from affliction is to rejoin the feasting of the worshiping congregation (22:26 [27]).

Chronicles is fond of noting that worship and other activities involve "all Israel." It emphasizes that Israel never wholly lost the form in which it began, the twelve-clan unit. All these clans are equal, though some are more equal than others: the entire story of Israel's origins led to the choice of Judah. That might glorify Judah, but it might also warn it to be careful lest it fall, as Ephraim had fallen (Ps 78:9–11; cf. the argument of Rom 11:20–21). Judah cannot take its position for granted. It was all Israel that had lived a life of recurrent rebellion and experience of God's grace (Ps 78:12–66). That might also hint that the merciful God has not yet finished even with Ephraim.

---

[3] Cf. Walter Brueggemann, *Israel's Praise* (Philadelphia: Fortress, 1988), 6–53.
[4] Cf. E. Gerstenberger, *Psalms, Part 1* (Grand Rapids: Eerdmans, 1988), 14.

In Chronicles, the story of the northern kingdom after its separation from Jerusalem is not part of Israel's story, and cooperation with the northern kingdom is a dangerous enterprise (2 Chr 20:35–37). But people in the north retain the potential to return to a relationship with Jerusalem and thus a proper relationship with Yahweh (11:13–17; 15:9–15; 30:1–27). The story of Israel's origins in 1 Chr 1–9 gives an honored place to exploits of northern clans, the story of the establishment of the monarchy and the worship of Jerusalem is told to show that these belong as much to the north as to the south, and the subsequent story shows that the division between north and south was never absolute.[5]

Israel's oneness also extends through the generations. Chronicles has a strong concern to link Israel's ancestors, the First Temple community, and the Second Temple community, not least via the pattern, the place, and the equipment of its worship. The belief that the worship of Jerusalem inherits the varied traditions of Israel further buttresses the conviction that it stands as Israel's one worship resource. Horeb (2 Chr 5:10), Shiloh (1 Chr 9:5), Gibeon (1 Chr 9:35–44; 16:37–42), and Moriah (2 Chr 3:1) all come together on Mount Zion. The wilderness sanctuary and its altar (1 Chr 21:29–22:1; 2 Chr 1:4–6) and the covenant chest (1 Chr 13; 2 Chr 6:41) find their place in the temple. Zadokites, Levites, and prophets all take part in its ministry. Communities that might value varying traditions are invited to see all as fulfilled in Jerusalem; they can and must make it their center.

Israel as an entirety stands within God's historical purpose. The history of Israel often threatens to break down but never does so. God's grace in the past is a basis on which to trust in such grace for the future, though the fragility of the community's sense of link with the past is hinted in Ezra 3. The story emphasizes continuity with Moses, with David, and with the period immediately before the exile (3:2, 10, 12). It also records the weeping that accompanied joy, which might denote tears of joy or might indicate that the people celebrating the occasion sensed discontinuity with the past as well as continuity (3:12–13).

Israel is Abraham's offspring, Jacob's children (Ps 105:6–11, 42): as such they have been protected, provided for, increased, and released (105:12–41), and therefore are called to obedience (105:45). The trouble is that as well as being one over the generations in God's giving, Israel is one in its own waywardness over the generations, a oneness in disloyalty, insubordination, and blasphemy in the face of God's giving (of promise, deliverance, rule of life, provision, territory, preservation). In its prayer (e.g., Neh 9) implicitly it pleads for the divine consistency to keep overcoming the human consistency, so that the pattern of grace, sin, loss, and restoration may never falter at the third stage. Explicitly it asks God not to make the ancestors' failures a basis for later judgment (Ps 79:8). One generation is not punished for an earlier generation's sin; if it turns back to God from waywardness, it can be forgiven and healed (2 Chr 7:14). Retribution is not an inexorable principle. Each generation stands before God with an open future, responsible for its own destiny.[6]

---

[5] Cf. H. G. M. Williamson, *Israel in the Books of Chronicles* (Cambridge / New York: Cambridge University Press, 1977), 89–140.

[6] See Gerhard von Rad, *Old Testament Theology* (2 vols.; Edinburgh: Oliver and Boyd / New York: Harper, 1962), 1:349.

2. A Family Community

The idea of seeking and valuing solitariness is alien to the First Testament; even in their individual prayers and praises people speak from within a rich community heritage and as members of the community.[7] The individual's hurt arises not least from being rejected and alone, "scorned by the people" and attacked by a "group of evildoers," people who belong to the same community and fellowship (Pss 22:6, 16 [7, 17]; 25:16; 55:12–14 [13–15]; 102:6–7 [7–8]). The individual abjures membership of a community of evildoers, in preference for membership of the community that worships Yahweh (26:5, 12). Survival (and even triumph) issues in part from seeing oneself in the context of a cloud of witnesses who have proved God in the past, of a supporting, worshiping community before which the sufferer testifies to God's responsiveness in the present and of another "people" who will still confess Yahweh on the basis of such testimony in the future (22:3–5, 22–25, 30–31 [4–6, 23–26, 31–32]; 35:27; 42:4 [5]). The interdependence of individual and community is thus important to the individual but also to the community itself. It shares in the blessing of the individual's experience of deliverance as it joins in the response of praise (30:4 [5]; 31:23–24 [24–25]; 32:11; 40:9 [10]).

The community is one that cares. Its vision is that all should have enough— indeed plenty—and that none should cry out in distress (144:12–15). It declares a blessing on people who do care about the powerless, feeble, and insignificant rather than despising them (Ps 41). Its vision is for a community that weeps with the weepers and rejoices with the joyful (34:3 [4]; 35:12–13). It knows that moral considerations determine whether someone can dwell on God's hill or join the circle of those who seek Yahweh's face (Pss 15; 24). Joyful praise is appropriate to the just or upright because the words and deeds of the one they praise are characterized by justice and uprightness (33:1–5). Thus "properly conceived, the Temple is a place of electrifying holiness that cannot tolerate injustice." The cultic and the ethical are "two sides of the same experience."[8]

Sometimes the vision just referred to meets no realization. Elimelech's community experienced famine, loss, and displacement, though his family's story also illustrates the way the community can care for its weak (Ruth 1–2). The weepers can have their pain exacerbated rather than relieved by the response of their community (Pss 42:3, 9–10 [4, 10–11]; 43:1–2). Worse than that, the community (or elements within it) is often characterized as wicked, recalcitrant, godless, mischievous, greedy, murderous, thieving, adulterous, oppressive, arrogant, scoffing, trusting in worldly resources, deceitful, and foolishly self-deceived (Pss 1; 5; 35; 36; 50; 52; 55). It knows conflict within as well as without. Power within it lies with the perjurous, the haves, the taunting, who stand over against the righteous, the godly, the com-

---

[7] Hans Walter Wolff, *Anthropology of the Old Testament* (Philadelphia: Fortress / London: SCM, 1974), 217; cf. Helmut Ringgren, *The Faith of the Psalmists* (London: SCM / Philadelphia: Fortress, 1963), 20–26; H.-J. Kraus, *Theology of the Psalms* (Minneapolis: Augsburg, 1986), 138–41.

[8] J. D. Levenson, *Sinai and Zion* (Minneapolis: Winston / London: SPCK, 1985), 170, 172.

mitted (to God and to others), the covenant-keeping and Torah-delighting, who are powerless, fearful, fleeing, vengeful, vulnerable, groaning, with God's promise all they have to trust in. In another sense the wicked belong only formally to the community. The real Israel is the community of the just (1:5). Widow, alien, and orphan comprise the people of Yahweh (94:5–6).

In part the expectation that Israel should behave as a community is based on a vision of Israel as a family of brothers and sisters. This image is explicit when all Israel's "kindred" join in great festive events (1 Chr 12:39; 13:2; 28:9). It is implicit in the genealogies that are a prominent feature of the Writings, though these also likely reflect the power struggles and identity crises of the Second Temple community. They indicate that like any family, Israel has its family arguments. This image is then the basis for prophetic appeal and rebuke (2 Chr 11:4; 28:9–15), but in such situations straight talking within the family can lead to matters being sorted out, and even issuing in worship (Neh 5).

3. A National State, a Warring Army

In the Writings, Israel is a state when the story opens; sanctuary and monarchy are of more dangerously unequivocal and mythical significance than is the case in the Torah and the Prophets. As a nation Israel is a territorial entity, by the inalienable gift of Yahweh (1 Chr 28:8; Pss 135:12; 136:21–22). When people do not enjoy the land as their ancestors had (Neh 9:36–37), the affirmation that it is their secure possession is the more important. However, Daniel, Ezra, Nehemiah, and Esther witness to the possibility of full life and political success in continuing dispersion.

As a nation Israel has a capital, which is the location of its sanctuary but is in its own right a place of fortified strength, material prosperity, and architectural splendor. The restoring of its walls and population is calculated both to bring its disgrace to an end and to improve its security (Neh 2:17; 7:1–4; 11:1–2; Ps 122:3). Jerusalem is the center of the nation's life. To Israel's rest in its country there corresponds Yahweh's rest in Zion after wandering (1 Chr 28:2; 2 Chr 6:41; Ps 132). Indeed, the country is Yahweh's place of rest first; only because it is that can it become Israel's (Ps 95:11).[9]

As a nation Israel has a leadership structure. Israel is both a theocracy, a kingdom over which Yahweh reigns, and a monarchy, a kingdom over which a human ruler reigns. The Davidic kings sit on Yahweh's throne reigning over Israel on Yahweh's behalf; Yahweh's kingdom lies in their power and will always do so (1 Chr 17:13–14; 28:5; 29:23; 2 Chr 9:8; 13:5, 8). David is made king in fulfillment of Yahweh's word concerning Israel; he is important for Israel's sake rather than vice versa (1 Chr 11:10; 14:2). By Yahweh's power he experiences victory over his enemies (Ps 18:46–48 [47–49]), but like the rest of Israel he moves between weakness, fear,

---

[9]On this idea see Gerhard von Rad, *The Problem of the Hexateuch and Other Essays* (Edinburgh: Oliver and Boyd / New York: McGraw-Hill, 1966), 94–102, though he is critical of Chronicles.

abandonment, and grief, and joy, confidence, strength, and acceptance (Pss 5; 6). The difficulty is that all leadership, which theoretically exists for the sake of those it leads, easily comes to be important in its own right. Psalms and Chronicles witness to a growing gap between people and king and a shrinking gap between king and God (Ps 45:6 [7]). In theory, worship of the one true God relativizes all other powers. "But what happens if one earthly norm becomes excluded from the relativization of all that is mundane?"[10]

Chronicles expresses no explicit hope regarding the future of the suspended monarchy. This silence has been variously interpreted. Daniel is more overtly concerned for the future, and its visions give a prominent place to earthly kings and to Yahweh's kingship, but it also expresses no hopes concerning Israel's own monarchy; its silence is less equivocal. In Dan 7, sovereignty is taken from four animals and given to a human-like figure; the animals stand for human kings, but the entity that apparently corresponds to the human-like figure is not another king but "holy ones on high" or "holy people on high," who in some sense represent Israel.

As a nation Israel is also a body involved in political relations with other nations over which it is destined to exercise authority. Its existence is lived like that of other nations in its world, and it is often in conflict with local peoples, some ethnically or religiously related, and with more distant imperial powers that might be a military or political threat (see Ezra 4–5; Neh 2; 6; Pss 46; 83). It prays as a political entity under pressure from enemies without as well as from enemies within (e.g., Pss 53; 54; 59).

Functioning as an army follows from being a nation. When Israel is under attack, Yahweh is the shield around Israel protecting it, or the stronghold or fortress hiding it, or the one whose aide surrounds it with a military camp, or the savior who arises in its midst to rescue it at the critical moment (Pss 2:11; 5:11–12 [12–13]; 34; 46; 125:2; 144:2). In success the plunder of battle belongs to God, so David's victories provide the resources for building the temple. The actual temple builder is not to be the bloodstained warrior (like sex, war does not fit well with who Yahweh is, so it involves ritual taboo). It is to be his son whose name marks him as a man of rest and in whose reign Israel will experience quiet and peace (1 Chr 22:8–9). Yahweh the warrior teaches Israel to fight (Ps 144:1) and uses Judah and Ephraim as baton and helmet (60:7 [9]), but war is destined to cease because Yahweh's purpose to subject the nations is destined to be achieved (Ps 46). The Writings' contrary attitudes to war are familiar in the modern world: it is better to be at peace than at war, but it is better to be dead than red, and it is necessary to fight with relish when that seems the only way to achieve your destiny.

While the offensiveness of David's census (1 Chr 21) may lie in its implicit trust in human military resources, foresight over fortification, resources, and defense is affirmed where these combine with urgent prayer, trust in Yahweh, and action "in Yahweh's name," as Yahweh's representatives (2 Chr 13–15). The most splendid, even baroque, embodiment of these attitudes appears in the story of Jehoshaphat's

---

[10] P. D. Hanson, *The People Called* (San Francisco: Harper, 1986), 122.

battle with peoples from the east (2 Chr 20).[11] The people seek Yahweh, fast, and lament; through a Levite Yahweh urges them not to fear, reminds them that the battle belongs to God, and gives them their battle instructions, which amount to an invitation to watch Yahweh act; the people bow down to worship, and the Levites stand up to praise; Jehoshaphat appoints a choir that sings while Yahweh sets an ambush involving the hostile armies self-destructing. The story ends with plunder, worship, astonishment on the part of the nations, and a period of quiet rest. Psalm 149 provides a lyric for this remarkable holding together of worship and war making, Ps 18 a testimony to deliverance of this kind, and Ps 47 a witness to the expectation that the nations will indeed come to acknowledge that God subdued peoples under Israel. The view that Chronicles' attitude is superseded by Jesus has not generally been held by Christians. Oliver Cromwell's troops and many others have sung psalms before battle, and levitical chaplains still accompany the armies of "Christian" nations.[12]

4. Yahweh's Flock, Yahweh's Possession, Yahweh's Servant

Israel is a flock provided for, rested, pastured, led, watered, refreshed, protected, and reassured by its shepherd (e.g., Pss 23; 95:7). The more general theme of Israel as a people under Yahweh's protection finds paradoxical expression in Esther. The story vividly portrays the reality of the world's pressure on Israel's existence and of Israel's miraculous survival and triumph. It provides the strongest scriptural assertion of the significance of ethnic Israel, one that Christian theology has often failed to come to terms with.[13] It is the one book in the First Testament that resists Christian supersessionism absolutely, as Luther saw, and one that the Holocaust might take from the periphery of the canon to its center.[14] Jews once more lament the way the nations seek to destroy them, but the response to their lament comes not explicitly through an act of God but through an act of a woman, and one who had concealed her Jewishness.[15] The result is not the exaltation and the reverential fear of Yahweh by people but the exaltation of Mordecai and the abject fear of the Jews by people.

All peoples owe allegiance to Yahweh as creator and lord, but Israel is Yahweh's particular inalienable possession (*nakhalah*), Yahweh's valued personal property

---

[11] See Gerhard von Rad, *Holy War in Ancient Israel* (Grand Rapids: Eerdmans, 1991), 129–31.

[12] See R. E. Prothero, *The Psalms in Human Life* (London / New York: Nelson, 1903), 228–36.

[13] Cf. W. Vischer, "The Book of Esther," *Evangelical Quarterly* 11 (1939): 3–21 (the date is significant); Brevard S. Childs, *Introduction to the Old Testament as Scripture* (Philadelphia: Fortress / London: SCM, 1979), 606.

[14] See E. L. Fackenheim, *The Jewish Bible after the Holocaust* (Manchester: Manchester University Press, 1990), 62, 90.

[15] See S. A. White, "Esther," in *Gender and Difference* (ed. P. L. Day; Minneapolis: Fortress, 1989), 166–73.

(*segullah*, a word sometimes used for "treasure") (Pss 33:12; 106:5; 135:4; cf. 28:9; 74:2; 78:62, 71; 94:5, 14; 106:40). If Israel is merely the part of the world over which Yahweh more overtly exercises sovereign rights at the moment, this in itself makes Yahweh's acts in Israel significant for other peoples. These acts are designed to enable the whole world to acknowledge the way Israel's God can deliver, and to do so with joy because this God also governs and guides all peoples (Pss 47; 66; 67). Israel's was not a missionary faith, but it was a faith which made universal claims.[16]

To put the point more centripetally, the peoples of the world are expected to gather together to worship in Jerusalem, declaring the praise of Yahweh as the one who hears and liberates the doomed and stripped captives (102:15–22). All the peoples of the earth in their apparent glory but actual fragility will pay attention and come to worship Yahweh as their sovereign (22:27–29 [28–30]). The story of Ruth encapsulates that purpose in a vignette, while Chronicles also notes the place of foreigners in the story and worship of Israel (1 Chr 2; 2 Chr 6:32–33; 30:25; cf. Ezra 1:1–11; 6:1–5). "What can one say about the self-consciousness of a provincial cultic community tolerated by the Persian Empire which yet portrays history from Adam onwards as taking place all for her own sake?"[17]

To say that Yahweh chose Israel is thus not to say that other peoples are rejected. Within Israel, Yahweh especially chose Levi, Judah, and David for particular purposes (1 Chr 15:2; 28:4–6; 2 Chr 6:5–6; 29:11; Ps 78:68, 70). This was more for the sake of the people as a whole than in rejection of the people as a whole. The same dynamic underlies the choice of Israel. It belongs in the context of Yahweh's will to be sovereign deliverer of the world as a whole, and it serves that end. There can be no ideological appropriation of belief in election.

Chosenness thus belongs with servanthood. As Yahweh's servant (Ps 136:22), Israel is called to obedience and trust as well as worship. A servant has a special relationship with a master or mistress and can rely on the latter's care and protection, and also one who is committed to do as the master or mistress directs. This trust and commitment stem from being in covenant relationship with a master whereby the latter promises to look after the servant's future and the servant is committed to obeying the master (cf. Ps 89:39; Ps 119). Israel is thus a people covenanted to be Yahweh's people (2 Chr 23:16; 34:29–33). It is the company of the committed (*khasidim*; Pss 50:5; 85:8 [9]; 97:10). Covenanting with other gods or other peoples is disallowed and disapproved because it indicates reliance on resources other than Yahweh (2 Chr 16:1–12; 25:5–13; 28:16–25; Ezra 8:21–23; cf. Ps 40:4 [5]).

The covenanted people is challenged to express its dependence on God and its commitment to God in simple worship and moral uprightness (Ps 50). Israel has known Yahweh releasing its back from its burdens: it is now expected to bow down to Yahweh and no other gods and to walk in Yahweh's ways, and it is invited to look to Yahweh alone for the satisfying of its needs and for deliverance from its pressures

---

[16]Cf. R. Martin-Achard, *A Light to the Nations* (Edinburgh: Oliver and Boyd, 1962), 54–60; Levenson, *Sinai and Zion*, 207–8.

[17]Von Rad, *Old Testament Theology*, 1:347.

(Ps 81). In the Psalms, Israel is challenged to trust in Yahweh, delight in Yahweh, commit its way to Yahweh, relax before Yahweh, wait for Yahweh, hide in Yahweh. If it does so and combines that with a commitment to walking in Yahweh's way, it will live long in possession of its country, enjoy security and prosperity there, be upheld and prevented from falling headlong, see the wicked off and be vindicated itself, have its deepest desires fulfilled and see its posterity (Ps 37; cf. 33:18–22). The narratives in 2 Chr 10–36 illustrate the life of Israel lived in trust and obedience— or not. In due course freedom from Yahweh takes Israel into servitude and exile (Lam 1:3), which continues in the Second Temple period in a bondage to Persian overlords (Neh 9:36–37).

Loyal servants "seek" the master, aim to attend on the master with loyalty, commitment, and energy, in a way that opposes anything conflicting with the master's interests (1 Chr 28:9; 2 Chr 31:21, where service and seeking are linked; also 1 Chr 22:19; 2 Chr 7:14; 14:4, 7; 15:2–4, 12–15; 17:3–4; 20:3–4; 34:3). They try to draw each other into fuller or renewed commitment to their master's service (2 Chr 17:7–9; 19:4; 29). They seek the master where he may be found (2 Chr 11:16); failure here is one basis for regarding the worship of northern Israel as illicit (2 Chr 13:8–11). Worship itself is one way of serving God (see Ps 102:22 for the verb); service of God is expressed in worship services, and in reforming the temple Hezekiah restores the service of Yahweh's house (2 Chr 29:35). Such seeking of Yahweh is thus the opposite of apostasy or trespass (*ma'al*), a way of worship or life that ignores Yahweh's rights and defers to other gods by seeking them rather than Yahweh, or by introducing their way of worship into worship of Yahweh, or by associating too closely with their worshipers (1 Chr 10:13–14; 2 Chr 28:22–25; 33:19; 36:13–14; Ezra 9:2; 10:2–3), doing what one likes and ignoring Yahweh's revealed way (2 Chr 12:1–2; 26:16–18; 28:19; 29:19; 36:14).[18]

Psalm 95 moves on from the enthusiasm and prostration already noted to testing interrogation, not by Israel but of Israel. Israel's voice is silenced by that of another voice challenging it to listen to God's voice. When Israel celebrated Sukkot, it celebrated the giving of the Torah, but the question was whether rejoicing in the Torah was only a matter of heart and lips and not of life. Israel is a community instructed in the Torah and committed in covenant to making the Torah its rule of life (Ezra 7–10; Neh 8–10). There is nothing intrinsically legalistic about Israel's commitment to live by the Torah. Joy in Yahweh and obedience to the Torah happily coexist in Ps 119, and Nehemiah encourages the people toward this combination when they are inclined to grief on discovering teaching in the Torah which puts them to shame (Neh 8:9–12).

5. A Crushed Remnant, an Exclusive Sect, a Theological School

Israel is a vine planted to flourish in ground Yahweh prepared for it, but a vine from time to time unprotected, ravaged, and cut down (Ps 80). Israel as a

---

[18] On *ma'al* see Jacob Milgrom, *Cult and Conscience* (Leiden: Brill, 1976), 16–35.

people is given up to subjection, death, exile, plundering, and shame (Ezra 9:7). It is rejected, abased, defeated, spoiled, slaughtered, scattered, discarded, taunted, shamed, broken, forgotten, cast off, oppressed, resourceless, and powerless, like a bird at the mercy of predators (Pss 44; 74:19, 21). The people of holy ones is subject to oppression and attack by mighty kings. Loyalty to Yahweh seems to stimulate suffering rather than evade it (Dan 7:21; 8:24–25; 11). Jerusalem is like a lonely widow, a serf, let down, disillusioned, weeping, betrayed, homeless, distressed, overwhelmed, desolate, bereft, defeated, dishonored, helpless, mocked, despised, fallen, comfortless, desecrated, hungry, despised, uncared for, trapped, stunned, crushed (Lam 1). In exile Israel weeps and remembers, is taunted and voiceless, reminds and looks for judgment (Ps 137). The people is a mere remnant of what it once was (Ezra 9:13–15). All that remains in Jerusalem or in dispersion is a group of survivors (Ezra 1:4; Neh 1:2–3).

The experience of being turned into a mere remnant can come despite the fact that Israel lives in loyalty to the covenant and shapes its life by Yahweh's ways (Ps 44:17–26 [18–27]). But this is not always so. Whereas the ideal Israel lives in trust and obedience, the actual Israel does no such thing, and it is cut down to size in the way appropriate to a servant who fails. From the beginning Israel forgets, rebels, hustles, craves, tests, envies, forsakes, despises, disbelieves, grumbles, disobeys, abandons, angers, provokes, compromises, nauseates (Ps 106). Jerusalem falls because it has become disobedient, sinful, rebellious, careless, polluted (Lam 1). Israel has failed, gone astray, done wrong, rebelled, trespassed, turned its back on Yahweh's commands, ignored Yahweh's prophets, and refused to turn from its waywardness (Dan 9). Moral and religious failure is a reality of both past and present (Ezra 9). Whereas Israel was designed to be a people where the kingship of God was a reality and thus to be a microcosm of what the world was called to be, it had rejected Yahweh's kingship and become a microcosm of what the world also is, and was therefore judged as such.[19]

It is a sign of God's grace that Israel survives at all with a toehold in its country and is able to feel encouraged that it experiences a little reviving even as it has to live under the authority of foreign kings (Ezra 9:8–9). Israel has escaped its enemies like a bird escaping a trap; if Yahweh had not been on Israel's side, its enemies would have devoured it (Ps 124). The history of rebellion never ends in Israel's annihilation, because saving Israel reveals Yahweh's power, because leaders such as Moses and Phinehas intervene on their behalf, standing between them and Yahweh's wrath, because Yahweh could not but hear their cry and remember the covenant relationship with them, because saving them could lead to testimony and glory (Ps 106). They are a people grieved for and prayed for, confessed for and argued for (Neh 1:4–11). As the preserved remnant, they are then challenged to be the responsive remnant (Ezra 10; Neh 9).

It is the Writings that contain much of the Hebrew Bible's material reflecting Israel's openness to learning from the world (in Proverbs) and reflecting Yahweh's purpose for the whole world (in Psalms and Ruth). They also contain much of its

---

[19] See chapter 7, § 4, above.

material that expresses an inclination to separate oneself from the world and from other groups that worshiped Yahweh, especially in Ezra-Nehemiah. The later controversies underlying Dan 7–12 also reflect the conflict between different groups within the community in Judea such as the party led by Tobias over against that led by Onias.[20]

Something of the theological rationale for exclusivism emerges from the crisis over "marrying out" in the time of Ezra and Nehemiah. The theological issue is expressed as a concern for holiness rather than pollution (Ezra 9:10–14) and for people not to lose the ability to speak Hebrew (Neh 13:24). Ezra requires the annulment of many mixed marriages (Ezra 10), but there were broader senses in which the people were expected to distance themselves from other local people as part of their commitment to observing the Torah, including observance of the sabbath, a distinguishing mark of a true Yahwist as Nehemiah sees it (Neh 10:28–29 [29–30]; 13:15–22). The Torah set limits on who could belong to Yahweh's congregation; people needed to be able to prove their genealogical right to membership of Israel, of the clan of Levi, and of the priestly line (Ezra 2), and many people of foreign descent were expelled from the community (Neh 13:1–3). Even the stories in Daniel that envisage Jews successfully involved in imperial politics stress the need for boundaries that preserve Jewish purity and avoid pollution (Dan 1:8). Israel is called to be the holy people of the holy God (cf. Ezra 9:2).[21]

The narrowness of the Second Temple community should not be exaggerated. As the Writings portray the matter, it was not ultimately ethnic; anyone who had broken with the pollution of the other nations in the country was welcomed to join in the worship of Yahweh (Ezra 6:21; cf. Neh 9:2). Although in a postmodern context the attitude of leaders such as Ezra and Nehemiah makes us feel uneasy, their rigor was a factor in enabling Israel to survive. The Second Temple community was beginning a new life, "trapped between a political and religious sense of identity" and encouraged by its political overlords to develop as a religious community. It had to define the nature and the boundaries of its identity if it was to maintain the distinctive witness to God for which it had been chosen.[22] "The recovery of ethnic rootage and the special histories of pain . . . may help us see that an alternative perception of reality is not simply a defensive measure but may be an act of identity, energy, and power." It may challenge the claims of the dominant reality. Admittedly it may fall into the trap of defensively keeping its alternative perception to itself lest this truth be contaminated, rather than openly making it available to the dominant community. We do not know enough about the communities of the Second Temple period to be able to offer an independent evaluation of Ezra-Nehemiah's stance in

---

[20] Among adventurous attempts to trace the development of the parties in Second Temple Judaism are M. Smith, *Palestinian Parties and Politics That Shaped the Old Testament* (New York / London: Columbia University Press, 1971); P. D. Hanson, *The Dawn of Apocalyptic* (Philadelphia: Fortress, 1975).

[21] Cf. D. Bossman, "Ezra's Marriage Reform," *Biblical Theology Bulletin* 9 (1979): 32–38 (36).

[22] See H. G. M. Williamson, *Ezra, Nehemiah* (Waco, Tex.: Word, 1985), 159–60.

relation to them, but the problem of assimilation to a powerful surrounding culture arises at both ends of the biblical period: Israel repeatedly experienced its conversation partners "as having a more fully adequate hermeneutic, rationality, or way of experiencing the world" and needed to be wary of their beguiling if it was to keep alive its distinctive memory.[23]

There is no mention of Israel in Proverbs (except Prov 1:1), Job, Song of Songs, or Ecclesiastes. Evidently Israel (like God) does not always need mention in theology; perhaps the servant status of Israel reaches its apogee when it can survive or even affirm its own dispensability. These books nevertheless emerge from the life and experience of Israel. Their theological concern suggests the image of Israel as a theological school. They bear the fruit of Israel's reflection on everyday questions about how to live in a way that is successful, godly, and moral, and on major theological issues concerning creation, revelation, the nature of God, and the basis of God's relationship with human beings. This theological school belongs within the life of the believing community. Solomon is its patron, as (with some irony) the great embodiment of God-given wisdom in Israel's story.

Israel is drawn to a theology that holds together confident affirmation and bold questioning. Confident affirmation is the dominant feature of Proverbs and the Song of Songs; limitations and ambiguities are the dominant feature of Job and Ecclesiastes, which focus on the degree to which the orthodoxies and promises of Proverbs and the Song of Songs do not work out for people.[24] Between them they enable Israel's theological school to avoid both the Scylla of simplistic triumphalism and the Charybdis of despairing agnosticism.

The wisdom of the Writings often profits from the wisdom of the world. But their conviction is that Israel's wisdom nevertheless quite outclasses that of the world. In Daniel, the young Judean youths enrolled in theological school in Babylon not only maintain their purity but also are wiser than their teachers in both the everyday life skills that make survival possible and in the capacity for far-reaching insight that makes it possible to understand the riddles of history.

In part they do that by utilizing the insights already expressed in their own scriptures, which provide key seed thoughts and clues for both stories and visions in Daniel. Israel's own scriptures are a key resource in its theological school. The sermons in Chronicles, too, utilize earlier scriptures to suggest how Yahweh's word speaks today (e.g., 2 Chr 16:9; 20:20).[25] In Chronicles in general Israel does its theological thinking by reflecting in narrative form on questions raised by its current context, in light of historical, prophetic, and worship traditions. In Ruth and Esther it does this by telling a less complicated story, though here too aspects of these

---

[23] See Walter Brueggemann, *Interpretation and Obedience* (Minneapolis: Fortress, 1991), 46–48, 54, though Brueggemann does not apply his observation to the Second Temple community. See also Hanson, *The People Called*, 291–300, for a more critical but still sympathetic evaluation of Ezra and Nehemiah.

[24] See the opening paragraph of chapter 5 above.

[25] See von Rad, "The Levitical Sermon in *I* and *II Chronicles*," in *The Problem of the Hexateuch and Other Essays*, 267–80.

traditions make an important contribution to it: there is a markedly intertextual relationship between these stories and those of the Torah.[26]

The Israel of the Writings is the Israel the New Testament presupposes. In its genealogical approach Matthew follows on from Chronicles. In its opening portrait of the worshiping community in the temple Luke does the same. In his parables Jesus invites both wise and simple into his theological school, and as they do theology the New Testament writers show that they themselves have learned from the Writings as much as from anywhere. In identifying "models for the church," the New Testament recycles the scriptures' images of Israel that we have considered.[27] These images continue to provide both the Jewish community and the church with identity and challenge.

---

[26] See, e.g., D. Nolan Fewell and D. M. Gunn, "'A Son Is Born to Naomi!'" *JSOT* 40 (1988): 103–7; G. Gerlemann, *Esther* (Neukirchen: Neukirchener, 1973), 11–23; S. B. Berg, *The Book of Esther* (Missoula, Mont.: Scholars Press, 1979), 6–8, 123–65, 174–77.

[27] See A. Dulles, *Models of the Church* (Garden City, N.Y.: Doubleday, 1974 / Dublin: Gill and Macmillan, 1976, 1988); also Paul S. Minear, *Images of the Church in the New Testament* (Philadelphia: Westminster Press, 1960 / London: Lutterworth, 1961).

9

WHAT IS A COVENANT?

The relationship between Yahweh and Israel involves a covenant (*berit*). What does that mean? A covenant is a solemn formal commitment made by one party to another party or by two parties to one another; its seriousness is normally undergirded by an oath or rite undertaken before God and/or before other people. A covenant is thus a little like a contract, but the commitment is moral, not legal. It lacks the legal framework and protection of a contract; we do not usually think of suing someone for failing to keep a covenant. A covenant involves something more like a personal relationship, but no ordinary relationship: it presupposes a level of commitment not required of most relationships, and it involves a formalizing of that commitment that shows we really mean it.[1]

In British English a covenant can be two-sided or mainly one-sided. Marriage is a two-sided covenant; a commitment to giving a certain amount of money to a charity is a one-sided covenant. American English uses the word "pledge" for the latter, and thus the word "covenant" refers more exclusively to mutual commitments. This keeps closer to the etymology of the English word "covenant," which suggests a coming together or an agreement. American English thus compares (though a little paradoxically) with the Greek of the Septuagint and the New Testament, which prefers the word *diatheke* to the regular Greek *syntheke*. The latter could perhaps suggest too mutual, too contractual an understanding of the relationship between God and Israel or the church. German *Bund* also essentially denotes a mutual relationship, often a contractual one; it covers both "covenant" and "federation."

In Hebrew, *berit* covers the ground both of a one-sided pledge like God's pledges to Noah or the pledges to God in which Josiah and Ezra lead their people and a two-sided covenant like that between God and Israel, and a legal contract, federation, treaty, or alliance. We here focus on the first two meanings, though in keeping with convention we will refer to both as covenants.

1. The Noah Covenant

The first covenant is made by God to Noah, his descendants and thus all future humanity, and all other living creatures (Gen 6:18; 9:8–17). It is a one-sided com-

---

[1] First published as "Covenant," in *The New Interpreter's Dictionary of the Bible* (ed. Katharine Doob Sakenfeld; 5 vols.; Nashville: Abingdon, 2006), 1:767–78.

mitment on God's part, by which God undertakes never to flood the earth and thus destroy life on earth.

Theologians have sometimes spoken of the original relationship between God and humanity (and/or God and creation) portrayed in Gen 1–2 as having the nature of a covenant. As happens with many other biblical terms, their use in theological discussion thus comes to be different from their use in scripture itself. This is not so much wrong as something we need to keep our wits about, so that we notice it happening in order to try to avoid reading our categories into scripture. The fact that Genesis does not use the word "covenant" until after the flood is unlikely to mean nothing. It suggests there is no need for the formalizing of the relationship between God and the world as a covenant when the relationship is in its unspoiled state. Creation established a natural relationship between God and humanity. In human relationships there is such a thing as a natural commitment of one person to another, specifically within the family. Parents do not covenant to look after their children; it is built into parenthood. But when the family relationship is extended to someone outside it, specifically when someone marries and brings a new person into the family, a covenant is involved. Covenants establish relationships where there was no relationship before. In the case of God and humanity, the natural relationship that came about by creation came to be devastated by humanity's being wrong-minded from youth and by God's destroying the world. A fresh relationship therefore needs to be established. That comes about by God's making the irrational promise that Noah receives and by God's sealing it with a covenant commitment.

The equivalent of a rite to back up the Noah covenant is a sign that God attaches to it. The rainbow that appears in the clouds after the rain, and has the shape of a bow, will henceforth not be a sign that God is acting as a warrior but will draw attention to the fact that the rain did not continue forever but yielded to fair weather. This natural event will become one of supernatural significance. While the rainbow will thus be a sign to reassure humanity that the flood will not recur, Genesis makes more explicit that it will be a sign for God: It will remind God of this undertaking.

The covenant is a "perpetual" one (*berit 'olam*). As long as human life continues on earth, this covenant commitment will hold. The Noah covenant is thus significant for all humanity throughout the ages. It guarantees the security of the human and animal creation from divine destruction, though it perhaps does not rule out humanity destroying the world.

Such one-sided covenants presuppose that the other party accepts the commitment (as happens when British people covenant their giving), and in that sense they presuppose an element of reciprocity. But no reciprocal commitment on the same scale is required; the only thing the other party has to do is accept the commitment. The point is highlighted by the nature of the sign that guarantees the Noah covenant, the appearing of the rainbow, which is a fact whether anyone sees it or not. Yet at the same time, the Noah covenant illustrates the ambiguity that often holds over whether a covenant is unconditional or conditional. God makes no reference to conditions, and earlier comments suggest that this would be no coincidence. The reason the flood came about was humanity's rebellion against God. God knows that "the inclination of the human heart is evil from youth" (8:21). It would therefore be no use making a covenant conditional on humanity's responsiveness to God. However, the covenant is preceded by statements of God's expectations of humanity (9:1–7). It is not clear how many of these statements should be seen as commands, but in some way statements of divine expectations preface God's making the covenant. God is permanently committed to humanity and will not go back on that commitment, but God does have expectations of humanity. This is confirmed by the apparent reference to this "perpetual covenant" in Isa 24:5, which identifies it with "instructions" and "statutes" that humanity has broken, thereby causing a curse to devour the earth (cf. also Amos 1:9).

2. The Abraham Covenants

Yahweh first makes a covenant with Abraham to give the land of Canaan to his descendants (15:18–21). Here for the first time the verb for "making" a covenant is *karat*, literally "cut." The preceding ritual seems to link with it. Yahweh had repeated a promise to give Abraham the land, and Abraham had asked how he can have some assurance of this. That leads Yahweh to bid him bring various animals and birds; Abraham cuts the animals in half then falls into a deep sleep. A terrifying darkness falls, and Yahweh reiterates the promise. It will not be Abraham himself who enters into possession of the land but his descendants, after four centuries' oppression in a foreign land; it will not be fair to dispossess the Amorites yet, "because the waywardness of the Amorites is not complete yet." Then a smoking fire pot and a flaming torch, representing Yahweh, pass between the dismembered animals. This is the sign that turns the promise into a covenant and explains why one "cuts" a covenant. It is tantamount to an enacted prayer or self-curse: "If I fail to keep this undertaking, may I be cut up as these animals have been" (cf. Jer 34:18–20).

Paul emphasizes (Gal 3:17) that this covenant with Abraham was an unconditioned promise. It did not depend on obedience to the law, which would also not be given for another four centuries.

In God's second covenant with Abraham (Gen 17; from the Priestly narrative) the focus of the covenant lies on the promise of offspring. Like the Noah covenant, this Abraham covenant issues entirely from God's initiative but leaves ambiguous the relationship between "divine commitment and human obligation."[2] Once again, it is God who opens the conversation and does so with imperatives, then goes on to promises (17:1–2). The word for "making" the covenant is here *natan*, the regular Hebrew word for "give," while subsequently (17:7) God speaks of "establishing" it (*qum* hiphil); both underline the extent to which God claims responsibility for making the covenant. The fact that it is "between me and you" does not mean that both parties have equal involvement in establishing it. At no point is Abraham given opportunity to decide whether he wishes to be party to the covenant or to

---

[2] Cf. David Noel Freedman, "Divine Commitment and Human Obligation," *Int* 18 (1964): 419–31.

negotiate its terms. He will be told something he has to do, though there will be a threat attached to failure to play one's part.

The covenant will apply to Abraham's descendants as well as Abraham himself, and the account emphasizes that like the Noah covenant, it will be a perpetual covenant (Gen 17:7, 13, 19; cf. Ps 105:10; 111:9). But in distinctively far-reaching fashion over against what has preceded, Yahweh describes this as "a covenant, to be God to you and to your offspring after you" (Gen 17:7).

The ambiguity over divine commitment and human obligation is underlined by the subsequent declaration that there is a covenant requirement laid on Abraham, but one of quite a different kind from the requirements stated in Gen 17:1. "This is my covenant, which you shall keep"; it also applies to Abraham's descendants and to the rest of his household, including foreign slaves. "You shall circumcise the flesh of your foreskins, and it shall be a sign of the covenant between me and you" (17:10–13). Accepting circumcision is the only requirement for the fulfillment of Yahweh's very far-reaching promises to Abraham; nothing like the detailed commitment of the Mosaic covenant is required. But it is a real requirement.

The Abraham covenant thus again parallels the Noah covenant in being supported by a sign. This sign, too, is given for God's sake; when God sees the sign, it reminds God that the divine covenant commitment applies to this person. But it will also function to reassure the recipient of this fact. When awareness of guilt threatened to overwhelm Martin Luther, he would remind himself, "I am baptized";[3] circumcision could function in a similar way.

Yet this is a very different sign from the rainbow. Like the rainbow sign, it is divinely mandated, but unlike that sign, it is humanly implemented. It can therefore be humanly ignored, though with fatal consequences: anyone who is not circumcised "shall be cut off from his people; he has broken my covenant" (17:14). The absence of the sign thus also speaks to God. The fact that Yahweh tries to kill the uncircumcised Moses but gives up when Zipporah circumcises their son (Exod 4:24–26) fits with this. Neatly but perhaps fortuitously, "be cut off" is the same verb as appears in the expression "cut a covenant." Yahweh's willingness to be cut for failing to keep the covenant has to be matched by human willingness to be cut, and in the absence of that, the whole person is cut. Once again "cut" is a metaphor, and the First Testament is not explicit on whether it means the person is to be executed, or excommunicated, or whether it means they lose their place in the register of the people of God.

The fact that humanity has the possibility of not playing its part in the working of the covenant introduces the notion of "breaking" the covenant (*parar* hiphil) rather than "keeping it"—that is, obeying it. "Breaking" the covenant could suggest annulling, making permanently ineffective, as when someone annuls a vow (Num 30:8, 13, where it is the opposite of "establish"). Or it could suggest violating, making ineffective at this point and imperiling but not annulling, as when someone violates a law (15:31). In the broader context of the First Testament, Israel's recurrent breaking of the covenant does not have the effect of annulling it but rather of

---

[3] See *The Large Catechism* on "Holy Baptism."

unleashing the sanctions that operate within the covenant's terms, as breaking a law does not make it any less of a law, though widespread breaking of a law can have that effect.

To speak of breaking the covenant does draw attention to the relationship between covenant and law or obligation. One way of understanding covenant is to see it as suggesting obligation, imposed on oneself or imposed on other people. Insofar as the covenant *is* the requirement to be circumcised, it is an obligation God imposes on Abraham's offspring, like a law that must not be broken.

If people accept that obligation, when things go badly Israel can urge, "Have regard for the covenant" (Ps 74:20), in the conviction that Yahweh "is mindful of his covenant forever" (Ps 105:8; cf. 111:5). In 1 Chr 16:15–18, David takes up this psalm in urging people to "be mindful of his covenant forever," which "he sealed with Abraham, his oath to Isaac, which he confirmed to Jacob as a statute, to Israel as a perpetual covenant, saying 'To you I will give the land of Canaan as your allocation, your possession.'" The next psalm observes how for all Israel's recurrent rebellions and Yahweh's consequent chastisements, "for their sake he was mindful of his covenant, and showed compassion according to the abundance of his commitment" (Ps 106:45). If Gen 17 was composed in the exile, when Israel had indeed systematically broken the covenant and it could seem as if Yahweh had therefore annulled it, the Abraham covenant underlines the permanence of Yahweh's covenant commitment. The fact that the covenant is not explicitly dependent on a response from its beneficiaries, except for the sign of circumcision, would also be significant in this context.

The Abraham covenant is to apply to his offspring. Does it apply to his first son, Ishmael, and his offspring, or only to Isaac and his offspring? Ishmael is circumcised along with the rest of the male members of Abraham's household (Gen 17:23–27). But before that happens, God reasserts the promise of a son to Abraham and Sarah, making clear that Ishmael does not count as the fulfillment of that promise, and declares the intention to "establish" the covenant with Isaac. Of Ishmael, God says, "I will bless him," in spectacular ways, so that he becomes a great nation, "but my covenant I will establish with Isaac" (17:21). Paul assumes there are two covenants here, though he speaks of them as covenants with Hagar and Sarah. They provide an allegorical picture of the faith in which Paul was brought up and the faith he now holds (Gal 4:21–31). As a slave, Hagar now stands for people in spiritual slavery, and thus, paradoxically, for Mount Sinai and the earthly Jerusalem. Sarah now stands for freedom and promise, and thus for "the Jerusalem above."

When the Israelites became serfs in Egypt, they groaned out, "God was mindful of his covenant with Abraham, Isaac, and Jacob" (Exod 2:24). For "was mindful" (*zakar*), English translations usually have "remember," but the verb indicates not so much the opposite of forgetting as an indication that God now gives thought to this covenant. One aspect of the covenant promise has been amply fulfilled; Abraham's descendants via Isaac and Jacob have become a huge company. But the covenant promise also involved their coming into possession of the land of Canaan. The time for this has now arrived. The covenant is therefore the basis for acting to release Israel so that it can return to the land not as "aliens" but to receive it as a "possession" (cf. 6:2–8).

God adds, "I will take you as my people, and I will be your God" (6:7). The second phrase takes up the expression from Gen 17:7; the first phrase complements it in such a way as to introduce the two-sided "covenant formula."[4] God's words signify an imminent nuancing of the Abraham covenant. The greater mutuality of the covenant will now mean that a commitment of Israel to God complements the commitment of God to Israel. Something of the ambiguity of the Abraham covenant will be resolved. God is still the one who takes the initiative in the words that announce the covenant and in the acts that set it up (see Exod 6:6), but the covenant will integrally involve a more wide-ranging response on the people's part and a mutual relationship.

3. The Sinai Covenants

In Exod 6:6–8, Yahweh had referred to delivering Israel from serfdom, establishing the mutual relationship, and taking them to the land. When they reach Sinai, in Exod 19:1–8 Yahweh points out that the first undertaking has been fulfilled; it is therefore possible to move onto the second. This will involve Israel keeping God's covenant. The phrase recurs from Gen 17:9–10, and the people could pardonably think that Yahweh is simply reasserting the demand for circumcision; this might link with the ease with which they agree, "everything that Yahweh has spoken we will do." But it will become clear that keeping the covenant will now have much broader implications.

At this point, however, Yahweh is more explicit about the special nature of the relationship that will issue from the mutual covenant commitment. Implementing the intention to "take you as my people" will mean Israel becoming Yahweh's "treasured possession out of all the peoples." That will spell itself out in Israel's becoming a priestly kingdom or holy nation. The two adjectives and the two nouns form more or less synonymous pairs. Israel is separated from other peoples in such a way as to belong distinctively to Yahweh in the way that the priesthood within a people belongs distinctively to the people's deity. As such they are a nation over which Yahweh personally reigns. They are not under the rule of some other people, as they were in Egypt. But they are freed from serfdom in Egypt not so that they can simply be free but so that they can be given to the service of Yahweh.

The people's initial commitment to keeping the covenant (19:8) clears the way for their meeting with Yahweh at Sinai. This is often thought to be *the* occasion of the making of a covenant between Yahweh and Israel, but the narrative is sparse in its reference to covenant.

In Exod 20–24 the word comes first in the requirement that Israel make no covenant with the inhabitants of Canaan or with their gods (23:32). The second requirement explains the first. A basic obligation of some covenants is a requirement of exclusive loyalty; some political covenants or treaties require a subordinate state to show exclusive loyalty to its imperial overlord (for instance, Israel in its

---

[4] So Rolf Rendtorff, *The Covenant Formula* (Edinburgh: Clark, 1998).

relationship with Assyria) and not to ally with other peoples. Analogously, Israel is expected to show exclusive loyalty to Yahweh and thus not to seek help from other deities. That is implicit in the idea of Israel being Yahweh's covenant people (e.g., 19:5–6) and explicit in the first of Yahweh's Ten Words (20:2–3). Exodus 23:32 makes the link with the covenant. Exclusive commitment to Yahweh rules out covenants with other peoples because these would involve or lead to acknowledgment of their deities. Either the making of a covenant is a religious act that would require recognition of each others' gods, or close relationship with these other peoples would lead to being attracted by their gods. Israel's looking at these other peoples as sources of help and strength instead of looking to Yahweh is indeed an issue in Israelite history. The Gibeonites' tricking the Israelites into a covenant or treaty (*berit* covers both) implicitly involves them in a contravention of this requirement. Hosea overtly critiques Ephraim for making a *berit* with Assyria (Hos 11:12–12:1). And when Judah makes a *berit* with neighbors in order to be able to resist Assyria, Isa 28:15, 18 declares that it has made a covenant with death.

The other references to covenant in the first stage of events at Sinai come in the account of the meeting between representative Israelites and Yahweh in Exod 24. This is often thought to be the occasion of covenant making, but Exodus does not describe it as such, perhaps because Exodus is clear that Yahweh and Israel are already in covenant relationship. What happens at Sinai reconfirms the covenant, specifically in light of the expectations of Israel and the undertakings Yahweh makes to take the people to the land and care for them there, which Yahweh has laid down in Exod 20–23. Moses now reads "the covenant book" to the people, and they make a commitment to obey Yahweh; the narrative thus repeats the scene in Exod 19:3–8, resolving an ambiguity we noted there. It is now explicit that "keeping the covenant" involves more than circumcision; it involves all that this "covenant book" requires. The people's accepting that commitment is part of what is involved in what we might call the confirming or renewing of the covenant in the form that Yahweh has declared that it will now have, with this new requirement in light of what Yahweh has done for the people in bringing them out of Egypt. In scholarly parlance the title "The Book of the Covenant" usually means Exod 20:22–23:33 or part of it. Exodus 20:1–17 is simply something that Yahweh says. It is separated from what follows by the further narrative in Exod 20:18–21, and it is often thought to be a later composition that has been placed at the beginning of the Sinai story because of its great importance as a summary of Yahweh's expectations. The Ten Words will later be described as the "declaration" written by God and to be put into the covenant chest (see 31:18; 32:15–16); "declaration" is *'edut,* a word translations sometimes also render by "covenant."

A sacramental confirming of the covenant is associated with this reading of the book of the covenant. Sacrifices have already been offered, and Moses has already taken half the blood drained from the sacrificial animals and spattered it on the altar. After the people's declaration of commitment, he spatters the other half on the people themselves, saying, "There is the blood of the covenant that Yahweh now seals with you in accordance with all these words" (Exod 24:8). The rite with the blood does not correspond to any regular worship practice, though it does recall the event narrated in Gen 15:7–21 and the idea that one "cuts" a covenant. Both Yahweh (represented by the altar) and the people are spattered with blood, sealing their commitment and bringing home the solemn undertaking that this meeting on Sinai represents. It is as if either will be torn apart for failure to keep their undertaking. The people have "sealed a covenant with me by sacrifice" (Ps 50:5), and the covenant blood subsequently undergirds Yahweh's promises to Jerusalem (Zech 9:11).

The people's making a gold calf brings about a crisis in the relationship between Yahweh and Israel as Yahweh contemplates annihilating the people. The account in Exod 32–33 does not refer to the covenant, but the incident and its aftermath implicitly raise questions about the covenant relationship. They show that Yahweh's permanent covenant with Abraham's descendants does not leave Israel able to get away with despising Yahweh. It is therefore significant that Yahweh now reaffirms a covenant commitment to Israel. Indeed, strictly and significantly this is the first time Yahweh makes a covenant commitment at Sinai. Yahweh did not need to do so earlier because Yahweh and Israel are already in covenant relationship. With events in Exod 32–33 having implicitly imperiled that, this is the moment when Yahweh declares, "I hereby seal a covenant" (34:10).

Yet again there is some ambiguity over the relationship of divine commitment and human obligation in this covenant. On one hand, in beginning to spell out the implications of the declaration about making a covenant, Yahweh first promises to do great wonders before the people; these will be the wonders that will be involved in giving the people the land, to which Yahweh immediately goes on to refer (34:10–11). But Yahweh precedes that declaration of intent by an exhortation to "observe what I command you today" and then spells that out as involving not making a covenant with the peoples of the land (34:11–16), renewing and expanding the earlier command about covenant making (23:32). Once again Yahweh thus emphasizes the exclusive aspect to this covenant relationship, then continues by detailing other expectations of the people (34:17–26) in a way that overlaps with the covenant book. This reformulating of the requirements laid down in the covenant book is implicitly an act of grace on Yahweh's part. The original revealing of expectations was an act of grace, insofar as once we know what God wants of us, we can do it; we cannot do that if we are left in the dark. Restating the expectations underlines the point. Yahweh is still reaching out in grace to Israel in being willing to do so.

So Yahweh's covenant making (34:10) might consist in making the promise about doing wonders, or in laying down those expectations, with the promise as a preamble, or it might involve both of these. The persistence of such ambiguity in references to the covenant is of theological significance. It does not imply that Yahweh fails to make things clear. It rather points to the fact that the relationship between divine commitment and human obligation is inherently ambiguous, dynamic, volatile, and changeable. A covenant is not a contract, as the adversary in Job 1–2 suggested Job thought his relationship with God was. The "covenant" Leviathan would not make to serve Job (Job 41:4 [40:28]) would be something like a contract, but the covenant that Job had sealed with his eyes (Job 31:1) was an inner commitment that no one could test.

A covenant does involve a mutual commitment, but it is not exactly conditional. In this respect it resembles marriage. This requires that both people commit themselves to the other, but we would not say that one person makes a commitment on condition that the other does. This would underestimate the element of trust and risk in the relationship. In a contract, the conditions are calculated to minimize the element of risk and make trust less necessary. This is good practice in certain areas of life; there is nothing wrong with contracts. But we would rather marriage were not contractual and calculating in this way. In this respect the relationship between Yahweh and Israel resembles a personal relationship such as marriage more than a contract, alliance, or treaty. The recurrent ambiguity in the texts about the relationship between divine commitment and human obligation is a sign of that.

It is possible that the First Testament itself sees marriage as a covenant,[5] though the texts that may indicate that (Prov 2:17; Ezek 16:8; Mal 2:14) are all allusive. It also refers to a personal covenant between David and Jonathan (1 Sam 18:3; cf. 22:8), a "sacred covenant" (lit., "a covenant of Yahweh"; 1 Sam 20:8), perhaps so designated because it was "a covenant before Yahweh" (1 Sam 23:18). A psalmist laments, "My friend . . . violated a covenant with me" (Ps 55:13, 20 [14, 21]).

After laying out those expectations in Exod 34, "Yahweh said to Moses: Write these words; in accordance with these words I have sealed a covenant with you and with Israel" (34:27). The reference is presumably to the words in Exod 34:10–26. The narrative goes on to tell us that "he wrote on the tablets the words of the covenant, the ten words" (34:28; they are not called "ten commandments" in scripture). Within the narrow context we would think that "he" is Moses. But the chapter began with Yahweh declaring the intention to rewrite what was written on the tablets Moses broke, and more likely "he" is Yahweh, who was the subject in the previous verse, "Yahweh said to Moses." Either way, "the words of the covenant" are here "the ten words," and they complement "the covenant book," both being integral to the covenant as statements of the obligations that Yahweh imposes and Israel accepts (cf. Deut 4:13; 9:9–15).

Near the end of the time at Sinai, Yahweh restates the point, in Lev 26 (to put it another way, Lev 26 is the Holiness Code's equivalent to Exod 34). Here the relationship between Israel's obedience and Yahweh's covenant keeping is less equivocal: "If you follow my statutes . . . I will give you your rains in their season . . . and I will establish my covenant with you. . . . I will walk among you, and will be your God, and you shall be my people" (Lev 26:3–12). The promise amounts to a renewed undertaking to make the covenant work, here in the context of the people's coming arrival in the land (cf. Deut 8:18).

Leviticus 26:15 again parallels Gen 17 in allowing for Israel's "breaking" the covenant, to which severe sanctions are attached. Persisting in disobedience will mean Yahweh "will bring the sword against you, exacting redress for the covenant" (Lev 26:25). Yahweh itemizes this redress in horrific fashion but then declares that if the people turn back to Yahweh, "then I will be mindful of my covenant with Jacob; I will be mindful also of my covenant with Isaac and also of my covenant

---

[5] So Gordon P. Hugenberger, *Marriage as a Covenant* (VTSup 52; New York: Brill, 1994).

with Abraham" (26:42). Being mindful of the covenant and thus taking action on the people's behalf is possible in the context of their wrongdoing as well as their undeserved oppression (Exod 2:24). No more than at Sinai will Yahweh annihilate them and thus "break my covenant with them; for I am Yahweh their God; but I will be mindful in their favor of the covenant with their ancestors whom I brought out of the land of Egypt" (Lev 26:44–45).

The ambiguity of the relationship between divine commitment and human obligation yet again reasserts itself. The warnings presuppose that the people have failed to keep their covenant obligations, and this would give Yahweh quite enough reason to terminate the covenant. The mere fact that the covenant was perpetual might not guarantee that it stays in force no matter what Israel does. Many things that God says will be permanent, such as the temple, the priesthood, and the Davidic monarchy, seem not to be permanent. That declaration only guarantees that Yahweh is not fickle and will not have a random change of mind. It does not stop Yahweh terminating them in light of people's intransigence. But Yahweh will not "break" the covenant (Yahweh uses the verb that describes Israel's failure) let alone terminate it; perhaps "break" and "annul" end up having the same meaning in this context.

Even in this connection Yahweh will not "put out of mind the covenant with your ancestors that he swore to them" (Deut 4:31). Admittedly, at the beginning of Judges Yahweh declares, "I said, 'I will never break my covenant with you. For your part, do not seal a covenant with the inhabitants of the land, tear down their altars.' But you have not obeyed my command" (Judg 2:1–2; cf. v. 20). Yahweh will therefore not drive these peoples out before Israel. Is Yahweh therefore breaking the covenant, on the basis of the fact that Israel has done so? Or does a responsive action such as that not count as breaking the covenant? However, even when Ephraim has long been unfaithful and has been chastised, "Yahweh was gracious and compassionate to them; he turned toward them, because of his covenant with Abraham, Isaac, and Jacob, and was not willing to destroy them; and he has not thrown them out of his presence until now" (2 Kgs 13:23). "Until now" apparently implies that even the fall of Samaria and the exile of its people did not constitute such destruction or banishment. In Jer 14:21, the prophet thus feels free to urge, "Do not break your covenant with us," despite our wickedness.

4. The Moab Covenant

A generation on from Sinai, on the edge of the land, Yahweh commands Moses to seal a covenant with the Israelites to supplement the covenant at Horeb, by means of which the new generation will "enter into the covenant of Yahweh your God and into his oath, which Yahweh your God is making with you today in order that he may establish you today as his people, and that he may be your God" (Deut 29:1, 12–13 [28:69; 29:12–13]). The terms of the covenant parallel those at Sinai, though they are adapted to aspects of life in the land in a way that reflects needs that arise in later contexts (for instance, the people wanting a king and the problem of false prophecy). This covenant making also has the effect of putting the obligation of the covenant on people who were not at Sinai. For the readers, that next generation stands for each succeeding Israelite generation, and thus for the readers themselves. "Not with you alone am I making this covenant and this oath but with whoever is standing here with us today before Yahweh our God and with whoever is not here with us today" (29:14–15 [13–14]).

Deuteronomy talks more about covenant than any other book in the Bible. Indeed, although the actual occurrences of the word come chiefly in chapters 4–11 and 29–31, Deuteronomy as a whole can be seen as a covenant document, a book structured to reflect and expound Israel's covenant relationship with Yahweh. Thus, if one-sided covenants are more like a pledge or a *diatheke*, this covenant is more like a contract, more of a *suntheke* or *Bund* (though the Greek translations still usually use *diatheke*). Israel can be and is sued for failing to keep its side of the contract. Its structure parallels that of a treaty between an imperial power and an underling such as Israel. It has been argued that it more closely resembles Hittite treaties from the second millennium than Assyrian treaties from the first millennium and thus that it more likely reflects the work of Moses than the work of the seventh-century theologians whom the scholarly world has more often thought to be the authors of Deuteronomy. But like most aspects of the history of covenant in Israel, this question is controverted. Either way, most Israelites would presumably be unaware of the treaty background of the work, but the theologians who drafted the text perhaps found that this political arrangement helped them articulate the dynamics of Yahweh's relationship with Israel, though we should be wary of exaggerating the importance of this factor in the development of covenant thinking.[6]

A political treaty could review the past relationship between the superpower and the underling, lay down the basic requirement of loyalty to the superpower, itemize specific requirements, describe the benefits and sanctions attached to compliance and noncompliance, and provide for the solemnizing and regular reading of the treaty. Deuteronomy is much longer than a treaty, but this comparison helps one see aspects of its dynamic and the way it could have communicated at least with Israel's leaders.

First, Deut 1–3 reviews the relationship between Yahweh and Israel since Sinai, as background to the reaffirmation of the covenant on the edge of the land, noting both the way Yahweh has supported Israel and the way Israel has been inclined to rebellion. Each of these is also background to the requirements that will follow.

Deuteronomy 4–11 lays down the fundamental requirement that Israel should respond to what Yahweh has done by showing unqualified commitment to Yahweh and having nothing to do with other deities. In a literal sense Yahweh made the covenant with the parents of the people about to enter the land, but Moses declares that Yahweh did not seal it merely with them but with this present generation (5:2–3). NRSV translates "ancestors" rather than "parents," which brings out the fact

---

[6]See Ernest W. Nicholson, *God and His People* (Oxford / New York: Oxford University Press, 1986); also A. D. H. Mayes and R. B. Salters, eds., *Covenant as Context: Essays in Honor of E. W. Nicholson* (Oxford / New York: Oxford University Press, 2003).

that Deuteronomy sees every later generation of Israel as faced with the same expectations that bind the Moab generation. In particular, each generation that hears Deuteronomy read is bound by the basic expectations laid down in the Ten Words that follow in Deut 5:6–21 (see also 4:23). Exclusive loyalty to Yahweh involves making no covenant with another deity (7:2). It is the converse of the fact that Yahweh keeps covenant with those who keep their side of this commitment (7:9, 12).

The itemizing of specific requirements in Deut 12–26 is much more extensive than the equivalent section of a treaty; in a way Deuteronomy combines the form of a law code with that of a treaty. This section contains one telling reference to covenant, in the course of another comment on serving other gods than Yahweh. A person who does that "transgresses his covenant" (17:2–3; the verb is used of Achan, Josh 7:11, 15). It is another way of saying that this action involves breaking the covenant.

Deuteronomy 27–31 provides for the memorializing of the words of the law when the people enter the land and for reading them out on subsequent occasions, describes the blessings and curses attached to obedience and disobedience, and provides for the solemnizing of the covenant. It has been thought that the festival of Sukkot in the fall was also an annual covenant renewal festival, though the First Testament does not directly suggest this.

Deuteronomy warns that Yahweh will implement "all the curses of the covenant written in this book of teaching" when people have "abandoned Yahweh's covenant" by turning to other gods (29:21, 25–26; cf. 31:16, 20). Joshua will reaffirm this at the end of his life; he also "sealed a covenant with the people" to confirm their commitment to exclusive service of Yahweh (Josh 23:16; 24:25).

5. The Covenant Broken

Psalm 25:10, 14 promises that Yahweh is faithful to people who "keep his covenant and his declarations" and that "his counsel is with those who revere him, and his covenant, in making them acknowledge him" (cf. 103:17–18), and Israel needs to be able to claim, "We have not . . . been false to your covenant" (44:17 [8]). But the references to covenant in Josh 9 and Judg 2 show how it did not take Israel long to break the covenant. Solomon does the same in making marriage alliances with foreign peoples, and he pays a severe penalty (1 Kgs 11:11). Elijah's critique of Ephraim is that they have "abandoned" the covenant, which sounds more far-reaching (19:10, 14). Hosea likewise critiques Ephraim for transgressing the covenant (Hos 8:1). Ephraim's "despising" and "transgressing" the covenant, failing to keep it in mind, is the basis for the fall of Samaria and Ephraim's exile (2 Kgs 17:15, 35, 38; 18:12). "They did not keep God's covenant, but refused to walk by his teaching" (Ps 78:10).

The same is true of Judah, though the narratives do not express the matter thus. Indeed, they emphasize the way Asa and his people, Hezekiah, and especially Josiah and his people sealed covenants that expressed an exclusive commitment to Yahweh, going back on the stance of the previous generation (2 Kgs 23:2–3;

2 Chr 15:12; 29:10; 34:30–32). The basis for Josiah's act is a "covenant book," earlier described as a "teaching book," a scroll found in the course of remodeling in the temple (2 Kgs 22). The expression "covenant book" recalls Exod 24:7; it occurs only in these two connections. But the usual critical view has been that Josiah's actions suggest Deuteronomy (2 Kgs 23:21 relates how Josiah also celebrated the Passover in accordance with the covenant book, and Exod 20–24 does not mention Passover).

Jeremiah does challenge Judah about its attitude to the covenant (Jer 11:1–13) and prospectively imagines other nations explaining Jerusalem's destruction by Judah's "abandoning" the covenant—again, a more drastic act than transgressing or breaking it (22:8–9)? The people have no right to "proclaim my statutes, or take my covenant on your lips" (Ps 50:16). "They were not true to his covenant" (78:37). Thus on the eve of Jerusalem's fall Yahweh declares, "I will act toward you as you have acted, you who have despised the oath, breaking the covenant" (Ezek 16:59; cf. 44:7). Apparently Yahweh does intend to break the covenant, though this need not mean annulling it, any more than it does when Israel breaks the covenant. And the fact that Yahweh immediately goes on to declare the intention then to bear the covenant in mind (16:60) suggests that this is not so. Yet Yahweh's subsequent declaration of intent to establish with Israel a perpetual covenant (another one?) (16:60) suggests that Yahweh's act in breaking the covenant is a serious one.

The enigmatic Zech 11:10 perhaps also refers retrospectively to the fall of Ephraim and Judah, occasions when Yahweh broke "the covenant with all the peoples." The First Testament does not elsewhere refer to a "covenant with all the peoples." A covenant that benefits the nations is hardly relevant in the context; this covenant is more likely one that makes the nations Yahweh's servants in protecting and blessing Israel (compare the covenant "with" the animals in Hos 2:18 [20]; also Job 5:23). By breaking that covenant, Yahweh freed the nations to devastate Ephraim and Judah. Ezekiel 17:11–21 applies covenant language to the nations and Judah in a rather different way. Nebuchadnezzar has sealed a covenant (that is, an agreement or treaty) with Zedekiah that involved Judah behaving itself, but Zedekiah has rebelled against Nebuchadnezzar. "Can he break the covenant and escape?" The answer is surely yes, in some circumstances. But Zedekiah has despised and broken "my covenant" (Ezek 17:11–21). Yahweh is in covenant with Nebuchadnezzar as Yahweh's agent in ruling Judah and controlling its destiny.

6. The New Covenant

Yahweh declares the intention to make a new covenant with both Judah and Ephraim (Jer 31:31–34; cf. 32:40; 33:23–26). It will be new because the thing Yahweh intends to do is different; it is new as the Sinai covenant was new over against the Abraham covenant. The Sinai covenant moved from a promise about Abraham becoming a great people to the setting up of a relationship between this people and God and a focus on giving this people the land. In addition, it added a whole corpus (indeed, several corpora) of requirements to the relationship, though much of this material spelled out the basic expectation that the people would indeed be Yahweh's people, and exclusively so; the heart of the people's covenant breaking thus lay in their serving of other gods.

Yahweh's intention now is to write this requirement on the people's wills. The nature of the Sinai and Moab covenants was to have Yahweh's requirements written on a scroll. The challenge to acknowledge Yahweh was therefore one that Israelites had to issue to one another. The work Yahweh will now do in transforming their attitudes will make this unnecessary, and the covenant aim that "I will be their God and they shall be my people" will be fulfilled. The last phrase in Jeremiah's promise is, "for I will forgive their iniquity, and remember their sin no more." It may indicate how Yahweh will do this writing onto the people's wills. The extraordinary nature of Yahweh's grace shown in not casting them off but rather being prepared to forgive and forget and restore will be what finally gets to them and changes their attitude.

Ezekiel makes the same point more sardonically. Although Judah has despised the oath and broken the covenant, Yahweh will bear the covenant in mind and in fact establish a perpetual covenant with them. That will lead to their feeling shame at their past behavior "when I make expiation for you for all that you have done" (Ezek 16:59–63). "I will bring you into the covenant bond" (Ezek 20:37). Yahweh adds, "I will seal for them a covenant of *shalom*," a covenant that guarantees security and blessing (Ezek 34:25–31; cf. Hos 2:18 [20]), and it "will be a perpetual covenant with them" (Ezek 37:26; cf. Isa 54:10; 61:8). Israel will thus "come and join themselves to Yahweh by a perpetual covenant that will never be put out of mind" (Jer 50:5). Perhaps the idea is that the people will make this covenant and never put it out of mind, but it would fit the other occurrences of such language if the verse again refers to a perpetual covenant that Yahweh will make and never put out of mind.

One aspect of Yahweh's covenant commitment will be that Yahweh will always be speaking through the kind of prophet who speaks in Isa 59:21. Isaiah 55:3 promises "a perpetual covenant, my steadfast commitments to David"; it takes up the charge at the end of Ps 89 that Yahweh has abandoned the covenant with David and offers a distinctive response. Yahweh will be true to the covenant with David by extending its application to the people as a whole. Israel can thus be "a covenant to the people" (Isa 42:6; 49:8). This expression recalls the idea that Abraham can be a blessing. Israel can be an embodiment for the world of what it means to be in covenant relationship with Yahweh and thus be a means of light coming to the nations.

The Second Temple period saw Israel keeping the covenant in a way they had not before. Under Jeshua and Zerubbabel the people establish the proper round of worship in the temple, with praise and joy, in accordance with the Torah (Ezra 1–6). Ezra comes to see that the people know the Torah, and the community join him in an act of repentance for failing to live by the Torah in their relationship with other peoples and make a covenant commitment to Yahweh (Ezra 7–10). They join Nehemiah in restoring to people their fields, vineyards, orchards, and houses and in stopping lending at interest to each other when they are in need, in accordance with the Torah (Neh 5). They ask Ezra to teach them Torah, and they listen with joy; they discover its regulations about Sukkot and implement them; Ezra emphasizes that Yahweh is a God who keeps covenant; and the people commit themselves to the offerings that are needed to maintain the temple worship (see Neh 8–10).

Nehemiah sees that the sabbath is properly observed and the Torah's regulations about marriage with other peoples accepted (Neh 13).

The basic requirements of the Torah as these are expressed in the Decalogue are thus implemented in the community's life. They have given up worship of other gods and worship by means of images, the key first two requirements. In accordance with the third command, they safeguard against wrongful use of Yahweh's name by giving up uttering the name, and in accordance with the fourth, they come to be committed to observing the sabbath, which itself can be seen as a perpetual covenant for Israel (Exod 31:16; Lev 24:8). Thus by the end of First Testament times these requirements can be taken for granted; the New Testament does not accuse the Jewish people of worshiping other deities, or making images, or profaning Yahweh's name, or breaking the sabbath. The story in Ezra and Nehemiah and books such as Malachi show that the community remains capable of great waywardness, but the Second Temple community is a religiously very different one from that which the eighth- and seventh-century prophets attacked. Conversely, by New Testament times the Jewish people is in occupation of something like the old bounds of the land, the area that belonged both to Judah and to Ephraim.

Yahweh has thus kept the promise to implement a new covenant. Indeed, the people *are* the "holy covenant" (Dan 11:28, 30), a strong way of defining them as the covenant people. Further, the spread of appreciation of Jewish religion through the diaspora means they have become a covenant to the people of the world. Yet they again come under the domination of a foreign empire and once again need God to "remember his holy covenant" (Luke 1:72). And most of them fail to recognize the Messiah when he comes. The situation with regard to the promise of a new covenant is thus similar to that with other promises, such as those of the physical restoration of city, community, and land. There is room for more fulfillment, but all receive some fulfillment in the shorter term.

7. The Jesus Covenant

The New Testament shows rather little explicit interest in covenant compared with some other Second Temple writings such as Ecclesiasticus, which emphasizes the successive covenants in its survey of biblical history as a celebration of "famous men" (Sir 44–45), or the Qumran writings. But early on, it declares that Jesus came because God did indeed "remember his holy covenant," and Jesus looks at his death in light of the First Testament talk of covenant: "My blood of the covenant . . . is poured out for many" (Mark 14:24). The covenant promise was not being fulfilled, and Jesus came to see that it was, but this involved his willingness to die. The references to "pouring out" and to "many" suggest a link with Isa 53 and thus ultimately with the "covenant for the people" in Isa 42:6; 49:8. The Jesus covenant will benefit the world more spectacularly than the previous versions of the covenant did. The idea of the "covenant blood" (Exod 24:8; Zech 9:11) is reworked in Jesus' words. In the First Testament, being unfaithful to the covenant could issue in the covenant maker's blood being shed. Here, blood is to be shed in order that the covenant may be operative.

In the parallel passage, Matt 26:28, Jesus adds that the pouring out of his blood brings about "the forgiveness of sins." He thus takes up Jeremiah's talk of a new covenant (Jer 31:31–34). This is explicit in a different way in the Lukan version, Luke 22:20, where Jesus speaks of "the new covenant in my blood" (cf. 1 Cor 11:25). Jesus is ignoring the question whether God has already fulfilled the new covenant promise in the life of Second Temple Israel and using the image of a new covenant to interpret the significance of his death. His way of speaking thus corresponds to the general dynamic of the New Testament use of the First Testament. What the New Testament calls fulfillment does not refer to the first time promises have been fulfilled. The New Testament characteristically uses First Testament passages to throw light on the new act of God to which it witnesses, but this does not mean that the First Testament promises referred exclusively or primarily or directly to the Christ event.

Matthew's formulation indicates the way this covenant is new. Jesus' death is of key significance for the forgiveness of the many, both Israel (cf. Luke 1:77) and the world. It will still be true that "to them belong . . . the covenants" (Rom 9:4), but people who are now "strangers to the covenants of promise" (Eph 2:12) will thus cease to be strangers. In keeping with this, Peter reminds Jews in Jerusalem that they are "the descendants . . . of the covenant that God established with your ancestors, saying to Abraham, 'And in your offspring all the families of the earth shall be blessed.'" This comes about through Jesus, who calls them to turn from their wicked ways (Acts 3:25–26). That is the way they will find forgiveness.

Apostles such as Paul are thus "ministers of a new covenant," whose novelty lies in its being "not of letter but of spirit" (2 Cor 3:6). This antithesis corresponds to but restates the one in Jer 31:31–34. The Jewish people of Paul's day have the written word, once "engraved in letters on stones," but their rejection of the gospel shows that this is all they have. When they read the old covenant, it is as if there is a veil over their minds, which is set aside only in Christ (2 Cor 3:14). Otherwise, they do not understand. Paul thus sees the new covenant as a present reality.

At the same time, Paul recognizes that the process of transformation is incomplete. As was the case in First Testament times, God's making this new covenant and writing the teaching in people's minds is not incompatible with their remaining sinful. Among the New Testament churches in which the new covenant is implemented, there is, for instance, fighting, deception, and sexual immorality. If we wonder how this is compatible with God's having kept those promises, we might infer that it is because human beings still have the free will to resist God's purpose. While this is true, it is not a satisfactory explanation, because the point about those promises was that God would do something that meant people exercised their free will in a more satisfactory way. A better explanation is to think that the general sense in which God's promise is fulfilled is not undone by individual examples of wrongdoing.

Further, Paul cannot believe that God will never take away the veil over the Jewish people's minds. This, too, points toward a sense in which the implementation of Jeremiah's new covenant still lies in the future. It will come at the time when God's ultimate purpose is fulfilled and all Israel is saved; "as it is written . . . 'And this is my covenant with them, when I take away their sins'" (Rom 11:25–27).

Hebrews develops the notion of the new covenant most systematically (see esp. Heb 8–9). Like Jesus, it takes up the expression "covenant blood," referring specifically to the Exod 24 narrative (Heb 9:19–20), and takes it in a new direction in order to expound the significance of Jesus' death. Whereas in the First Testament the sacrifice involved in confirming the covenant at Sinai was separate from the regular sacrificial system, Hebrews brings these two together; it can then see the covenant sacrifice as a cleansing sacrifice (Heb 9:21–22). But the fact that Jer 31:34 speaks of forgiveness as still future shows that these cleansing sacrifices did not really work. So "Jesus is the mediator of a new covenant" by virtue of the fact that "a death has occurred to redeem them from the transgressions under the first covenant" (Heb 9:15). The old covenant with its shortcomings is thus obsolete and about to disappear (Heb 8:7–8, 13). The single definitive sacrifice that Christ offered makes the regular sacrifices now unnecessary (cf. Heb 10:14–18).

This puts people who believe in Jesus in a privileged position, though also in a solemn one, because the superiority of the new covenant is matched by a greater enormity involved when someone has "profaned the covenant blood by which they were sanctified" (Heb 10:29). But Hebrews has better hopes of its readers and prays that "by the blood of the eternal covenant" God may take them to complete maturity (Heb 13:20–21).

The Jesus covenant is thus a reworking of the First Testament covenant, analogous to the several reworkings that have preceded it. It is the means whereby the Gentile world is drawn into the covenant relationship that goes back to Abraham. There is not one covenant for Jews and one for Gentiles.

8. Covenants between God and Individuals or Groups

In the First Testament, Yahweh also makes a covenant commitment to the clan of Levi in connection with the priesthood and to the household of David in connection with the monarchy. Malachi 2:1–9 speaks most systematically about a covenant with Levi, a "covenant of life and *shalom*." Levi made an appropriate response to that covenant, but his descendants have "corrupted" it. They may have done that by colluding with the unworthy offerings condemned in Mal 1, but in addition the priests who have married foreign women "have defiled the priesthood, the covenant of the priests and the Levites" (Neh 13:29). In this context, the covenant may be the priesthood's covenant commitment to Yahweh rather than Yahweh's to them. Similarly, Mal 2:10–16 goes on to speak of Judah "profaning the covenant of our ancestors" because it has "married the daughter of a foreign god." You have "broken faith" with "the wife of your youth" although she is "your partner, your wife by covenant." The juxtaposition of these passages suggests another reference to the involvement of Levi as well as the other clans in marriages with people committed to other gods. Apparently these marriages first involved divorce from an Israelite wife, "your wife by covenant." This might imply that the first marriage was understood as a covenant or that the first wife was an Israelite, someone within the covenant between the people and Yahweh, whereas the new wife was outside that covenant. It is then another way of noting how such a marriage "profaned the covenant of our ancestors."

In the context of the imminent destruction of the temple, Yahweh had declared that it would be no more possible to break the covenant with the Levites as people ministering to Yahweh than to break the covenant of day and night (Jer 33:19–22). But this commitment might presuppose the assumption that they stay faithful to their own covenant commitment

Yahweh gives a specific covenant to Aaron's son Phinehas, because of his passionate zeal for Yahweh in killing an Israelite who took a Midianite wife (Num 25:10–13). This, too, is a "covenant of *shalom*" and "a covenant of priesthood," perhaps a promise that his line will always have a place in the Aaronic priesthood. The "prince of the covenant" (Dan 11:22) is likely the high priest.

In his "last words" David says that God "laid down for me a perpetual covenant, ordered in every respect and secured" (2 Sam 23:5). The narrative has not recorded this, though one could see Yahweh's promise in 2 Sam 7 as covenant-like. More emphatically, Ps 89 observes to Yahweh, "You said, 'I have sealed a covenant for my chosen one, I have sworn to David my servant: "I will establish your offspring forever, and build up your throne for all generations. . . . Forever I will keep my commitment to him, and my covenant will be true for him. . . . I will not profane my covenant, or change what has come forth from my lips"'" (Ps 89:3–4, 28, 34 [4–5, 29, 35]). The promissory nature of the David covenant makes it comparable with the Abraham covenant.

The Judean king Abijah reminded Ephraim that Yahweh gave the kingship forever to David and his sons "by a salt covenant" (2 Chr 13:5). We do not know the background of this expression (for which see also Num 18:19; Lev 2:13), but it seems to underline the notion of permanency. Second Chronicles 21:7 notes that despite its wrongdoing "Yahweh was not willing to destroy the household of David, for the sake of the covenant that he had sealed for David." The same undertaking that made it impossible to break the Levi covenant would make it impossible to break the David covenant so that his heirs would not sit on the throne (Jer 33:19–26).

Yahweh has abandoned the Davidic king: "You have renounced your servant's covenant" (Ps 89:39 [40]). But then, according to another psalm, what Yahweh had said was, "If your sons keep my covenant and my decrees that I shall teach them, their sons also, forevermore, will sit on your throne" (Ps 132:12).

9. Covenant as a General Term for Relationships between God and People in the Bible

In the history of theology, the significance of covenant broadened so that it came to be used as a term for the relationship between God and Israel even where the word *berit* does not occur in the First Testament. Indeed, the original relationship between God and humanity in the garden of Eden has been seen as covenantal. Specifically, federal theology sees this as the covenant of works that was the original basis for the relationship between God and humanity. But not only does Genesis fail to refer to that original relationship as covenantal; it does not imply that the relationship was based on works but rather on the same interrelationship of God's grace and human response as obtains when it does talk in terms of covenant. Hosea 6:7 does refer to Israel transgressing the covenant "like *'adam*," which could imply that Adam transgressed a covenant, but translations assume the text either refers to humanity in general or to the place Adam on the Jordan, though we do not know what event this then refers to.[7]

Thus where the First Testament is talking about a relationship with God that "has the character of a relationship of grace, that is to say, it is founded on a primal act in history, maintained on definite conditions and protected by a powerful divine Guardian," it can be reckoned to be talking about a covenant relationship whether or not it uses the word *berit*.[8] On this basis, covenant can be seen as providing the framework for First Testament theology. Likewise one could term the description of the mutual relationship between Yahweh and Israel in passages such as Jer 7:23; 24:7; 30:22 as "the covenant formula" even though there is no explicit reference to the covenant in the context.[9] Thus different theologians can both affirm and deny that the idea of covenant dominates the First Testament, and both can be right, depending on whether they are talking about covenant in the broader or narrower sense. We have noted that the New Testament, too, rarely refers to covenants, but in the broader sense it also thinks covenantally (consider its very title *he kaine diatheke*, "the new covenant"; the translation "New Testament" obscures the point).

The prophets, too, refer to covenant rather infrequently; it is a matter of guesswork why this is so. But they, too, in the broader sense think in covenant terms, and this may lie behind the way they sometimes imply that they are issuing a formal charge against the people, accusing them of covenant breaking, and warning that covenant sanctions are to be imposed on them. Yahweh thus has a *rib*, an indictment, against the people (Hos 4:1; 12:2; Mic 6:2). The form of speech would correspond to the way an imperial power brought a charge of disloyalty against one of its underlings and threatened it with punitive action. If there is a connection with covenant thinking, then this prophetic lawsuit might also be described as a covenant lawsuit.

We have noted the key theological issue that covenant raises, the relationship between divine commitment and human obligation. Covenant can put the stress on divine initiative and commitment, though it will then regard human obedience as absolutely required. Or it can put the stress on human commitment to obey an obligation set forth by God, though it will assume that this commitment is offered in the context of the framework of divine grace. Or it can hold these two in balance in the way marriage does; Yahweh initiates the covenant, but it becomes properly

---

[7] Isaiah 24:5 and Amos 1:9 might be taken to refer to a creation covenant; I have commented on these passages in section 1 above.

[8] Walter Eichrodt, *Theology of the Old Testament* (2 vols.; Philadelphia: Westminster Press / London: SCM, 1961), 1:36–37.

[9] So Rendtorff, *The Covenant Formula*.

operative only when humanity responds to "Yahweh's covenant." The dynamic tension between these ways of looking at the matter means God can never be taken for granted but can always be appealed to.

To put it another way, covenant reframes the debate about election and free will, about which one might say the following:

1. God chose certain individuals, such as Moses and Paul, in order to use them. This election does not apply to every Israelite or every believer in Christ. It relates to individuals God intends to use in particular ways.

2. God chose the people of Israel and the church in order to use them. This is the election of a people, not of individuals.

3. Nothing about these individuals or about Israel or about the church makes them warrant or deserve election.

4. The stories of Moses or Jeremiah or Paul show that when God chooses people, they do not have much option about responding.

5. While being chosen may convey the privilege of a relationship with God and eternal life, God's object in the choosing is not to convey privileges but to use the chosen ones, as when we choose a pan to cook with.

6. Election is designed to be inclusive not exclusive. God chooses Israel and the church so as to reach other individuals and other groups.

10. Covenant as a Term for the Basis of Community Life

In the history of the United States, the significance of covenant has broadened horizontally as well as vertically—that is, covenant has often been a key image for human relations. Etymologically, a covenant is something people come together to agree, and "agreement" is the first dictionary definition of "covenant." Such an idea of covenant was influential in the development of American democracy. It has a background in the federal or covenant theology of the sixteenth century. This received political expression in, for instance, the Church of Scotland's National Covenant of 1639, one of whose preliminary texts was 2 Kgs 11:17: "Jehoiada sealed a covenant between the Lord and the king and the people, that they should be the Lord's people; between the king also and the people." This is a rare instance of a biblical passage where people are making a covenant with one another as well as with God. Another example of horizontal covenanting is King Zedekiah's covenant with the community that people should set free indentured servants whom they have held onto after the end of their six-year period of work, though they soon renege on this commitment and re-enslave these servants (Jer 34:8–11). This may presuppose that the people who were freed had no resources, which is what would have driven them into servitude, and if people will not relate to them as free people and help them reestablish themselves as free citizens, then they have no alternative but to return to servitude. That means they have both transgressed the original covenant that Yahweh laid down, which limited servitude to six years, and not kept the terms of the covenant they had just made with each other before Yahweh (Jer 34:13, 15, 18).

In 1620, the settlers at New Plymouth formulated the Mayflower Compact by which they entered into covenant with one another for their "better ordering and preservation" under God. The nation is then a group of people who live in covenant with one another, accepting responsibility for one another under God. A little later in the seventeenth century there was also developing in Europe a secular form of covenant-based political thinking in the work of Thomas Hobbes and John Locke, and this also subsequently came to influence American thinking and made it possible to formulate constitutions that were covenantal without being religious.

Inspired by God's covenantal self-giving, the church makes a commitment to mutual solidarity and to embodying this in a covenantal life, though it also sees the world as "intended by God to be a community that covenants, that distributes its produce equally, that values all its members, and that brings the strong and the weak together in common work and common joy."[10] Demythologized, covenant is "the bonding of decentralized social groups in a larger society of equals committed to cooperation without authoritarian leadership and a way of symbolizing the locus of sovereignty in such a society of equals."[11]

The notion of covenant emphasizes the relational and communal aspect to life, expressed in human relationships and in humanity's relationship with the rest of creation. We do not live to ourselves but in mutual commitment. It has been argued that there is a close connection between covenant and *khesed*, "steadfast love" or "commitment." Yahweh is one "keeping covenant and commitment for your servants" (1 Kgs 8:23; cf. Deut 7:9; 2 Chr 6:14; Neh 1:5; 9:32; Ps 89:28 [29]; Dan 9:4), and *khesed* is the kind of commitment that people show one another when they are in covenant. One could extend this to other classic Hebrew expressions for community values such as those listed as characteristics of Yahweh in connection with the remaking of the covenant in Exod 34:6–7. On the basis of the conviction that our human action in covenant is an imitation of God's action in covenant, one could infer that these are the qualities of human covenantal living. But all this develops First Testament ways of thinking rather than directly following it.

---

[10] Walter Brueggemann, *A Social Reading of the Old Testament* (Minneapolis: Fortress, 1994), 50.

[11] Norman K. Gottwald, *The Tribes of Yahweh* (Maryknoll, N.Y.: Orbis, 1979 / London: SCM, 1980), 692.

10

What Is the Meaning of Sacrifice?

If one were to ask a Christian about the meaning of sacrifice, it is likely that it would be seen as a way of getting right with God. And in expounding the significance of Christ's death in this connection, the New Testament often speaks in terms of its being a kind of sacrifice and refers to sacrifice in the First Testament in doing so. Yet the New Testament also uses the imagery of sacrifice in a number of other connections, and it thus reflects the fact that sacrifice has broader significance than the one Christians usually assume. I shall consider four approaches to interpreting sacrifice.[1]

1. Sacrifice as a Way of Giving a Gift

A man returns home clutching a bunch of cut flowers. He presents these to his wife, who perhaps bursts into tears (or perhaps slaps him in the face). What is going on? In their culture, the gift of flowers is recognized as a positive gesture in the context of a relationship. But the gesture may have various significances. It may express or accompany gratefulness for some act, appreciation for the person, hope for some favor, sorrow for some wrongdoing, or regret for some non-culpable failure (he arrived home late because the train broke down). The implicit feelings (for instance, of appreciation or regret) may be genuine or false.

Giving a gift is one central aspect of the meaning of sacrifice.[2] As gifts to God, sacrifices can have a parallel range of significances to those of the giving of flowers. A thank offering expresses gratitude for some act on God's part. A whole offering suggests the commitment of the person to God; the offerer surrenders every part of the animal. Sin offerings and guilt offerings, as they are traditionally called in English, provide ways of finding cleansing when one is taboo and of making up for the consequences of some offense. Parallel to the gift of flowers in human relationships, then, sacrifices give the appropriate concrete, material, symbolic expression and evidence of a response to God of commitment, appreciation, gratitude, hope,

---

[1] First published as "Old Testament Sacrifice and the Death of Christ," in *Atonement Today* (ed. John Goldingay; London: SPCK, 1995), 3–20.

[2] See George B. Gray, *Sacrifice in the Old Testament* (Oxford / New York: Oxford University Press, 1925), 1–20.

shame, and regret. Without the attitude, the sacrifice would be meaningless; without the sacrifice, the attitude would be a mere head trip. The analogy with a practice such as the giving of flowers may help Western Christians appreciate some aspects of the logic of sacrifice.

First, the practice presupposes a framework of interpretation within a culture; as with other aspects of Western culture, someone from outside might find it puzzling. The significance of the practice is assumed rather than stated.

Second, Protestant interpreters have understood passages in the Prophets and the Psalms that raise questions about sacrifice to be suggesting that there is no need for sacrifice in principle. One might similarly argue that there is no need for a man to give his wife flowers, especially as this can easily be a substitute for real commitment, or a disguise rather than an expression of feelings, or a sexist gesture. One fault in that argument lies in its failure to take account of the fact that men and women are material human beings and that symbolic gestures are built into being human. It is appropriate for people to have concrete and outward, practical and symbolic ways of expressing attitudes of will, mind, and feeling. In a parallel way people relate to God by symbolic actions as well as by words, thoughts, and feelings. The analogy with the giving of a gift such as flowers hints at the person-to-person nature of the relationship between God and people. To put it another way, a gift is an act that does something. The giving of flowers can have a magical effect on a relationship; sacrifice, too, can act like magic. Something happens when either offering is made.

Third, it is not merely their inherent commercial value that gives the gift of flowers its significance and its effectiveness, but the gift's symbolic significance in a culture. If the giver had caused his wife some loss (e.g., had crashed her car), he would need to put that right; the gift of flowers adds to this practical act rather than replacing it. If the loss he had caused could not be made up (as when I accidentally threw away a package of photographs of our wedding and honeymoon), some symbolic gift may help to compensate for it (though I do not remember making one). In the Day of Atonement ritual, two goats correspond to the entire body of wrongdoing committed by the community in a year.

Fourth, both forms of gift also presuppose that right attitude of spirit and will is indispensable if the gift is to be significant and effective. The gift works only if it is the symbolic expression of a personal attitude that characterizes the giver's life as a whole. A woman whose husband brings her flowers that she has reason to believe hide rather than express his true attitude may well respond, "Stuff your bloody flowers." In a parallel way Yahweh says, "Stuff your bloody sacrifices" in equivalent circumstances.

Fifth, it is possible for the giving of flowers to be the beginning of a relationship, but more commonly it belongs in the context of an existent one. Sacrifice, too, is not a means of establishing the relationship between people and God but a means of expressing, developing, and healing it.[3]

Sixth, when the man offers his flowers to his wife, as much significance attaches to their reception as to their being offered. In parallel, a "'theology of acceptance'

---

[3] Cf. Derek Kidner, *Sacrifice* (London: Tyndale, 1952), 23.

pervades Old Testament attitudes towards sacrifice."[4] This begins with Gen 4. The story of Cain and Abel already illustrates that acceptance cannot be presupposed, that everything depends upon it, and that questions of moral stance and questions of acceptance interweave, though not always in the way we might expect (see further Jer 6:20; Hos 9:4; Amos 5:22).

God offered Jesus Christ as a sacrifice, Jesus offered himself as a sacrifice. What does this statement suggest regarding the significance of his death?

First, the offering of Christ was an outward act. The statement that Jesus' death was a sacrifice is a metaphorical one. Jesus was not literally a priest, his offering did not take place in a temple, and he did not kill himself. Describing his death as a sacrifice is a way of gaining an understanding of its deep significance. It is an example of typological thinking. But as a sacrifice, Jesus' person, his life, and his death—the totality of his self-offering—were concrete, outward, historical, this-worldly events.

Second, the offering of Christ took place within the context of a person-to-person relationship. To see Christ's death as effecting the satisfaction of God's honor or the achievement of God's victory or the redemption of God's possession or the acceptance of God's punishment sets it in the context of intrinsically hierarchical and/or contractual webs of relationships, those of authority, power, business, or law. To see Christ's death as a gift offered to God sets it in the context of a person-to-person relationship of mutual commitment with its potential for love, favor, generosity, self-sacrifice, gratitude, and forgiveness, as opposed to pardon, which is a more hierarchical idea.[5]

Third, this relationship in whose context Christ's offering took place is an already existing one. It is not the case that people were unable to relate to God before Jesus' act of self-offering to the Father. It is precisely because they were in relationship to God that there needed to be an offering of themselves to God in appreciation, gratitude, joy, commitment, hope, penitence, and recompense, expressed in the self-offering that characterizes Christ's life as a whole.

It was because God chose us that God gave Jesus for us, rather than vice versa. Sacrifice was the seal of a relationship rather than the means to it. Because my wife is disabled and cannot get out to the shops on her own, when Christmas draws near I have sometimes said to her, "Would you like to give me that shirt?" And if she liked it too, I would buy it, wrap it, attach a tag that says it comes from her to me, put it with the other family presents, and in due course receive it from among them as a gift from her that I knew she was glad to give me.

The same point may be made by noting that Christ is both priest and victim at his sacrifice. He is not given by someone else. When this form of self-sacrifice is required by the path he has to walk, he freely gives himself; it is a positive act of self-giving rather than a hopeless giving up. Indeed, we may go further. It was already the case that Israel's sacrifices involved the offering of something God provided. The point is particularly explicit in the prayer with which Israel brought

---

[4] Robert J. Daly, *The Origins of the Christian Doctrine of Sacrifice* (Philadelphia: Fortress, 1978), 23.

[5] See Vincent Brümmer, "Atonement and Reconciliation," *Religious Studies* 28 (1992): 438–52, for further analysis.

firstfruits (Deut 26:10–11) and in David's prayer regarding the offerings for building a temple (1 Chr 29:14). God is the origin of Christ's sacrifice in a more direct or specific sense. Such sacrificial notions are implied when the New Testament says that God "gave his only Son" (John 3:16) or "put [Christ] forward as a sacrifice of atonement" (Rom 3:25) or "did not withhold his own Son, but gave him up for all of us" (Rom 8:32, following the language of Abraham's offering of Isaac).[6]

2. Sacrifice as a Way of Finding Cleansing and Restoration

The giving of flowers, then, can have various meanings. These are not confined to the expression of sorrow for some failure, but they do include that. Likewise some sacrifices expressed God people's commitment, gratitude, appreciation, or need. Others were more concerned with the problems caused by human wrong-doing. Indeed, the account of Israel's sacrificial system in Leviticus does hint at a general concern to allow for the fact of human failure (1:4). It may suggest the idea that even in expressing our commitment, gratitude, appreciation, and prayer, we do so as people sharing in this failure.

In Richard Swinburne's analysis,[7] in human relationships doing wrong to someone has two sorts of moral consequences. It puts us in a situation in relation to the person something like that of a debtor: there is a wrong that needs righting. In addition, we acquire a status "something like being unclean."

Leviticus 4–5 presupposes an equivalent dynamic in our relationship with God and provides for two corresponding forms of offering. They have traditionally been called "sin offering" and "guilt offering," but "purification offering" and "restitution offering" are better renderings of the words.[8] The first deals with the stain or taboo that some acts bring on a person or a place, the second with the position of indebt-edness it puts the person in. They apply whether or not the event involved moral blame (that is, they deal with events that were objectively wrong whether or not the person was culpable), and they offer ways of finding cleansing and of making up for the wrong in certain respects. It is the restitution offering with which the servant's death is metaphorically identified in Isa 53:10. Here sacrifice is already spoken of typologically within the First Testament. Misunderstanding of Isa 53:5–6, 10–12 as if it implied a punitive understanding of sacrifice is one root of the idea that there is a link between atonement and punishment.[9] Indeed, Isa 53 (misunderstood) and

---

[6]See Colin E. Gunton, *The Actuality of Atonement* (Edinburgh: Clark, 1988 / Grand Rapids: Eerdmans, 1989), 125; James D. G. Dunn, "Paul's Understanding of the Death of Jesus as a Sacrifice," in *Sacrifice and Redemption* (ed. Stephen W. Sykes; Cambridge / New York: Cambridge University Press, 1991), 35–56 (41).

[7]*Responsibility and Atonement* (Oxford / New York: Oxford University Press, 1989), 74.

[8]See, e.g., Gordon J. Wenham, *The Book of Leviticus* (Grand Rapids: Eerdmans, 1979), 88–89, following, e.g., Jacob Milgrom, "Sin-offering or Purification-offering," *VT* 21 (1971): 237–39, and Baruch A. Levine, *In the Presence of the Lord* (Leiden: Brill, 1974), 101–5.

[9]See John Calvin, *Institutes* II.16.5–6; Karl Barth, *Church Dogmatics* IV/1 (Edinburgh: Clark, 1956), 253.

Hebrews form the restrictive prism that has dominated Christian thinking about the atonement.

The notion that wrongdoing leaves us in debt or under obligation to the person we have wronged is a familiar one, and the giving of flowers as a recognized expression of contrition and of the desire to make up for what we have done illumines some aspects of the logic of sacrifices concerned with sin. Swinburne's analysis and the comparison with the Levitical offerings draws attention to another aspect of the problem caused by our failure and wrongdoing, the stain it leaves. Contact with blood and with death was a major cause of stain or taboo as well as indebtedness in Israel. It parallels our own sense of stain as well as indebtedness when we are in contact with blood or death or are (even unwittingly) the cause of injury or death.[10]

It is not that we first experience failure and then consciously utilize the imagery of pollution to express its significance. If a child escaped its mother's grasp and ran into the road, and I could not avoid running it over, I would instinctively feel stained by its blood. I would find myself distasteful. I would be guilty of killing someone, even though it was not my fault, and I would feel the shame of guilt. This would be the case all the more, of course, if I were slightly exceeding the speed limit at the time, as is likely, for then I have to accept more responsibility for the event; but even without that, guilt, stain, and shame are involved.[11] If a wife discovers her husband has been unfaithful to her, among other things he may well seem stained to her. Even if he takes an initiative in confessing the wrongdoing and seeks a new beginning to the relationship, he may well nevertheless seem stained both to her and to himself, and she may find it difficult to approach him. In neither case are we speaking of a mere subjective feeling of stain. And in either case, the mere giving of flowers would have no effect. How does the stain come to be removed?

If I am morally in the wrong and am stained, restoration and cleansing may involve at least five factors.[12] There is repentance, in the two Hebrew senses of regret and turning to a new pattern of behavior, and in the Greek sense of a change of attitude. There is the open expression of that repentance in acknowledgment of the wrongdoing as what it was, in confession or apology. There may be some symbolic act of which the gift of flowers is a trivial example. There needs to be some substantial act that replaces my wrongdoing with something positive. Where possible this involves at least the restoring of the situation to what it was before (if I have crashed your car, I see it is repaired). In the situations that trouble us most, such as death or unfaithfulness, that is impossible, and some other more imaginative act may be required. Finally, there is time, for somehow restoration cannot be instant.

A similar set of factors may be identified in relationships between human beings and God. Deliberate wrongdoing in defiance of God's word should issue in being cut off from the community, and sacrifice alone cannot make up for such

---

[10] Cf. G. B. Caird, *The Language and Imagery of the Bible* (London: Duckworth / Philadelphia: Westminster Press, 1980), 17; Paul Ricoeur, *The Symbolism of Evil* (repr., Boston: Beacon, 1969), 25.

[11] Cf. Swinburne, *Responsibility and Atonement*, 73–74.

[12] I partly follow the analysis in Swinburne, *Responsibility and Atonement*, 81–84.

wrongdoing (Num 15:30–31). If a person repents of wrongdoing and confesses, he or she ceases to be in defiance of God, but this does not solve the entire problem, and that person must also make restitution for the wrongdoing, in relation to human beings who were involved and in relation to God. People also have to take the appropriate action with regard to the defilement that their action has brought upon them; in itself their repentance and confession cannot remove that, but it perhaps puts them into a position like that of an inadvertent offender who can offer the customary sacrifice in connection with their offense and thereby find purification (Lev 6:1–7).[13] With offerings for purification, too, time is one of the great healers: "purification is achieved principally by an appropriate ritual and a lapse of time."[14] And if the offering is not set in the context of the right attitude, to judge from the prophets Yahweh may indeed say, "Stuff your blood sacrifices."

Directly or indirectly a giver is personally identified with a gift. Usually the husband personally hands over the flowers; commonly the offerer lays hands on the offering. Like flowers, offerings do not generally substitute for people (except in the case of the dedication of the firstborn), but neither do their offerers merely own them. The laying on of hands identifies offerers and offerings and indicates that they truly represent them; something of themselves passes over with the gift to the recipient.[15] In the case of a purification offering and of the Day of Atonement ritual, the stain is transferred to the offering (cf. Lev 16:21) and is destroyed in it. Here there is indeed a sense in which the offering substitutes for the offerer, though it is not that the offering is vicariously punished. The idea of punishment belongs in the framework of law rather than the framework of worship, and we get into difficulties when we mix ideas from the different frameworks such as these. Sacrifice does not involve penal substitution in the sense that one entity bears another's punishment. By laying hands on the offering, the offerers identify with it and pass on to it not their guilt but their stain. The offering is then not vicariously punished but vicariously cleansed.

A common illustration of the need and achievement of atonement pictures God and humanity on either side of a chasm carved out by human sinfulness; the cross then makes it possible for the chasm to be bridged and for human beings to be one with God. The sacrificial model presupposes that God and human beings stand together in love and mutual self-offering. Insofar as sin becomes a problem in the relationship, in the sacrificial system God provides the way for it to be handled (even while drawing attention to it) as part of providing the means in general for expressing and developing a relationship with people. Our situation is not one in which God and ourselves are set over against each other with sin causing a gulf between us but one in which God is on the same side as us over against all that spoils and offends. "Whereas our rebellions are too mighty for us, you are the one who expiates them" (Ps 65:3). In Leviticus it is our job to expiate our wrongdoing,

---

[13] Cf. Jacob Milgrom, "The Priestly Doctrine of Repentance," *RB* 82 (1975): 186–205.
[14] Philip P. Jenson, *Graded Holiness* (JSOTSup 106; Sheffield: Sheffield Academic Press, 1992), 165.
[15] Cf. Dunn, "Paul's Understanding of the Death of Jesus as a Sacrifice," 44–45.

by following the procedure God has laid out; the psalm sees God as doing that. Of course people could decline to turn back to God, to seek forgiveness, and to offer the appropriate sacrifice, and then the relationship would remain disturbed. There would be tension between them and God. If we thus resist God, we do not stand together on the same side over against sin.

In Christ, as happens in connection with a purification offering or the Day of Atonement ritual, God is willing to transfer to something else the stain that rests on human beings so as then to destroy it and render the people clean. A sinless one is "made sin," or perhaps "made a sin offering" (2 Cor 5:21).[16] What was polluted can be restored through contact with the clean, as is announced by Jesus' unhesitating willingness to reach out to touch the polluted. They are no danger to him; he brings cleansing and restoration to them.[17]

Christ offers himself on our behalf; his self-offering becomes effective for us as we associate ourselves with it. It would be natural for the woman whose child I killed to feel negative toward me and for me to share that feeling toward myself. Imagine that God brought the child back to life and gave it to me to restore to its mother. As I did so, my stain would surely go, and this would be recognized by her and by me. Indeed, the relationship between us might now gain a depth it would never otherwise have had (though all this only if God brought me into the process of restoring).

3. Sacrifice as a Way of Enabling Movement between This World and the Realm of the Holy

Sacrifice, then, is a way of making a gift and a way of bringing about restoration. But it commonly involves the gift's destruction, a strange way of making a gift. Why is this so?

As with the giving of cut flowers (which also die as a result of becoming a gift), one can suggest a down-to-earth reason. There is a substantial overlap between sacrifice and feasting, and an animal has to be killed before it can be eaten. Generally the killing of the animal was a preliminary to the rite at the altar, undertaken by the offerer rather than by a priest. In the First Testament, at least, it is not the case that the animal's death is the climax of the rite.[18] What is central is what is done with its blood and with fire.

The varied acts involving blood indeed emphasize that sacrifice is about life poured out in death. Perhaps this reflects a distinctive feature of this occasion of giving. The gift is given to someone invisible, someone who belongs in a realm other than the earthly, the one who inhabits eternity, whose name is holy. There is a metaphysical distinction between the offerers and the recipient, even apart from

---

[16]Cf. Roland de Vaux, *Ancient Israel* (London: DLT, 1961), 420.

[17]Daly, *The Origins of the Christian Doctrine of Sacrifice*, 26–27.

[18]Contrast J. H. M. Beattie, "On Understanding Sacrifice," in *Sacrifice* (ed. M. F. C. Bourdillon and Meyer Fortes; London: New York: Academic, 1980), 29–44 (34).

any moral distinction. To describe God as the holy one is to acknowledge this distinction: God is spirit, humanity is flesh. If sacrifice is to be a means of expressing their mutual relation and of facilitating the step of faith into the unseen world of spirit, it has to belong to both realms.[19] Fire takes the offering from the material, earthly realm to the immaterial, heavenly one.[20] It crosses the threshold between the visible and the invisible.

· In Eden God takes the initiative in providing a sacramental means whereby the divine life is shared with human beings through their eating the fruit of a certain tree. This illustrates how it is appropriate for there to be ways of mediating between the realm of the holy and the created realm even before sin is a problem. East of Eden human beings follow God's example and offer God of their produce and their flocks. The mutual giving of fruit, produce, and flocks is designed to express the relationship between God and humanity, to facilitate movement between people and God, again independently of questions about sin. (In practice it can contribute to the process whereby the metaphysical distinction is turned into a moral one as it tempts the human beings into misplaced assertiveness and aggression.)

Sacrifice facilitates movement between different worlds. It is a ferryboat between heaven and earth.[21] Sacrifice is a *"rite de passage"*[22] (a ferryboat is a *bateau de passage*). The imagery was extensively used in the twentieth century, but it already appears in Luther's comments on Heb 10:19–22, where Christ is the ferryman who transports us safely from this realm to that of heaven.[23]

Sacrifice can also be part of a *rite de passage* in another sense, in that it can facilitate movement at moments of transition in the life of individuals or communities.[24] There is thus a sacrifice associated with birth and with the rite of circumcision. It is striking, however, that there are no such sacrifices associated with other transition events such as puberty, marriage, and death, nor is it the case that the regular Israelite sacrifices belonged in this context. Again, the Day of Atonement takes place in September-October in proximity to the New Year and thus facilitates the transition from one year to the next as God's means of ensuring that one year's failures are eliminated as a new year begins. But it is also striking that Lev 16 and Lev 23, far from making anything of this point, date the Day of Atonement, like other festivals, not by the autumn calendar but by the spring calendar, in which it comes in the seventh month.[25]

---

[19] Cf. Godfrey Ashby, *Sacrifice* (London: SCM, 1988), 1.

[20] Cf. Henri Hubert and Marcel Mauss, *Sacrifice* (Chicago: University of Chicago Press, 1964), 97.

[21] See Ashby, *Sacrifice*, 24–25, quoting Sylvain Lévi, *La doctrine du sacrifice dans les Brâhmaṇas* (2d ed.; Paris: Presses Universitaires de France, 1966).

[22] See A. van Gennep, *The Rites of Passage* (London: Routledge / Chicago: University of Chicago Press, 1960).

[23] Cf. Christopher Cocksworth, "The Cross, Our Worship and Our Living," in *Atonement Today* (ed. John Goldingay; London: SPCK, 1995), 111–27.

[24] See Edmund R. Leach, "The Logic of Sacrifice," in *Anthropological Approaches to the Old Testament* (ed. Bernard Lang; London: SPCK / Philadelphia: Fortress, 1985), 136–50.

[25] See John W. Rogerson, "Sacrifice in the Old Testament," in *Sacrifice* (ed. M. F. C. Bourdillon and Meyer Fortes; London: New York: Academic, 1980), 45–59, for further critique.

Exodus 12 similarly begins by asserting that Passover comes at the beginning of the year, implying that if the Israelite calendar year has a transition point, this occurs in the spring, with Passover as its transition ritual.[26] Passover marks the shift from the old year to the new, symbolized by the clearing out of the old leaven in favor of the new. It also marks the transition from the rainy season/winter to the dry season/summer. Further, and more importantly in the First Testament's explicit commentary, it commemorates the Israelites' passing from bondage to freedom, from Egypt to Canaan, and from death to life. The rite takes place chronologically at the transition point from one day to another, at midnight, and geographically emphasizes the transition point from inside to outside, the door of people's houses where the blood is daubed. Historically and then experientially these transitions are facilitated by means of sacrifice.

Christ relates to us not merely by taking our place in a legal or cultic transaction between humanity and God but by being our "representative or mediator who in his very person presents or mediates God to us and us to God, thus showing the vital differences between the creator and the creation not to be a lethal separation: in and through him we, though mortal beings, live in the eternal community with the immortal God."[27] He "is our substitute because he does for us what we cannot do for ourselves," because we need to have our being formed not by ourselves but by God, but he substitutes for us in order to free us then to be ourselves and to go where he has gone, into God's presence.[28] His death makes possible our movement into God's presence.

In theory, the dying of Christ thus fulfills and terminates any need for special places, rites, castes, or times. In Christian faith there is no longer sanctuary, sacrifice, priesthood, or sabbath, because there is now open access to God for all time, people, and places.

In practice, the Christian church found itself reinventing holy place: churches became the house of God (commonly following the threefold architectural structure of the Jerusalem temple) and not merely convenient places for the temple of God to meet. It reinvented holy time, Sunday as the sabbath and not simply resurrection day. It reinvented holy caste, a structured patriarchy of bishop, priests, and deacons corresponding to that of high priest, priests, and Levites, rather than the more egalitarian male and female apostles, prophets, teachers, and leadership groups of the New Testament. It reinvented holy rites: baptism in the street and eucharist in the home become holy baptism and holy communion.

Is it the same instinct that underlies the notion of eucharistic sacrifice? If we accept the notions of Christian sabbath, priesthood, and church buildings, do we also have to accept that there needs to be some continuing outlet for the God-approved instinct that led to the institution of sacrifice? Or is sacrament enough? Passages

---

[26] So J. B. Segal, *The Hebrew Passover from the Earliest Times to A.D. 70* (London / New York: Oxford University Press, 1963), 186–87.

[27] Ingolf U. Dalferth, "Christ Died for Us," in *Sacrifice and Redemption* (ed. Stephen W. Sykes; New York: Cambridge University Press, 1991), 299–325 (321).

[28] Gunton, *The Actuality of Atonement*, 165–66.

such as Rom 12, Rom 16, and 1 Pet 1 imply that there is indeed a continuing expression of the sacrificial death of Christ, but it is one made in the world rather
than in the church building. Sacrifices are offered in service, proclamation, and
winning people for Christ. If this is so, is there a place in Christian faith for holy
place, holy time, or holy caste? I think not. But then, God has to put up with what
we cannot do without.

4. Sacrifice as a Way of Handling the Violence in the Community

Humanity's first sacrifice leads to humanity's first act of violence, the act that
Genesis itself describes as the occasion of a "fall" and of the first "sin" (Gen 4:5-7).
The essence of sin east of Eden seems to lie in violence; it is for the pursuit of violence that Lamech adapts the first technology and for the glorification of violence
that he adapts the first art (Gen 4:23-24). It is because the world is filled with violence that God determines to destroy it (Gen 6:11-13). The First Testament's hope
is of an era of peace when people are free to sit under their own vine and fig tree.

Animal and human sacrifices by their very nature involve violence on an object
that did not deserve it. The substitutionary aspect to sacrifice is clearest in the Day
of Atonement ritual, where one goat is sacrificed and a scapegoat is driven into
the open country. The rite is an act of catharsis.[29] The link between sacrifice and
violence is also hinted at by the Passover festival, which in Israel's own history with
God begins with a reversal of the violence of Egypt.

In *Violence and the Sacred*, René Girard has made the link with violence the key
to understanding sacrifice. Even less than other understandings is this overt in the
First Testament (in that respect it is reminiscent of Freudian or Marxist understandings of aspects of scripture), but it is a suggestive thesis. Violence has the same con-
tagion as pollution. It has the power to spread its contamination. It is infectious. The
only power that can counter violence is more violence, but then "whether we fail or
succeed in our effort to subdue it, the real victor is always violence itself. . . . The more
men strive to curb their violent impulses, the more these impulses seem to prosper.
The very weapons used to combat violence are turned against their users. Violence
is like a raging fire that feeds on the very objects intended to smother its flames."[30]

Blood speaks of violence and taboo. This may be one reason why even men-
strual blood causes taboo and requires a purification sacrifice, though this perhaps
also hints at a deeper link between sex and violence, hinted at further in a book such
as Judges that interrelates the two so systematically.[31] Our own culture has become
newly aware of the link between sex and violence within marriage and outside it.
"Sexuality leads to quarrels, jealous rages, mortal combats. It is a permanent source

---

[29] Cf. Beattie, "On Understanding Sacrifice," 43.

[30] René Girard, *Violence and the Sacred* (London / Baltimore: Johns Hopkins University
Press, 1977), 31.

[31] See Mieke Bal, *Death and Dissymmetry* (Chicago / London: University of Chicago Press,
1988); cf. further Ricoeur, *The Symbolism of Evil*, e.g., 28, 36, on the link between them in
the symbolism of pollution.

of disorder even within the most harmonious of communities."[32] It is said that rapists are often motivated by a desire to defile and pollute their victims.[33] The nature of the manifold links between blood, sexuality, and violence gives gloomy plausibility to "the proposition that all masculine relationships are based on reciprocal acts of violence"[34] which is disturbingly paralleled by the feminist proposition that violence is a distinctively male problem, the converse of the characteristic female need to emerge from passivity.

Sacrifice channels violence, gives it a legitimated context for ritual expression, and thereby exercises a measure of control over its effects in the community. Sacrifice is thus a means of maintaining order in the community.[35] Sacrifice and violence are therefore alternatives. A community given to violence gives acted testimony to the inefficacy of its sacrifices, as is reflected in the famous contempt for people's sacrifices shown by prophets such as Amos, Micah, Isaiah, and Jeremiah in the midst of communities characterized by violence.[36]

Jesus' death was not effected in a ritual context but in a political one. He was killed by soldiers, not priests. The Torah of course had no place for the sacrifice of a human being.[37] And Jesus was killed as a result of a judicial process: his death was indeed punitive or penal, but to satisfy human rather than divine justice. Whereas sacrificial animals were not killed particularly "violently" (Girard's interpretation looks beneath the surface of what is going on symbolically), Jesus' sacrificial death was a more intrinsically violent event.

Admittedly there are commonly ritual features about an execution, particularly when the charge has a religious aspect, as was the case with Jesus.[38] Jesus' death was a political event but at the same time a religious one because of the interweaving of religion and politics. To say that the people who brought it about were Jews can imply that Jews rather than Gentiles bear responsibility for it, and this can encourage and has encouraged anti-Semitism. To guard against that, it is now common to emphasize that Romans rather than Jews were responsible for Jesus' death. Historically this is a half-truth; Jewish and Roman leaders surely collaborated in the event, and the New Testament attributes responsibility to both parties. Further, there were both Jews and Romans who tried to avoid Jesus being killed; that in itself suggests that responsibility does not lie with a particular national group as such. Theologically the significant point is not nationality but status. Jesus' death was a religio-political event. It was the desire of the members of his own religious group, but in particular of their leaders, who were able to enter into alliance with the political leadership of the imperial power.

---

[32] Girard, *Violence and the Sacred*, 35.

[33] So Gunton, *The Actuality of Atonement*, 119.

[34] Girard, *Violence and the Sacred*, 48.

[35] Cf. Douglas J. Davies, "An Interpretation of Sacrifice in Leviticus," in *Anthropological Approaches to the Old Testament*, 151–62, from an anthropological perspective.

[36] So Girard, *Violence and the Sacred*, 43.

[37] Cf. Gunton, *The Actuality of Atonement*, 122.

[38] Cf. M. F. C. Bourdillon, "Introduction," in *Sacrifice* (ed. M. F. C. Bourdillon and Meyer Fortes; London: New York: Academic, 1980), 13–14, 27.

Jesus did not simply die. He was killed. Now sacrifice intrinsically involved bloodshed and death but not suffering or cruelty. Jesus' death was a deliberately violent, unpleasant event. His killing was an act of violence against him, but not merely for his own sake. He represented God. Whether people recognized it or not, their violence against Jesus was violence against God. "At the cross our human righteousness and piety found themselves ranged in murderous enmity against the God whom they proposed to honor."[39] Certain religious who exhibit "passionist" manifestations present themselves as a sacrifice to the destructive impulse in the world rather than "hitting back";[40] Ann Loades instances Simone Weil.[41] God's own reaction to the violence of the world was to think that the power of evil needs to be neutralized and brought to nothing by being absorbed; hence the significance of Jesus' not defending himself when attacked. Forgiveness is "a certain way of absorbing pain," one that refuses to let it engender bitterness, resentment, hatred, and revenge.[42] God "comes into the world as the 'Innocent Victim'" and "defends and frees victims."[43] In the end the death of the victim had to be a death of this kind of victim and not merely a ritual one. In the end Israelite sacrifices were indeed but types of the real thing.

According to Hosea, God desires commitment not sacrifice, and according to Matthew, Jesus concurs (Hos 6:6; Matt 12:7). Elsewhere Jesus makes the comments that, Mark observes, abolish the categories of cleanliness and pollution (Mark 7:19). Why, then, does God offer and accept the sacrifice of Jesus or accept an interpretation of his death along such lines? Perhaps God is again characteristically condescending to where humanity is: we desire sacrifice, so God gives it, as was the case with the gift of the temple and the institution of the monarchy in Israel. "We strain to glimpse your mercy seat and find you kneeling at our feet."[44]

It is tempting to believe that we live in a time of unprecedented human violence. This includes the political violence of two intercontinental wars, of Vietnam and the Balkans, of Ireland and the Middle East, and of oppression within the USSR and China and within Latin American and African states. The killing of human beings as a ritual sacrifice was an unusual event in the ancient world; the killing of human beings as a metaphorical sacrifice has become a more common phenomenon in the national warfare of the modern world. The violence of our time also includes interpersonal violence, in particular marital violence, sexual violence, and parental violence, but also violence in connection with theft, and police violence.

The fact that we belong to such a violent humanity must give great significance for us to the fact that the First Testament understanding of human life gives a

---

[39] Lesslie Newbigin, *The Open Secret* (Grand Rapids: Eerdmans, 1978 / London: SPCK, 1979), 200.

[40] M. Masterman, "The Psychology of Levels of Will," *Proceedings of the Aristotelian Society* n.s. 48 (1947–48): 75–110H (88).

[41] "Eucharistic Sacrifice," in *Sacrifice and Redemption* (ed. Stephen W. Sykes; New York: Cambridge University Press, 1991), 247–61 (247–48).

[42] Leonard Hodgson, *The Doctrine of Atonement* (London: Nisbet / New York: Scribner's, 1951), 63–64.

[43] James G. Williams, *The Bible, Violence, and the Sacred* (San Francisco: Harper, 1991), 2.

[44] Brian Wren, from the hymn "Lord God, Your Love Has Called Us Here," in *Faith Looking Forward* (Oxford / New York: Oxford University Press, 1983).

prominent place to national and interpersonal violence. Its spirituality is a spirituality of violence, one whose prayer often focuses on violence received and seeks for God to reverse it. In talking about the Psalms, I often find people offended at their violence, but I then suspect that this reflects their not having come to terms with the violence in their own spirits. The real problem lies not in the presence of violence and anger in the Psalms but in their presence within and among us, so that the Psalter is attuned to what goes on among us: there is "an acute correspondence between what is written there and what is practiced here."[45] The Torah and the Psalms offered people the opportunity to face their violence and anger and to express it in ritual and in words rather than in ordinary actions. The cross is also God's affirmative response to the Psalms' prayer for violence.

If ours is a time of unprecedented violence, might it be no coincidence that it is also an unprecedentedly post-Christian time? "When the religious framework of a society starts to totter, it is not exclusively or immediately the physical security of the society that is threatened; rather, the whole cultural foundation of the society is put in jeopardy. The institutions lose their vitality; the protective facade of the society gives way; social values are rapidly eroded, and the whole cultural structure seems on the verge of collapse. The hidden violence of the sacrificial crisis eventually succeeds in destroying distinctions, and this destruction in turn fuels the renewed violence. In short, it seems that anything that adversely affects the institution of sacrifice will ultimately pose a threat to the very basis of the community, to the principles on which its social harmony and equilibrium depend."[46] Might the preaching of the cross as God's once-and-for-all absorbing of human violence be the key to the peace of the world? But does that preaching first have to be heard by the Christian community (that locus of violence), so that it may then be preached in its life?

People in Christian ministry are often on the receiving end of anger and violence, much of it transferred from the appropriate object.[47] The first temptation for them, as for anyone else, is to retaliate. The second temptation is by superhuman effort to absorb and neutralize the violence and thereby end the cycle of violence. It is a temptation, because the mere effort to imitate Jesus, at this point as at others, is ultimately bound to fail. There needs to be an intimate interrelation between this imitation and Jesus' own atoning death that enables us to pass on the violence and anger to Jesus on the basis of his having already absorbed it, rather than keeping it within ourselves where it can continue its negative work.

5. Sacrifice as an Image for Today

According to a common understanding noted above, human beings are on one side of a chasm and God is on the other side. The chasm is caused by human sin.

---

[45] Walter Brueggemann, *Praying the Psalms* (Winona, Minn.: St Mary's Press, 1982), 68.
[46] Girard, *Violence and the Sacred*, 49.
[47] I owe this point and the seed thought of what follows to my former colleague Colin Hart.

Alongside that is the implication that God relates to humanity chiefly as a judge, with justice and judges understood in a Western sense: the key point about justice is treating everyone the same, and a judge's key role is to safeguard standards of justice. God therefore cannot relate to us because of our legal guilt, which makes it necessary for us to be punished. In terms of the picture, human beings cannot cross the chasm except by means of Christ as bridge. This works within the legal image because he bears the legal punishment for sin, thereby making it possible for God the judge to relate to us.

From a First Testament perspective, this looks unscriptural as well as unlikely to aid the proper preaching of the gospel. Both issue from the way it emphasizes the image of God as lawgiver and judge. Although God is indeed both of those, the First Testament does not draw the same inferences from the fact. As lawgiver, God is entirely free to pardon people if they repent. And as judge, God is committed to taking the side of people in the context of relationship, even when they are in the wrong. This understanding emphasizes a more relational understanding of God than the Christian one. Thus Jewish theologians contrast faith within Judaism, which is a matter of a relationship of trust, and faith within Christianity, which is a matter of believing correct doctrine.

Although Christians link sacrifice and atonement with law and punishment, as if an animal (or a person) that is sacrificed is being punished in someone else's place, the First Testament does not link sacrifice with legal categories. And although a price has to be paid before someone is forgiven, this need not be understood in a legal way. A more relational understanding of God fits scripture better and seems more likely to bring the gospel home to people who think more relationally. In Christian doctrine, it fits Irenaeus's understanding of God the Father as one who faces us holding out two arms, Christ and the Spirit, to embrace us. This is different from the picture of the angry Father placated by the nice Jesus.

The First Testament has a number of relational pictures of God, as friend of Abraham, as husband of Jerusalem, as next of kin (restorer/redeemer—*go'el*) of a needy relative, as mother/father in relation to son/daughter. Those relational First Testament images may help us understand what Christ achieved on the cross.

a) In 1969, Eric Clapton fell in love with the wife of his best friend, George Harrison, and wrote about her the song "Layla," "the most tortured rock song about unrequited love" (Paul Gambaccini), and eventually stole her from Harrison. Whereas one would have expected Harrison at very least never to want to talk to Clapton again, they stayed as friends. That implies that Harrison absorbed within himself the pain of what Clapton did and the anger it surely aroused. Their friendship could therefore survive the wrong. (I do not know whether this is what Harrison did, but the story nevertheless illustrates the point.)

b) Imagine a professor coming home after a faculty meeting. It has reinforced her feelings of being powerless, underpaid, undervalued, and put down. She thus acts "crabby" in relation to her husband, who has been cooking the dinner and looking forward to enjoying a glass of wine with her. She complains that the curry is too hot and the wine isn't properly chilled. He has two choices. He can respond in kind, "I've been here slaving over your dinner, and all you do is complain." Or he can lean into the wind and absorb the bitterness that he did not earn. He can wait till it is used up and thus look for the moment when they can relate to each other because it is gone.

c) The year I went to university, my sister married a man who my parents thought was no good. Six years later he abandoned her just after their first baby was born. Our parents had enjoyed the opportunity to begin a new life after their children had left home, but they welcomed her and her baby back home. Without a murmur they reshaped their life again so that my sister could go to work while my mother looked after the baby, and they helped her gradually to get back to independence as a single parent. They acted as parents and next of kin to her, paying the price to redeem/restore her.

d) The Hebrew word most commonly translated "forgive" is a word whose ordinary meaning is "carry."[48] This is a fair description of what parents do for their children's wrongdoing, and it is what God was doing with Israel through First Testament times. It was a process that came to its climax with the cross, which is the logical end to the First Testament story. Thus, seeing the way the relationship between God and Israel worked helps us see why the cross was necessary. Through God's life with Israel God was paying the price for that relationship, making the sacrifices to keep it going. God's people keep doing their worst to God, so eventually God paid the ultimate price for them. God showed that even killing God cannot put God off from relating to them. God will just come back from the dead.

That is the nature of sacrifice and the nature of what Christ did for us in making atonement.

---

[48] See further chapter 2 above.

11

WHY CIRCUMCISION?

1. The Puzzle and the Problem

Of the signs of the covenants, circumcision is the most troubling.[1] It is no less uninterpreted than other rites, and to the Western mind it is no stranger than rites such as sacrifice, which itself seems more troubling in the light of developing "animal theology."[2] A feeling that it has its amusing side may be an ancient as well as a modern one, and a feeling that can turn circumcision into black comedy (see Gen 34:25). But it is troubling because it is the most exclusive of covenant signs; most can apply to everyone, but circumcision (at least this particular rite of circumcision) applies only to males.

The point is made forcefully by Judith Plaskow in dialogue with Michael Wyschogrod. Over against the unbodily, flesh-denying, world-denying spirituality of Christian faith, Wyschogrod emphasizes the flesh-affirming, world-affirming bodiliness of Judaism. God's election takes seriously the embodied, corporeal life of the Jewish people. God requires "the sanctification of human existence in all of its aspects." And circumcision is the core symbol of this election, "a searing of the covenant into the flesh of Israel and not only, or perhaps not even primarily, into its spirit."[3]

But this leaves Jewish womanhood in a systematically ambiguous position. Women represent Israel's unredeemed flesh.[4] Indeed, it has been suggested that the Priestly narrative in Genesis especially emphasizes circumcision precisely because it epitomizes male privilege in worship[5] or because it safeguards patrilineal descent.[6] Subsequently, circumcision "has symptomatized a deep gender dichotomy in the course of rabbinic Jewish history"; it was men who emphasized the rite of circumcision as the symbol of "a covenant presupposed as existing between men and

---

[1] First published as "The Significance of Circumcision," in *JSOT* 88 (2000): 3–18.
[2] See chapter 21 below.
[3] *The Body of Faith* (repr., San Francisco: Harper, 1989), 67.
[4] Judith Plaskow, *Standing Again at Sinai* (San Francisco: Harper, 1991), 82–84.
[5] So R. B. Coote, "The Book of Joshua," *The New Interpreter's Bible* (ed. L. E. Keck et al.; 13 vols.; Nashville: Abingdon, 1998), 2:553–719 (see 608).
[6] See the general argument regarding priesthood and sacrifice in N. B. Jay, *Throughout Your Generations Forever* (Chicago / London: University of Chicago Press, 1992).

God, a covenant . . . to which women are party only in a secondary way, through their relationship with fathers and then husbands." "Circumcision was a rite of masculine status bestowal in which one man, the father, initiates a man-to-be, his son, into the covenant with God (conceived as a man)."[7]

There have been various attempts to take the edge off the significance of circumcision's gender exclusiveness. V. P. Hamilton suggests that because two people become "one flesh" (Gen 2:24), only one of them needs the mark of the covenant.[8] This is not convincing. Alice Laffey suggests that the First Testament's emphasis on the importance of metaphorical circumcision (of mind and lips) takes the edge off the confinement of the covenant sign to males; inner circumcision is open to both sexes.[9] We will have cause to note that this advantage has a down side; metaphorical circumcision is introduced with a two-edged sword. Again, the horrific consequences of female circumcision might make us grateful that circumcision was confined to males; feminist critique would take a different form and would be much sharper if Israel had circumcised females. But this heightens rather than reduces the question why the sign of the covenant was one best confined to males.

The mystery of circumcision increases when one reviews the First Testament's major references to it, especially in connection with the great figures of Abraham, Moses, and Joshua. In the account of its origin in Gen 17, God simply tells Abraham that circumcision is required, and the narrative relates its immediate application to Abraham's family and household (in 21:4 we are later assured that Isaac was also circumcised). It is clear that circumcision is to be an indispensable mark of being a (male) member of the people of promise (cf. Exod 12:44, 48; Lev 12:3). But it is not clear why. Indeed, it is not explicit whether circumcision is a sign for God, or a sign for its recipients, or both, though I incline to the last view.

The circumcision story in Exod 4:24–26 is notoriously enigmatic; it has stimulated a wide variety of theories regarding its origin and meaning but no consensus on the most basic questions.[10] That the circumcision story in Josh 5:2–9 raises difficulties is reflected in the textual tradition itself, where for the first time in Joshua the Masoretic Hebrew Text is significantly longer than the Old Greek text.[11] The latter suggests that some people left Egypt uncircumcised, implying that circumcision had not been properly administered there. The Hebrew Text reassures us that circumcision had been properly practiced in Egypt, but not during the wilderness journey, though it does not make clear why this was so, and it perhaps introduces a further unclarity regarding what the "shame" of Egypt consisted in. Nor is it clear in what sense people were being circumcised for a second time (so the Hebrew Text), and why. J. M. Sasson suggests that the second circumcision was a more radical version of the operation than the one applied in Egypt, cutting off skin rather than merely

---

[7]L. A. Hoffman, *Covenant of Blood* (Chicago / London: University of Chicago Press, 1996), 2, 26, 80.

[8]*The Book of Genesis Chapters 1–17* (Grand Rapids: Eerdmans, 1990), 470.

[9]*An Introduction to the Old Testament* (Philadelphia: Fortress, 1988), 62–64.

[10]See now Athena E. Gorospe, *Narrative and Identity* (Leiden / Boston: Brill, 2007).

[11]See conveniently R. D. Nelson, *Joshua* (Louisville: Westminster John Knox / London: SCM, 1997), 72–77.

slitting it.[12] But during the First Testament period Israelite circumcision itself seems to have been of a not very radical kind. It was Jewish attempts to reverse it in the Greek period that led to the introduction of the version with which we are familiar, involving the exposure of the crown of the penis and not merely the cutting off of the foreskin.

2. The Disciplining of Sexuality

Biblical scholarship has generally assumed that we need to dig beneath the surface of the text if we are to understand it, and the digging has produced an impressive variety of theories about the religious history of the rite, especially in connection with Exod 4. But the variety depresses as well as impresses. Apart from not producing any consensus, this form of digging does not seem destined to produce any usable results. Thus Athena Gorospe focuses on studying Exod 4:24–26 in its narrative context in light of the work of Paul Ricoeur.[13]

Since the time of Sigmund Freud other writers have attempted psychological excavation of circumcision instead of religio-historical excavation, and my aim here is to try a version of that, informed by feminist questions and interests, of the kind that has produced creative results in connection with some other passages that may be related. Perhaps this may turn out to have the "power to make intelligible that which had been unintelligible."[14]

This has worked elsewhere. J. C. Exum suggests that we move the focus of the stories of the patriarch passing off his wife as his sister to the questions, "Why should Israelites tell this story three times? What issue are they enabling to come to the surface?" Her answer is that they give expression to male ambiguity about their wives' sexuality.[15] Telling the story then gives men the opportunity to speak indirectly about an issue that is hard to discuss directly. But the cat is now out of the bag.

I. L. Rashkow offers a parallel reading of the stories of Noah and his son and Lot and his daughters.[16] The reticence of the first story prevents our knowing whether it implies a sexual relationship between Noah and Ham, while the second story attributes the initiative in events to Lot's daughters, but if we again ask, "Why should Israelites tell such stories? What issues are they enabling to find expression?" then the answer that suggests itself, in parallel with the first example, is that they give expression to fathers' ambiguity about the sexuality of their children. Telling these stories, too, gives men the opportunity to speak indirectly about an issue that is hard to discuss directly and that (we have become aware, over recent years) desperately needs discussing.

---

[12] "Circumcision in the Ancient Near East," *JBL* 85 (1966): 473–76.

[13] See *Narrative and Identity*.

[14] Jay's claim for her feminist anthropological interpretation of sacrifice (*Throughout Your Generations Forever*, 97).

[15] "Who's Afraid of 'The Endangered Ancestress'?" in *Fragmented Women* (JSOTSup 163; Sheffield: Sheffield Academic Press, 1993), 148–69.

[16] "Daddy-dearest and the 'Invisible Spirit of Wine,'" in *Genesis* (ed. A. Brenner; The Feminist Companion to the Bible II/1; Sheffield: Sheffield Academic Press, 1998), 82–107.

These strange stories about circumcision are open to an analogous reading. They witness to subconscious awareness of issues regarding male sexuality. This is not the whole truth about circumcision; its nature as a rite in itself perhaps precludes the idea of its having one meaning, for rites tend to be multivalent. But this reading opens up part of its meaning, the evidence being that it makes sense of some otherwise puzzling features of the biblical material. Looking at them in this way does not solve their religio-historical problems, but it does suggest one answer to the question why Israel preserved these religio-historical mysteries, and it enables us to bring out into the open the issues to which they give indirect expression.

Way below the surface, requiring and accepting circumcision may be merciful alternatives to requiring and accepting castration,[17] but the stories themselves point to more concrete concerns with male sexuality. They point to the disciplining of procreation, of sexual activity itself, and of masculinity. It is then a nice fact that circumcision is not merely a covenant sign for Israel alone but the sign of a covenant with all Abraham's descendants (the descendants of Ishmael as well as Isaac, of Esau as well as Jacob, and of the foreigners who lived in their households). It is not only Israelite men who need this sign.

Having formulated this view of circumcision's significance, I was humbled to find much of it anticipated in Philo of Alexandria's typically systematic and instructive consideration of the matter. At the opening of his study of "The Specific Laws" (I.1–11 [I.i–ii]) he notes six reasons for the practice. The traditional rationales are that circumcision avoids infection, contributes to hygiene, symbolizes the disciplining of the whole person's creativity, and encourages fertility. Philo's additional suggestions are that it symbolizes sexual discipline in particular and cuts back human pride in the capacity to procreate. It is further interesting to be told that "four interrelated themes are frequently embedded in African rites of circumcision: fertility, virility, maturity, and genealogy."[18]

3. The Disciplining of Procreation

On its first appearance in Gen 17, it seems plausible that circumcision signifies the disciplining of procreation. K. E. and J. M. Paige have apparently suggested that circumcision was a ritual that tested a man's trust in his wider community, as he lets his son be circumcised and thus lets this son's reproductive potential be both threatened if the operation goes wrong and realized if it is effective.[19] This precise rationale must lie somewhat behind Gen 17, for here Abraham does the

---

[17] So Sigmund Freud, *Moses and Monotheism* (New York: Knopf, 1939), 192. For such theories which he calls "reductionist," see Hoffman, *Covenant of Blood*, 28, and n. 5; but see also I. N. Rashkow, *The Phallacy of Genesis* (Louisville: Westminster John Knox, 1993), esp. 92–93.

[18] Howard Eilberg-Schwartz, *The Savage in Judaism* (Bloomington: Indiana University Press, 1990), 144.

[19] So according to R. B. Coote and D. B. Ord, *In the Beginning* (Minneapolis: Fortress, 1988), 68–70, referring to *The Politics of Reproductive Ritual* (Berkeley: University of Cali-

circumcising on a son who is a baby, but the general suggestion of a link with procreation fits the context and matches the extension of circumcision thinking to fruit trees (Lev 19:23–25). The covenant with Abraham here seals the promise of progeny; this promise dominates Gen 17 as it does not Gen 12 or 15.

Historically it seems that the circumcision of infants is a distinctive Israelite version of a rite practiced widely among Semitic peoples and elsewhere, but here it becomes a sign of God's covenant commitment to the individual and his acceptance of that commitment, even though he has no say in the matter.[20] M. G. Kline thus sees the act of cutting as symbolizing the cutting off that he wishes upon himself for failure to keep the covenant; it carries an implicit "God do thus to me, and more."[21] The application of the sign to the organ of generation suggests specifically the cutting off of one's descendants but also the consecration of one's descendants.[22]

It would be a frightening oath. The covenant sign requires the cutting not of some random part of the body such as the hair, or the piercing of the nose, nor an operation such as the piercing of the ear, which might have had huge symbolic significance in terms of a commitment to listening to Yahweh. It requires the cutting of the part of the male body through which God's promise will be fulfilled. "God is demanding that Abram concede, symbolically, that fertility is not his own to exercise without divine let or hindrance. A physical reduction in the literal superabundance of Abram's penis is a sign with an intrinsic relationship to what it signifies. . . . The organ and the power behind it now belong partly to God."[23] It is striking that this assertion on God's part follows on Abram and Sarai's taking the initiative in the exercise of the power and the organ in Gen 16.

In a traditional society, the disciplining of procreation may thus relate in particular to male desire for male offspring who will both signify achievement and status (cf. Job 1:2; 42:13) and will also in real terms add to economic power. The disciplining of procreation puts such instincts under God's sovereignty, which could have the capacity to be a protection, for instance, both to a woman who could not have children and to one who all too easily could. In a modern society its significance might be the reverse. The original blessing of procreation designed to encourage it to fill the earth has been more than fulfilled, and the capacity to procreate needs disciplining. On the micro-level that is also true in the context of the breakdown of social structure in an urban society such as the one where I live (where the prevalence of the fatherless family has led to advertisements on buses to remind men that fatherhood is forever).

According to the common view, "circumcision was originally and essentially a fertility device associated with puberty and marriage."[24] If circumcision were administered at puberty, then in particular it might suggest the disciplining of

fornia Press, 1981). Eilberg-Schwartz (*The Savage in Judaism*, 141–76) especially emphasizes the procreative significance of circumcision.

[20] Cf. N. M. Sarna, *Genesis* (Philadelphia: Jewish Publication Society, 1989), 386.

[21] See further chapter 9 above, § 2.

[22] *By Oath Consigned* (Grand Rapid: Eerdmans, 1968), 39–49 (86–89).

[23] J. Miles, *God: A Biography* (London / New York: Simon and Schuster, 1995), 53, 90.

[24] M. V. Fox, "The Sign of the Covenant," *RB* 81 (1974): 557–96 (see 591).

sexuality. Now after the birth of Isaac, the first mention of circumcision in the First Testament comes in the story of the hapless Shechemites in Gen 34. In light of this aspect of the possible implicit significance of circumcision, the story carries some irony. Shechem has demonstrated that his sexuality is not circumcised, and it may seem quite appropriate for Jacob's sons to require his circumcising (along with that of the other men in his family) before he can marry their sister.[25] But that is not Jacob's sons' concern. For them, circumcision is merely the means to a wholly other end. It has become "a means of social control and exploitation."[26]

4. The Disciplining of Machismo

Circumcision next features in the supremely enigmatic Exod 4:24–26. Yahweh has commissioned Moses to go back to Egypt and to begin confronting Pharaoh so that he will let Israel leave Egypt. On the way back there, "Yahweh met him and tried to kill him." A story about a threat to the life of Moses' and Zipporah's son would fit well in the context in general, but the specific preceding context suggests that "him" must be Moses, and the specific reference to their son that follows confirms this, but perhaps it makes little difference. Zipporah takes decisive action. She circumcises her son and touches Moses' legs (which might or might not be a euphemism for genitals) with her son's foreskin, and says, "You really are a bloody bridegroom for me."[27] Then Yahweh let Moses alone. Only here is the bloodiness of circumcision noted and a link therefore hinted with bloodiness as a means of pollution and blood as a means of expiation. The Septuagint and the Targum thus assume that the blood has expiatory significance.[28] The smeared blood is graphic evidence that the child's blood has been shed.[29] The preceding reference to Moses' killing the Egyptian might hint at the reason why he needed a quasi-expiatory rite;

---

[25] Cf. Sarna, *Genesis*, 236.

[26] Walter Brueggemann, *Genesis* (Atlanta: John Knox, 1982), 278.

[27] A translation such as "a blood-circumcised one" (referring to the boy, not to Moses) would be easier in the context and has been argued, e.g., by J. de Groot, "The Story of the Bloody Husband," *OtSt* 2 (1943): 10–17 (see 13), H. Kosmala, "The 'Bloody Husband,'" *VT* 12 (1962): 14–28 (see 27), and E. Kutsch in his article on *khtn* in *Theological Dictionary to the Old Testament*, on the basis of the link between its root and an Arabic cognate meaning "circumcise." But Brevard S. Childs (*Exodus* [London: SCM, 1974] = *The Book of Exodus* [Philadelphia: Westminster Press, 1974], 98) makes the crucial point that in Arabic the verb refers not to circumcision in general but to the circumcising of a bridegroom. T. C. Mitchell ("The Meaning of the Noun *ḥtn* in the Old Testament," *VT* 19 [1969]: 93–112) concludes that the word means a relative by marriage, and B. P. Robinson ("Zipporah to the Rescue," *VT* 36 [1986]: 447–61 [457–58]) argues that here it describes Moses as a son-in-law by virtue of blood, because circumcision was a father-in-law's task.

[28] See Geza Vermes, "Baptism and Jewish Exegesis," *New Testament Studies* 4 (1957–58): 308–19 (see 310–13); J. D. Levenson, *The Death and Resurrection of the Beloved Son* (New Haven, Conn. / London: Yale University Press, 1993), 50–52. For subsequent Judaism, see Hoffman, *Covenant of Blood.*

[29] J. Morgenstern, "The 'Bloody Husband' (?) (Exod 4:24–26) Once Again," *HUCA* 34 (1963): 35–70 (see 70); though he thinks it is the child whom Yahweh seeks to kill.

blood guilt attached to him.[30] That is then why he is an in-law characterized by bloodiness. His son's blood has cleansed him from his bloodiness.[31]

If we read the Torah as we have it, clearly Moses is in breach of the crucial covenant requirement in Gen 17. If Zipporah's action implies Moses is also uncircumcised, that is also odd. Moses, and perhaps his father, have neglected to administer the sign of covenant commitment. Moses is "in peril of the curse that was invoked against him in his own circumcision."[32] On a traditional critical view of the Pentateuch, we have had no instruction regarding circumcision in the pre-P narrative of Israel's story up to Moses' day. But the narrative would be quite capable of presupposing the practice nevertheless, and it may thus still imply that Moses' or his son's being uncircumcised is somewhat odd. Or, in the case of the son it may assume some defensible explanation (see Josh 5:2–7, even if the logic there is obscure).[33] But in any case the narrative does not indicate that the uncircumcised state of Moses or his son is the reason for God's attack. As is the case with God's acceptance of Abel, and God's attack on Jacob, and God's later confrontation of Balaam, we may be able to infer reasons from hints in the context,[34] but that is all, and it suggests that the point of the story may lie somewhere else.[35]

What issues regarding maleness might be expressed in this enigmatic story or might have led to its preserving? In the modern world we are familiar with the assumption that a man's sexual instinct is for him a symbol of his manliness, his machismo. While Gen 16 marks Abraham as needing the circumcising of his manliness in the narrowly reproductive sense, it also provides some of the evidence that in general Abraham was something of a wimp (see, e.g., Gen 16:2, 6) and had less need of the circumcising of his manliness in this connection. Robinson suggests that Yahweh attacks Moses because of a continuing annoyance at his wimpishness (Exod 4:14a).[36] But the instructions and events that follow (Exod 4:14b–23) constitute the resolving of this matter. It is they, not Moses' resistance to being drafted, which provide the background to Yahweh's attack. Moses has already proved himself a more macho figure than Abraham (Exod 2:11–13, 17). Yahweh's instructions to Moses (Exod 4:19) have referred to the exercise in machismo that got him into trouble and to the fact that the people who might have brought restraint to this instinct are now dead. So perhaps his vicarious circumcision has this symbolic

---

[30] So P. Middlekoop, "The Significance of the Story of the 'Bloody Husband,'" *South East Asia Journal of Theology* 8/4 (1966–67): 34–38 (see 35).

[31] W. H. Propp ("That Bloody Bridegroom," *VT* 43 [1993]: 495–518 [501–6]) provides a detailed but rather speculative account of precisely how this logic worked in the minds of the narrator and the audience.

[32] Kline, *By Oath Consigned*, 88.

[33] Cf. Umberto Cassuto, *A Commentary on the Book of Exodus* (Jerusalem: Magnes, 1967), 59.

[34] See, e.g., Robinson, "Zipporah to the Rescue," 456–57.

[35] Walter Brueggemann thus comments that the story witnesses to the deep, untamed holiness of God and to the risk involved in coming close to this God or being this God's servant ("The Book of Exodus," *The New Interpreter's Bible* (Nashville: Abingdon, 1994), 1:675–981 (see 718, 720).

[36] "Zipporah to the Rescue," 456.

significance. His attack by Yahweh demonstrates an irony in Yahweh's statement about the death of all the human beings who had sought his life. This does not solve all Moses' problems; Yahweh now seeks his death (the verb "sought" recurs). This happens at a moment resembling Yahweh's fight with Jacob, at night on a crucial journey. Jacob was a man who was literally circumcised but whose character was never subjected to Yahweh's constraint, even after the fight that Yahweh wins only by hitting below the belt. The symbolism and the parallelism will be the more powerful if Yahweh's attack was aimed at Jacob's genitals.[37] In Jacob's case, as in Moses', the timing means that Yahweh is not asserting authority over Jacob's capacity to procreate,[38] but he could well be asserting authority over his masculinity.[39]

As Yahweh had once taken on the "old" Jacob, so now Yahweh takes on the "old" Moses, yet again in such a way as not to overwhelm him by divine firepower. "Yahweh tried to kill him": what does that say about Moses' will to live, Moses' machismo? But the old Moses must die and a Moses under Yahweh's control be born. If he will not agree to that, his vicarious circumcision by Zipporah will symbolize it. "The blood of circumcision is a symbolic acknowledgment that a man's masculinity belongs to God."[40] Perhaps after this encounter Moses becomes a decisive figure instead of someone who shirks God's call and incurs God's wrath, rather than that after this encounter Moses is prepared to submit his decisiveness to Yahweh.[41] Perhaps it makes little difference why Moses' machismo needs to be circumcised: either he needs to be prepared to act the man for Yahweh's sake or he needs to be held back from acting the man for his own sake.

It is nice that a woman has the opportunity to be involved in making the point. She is a sister to the women in Exod 1–2[42] and to the mothers over far distant centuries who will have "brought their children, held them during the rite, had prayers said for their recovery from childbirth, and drunk some of the wine intended for their recuperation" until circumcision was turned into a male-only ritual.[43] If Moses' capacity to resist being killed by God suggests his strength, Zipporah's capacity to resist the loss of her husband and find the way to avoid this loss suggests hers. Perhaps it is in her interests to have her husband's masculinity subordinated to God.

The act of circumcision in Exod 4 is a rite of passage: Moses, Zipporah, and their son(s) are on the way from Midian to Egypt, as Jacob had been on the way back from Syria to Israel. The same is true of the act of circumcision in Josh 5. Indeed, the moments when Abraham, Moses, and Joshua's people are circumcised

---

[37] So S. Gevirtz, "Of Patriarchs and Puns," *HUCA* 46 (1975): 33–54 (see 52–53).

[38] So S. H. Smith, "Sexuality in the Jacob-Esau Narratives," *VT* 40 (1990): 464–73 (see 466–69).

[39] Cf. H. Eilberg-Schwartz, *God's Phallus* (Boston: Beacon, 1994), 154–56.

[40] Ibid., 160.

[41] So Robinson, "Zipporah to the Rescue," 452. In contrast, Middlekoop ("The Significance of the Story of the 'Bloody Husband,'" 37) notes the contrast between the Moses of Exod 2 and the supremely "meek" Moses of Num 12:3.

[42] Cf. C. Houtman, "Exodus 4:24–26," *Journal of Northwest Semitic Languages* 11 (1983): 81–103 (see 102).

[43] Hoffman, *Covenant of Blood*, 207.

are all moments when God is in the midst of fulfilling a creative purpose—to give Abraham and Sarah children, to bring Israel out of Egypt, to give Israel its land. In each story the protagonists have taken some action—begetting a child by means of Hagar, killing an Egyptian, crossing the Jordan. In each story their key work and the fulfillment of God's promises in an impossible event is imminent—the begetting of Isaac, the victory over Pharaoh, the conquest of Jericho. In each story the cutting back of the flesh with its potency might imply the subordinating of human strength to the divine plan. Joshua 5 may imply that "only a circumcised Israel could become a conquering Israel."[44] More immediately, only a circumcised Israel could celebrate Passover. Exodus 4 perhaps links implicitly with Exod 12:48, and neither Moses nor his son can be imagined taking part in that first Passover if uncircumcised, but the two rites are juxtaposed in Josh 5.

5. The Disciplining of Men

Beyond these stories about physical circumcision in the Hexateuch, the Torah and the Prophets also make a number of references to metaphorical circumcision. Although the rite of circumcision itself, like many other rites, is not explicitly interpreted, like other rites it seems likely always to have been a practice with a significance. It was a symbol and not merely a sign.[45] G. von Rad comments that circumcision must surely have been implicitly an act of bodily purification and dedication; otherwise it could hardly have become a metaphor for inner circumcision.[46] Within Gen 17, G. J. Wenham suggests a link with the call to live whole before God (Gen 17:2).[47] Sarna goes further and insists that it inherently "betokened dedication and commitment to God."[48]

If this is right, then passages referring to metaphorical circumcision do not spiritualize what was earlier a "merely" external rite, though they may extend the rite's inherent symbolic significance. Indeed, the talk of metaphorical circumcision is probably as old as the talk of literal circumcision. While the rite of circumcision apparently goes back to the time of Israel's ancestors, it does not become a sign of the covenant until the time of the Priestly writing. This at least belongs to the same period as the passages about metaphorical circumcision and may be later than most of them. There is no development whereby the physical comes to be taken for granted and emphasis is removed to the spiritual.

Moses sees himself as someone of uncircumcised lips (Exod 6:12, 30), one who has not been trained to speak; it would not be surprising if the man who is hasty to action is also inclined to speak before his brain is engaged. God fears that the people as a whole will turn out to be uncircumcised in mind (Lev 26:41); they will not

---

[44] So T. C. Butler, *Joshua* (Waco, Tex.: Word, 1983), 56.

[45] Cf. the discussion in Hans-Jürgen Hermisson, *Sprache und Ritus im altisraelitischen Kult* (Neukirchen: Neukirchener, 1965), 64–76.

[46] *Genesis* (2d ed.; London: SCM / Philadelphia: Westminster Press, 1963), 196.

[47] *Genesis 16–50* (Dallas: Word, 1994), 24.

[48] *Genesis*, 387.

have the mental and spiritual discipline to live in accordance with God's teaching. Moses himself urges them to circumcise themselves mentally and spiritually and not be resistant to God's teaching (Deut 10:16) and promises that God will do that for them (Deut 30:6). Jeremiah issues the same exhortation to people and warns of the trouble to come to peoples who are merely physically circumcised—including Israel (Jer 4:4; 9:25). They need their ears circumcised (Jer 6:10). With some irony, then, Ezekiel has Yahweh insisting that foreigners must be circumcised both spiritually and physically if they are to enter Yahweh's sanctuary (Ezek 44:7, 9). Thus, Paul argues, a Jew who is circumcised externally but not inwardly ceases to be a real Jew (Rom 2:25–29).

A sign applied only to males thus provides a metaphor for the need to be trained and disciplined if one is to speak well and to live well. What might this imply?

Let us put alongside it an interesting feature of the New Testament story. To the chagrin of a feminist, Jesus appoints only men as members of the group of twelve whom he gathers round him as the nucleus of a renewed Israel. But to the relief of the feminist, there turns out to be method or at least irony in his omission. The twelve male representatives of Israel misunderstand Jesus, betray him, and abandon him. At the moment when he sets about his most decisive act in achieving that renewal of Israel, he is accompanied only by a large crowd of women (Mark 15:40–41). It is some of them who are also the first people to discover that the tomb is empty and who are commissioned to tell the men that Jesus has been raised to a transformed life and has gone off to Galilee, where they will also see him in due course (Mark 16:1–7). The events that follow Jesus' appointment of the twelve men thus explode any suggestion that there is something distinctive about men that provides a positive qualification for their being the exclusive leaders of the renewed Israelite community.[49]

A similar implication emerges from the First Testament references to physical and metaphorical circumcision. It starts off (in the order of the text itself) looking like a sign establishing that full membership of the Israelite community belongs especially to males. I say "it starts off" as such, referring to the order within the text itself; we have noted that historically this seems to have been a Priestly innovation. In origin, full membership of Israel did not depend on accepting a sign that by its nature could apply only to males. But it becomes (again, following the order of the text) a sign of a disciplined-ness that the Israelite community lacks. The very fact that it is the males who bear this sign means that it is the males who embody spiritual and mental unfitness to belong to the people of promise.

It is further suggestive that this sign is one the male bears in his sexual organ. Abraham was supposed to see the fulfillment of God's promise through his sexual activity, but before this happens his sexual activity is the means whereby he seeks to engineer his own fulfillment of God's promise. His antitype, David, notoriously

---

[49] See, e.g., E. Moltmann-Wendel, *The Women Around Jesus* (London: SCM / New York: Crossroad, 1987), 109–13; *A Land Flowing with Milk and Honey* (London: SCM / New York: Crossroad, 1986), 82–83.

fails Yahweh in his sexual activity (2 Sam 11), being a true descendant of Judah (Gen 38). David's son, Solomon, the great temple builder, does the same in his own way (1 Kgs 11). Proverbs suggests that the distinctively male sin is sexual failure (e.g., Prov 5:16–23). Job begins his claim to having lived a wholly committed life by declaring that he has not "looked on a virgin" (Job 31:1).

Moses is the exception who proves the rule. There are no skeletons in his sexual cupboard (none that Exodus-Deuteronomy exposes!), except whatever is the one implied by Exod 4. But that failure would suggest he had not taken seriously the significance of the sign of circumcision. It draws attention to the fact that men in particular lack the moral and spiritual commitment and discipline that make holiness possible (no more than women, no doubt, though they have sometimes implied that women are the origin of sin) and that their sexuality is a focus of this lack. It is a potentially fatal failure on Moses' part, and God confronts him with it in a potentially fatal way. For this reason, turning circumcision into a metaphor for discipline of mind and speech may have the advantage of letting the sign apply metaphorically to women, but it has the disadvantage of robbing circumcision of its cutting edge with regard to men. In letting women in, it lets men off. Indeed, perhaps Christian abandonment of circumcision was a mistake. The Christian church needs its symbolism.

If God gives men this sign of a covenant commitment despite—even because of—their lack of that commitment and discipline and on the basis of the focus of this lack, there is indeed hope for them and for the world. But they can no more make their receiving this sign a basis for claims to authority that exclude women than they can make such claims on the basis of Jesus' twelve comprising only men.

12

SHOULD I TITHE NET OR GROSS?

In 1980, the State of Israel reformed its currency and replaced the lira with the shekel. This sent Israeli cartoonists back to the Bible to discover what you could buy with a shekel in scriptural times. More seriously, in the 1990s the emergence of the Jubilee 2000 movement sent some people back to the Bible to discover what it had to say about the idea of canceling punitive Third World debts to Western banks and governments. In the 2000s, I was asked to take part in a conference on Muslim banking and to speak on lending in the Bible. This sent me back to the Bible as well as to Islamic law, to discover how biblical law compared with the teaching of Islamic law. And in the 2000s, a student told me he had been given the impression that tithing and giving your tithe to your local church was the one First Testament law that Christians had to obey. All this set me thinking.[1]

1. The Significances of Lending

The First Testament prohibits Israelites to lend to each other at interest. "Interest" is usually *neshek*, literally a "bite"; some passages also use the words *tarbit* or *marbit*, literally "increase," with similar meaning. Older English translations understand these words to refer to usury (that is, excessive interest, however that may be defined), but this is mistaken. The texts forbid any lending at interest. Many English translations also introduce the ideas of interest or usury into the use of the verbs *nasha'/nashah* and related nouns, though in themselves these verbs simply refer to lending. But the first passage about lending in the Bible, Exod 22:25 [24], tells people not to behave like lenders (*nosh'im*) when they lend (*lawah*) money to people. Perhaps *lawah* refers to lending in general, as when an ordinary person lends something to a friend, while *nasha'/nashah* refers to something more formal or commercial, which by its nature would be likely to involve interest.

Exodus 22 forbids Israelites to impose interest on poor members of "my people" when making a loan. The reference to the poor indicates that the text does not refer to commercial loans. One can imagine successful Israelite farmers borrowing, for instance to enlarge their herds, but the First Testament does not refer to such loans.

---

[1] First published as "Jubilee Tithe," in *Transformation* 19 (2002): 198–205.

It rather presupposes a situation in which, for instance, a farmer's harvest has failed and he needs to borrow to feed his family or sow for the next year. It implies the motivation that these are "my people": so be careful how you treat them.

The exhortation about not behaving like a lender shows how it is quite possible for creditors to keep the regulation prohibiting lending at interest, yet still treat debtors oppressively. The First Testament refers to this in different connections. In no case need it imply charging excessive interest or even charging interest at all.

Treating debtors oppressively can be a personal issue. Individual lenders are not to take the necessities of life as pledges, such as an ox or donkey, or a garment, or a millstone—or a child (Deut 24:6, 17; Job 22:6; 24:3, 9). One oppressive lender is a man who insists on taking away a widow's children so that they can work for him because of the family's debt (2 Kgs 4:1).

It can be a community issue. Nehemiah 5 tells the story of a community controversy over oppressive lending: it may refer to charging interest or to other tough actions such as foreclosing on loans. It alludes to two reasons for debt, crop failure and imperial taxation. The two stories also make clear the results of default. One may forfeit fields, orchards, and houses, or one may end up in servitude. Translations have "slavery," but that conventional term is misleading, since the person's position resembles temporary indentured labor, something more like employment (but without freedom to leave) instead of the normal arrangement whereby one works for oneself on one's own land or in one's own business; it has little in common with the chattel slavery imposed on the ancestors of most African American and Afro-Caribbean people.

Treating debtors oppressively can be a national issue. The way imperial taxation thus burdens individuals and leads to debt was anticipated in the way national taxes burdened people when Israel was an independent state. When Israel asked for stronger central government, Samuel warned them of the burden such government would be on them (1 Sam 8:10–17).

It can be an international issue. Habakkuk 2:6–7 warns or promises that a major power that has behaved like a creditor accumulating pledges from weaker and poorer countries will in due course become the victim of its debtors. The tables will be turned.

Leviticus 25 expands on the point in Exod 22, referring to the poor person as "your brother" and to the need to "revere God." It also includes reference to lending food, which makes more explicit the kind of predicament, of poor harvest, that the texts are concerned to regulate. The passage urges that you let your brother live with you as a resident alien, someone who can maintain himself even though he has no land (Lev 25:36–37). People who are doing well are expected to lend freely to the needy and to accept payment in the form of labor or of the eventual repayment of the debt in money that the person had earned through labor. So the debtor would seek to work his way back to solvency by committing himself to indentured labor for a set period or to paid employment in relation to someone who did have land.

A third passage in the Torah makes explicit that people must not impose interest on any form of loan, in money or in kind (Deut 23:19–20 [20–21]). It also makes explicit that Israelites are permitted to impose interest in lending to a foreigner, as one does not have to remit a foreigner's debts in the sabbath year (Deut 15:3). This is an example of a number of obligations that did not apply to foreigners. The exemption has been of considerable influence in encouraging Jewish people to be involved in the commercial world, though we do not know its original background or significance. Perhaps it allows commercial loans to people such as local Canaanites or foreigners involved in trade. Perhaps it refers to resident aliens who choose not to take up full membership of Israel. Or perhaps it is a purely theoretical rule; permitting loans at interest to non-Israelites underscores the prohibition on loans at interest to nearly all the people that anyone would be asked to make a loan to.

Beyond the Torah, Prov 28:8 promises that people who augment their wealth by lending at interest "gather it for people who are kind to the poor"—that is, they will not see the profit themselves. It is a personal experience of this that Habakkuk envisages for the leading world power of its day. Psalm 15 asks the question, "Who may sojourn in God's tent," stay in God's presence. Its answer includes the general requirement of a life of integrity and truthfulness, and some concrete expectations such as avoiding slander, keeping oaths, refusing bribes—and not lending at interest. Ezekiel speaks in similar terms in listing obligations that people should fulfill if they wish God to treat them as righteous, such as not worshiping by means of images, defiling their neighbors' wives, robbing people—or lending at interest (Ezek 18:8, 13, 17). Ezekiel implies that people were not fulfilling these obligations and later makes explicit that the well-to-do in Jerusalem have committed many of the wrongs he lists, including this one (Ezek 22:12).

Exodus 22:25 [24] begins, "If you lend," but it presupposes that you will do so. To refuse to lend would contravene other exhortations regarding concern for the needy. The point is explicit in Deut 15, which urges people to lend generously to poor members of their "family." Righteous people do well in life and are therefore in a position to give and to lend and thus to be a blessing (Ps 37:25–26). Things go well for the person who deals generously and lends (Ps 112:5).

The New Testament confirms this stance. It refers to lending at interest only in the context of a parable, about a man entrusting his assets to his servants (Matt 25:27; Luke 19:23). One cannot infer an ethical position from such parables, which start from realities of life in order to make a point about something else. Jesus does urge his followers to lend to whoever asks for a loan (Matt 5:42) and makes explicit that this applies even to enemies and applies even if you do not expect to gain in any way from the act (Luke 6:34–35). This, too, would be in keeping with the Torah, where the exhortation about loving one's neighbor offers no exemption if one's neighbor is one's enemy and specifically requires one to help one's enemy (Exod 23:4–5). It would also imply that one should not hold back from lending because the needy person was one's enemy. Fourth Maccabees, a Jewish work from about the same period, which some Christians came to treat as near-canonical, claims that when people start conforming their lives to the Torah, even if they are by nature greedy they start lending to the needy without charging interest (4 Macc 2:8).

Through the first millennium of its existence the Christian church affirmed the First Testament principle that lending on interest was disapproved, on the continuing presupposition that lending was an aspect of care for the needy. But in practice lending on interest was tolerated as long as rates were not judged excessive. Where Christians refused to engage in commercial lending, Jewish moneylenders were able to fill the vacuum on the basis of the Deuteronomic permission to charge interest to foreigners.

In the second millennium, commerce began to develop in new ways, and the practice of lending on interest became prevalent, initially despite the church's opposition. In due course, however, in keeping with the usual pattern the church conformed itself to the secular practice and provided a theological rationale for it. In fifteenth-century Italy, public pawnshops developed with Franciscan support to offer loans to the poor more cheaply than those offered by regular moneylenders, charging a very low interest rate designed simply to cover expenses, and in 1516 the Fifth Lateran Council approved these. As years went by these pawnshops began also to lend for commercial purposes at higher rates.

Feeling unbound by the course of discussion within the medieval church and perceiving that the First Testament was concerned with caring for the poor and not with commercial loans, John Calvin removed the ban on lending at interest, with safeguards that predictably were conveniently forgotten. In due course the Roman Catholic Church also removed its ban on lending at interest. More seriously, as the capitalist world developed, it lost the idea that the point about lending is to be caring toward the needy. In Victorian Britain, the development of the Co-operative movement and the Building Society movement attempted to recover it. In effect the customers of the Co-op were the shareholders, while building societies worked by attracting safe investments from people who hoped eventually to buy a house and lending the money to people who were already in a position to do so. Until a generation ago, it was often difficult to get Anglican clergy in England to retire when they should do so because they had always lived in a parsonage and had nowhere else to go. When the church wanted to introduce compulsory retirement it had to solve this problem. So to get clergy out of their parsonages, it began lending them the money to buy a house—on interest (but a very low rate).

For the sake of argument we may grant that, for instance, if I want to buy a car or develop my company, someone has the right to charge me interest on a loan. But we have come to think about lending primarily in such commercial terms, and scripture invites us to change that. The focus of the scriptural material is on the predicament of needy people, and lending is a way you care for the needy, not a way you make money. The haves share with the have-nots by lending. Lending is a means of being a blessing. It seems self-evident that we have treated countries in the two-thirds world on a commercial basis when we should be thinking about them on a need basis. That in turn suggests that we have to think about whether we want to view people outside our communities or nations as aliens or as like members of the family. Further, the scriptural material gives membership of one's family priority over the question how good or bad are the relationships between lender and borrower.

2. The Significances of Jubilee

Sometimes we come to perceive the significance of scripture by an analytical, linear, left-brain process. We use our minds to work out the principles behind biblical teaching and to see how to apply them to today. But sometimes we see scripture's significance by jumping to a more intuitive, right-brain, imaginative, visionary, prophetic insight. The Holy Spirit can work both ways, and both appear within scripture itself. The jump from Lev 25 to Jubilee 2000 was an imaginative, visionary leap, not a linear step. As such it was in keeping with the way the jubilee vision fired people within biblical times.

The explanation of the jubilee in Lev 25 begins from the requirement that farmers observe a sabbath year, so that once every seven years they sow no crops in their fields. People thus acknowledge that the land belongs to God. Once in a while they leave the land alone, as the weekly sabbath acknowledges God's right to time and leaves that chunk of time alone.

The requirements of Exod 23:10–11 had already turned this religious instinct embodied in the sabbath year into a practice that could benefit the needy, who were to be allowed to gather what grows naturally in the sabbath year. Deuteronomy 15 and Lev 25 take up that concern for the poor and on its basis develop imaginative and radical visions of how to deal with situations of poverty that arise as Israel becomes a more complex society. Theologically they start from the nature of Israel's exodus faith and ask what that implies for such situations. They also link with the vision of the prophets and suggest how prophetic principle could be expressed as practical policy.

Leviticus 25 comes at the end of the Holiness Teaching that begins in Lev 19. Like Deuteronomy, Leviticus as a whole constitutes a God-inspired dream of a new foundation for Israel's life as a people, a new style of life. The book presupposes that the people will not live the life that exodus faith requires and will find themselves in exile but that this need not be the end of their story. God will give them another chance after exile (see Lev 26).

Leviticus 25 is the only place in scripture that describes the jubilee year (it is also mentioned incidentally in Lev 27:17–25 and Num 36:4). The jubilee was to happen every forty-nine years; perhaps Leviticus is being more realistic than Deuteronomy with its freeing every seven years. The word "jubilee" comes from the Hebrew word for the blowing of a trumpet, because that was the signal that this year was starting (Lev 25:9–10). The jubilee involved "proclaiming release" (*deror*); that expression is the one Jer 34 uses for what happened in the seventh year.

In both the sabbath and the jubilee years, things were to go back to square one in some way. In general, when someone got into economic difficulty, first obligation to help rested within the extended family. The nearest relative was under moral obligation to come to the person's aid in these circumstances and thus to act as a "redeemer" (*go'el*; "restorer" might be a better translation), in order to get things back to square one. In the sabbath year, people who had been forced by hardship to hire themselves to someone as workers were to become free. In the jubilee year, people who had been forced by hardship to rent their land to someone else were to receive their land back. An underlying principle is the assumption shared by the Navajo and other traditional peoples, that you cannot own land. You can own buildings, which you make, but land belongs to God.

Leviticus recognizes that human selfishness means people would resist the jubilee principle. They would be tempted to try to make a profit out of other people's need. They would not want to lend money if they were not going to be able to make their profit and would try to get round the regulations. The regulations thus remind them to keep God in mind, to "revere God." In some ways the regulations are impractical in that one cannot see how they could be implemented, but they are practical in recognizing that the value of the "lease" on land will diminish as the jubilee draws near. They thus try to think through the practical outworking of the vision and to take account of the perspective of lender as well as borrower.

It may be that throughout its history Israel did leave the land fallow for one year in seven as Exodus says, but there is no reference to its doing so in the First Testament. Nor is there any reference to Israel ever observing the sabbath-year freeing of people who were working for other people because of debt, in the way Deut 15 says. The nearest to an exception (significantly) is a story in Jer 34:8–17 about it *not* happening. Likewise, there is no indication that the jubilee year was ever implemented. Nor is there any reference to people lending without interest, while there are many passages that imply that people did lend at interest. In any group, the regulations or exhortations that leaders give do not necessarily tell us anything about how life was.

This might only resemble the way the church has not usually implemented the Sermon on the Mount, though that analogy indicates that Israel may not have been simply being disobedient. When Jesus told people to cut off their hands, he probably did not mean it. There are other examples of teaching in the Torah that were not implemented, and the implication may be that the people knew that this was a vision rather than a policy. We misunderstand the Torah when we think of it as a law book. It is more like a vision. This does not mean it was not to be taken seriously, any more than Jesus' comment about cutting off hands. It means scripture is offering us a vivid picture; we have to work out how to put it into practice. The awareness that it is a vision rather than a piece of law may help us handle the fact that as a literal practice it would have its disadvantages: for instance, it could end up penalizing people who work hard and rewarding the lazy. While the Torah includes regulations that look designed for quasi-legal literal implementation, other material looks more like concrete embodiments of a style of life. We would miss the point if we took it legally. We might fulfill the law's letter but not its visionary demand.

The problems the jubilee vision was designed to handle appear in Neh 5:1–13, where we have seen that the Torah's teaching about lending was being ignored in the context of pressures issuing from the failure of harvests and the demands of taxation placed upon people by a foreign government. Those have forced people to borrow money against the surety of their land, their children's freedom, and their own freedom. Even if they regain their freedom in the seventh year, they are very unlikely to be able to regain self-sufficiency as a family if they have lost their land. They will never be able to escape the poverty trap. Nehemiah insists that the well-off return property and land and cease foreclosing or charging interest on loans. There is no reference to the jubilee, but it is a jubilee vision that Nehemiah implements.

The function of the requirements in Lev 25 for us (like the function of the story in Neh 5) is to stimulate the theological and ethical imagination. No part of the First Testament binds us as law, because we do not live by law. But the whole First Testament is designed to shape the life of the people of God (2 Tim 3:15–16: in speaking of "scripture" it is referring to the First Testament, of course, because the New Testament did not exist). It shapes us by portraying God's vision for human life by suggesting ways this could be worked out in practice in different contexts and challenging us to discover what this will look like in our own context.

Apart from Neh 5, we know of three occasions in scriptural times when people did thus take the jubilee vision and apply it in fresh ways in their context. First, in Isa 61 the prophet testifies to having been called by God "to proclaim release to captives." This is the one other place where that word "release" comes in the First Testament. The captives are the people of Judah who are oppressed and depressed as a result of the devastation of Jerusalem and the decimation of its population. The whole people and the whole land are in a position like that of individuals who have become impoverished through bad harvests and have lost their land or freedom, and the chapter applies the image of release to them.

Second, the Qumran "Melchizedek" prophecy (11QMelchizedek) explicitly puts together Lev 25, Deut 15, and Isa 61 and promises that in the last days, which the Qumran community believed were imminent, people will be released from their sins.

Third, Luke 4 tells the story of Jesus following the Qumran prophecy in declaring that the last days have arrived and that he is bringing about another embodiment of the ministry described in Isa 61. The context of his ministry suggests that the release of which he speaks is release from illness, demonic oppression, and guilt.

The image of a special occasion when release is proclaimed is thus one capable of being applied to different contexts when believers of vision see people in bondage and see this is God's moment for their release. The Jubilee 2000 movement saw the new millennium as another such moment. It saw that jubilee was not essentially eschatological or spiritual or christological. The indebtedness of Third World countries puts them into another form of bondage, different from that in Leviticus, Nehemiah, Isaiah, 11QMelchizedek, and Luke. The visionaries who gave birth to the Jubilee 2000 idea invited us to hear God calling us to see here another way in which the image of release can be realized in the world. God did not require Israel to apply the jubilee vision outside the people of God, but it would make sense if God now does want that, as the renewed Israel is to reach out to the entire world. As Leviticus envisioned, the cancellation of debts gives people a new start rather than leaving them permanently oppressed by debts from which they can never recover.

3. The Significances of Tithing

The Bible talks about tithing more often than it does about jubilee, but it does so in a way that instructively parallels its references to jubilee and release. From Genesis to Malachi and on into the New Testament tithing is a norm, but the significance of tithing is understood in a number of different ways. The practice hardly changes, but its aim and its meaning are worked out anew in different contexts and connections. The implication would be that tithing remains a norm today but that we may need to discern afresh what God wants to do through tithing.

Tithing starts in Gen 14; translations vary over whether they use the word "tithe" or the word "tenth," but in Hebrew it is the same word. Abram has gone off on a risky expedition to fight with forces that have taken Lot as a prisoner of war. He has returned not only with Lot but also with much plunder. Some of Abram's allies come to see him on his return, and one of them is the king of Salem, Melchizedek, who is also "priest of God Most High." He blesses Abram, and Abram gives him a tenth of his plunder. Like sacrifice in Gen 4, and the leaving of the ground fallow in the sabbath year, evidently tithing is not a special revelation from God but a human instinct or a part of general revelation. Special revelation comes in due course in the way God harnesses these natural human instincts and instructs people to express them. Abram knows tithing is a human thing to do, as faithfulness, love, justice, worship, and prayer are human things to do. People are made that way. He can assume that the king of Salem understands this, too. When God gives you something, you recognize where it came from by giving some of it back to God.

Tithing next appears in the story of Jacob (Gen 28:10–22). Jacob is on his way out of the land of promise, on the run from the brother whom he has swindled of his rights as firstborn. God appears to him and promises to keep him safe and bring him back to the land. "Well," says Jacob, "if you are going to look after me and give me food and clothing and bring me back here in prosperity and peace, then you can be my God, and I will give you a tithe of all that you give me." We know the calculating nature of Jacob, grabber by name as well as by personality, and there is surely an irony here. "You give me everything, and I will give you a tenth." Tithing can be a means of indulging in our instinct to calculate, a means of being selfish.

God's own first instruction about tithing comes in the verses that close off Leviticus (Lev 27:30–33). They constitute a warning about how we may try to evade the demand of tithing. Tithing applies to produce and to animals, and the way you tithe animals is by giving up every tenth animal that passes under the shepherd's staff. But what happens if your best sheep happens to be the tenth? Can you substitute a less flourishing sheep for that one? You cannot. No substitutions are allowed.

What happens to tithes? The next passage on tithing (Num 18:21–32) gives one answer. Tithing is a means of seeing that the ministry is supported. Tithes go to the clan of Levi, whose task is to look after the services at the sanctuary and who have no land to work. So the tithe of the rest of the clans' work and land goes to them.

Deuteronomy also affirms that tithes go to the Levites (Deut 12), but it adds a special provision for every third year (Deut 14:22–29; 26:12–13). The calendar is thus divided into seven-year periods in which there are two "regular" years, a "third" year, two more "regular" years, another "third" year, then a sabbath year, after which the cycle starts again. In the "third" year, the tithes are to benefit not only Levites but also aliens, orphans, and widows, who are in the same position as Levites in having no land from which to gain their livelihood. This might seem an impractical provision. What are these needy groups supposed to do for the two intervening years? We have noted that questions such as this arise with other policies in the Torah, not least the jubilee regulations, and they may again show that these are more God-given dreams than God-given policies. People have to work out how to realize the dream.

In Joshua to Kings, there is only one reference to tithes, and it is a solemn one. If you insist on having kings, Samuel warns Israel, you will pay for it, literally (1 Sam 8:15–17). Kings will take a tithe of your grain, vines, and sheep for their staff. Perhaps Samuel means they will appropriate the tithes that are due to the ministry and to the needy, or perhaps he means they will add a second tithe to the first, to pay for the cost of having a monarchic state. Either way it is bad news. It is an indication that tithing can be a means of leaders oppressing ordinary people.

Unsurprisingly, there are indications in the First Testament that people often failed to tithe (e.g., Neh 13:10–12), but there is also a reminder that the practice of tithing can be a substitute for real commitment. Amos 4:4 implies that people were faithful in tithing as they were faithful in worship, but their giving was not matched by a commitment to faithfulness within the community. Some believers lived in fine homes, had good incomes, and enjoyed a cultured life, but they thus benefited from the fact that the way society worked made other believers much more poorly off (e.g., Amos 5:10–13; 6:4–6). They could afford to tithe and still be very well-off, and thus their tithing had become one of the ways they avoided God's lordship of their lives.

So tithing can have a variety of significances, and God had different things to say about tithing in different contexts. What might tithing mean now? We might discover this by relating tithing to jubilee.

4. Jubilee Tithing

The organization World Vision suggested ten urgent millennial issues: that the world's people have livable incomes; that people have enough food; that all children have primary schooling; that all people have clean water; that poor nations' debts to richer nations be cancelled; that we develop peace building programs at the community level; that girls grow up as equals of boys; that the earth's resources be used in a way that opens up a sustainable future; that child exploitation be ended; and that people have freedom of belief. It thinks that the material cost of handling these questions is only a fraction of world expenditure on arms; the question is whether we can raise the moral will to handle the questions.

I suggest that Christians are now called to tithe their income and to direct their tithes to causes that will thus provide nourishment, education, basic health care, and health education for people in the two-thirds world. I suggest that this is the purpose that God wishes tithes to fulfill in the twenty-first century. In the Christian dispensation, the gospel came to belong to the world and not just to the chosen people. It was a logical extension of this that we should apply the jubilee to the world and not only to our fellow believers. It is the next logical extension of this principle of God's care for the whole world that tithes should be applied for the benefit of peoples left behind by economic rules. The object is not the relief of immediate pressing needs but ongoing development that can encourage the realization of people's physical, intellectual, and spiritual potential to something nearer the realization possible in the West.

At the moment, people who tithe do so primarily for the benefit of the congregations they themselves belong to. I have heard it suggested that tithing is an essentially selfish exercise: it is the way we ensure we receive goods we desire such as people to pastor us or heating/air conditioning in church. In this sense it is not giving to God at all. If we tithe to maintain our churches and their ministry, this should perhaps be a second tithe, following on a tithe that benefits peoples who are more needy than us (there is no basis in scripture for the conviction that we give our tithe to our local church and let it decide what to do with it). Judaism came to understand the instructions about tithing in Deut 14 and Deut 26 to require a second tithe once every three years, and the Worldwide Church of God used to require of its members a double tithe every year. These practices probably involve misunderstanding of the instructions in the Torah, but the idea of a second tithe may nevertheless be helpful. Believers in the West could first tithe their income for the sake of the two-thirds world. They might then tithe again to pay their pastors and keep their churches ambient.

To tithe in this way would imply a significant reduction in our standard of living, and that is part of the point. We need to reduce the amount we spend on "necessities" such as education, health care, housing, transport, and saving for retirement, in order to reduce the gap between what we have a right to and what we possess. Unbelievers often take the lead in concern for the two-thirds world. Theologically and morally we should be able to expect believers to be the first to want to stop appropriating an excessive share of world resources and to be looking for ways of doing so.

I do not know how to quantify the reduction we should seek for ourselves or how to quantify what our income would be if it were to be "fair." I do not know whether tithing will be enough of a gesture to hold God back from acting in punitive discipline on the West for our misappropriation. But I suggest that the biblical practice of tithing gives us something to work with that would make a significant difference to us and to the two-thirds world. There might be at least four ways in which it could do that.

First, such tithing would in itself bring about a significant redistribution of resources. Second, in the West our lives as believers are characterized by a series of commitments for ourselves. These include high educational standards in school, university, and graduate education, ever-increasing expenditure on health care, comfortable and gracious housing, driving and flying many miles, and saving so that we can live in the same way when we retire. It is our appropriation of a disproportionate amount of the world's resources that enables us to do that, but one of the striking features of our lives is that believers generally look no happier with their lives than unbelievers are. By reducing our expenditure on these "necessities" that have not produced the happiness we expected, we could discover that we can live a fuller life on less. Third, it would not be surprising if the church's calling was to model the fact that human life finds fulfillment and happiness elsewhere than in the abundance of the things we possess. Fourth, if we tithed in order to contribute to a better distribution of resources, we might find that God will pour out a blessing on us because we are honoring God (Mal 3:8–12).

13

WAS THE HOLY SPIRIT ACTIVE IN FIRST TESTAMENT TIMES?

What was new about the Christian experience of God? After Jesus breathed the Holy Spirit on his disciples and after the Holy Spirit fell at Pentecost, in what sense was the first Christians' experience something novel?[1]

1. Talk of the Spirit of God in First Testament Times

> On the last day of the festival . . . Jesus cried out, "Let anyone who is thirsty come to me, and let the one who believes in me drink. As the scripture has said, 'Out of the believer's heart shall flow rivers of living water.'" (John 7:37–38)

Those two sentences raise a number of questions. It may be more likely, for instance, that the one out of whose heart the rivers flow is Jesus, not the believer. But the issue I am concerned with here arises from the comment that John goes on to make:

> Now he said this about the Spirit, which believers in him were to receive; for as yet there was no Spirit, because Jesus was not yet glorified. (John 7:39)

Thus the NRSV. It differs from the original RSV, which has "the Spirit was not yet given," the reading in some Greek manuscripts. The NRSV assumes that the manuscripts that say "given" are seeking to reduce the scandal of a difficult statement. "The Spirit was not" could sound as if it implied that the Spirit did not exist, which is the kind of misleading impression that a scribe might seek to remove. I think it likely that the NRSV is right and that John wrote "the Spirit was not," though this question, too, need make little difference to the issue we are concerned with here. For if John did write "the Spirit was not," he hardly meant that the Spirit did not exist; he has already referred to the Spirit's activity (see John 1:32–33). Rather, he must mean that the Spirit was not generally about, was not obviously there, was not active in relation to believers, or something of that kind. John will tell us later how Jesus breathes the Holy Spirit onto his disciples after his death and resurrection and how he commissions them for their ministry of bringing God's forgiveness

---

[1] First published as "The Holy Spirit in the Old Testament," in *Ex auditu* 12 (1996): 14–28.

(John 20:22–23). Scriptures such as Zech 14:8, which promise a flowing out of living waters, will then be fulfilled. Until that happens, there is no Spirit, the Spirit is not obviously about or active, or the Spirit is not given, says John. The comment parallels the remark attributed to some disciples in Ephesus who knew only John's baptism and had not even heard that there was a Holy Spirit (Acts 19:2); apparently they did not know that Pentecost had taken place. They were still looking forward to the manifestation of the Holy Spirit.

The trouble is that according to the other Gospels the spirit of God has been very active before Jesus' ministry, and not just in relation to Jesus himself, as in John 1:32–33. At the beginning of Luke, Elizabeth is "filled with the Holy Spirit," so is her husband Zechariah, and so will be their son John (Luke 1:15, 41, 67). The Holy Spirit was on the elderly Simeon, who had received a revelation from the Holy Spirit and came "in the Spirit" to the temple (Luke 2:25–27). Long before that, according to Jesus himself David had spoken "in the Holy Spirit" (Mark 12:36).

All those passages mesh with the descriptions of the activity of God's spirit in the First Testament.

In considering these, we need to keep in mind a vital broadness and ambiguity in the Hebrew and Greek words for spirit. Both *ruakh* and *pneuma* cover breath and wind and spirit. Wind suggests something of the mysterious, invisible, dynamic power of God. Breath stands for life in its own mysterious nature, with its origins and its end outside our control. The wind is the breath of God, and we breathe because God breathes breath into us. The spirit of God or of a human being suggests personal liveliness and dynamism, motive power or will. According to the First Testament, from the beginning this spirit of God has been involved in the process whereby God determined what do in creating the world and in shaping events in the world. "Who has directed the spirit of Yahweh" in the fulfillment of that task (Isa 40:13)? Genesis 1:2 with the *ruakh* of God moving over the waters, and Job 26:13 with God's *ruakh* involved in creation alongside God's power, understanding, and hand, associate the activity of God's *ruakh* with God's activity from the beginning. Indeed, the very breath of humanity comes from that breath/wind/spirit of God. Psalm 104:29–30 assumes that human beings and animals breathe in because God's *ruakh* breathes out (cf. Gen 6:3; Isa 42:5; Job 27:3; 33:4; 34:14; Eccles 12:7).

The First Testament thus begins by associating the activity of God's spirit with the world and not merely with the people of God. In the New Testament, this activity is narrowed down. Here, talk of God's wisdom or word can relate to the whole cosmos, but God's spirit is confined to the church. From a First Testament perspective, however, "to experience the fellowship of the Spirit inevitably carries Christianity beyond itself into the greater fellowship of all God's creatures. For the *community of creation*, in which all created things exist with one another, for one another and in one another, is also *the fellowship of the Holy Spirit*,"[2] so that experience of the latter leads us into concern for the former.

---

[2] Jürgen Moltmann, *The Spirit of Life* (London: SCM / New York: Harper, 1992), 106 (his emphasis); see also *God in Creation* (London: SCM / New York: Harper, 1985), 9–13, 98–103, 255–70.

For our understanding of Christian experience, a further implication of the link between God's spirit and creation is that when God's Spirit comes to fill the Christian church or the Christian believer and comes to produce the moral fruit of the Spirit or to release gifts of the Spirit, these are not bolt-on additions to human nature as created by God, essentially novel enlargements of it. They are the fulfillment of what created human beings were intended to be and have the inherent potential to be. The life of holiness or the utterance of tongues or the ministry of healing are the most natural things in the world, even if they become actual only through supernatural release. And the renewing of the church is the shaping of a microcosm of creation. The breathing of John 20:22 is a repetition of the event of creation; it is an act of new creation. The groaning on the part of the Spirit in Rom 8:23–27 is a sighing for the fulfillment of creation. It is because human beings in general are divinely created beings inbreathed with God's breath that they sometimes live holy lives, say things that are true and illuminating, and exercise gifts of healing.

Not surprisingly, the First Testament has further statements to make about the involvement of God's spirit with Israel in particular. When Israel was delivered at the Red Sea, this involved God's holy spirit being in their midst and giving them rest (Isa 63:11, 14). When Israel was then directed through the wilderness, this was by God's good spirit (Neh 9:20). As Israel lived their life in the land over the centuries, God's spirit lived among them (Hag 2:4–5). When they ignored God's expectations and standards, they grieved that holy spirit among them (Isa 63:10) and risked its being withdrawn (Ps 51:11 [13]), or they experienced God's *ruakh* as a scorching blast from which they might like to escape but could not (Isa 4:4; 40.7; Ps 139:7). They thus prayed for God to renew and uphold them with the steadfast, holy, and generous spirit of God that can act on their spirit and make it more like God's (Ps 51.10–12 [12–14]).

The spirit of God also breathed into particular individuals within Israel. This happened to the craftworkers in the sanctuary, to leaders such as elders, to prophets, and to liberators such as the judges. Things that they did suggested the life and energy of God; they reflected the active presence of God's *ruakh*.

On the First Testament's own understanding, then, there is no doubt that the spirit of God was about and active in First Testament times, and the attitude that surfaces in the synoptic Gospels makes the same assumption. So what are we to make of John's comment? What was new about the giving of the Spirit through Jesus?

2. When the Spirit of God Is Active but Unnamed

Before coming to that question, with John's help I want to make it sharper. There is another significance about that comment in John 7:39. When Jesus talks about rivers of living water, he does not explicitly allude to the spirit of God. It is John who assumes that he refers to the Spirit, that the Spirit will bring about the fulfillment of Jesus' words. So why does Jesus not mention the Spirit? John implies that it is the fact that the Spirit "was not yet [given]" that explains this. In other words, the spirit of God can be being referred to even when the words *ruakh* or *pneuma* do not appear.

That provides us with an important clue for our reading of the First Testament. The actual phrase "holy spirit" comes in only two passages in the First Testament, Isa 63 and Ps 51, but this is in a sense a misleading observation. Arguably, we should note, in First Testament thinking either adjective or noun is redundant in this expression. "Spirit" defines the being of God, in dynamic power (cf. Isa 31:3). And "holy" defines the being of God, in supernatural awesomeness (cf. Hos 11:9b). It is therefore hardly surprising that the two words are so rarely combined; they risk tautology. Any reference to the spirit of God must be a reference to the holy spirit of God. John's comment puts us on the track of the suspicion that there are many First Testament references to the work of the Holy Spirit that are not identified as such. These include passages that use the word *ruakh*, but also other passages that do not. With hindsight, John implies, we can recognize reference to the Holy Spirit even where the Holy Spirit is unmentioned.

This issue surfaces within the First Testament itself. Whereas it talks of the activity of the spirit of Yahweh in connection with some prophets, such as Elijah, Elisha, and Ezekiel, it does not do so in connection with others, such as Jeremiah. Jeremiah's experience of the pressure of Yahweh upon him was in its way as tumultuous as Ezekiel's, but he did not describe it in terms of Yahweh's spirit. He is usually thought to be avoiding such language because it is in some way discredited, perhaps through its use by other prophets from whom Jeremiah wished to distance himself. But if we think that Ezekiel was acted on by the Holy Spirit, it is natural to think that this was also true of Jeremiah, even if Jeremiah avoids saying so. There is no systematic tension between God's word and God's spirit in the First Testament (see Ps 33:6).

It can be dangerous to read back Christian theological ways of thinking into the First Testament. We can easily miss the thrust of what the First Testament has to tell us by reading it through Christian spectacles too quickly. When translations translate *ruakh* by Spirit with a capital S, they risk misleading us. In Ps 51:11 [13], TNIV has Holy Spirit with capital H and capital S, the RSV has holy Spirit with small h and capital S, while the NRSV has small h and small s. There are snags about the use of capitals which may make us read later meanings back into the passages and thus miss the passages' own meaning, miss what God's very spirit had to say to people through the words as they would hear them in their day. But at some stage we may properly look at the First Testament with Christian theological categories in connection with reaching a theological understanding of it that will enable us to interpret God's activity in the world and the church today.

In the First Testament, talk of the spirit of God is one of a number of ways of talking about the presence and activity of God. One can speak of God's arm, or hand, or finger, or face, or eyes, or wisdom, or name, or angel—or of God's breath. All these are ways of speaking of God's presence and activity. There are two strengths in this way of speaking. One is that the terms refer to these realities in a way that is more concrete than mere general reference to God. God's arm suggests God's power, God's hand suggests God's direct activity, God's face suggests God's personal concern, and so on. They also have the advantage of providing ways of speaking of God's presence and activity that preserve an awareness of God's absoluteness and transcendence. We experienced God's arm or hand; we do not pretend to have experienced all of God.

Reference to God's *ruakh* is an instance of such speech. It suggests that God is truly present and active, with the power of wind and the liveliness of breath and the personal decisiveness of human decision making, but it does so in a way that safeguards God's mystery. Wind and breath are invisible and are known only by their effects (cf. John 3:8).

In early Christianity, the metaphor of God's breath/wind/spirit became so dominant among those First Testament anthropomorphic expressions that it largely subsumed all the others. People stopped talking so much about God's arm or God's face. The process can be seen within the New Testament in the parallel between the casting out of demons by God's finger (Luke 11:20) or by God's spirit (Matt 12:28). Talk of God's spirit became *the* way of envisaging the presence and activity of God in the world. Perhaps, a colleague suggests to me, a reason for the dominance of spirit language henceforth was the emergence of body-of-Christ language. Arms, fingers, and face now belong to that divine-human body, itself indwelt by divine breath.

An implication of this development is that wherever within the First Testament there is talk of God's arm or hand or finger or face or eyes, in our terms what it is speaking of is the activity of the Holy Spirit. To use John's formulation, it did not speak in terms of the Holy Spirit because the Spirit was not yet [given]. That talk would become dominant only after the events referred to in John 20 and Acts 2. The Holy Spirit was there and active in First Testament times, but the language for expressing the Spirit's activity was more varied than was later the case.

Another example of the Spirit's being involved though unnamed in First Testament times emerges in the realm of worship. The New Testament assumes that the Holy Spirit inspires our worship. It is because the Holy Spirit is present and active among us that we sing God's praise and call upon God in prayer. It is as we are filled with the Spirit that we sing psalms and hymns and spiritual songs (Eph 5:19–20). So what is going on when First Testament Israel sings psalms? When the church took over the Psalms and made the Psalter its own hymnbook, one implication was that these hymns, thanksgivings, and prayers were ones inspired by the Spirit. That is the point Jesus makes with regard to Ps 110 in Mark 12:36. And presumably we are to apply to the Psalter the generalization in 2 Tim 3:15–16 about the First Testament scriptures being *theopneustos*, God-breathed, inspired or exspired by God's Spirit, or (as I incline to think the word suggests) produced as a result of people being blown over by God. In New Testament terms, these praises and prayers are a fruit of the Spirit, even if they are not described as such in the First Testament (though see passages such as Pss 45:1 [2]; 49:1–4 [2–5]). The Holy Spirit was involved in First Testament worship.

In Israel, people were not much inclined to speak of themselves as sons and daughters of God and of God as their Father, though they sometimes did so (Isa 43:6 is noteworthy as the only passage in the entire Bible—except where it is quoted in 2 Cor 6:18—where God says "my daughters"). That may have been because it was too cheap and easy an idea. In the First Testament world, as in ours, people assumed that God was their father, and the First Testament perhaps distanced itself from that assumption as it distanced itself from the usually accepted idea that there would be an afterlife. But the confidence, lack of inhibition, and enthusiasm of First Testament prayer and praise indicate that the people who prayed the Psalms enjoyed the same relationship as the one the New Testament speaks of in terms of being sons and daughters. People prayed in the Spirit to the Father, even if they did not put it that way.

The Holy Spirit was also involved in the everyday lives of people who produced the fruit of the Spirit. The fruit of the Spirit is love, joy, peace, patience, kindness, generosity, faithfulness, gentleness, and self-control. When I read First Testament stories of Ruth, Hannah, Josiah, or Nehemiah, I read stories of people whose lives have such features. They are not described as people in whom the Holy Spirit is active, but that is what they are. Further, this feature of First Testament experience seems to rule out some ways of seeking to articulate the difference between experience of the Holy Spirit in the two Testaments, as an intermittent rather than continuing matter, or corporate rather than individual, or affecting some special leaders rather than ordinary Israelites. The Holy Spirit was active on an ongoing basis in the lives of ordinary individuals in the First Testament as well as being involved on an occasional and a corporate basis and with leaders. All this adds force to the issue John raises for us. There is so much activity of the Holy Spirit in First Testament times, so how can John speak of the Holy Spirit as not yet given?

3. When the Spirit of God Is Hoped for

One reason for John's speaking of the Holy Spirit as not yet given will be the way the First Testament speaks of a future endowment of God's spirit. It appears in Ezek 36–37 (anticipated in Ezek 11:17–20). There it is one of a number of images of God's future work in Israel. Some are literal: the people will return to their land, will obey God's commands, and will prosper in the land. Others presuppose the metaphor of the people as having one body, one heart, and one spirit. The heart in First Testament thinking corresponds most closely to the mind in ours. Currently the people's heart or mind is like stone. This image suggests inert, inactive, and lifeless (Exod 15:16; Hab 2:19), not directly "resistant," as we may assume, though that doubtless follows. God will replace their stone-dead mind with a mind that is more like flesh—vital and lively, or spirited (as we might say). A mind like flesh, a new spirit, and God's spirit are parallel expressions in Ezek 36:26–27. In the New Testament it will become pejorative to describe someone's mind as fleshly, and in subsequent Christianity it will become customary to assume an antithesis between the spiritual and the bodily. In the First Testament to describe the mind as fleshly is a positive statement, and the spirit is at home in the body. The image of people being made fleshly, lively, and spirited becomes an allegory in the following vision in Ezek 37, of the dry bones that are turned first into corpses and then into living people by the infusion of the divine spirit/wind/breath. All this will lead to the world coming to recognize that Yahweh is God; the worldwide perspective of Gen 1–11 will be regained.

The image recurs in Isa 44:15, where "my spirit" is parallel with "my blessing" and these two are parallel with water and streams. It is the very imagery of John 7, though Isa 44 is not a passage that the New Testament directly appeals to. In Isa 44, the imagery suggests a renewal of the community at all levels, in its numbers, status, morale, faith, and social life. It recurs again in Joel 2:28–29 [3:1–2] in a promise for all people. There the fulfillment of this promise will issue in prophecies, dreams, and visions. The promise is followed seamlessly by reference to the great and terrible day of Yahweh. And it is this passage that provides Acts 2 with the clue to understanding what is going on at the first Pentecost after Jesus' resurrection.

What do prophecies such as these imply regarding God's activity in First Testament times? Do they indicate the assumption that God's spirit was not active, was not obviously there?

The perspective suggested by a number of passages is that God's spirit was indeed not obviously active in these prophets' day but that people were aware of such an activity in the past. The possibility of God's spirit being withdrawn is presupposed by Ps 51:10–12 [12–14], a psalm that brings several issues into focus. Its heading suggests a connection with David and in modern parlance invites us to take this as a royal psalm. That would make good sense of the reference to Yahweh's holy spirit, for the king is one with whom Yahweh's spirit is especially associated. It is evident that hopes of the king being filled with Yahweh's spirit were often disappointed, so that this is the content of the promises in passages such as Isa 11:1–5. But aspects of the content of Ps 51 make it unlikely that its heading tells us its actual origin; from the David who had had an affair with Bathsheba and arranged for her husband's death Yahweh could hardly have accepted a prayer in which David professed to have sinned against Yahweh alone (Ps 51:4 [6]), and the closing verses seem to presuppose a setting after the fall of Jerusalem. Perhaps, then, headings such as that to Ps 51 are lectionary notes, designed not to determine authorship but to suggest contexts against which to read the psalm in question.[3] The headings link the psalms in question with essentially private events in David's life of the kind that can have equivalents in the lives of ordinary people. They thus imply (in this case) that ordinary people might see themselves as knowing the presence of Yahweh's holy spirit; this was not confined to people such as judges, kings, and prophets. If we leave the heading on one side for a moment, it makes good sense to see the psalm as a communal one, spoken by the community after the fall of Jerusalem, its "I" either indicating its awareness of itself as a corporate entity or being the "I" of each individual within the community that prays it (compare the "I" of the prayer in Lam 3). It is then the community that asks that God's holy spirit be not withdrawn from it.

---

[3] So Brevard S. Childs, "Psalm Titles and Midrashic Exegesis," *JSS* 16 (1971): 137–50; *Introduction to the Old Testament as Scripture* (London: SCM / Philadelphia: Fortress, 1979), 520–22.

Whoever prays the prayer mentions the spirit three times in Ps 51:10–12 [12–14]. Each time, the word begins the second half of the line and is followed by a qualifying adjective. It seems natural to take "spirit" to refer to the spirit of God each time, or to the spirit of God at work on the human spirit.[4] The only point at which the psalm refers unequivocally to the human spirit is the later allusion to a broken spirit (Ps 51:17 [19]). In Ps 51:10–12 [12–14] the psalm prays that God's upright, holy, generous spirit may be given, may not be withdrawn, and may sustain. The failures of the past make it entirely possible to envisage Yahweh's withholding that spirit; but if Yahweh does, that is the end.

The experience of God's spirit being known in the past but not now is explicit in Isa 63, which speaks of the presence and activity of Yahweh's holy spirit within the people at the time of the exodus, the escape from the Red Sea, and the entering into the land. That was once a reality, but the people now see no evidence of such activity. A similar perspective is implicit in Isa 44. The kind of refreshment, blessing, flourishing, and recognition of Yahweh of which Isa 44:1–5 speaks and which can also be envisaged by the figure of Yahweh's *ruakh* being poured on people has been known in the past but seems to be missing in the community's present experience of Yahweh's punishment.

Something more equivocal has to be said about Ezekiel. The community that is now lifeless and hopeless will be brought back to life by the inbreathing of Yahweh's *ruakh*. That suggests the assumption that before their death this *ruakh* was present; what is needed is its return. However, Ezekiel has a radically negative view of the people's previous life, and the promise in Ezek 36:26–27 implies a radically negative assessment of the people's spirit. Only if Yahweh's spirit is put within them will they come to live Yahweh's way. By implication, their failure over many centuries reflects the fact that this spirit has not been put into them before. Something creatively new is needed, and the inbreathing of Yahweh's spirit is that new thing.

In Joel, the implication seems to be that the pouring of Yahweh's spirit is a repeat of something that has been known in the past but is not known now, yet that this pouring will surpass what has been known before. It will envelop not merely isolated individuals but people of all ages and classes and both sexes. Joel thus implies the conviction that God intends to do something in the future that will be even more splendid than what God has done in the past. He thus most clearly implies a typological way of thinking in which future events will parallel past events but exceed them in wonder.

4. When Are These Hopes Fulfilled?

In some sense these prophetic promises were fulfilled in the Second Temple period. The community was renewed; the presence of Yahweh returned. At the same time, passages such as Isa 63 themselves witness to the recognition that many hopes were unfulfilled. John then implies the conviction that the new thing that

---

[4]See M. E. Tate, *Psalms 51–100* (Dallas: Word, 1990), 22–25.

God promised has now come about in true fullness in Jesus Christ. It is part of God's ultimate act having taken place in him. The end has come in Jesus. The last days have arrived. The Spirit is now about and active because Jesus has been about and active; the Spirit, we now realize, is the Spirit of Jesus.

Yet that is not the whole truth. In another sense the end has still not come, any more than it had in Second Temple Judaism. The last days have still not arrived. Everything continues as it did before, to echo the complaint reported in 2 Pet 3:4.

This is not merely a chronological point. We must consider the question in what sense God really has now fulfilled the promises in Ezek 36–37. Ezekiel envisages the people given a lively, spirited, flexible mind such as will enable them to walk in God's ways and share God's perspective and concern for the world. The Jewish-Gentile church sees itself as the heir to that promise. Yet it is not obvious that this church any more possesses a consistently lively, spirited, flexible, responsive, God-aware, world-aware mind than First Testament Israel did. The promise has not been fulfilled.

A consideration of the parallel prophecy in Jer 31:31–34 may help to sharpen the point, though in keeping with the apparent avoidance of spirit language in Jeremiah it does not explicitly mention God's spirit. It promises that Yahweh's teaching will be written into the attitudes of the people rather as regulations are written in a registrar's mind. As a result they will not need to teach or exhort each other to acknowledge Yahweh because they will all individually do so instinctively. Hebrews at one point says that this promise has been kept (Heb 8:8–12; 10:14–17), yet it may seem to deny it by the extent to which it offers teaching and exhortation. And in due course the New Testament encourages the development of an institutional ministry corresponding to that of First Testament Israel whose end Jeremiah heralds (further, Rom 11:27 locates the realization of Jer 31:31–34 in the future).[5]

Joel similarly promised that the spirit of Yahweh would make it natural for people of all ages and classes and of both sexes to prophesy, in keeping with Moses' longing (Num 11:29). Acts declares that Joel's promise has been fulfilled. But in the history of the church the gift of prophecy has been hardly more prevalent than was the case within First Testament Israel, and the priesthood of First Testament Israel has been reestablished in the church.

Paul pictures the Holy Spirit as dwelling in the Christian community as if the community were a temple, and he speaks of this as a fulfillment of First Testament hopes that built on the recognition that the God who dwelt and traveled with the people of Abraham and Moses cannot be contained in stone buildings (2 Cor 6:16). The Christian church then rebuilt the First Testament temple in its buildings with their common tripartite structure and transferred the word "church" to these buildings.

In practice, the position and lives of Christian believers are not so very different from that of First Testament believers. We are like Ruth and Daniel who produce the fruit of the Spirit, but also like Jacob and David who more obviously live more according to the flesh. It is as if the Spirit is not yet [given].

---

[5] See further chapter 9 above, §§ 6–7.

5. The Witness of the Spirit

So what did Jesus achieve? What difference did his coming make? Classically there is an objective, datable aspect to this question, and a subjective, experiential aspect. Jesus was the first human being to live his whole life by the Spirit in obedience to the Father; it was this that enabled him by his final act of obedience to make atonement for the rest of humanity. Henceforth, the whole world is to be invited to live with God on the basis of this act of self-offering. On what basis did First Testament Israel live with God before this event, then, given that it had been invited to do so? It was surely on the same basis, though the event had not yet taken place. Jesus' act of obedience by anticipation applied to those First Testament believers too. They lived with God on the same basis as we do. They too prayed in the Spirit to the Father through Christ, though they used none of these prepositional phrases.

Or suppose we put Jesus' achievement in terms of his winning a unique victory over powers of evil, whose fruits can also be enjoyed by people who belong to him. Did First Testament Israel exercise victory over powers of evil? That was intended from Gen 1 and experienced in Egypt and at the Red Sea, while in the Psalms, Israelites put evil to flight and enjoy the freedom to bless and to curse. Again the effectiveness of Jesus' act applied to First Testament believers.

Or suppose we put Jesus' achievement in terms of the opening of the door to eternal life. Were First Testament believers to stay dead when they died? Here more explicitly New Testament writers imply the conviction that this door is opened for people who lived before Christ as well as for his contemporaries and for people who would live afterwards (e.g., Matt 27:51–53; 1 Pet 4:6).

Or suppose we put Jesus' significance in terms that have been more appealing over the past century. Jesus took experience of human life, suffering, and death into the Godhead. Here something novel happened, though again it is something in continuity with the First Testament, for the possibility of God's becoming human was grounded in humanity's having been made in God's image, and the First Testament hints at the pain in the heart of God at the awareness of human pain. It was not least in the context of their distress that Israel knew the manifestation of Yahweh's personal presence in the form of the dynamic presence of Yahweh's holy spirit (Isa 63:8–14). Even the capacity to die was a capacity in God from the beginning.

In the datable once-for-all Christ event with a before and after, however, Jesus did make his offering, win his victory, open a door, and take the experience of death into the Godhead. And all that gave the Spirit something to witness to (John 14:26; 16:14).[6] The nature of witness is that its object is something that has happened. Objectively and in theory it might make no difference to believers whether they lived before or after Christ, because Christ's achievement applies to people before him as well as after him. Subjectively, however, it would make a significant difference,

---

[6]Cf. H. F. Woodhouse, "The Holy Ghost Was Not Yet Given," *Theology* 167 (1964): 310–12.

because to people who live after Christ the Spirit can give explicit witness to what Christ has now done, as something that can be directly reflected on and appreciated.

So after the death of Christ, people can understand directly how it affects them; and to judge from a passage such as Rom 6, understanding this can be expected to make a difference to their experience of its fruits. After the death of Christ, people can know that the great victory over evil has been won. This will naturally add to their expectations of what God can achieve through them. After the death of Christ, people can know that they will enjoy eternal life, rather than being ignorant of this fact. They can know the Spirit as the spirit of eternal life, not just of this life. That, too, will make a difference to their present experience as they now live their life in new hope. After the death of Christ, people have new concrete evidence of the length, depth, height, and breadth of the love of God, and the Spirit has more basis on which to overwhelm them with the love of God (Rom 5:5).

In each case the difference in the nature of the Christian experience of God comes not simply because of what Christ has done; First Testament believers also enjoyed the benefits of that. It comes from their being able to know about what Christ has done, to receive the Spirit's witness to it, which can be given because it is now something actual. It is this that makes for a difference between Abraham's experience of God and Paul's. And it is for this reason that God's expectations of the people of Jesus can be higher than God's expectations of First Testament Israel. Whereas they lived by faith, in this sense we live by sight. The Spirit can explicitly work to the expression in us of a cross-shaped life.

That also makes it the more pathetic that the people of Jesus are as much like Jacob and David as like Ruth and Hannah, and that the Christian community may seem to experience less victory over evil than Israel did, and less freedom in prayer and praise than the First Testament envisages.

Taking John 7 in isolation could lead to Christians operating with a once-for-all-step-upwards model of the relationship between the activity of the Holy Spirit in First Testament times and New Testament times. More appropriate is an up-and-down model that presupposes gains and losses within First Testament times and recognizes that the Holy Spirit has by no means yet finished with us (which had better be so, after all).

On the one hand, then, the nature of First Testament believers' relationship with God in the Holy Spirit needs to be taken seriously; they model for us a life lived in the Spirit. On the other, all the potential of God's ultimate act in Jesus lies before us in a more explicit way than was the case for them. A crucial key to entering into it is knowledge of it, because that is the one thing we have that the First Testament saints did not have. This key, in fact, is the study of scripture. It is a potential key to discovering the riches we have in Christ Jesus in the Spirit, riches that far exceed anything we have begun to enjoy. Like First Testament Israel, we are invited to live in hope, in the sense of living in the conviction that what God intends for us far exceeds what we now experience. It is the Holy Spirit who encourages that hope, who is the guarantee that it is not empty hope, who works in us whatever fulfillment of it we now experience, who has the capacity to work in us that fulfillment that goes far beyond what we have begun to enjoy, and who invites us actively to seek that fulfillment.

14

HOW DOES PRAYER WORK?

Intercession, praying for someone else, may seem the strangest form of prayer. What kind of father refrains from giving good gifts to his children until another member of the family asks him to do so? What is the logic of intercession? Why does it work (when it does)?[1]

1. Intercession Presupposes That God's Policy Is to Involve Us

The Bible's first intercessor provides a starting point for understanding intercession (see Gen 18:17–33). Abraham is destined to be a blessing to the world and has a related obligation to the faithful exercise of authority. It is in this double connection that Yahweh reveals to him the calamity that is to come on Sodom and waits to discover his response. We might expect Abraham to enthuse over this disaster because it constitutes good news for Sodom's victims. In fact, it leads Abraham to challenge God about how authority is to be implemented. The expectations Yahweh has of Abraham are turned back on Yahweh. In the conversation that ensues, Yahweh agrees to see that the authority is indeed exercised in a proper way.

A pattern about God's activity in the world, especially with regard to the exercise of authority in relation to wrongdoing, appears for the first time here. God announces an intention, but then, strangely, does not set about putting the intention into effect. What goes on between God and people who are not directly affected will decide whether God's intention is implemented. Abraham plays a role God intends for him, the taking of a share in the process whereby decisions are taken and implemented in the world. For some reason, God does not do that alone but involves Abraham. What we call intercessory prayer is the way Abraham fulfils this calling.

If intercession is a way Abraham accepts an involvement in God's working in the world, the background to intercession lies even further back in the Bible, in its first chapter. In general, indeed, Abraham's role is to be God's means of realizing the purpose that goes back to creation, a purpose to bless the world that failed to find realization in Gen 1–11. God recalls that purpose when telling us the thinking that led to explaining to Abraham what was to happen (Gen 18:18). This particular role of intercession in Gen 18 is part of Abraham's bringing about the blessing of the

---

[1]First published as "The Logic of Intercession," in *Theology* 99 (1998): 262–70.

world that God intended from creation. His prayer works on the basis of a fundamental aspect of the way God intended to relate to human beings as created. God created us as God-like and commissioned us to share in God's work in the world. The Abraham story suggests that intercession is one of the ways in which human beings do that. Indeed, this makes intercession an inevitable part of human life.

Abraham is intended not only to pray for the world's blessing but also to stimulate the world into praying for blessing for itself. All peoples are to "be blessed" or to "bless themselves" by Abraham. The promise appears in two different forms of the verb; in some, at least (namely, in Gen 22:18 and Gen 26:4) Yahweh speaks unambiguously of people "blessing themselves" by Abraham. To "bless yourself" is to "pray to be blessed as he is blessed" (NEB).

That is not intercession but supplication, prayer for oneself, but it links with another element in the Abraham story, for already Melchizedek has "blessed Abraham" (Gen 14:19). What does it mean to bless someone else? Melchizedek blesses Abraham by saying "blessed be Abraham by God Most High." There is no "be" expressed in that sentence; Melchizedek declares that Abraham is blessed. It looks as if Melchizedek has power to bless Abraham. If that were uncertain, it becomes more explicit the next time a human being blesses another, when Rebekah's family bless Rebekah (Gen 24:60): "Become thousands of myriads; your offspring are to gain possession of the gates of their foes." Here the first verb is an imperative, a verb that sounds like a command but as much suggests a commission, a promise, and a declaration of what will be. "Become thousands of myriads." The second verb is a jussive, a third-person imperative; we do not have an equivalent in English. We might think of it as a third-person command, a declaration of what must and shall be: "Your offspring are to gain possession of their foes."

Human beings sometimes have the power to tell other people in God's name that they can, must, and will enjoy certain blessings and achievements. Where does that power come from? Theologically it is the same commission in Gen 1:26 that lies behind the human power to bless and the human power to curse, which Noah had (Gen 9:25) and which ordinary people evidently also have (e.g., Lev 20:9). References by Jesus and Paul to blessing and cursing, and actual blessings and curses, show how this power continues in the New Testament (e.g., Luke 6:28; Rom 12:14; Gal 1:8–9). The movie *Antonia's Line* contains a frightening scene where a woman curses a would-be rapist, who then experiences a terrible beating. The power to curse is part of God's delegating authority to us as human beings. Human words can have the power and effectiveness of God's own words.

Prayers of blessing and cursing are relatives of prayers of intercession. They are part of the way we are involved in running the world on God's behalf.

2. Intercession as the Task of a Prophet

The point about the significance of intercession may be made in another way by noting that Abraham is the first prophet in the Bible; he is called such explicitly because he is an intercessor (see Gen 20:7, 17). One of the implications of this story of Abraham and Abimelech is that there are apparently no moral conditions attached to intercession. The answering of prayer does not depend on the uprightness of the person praying, just as the uttering of a divine word does not imply the uprightness of the prophet (compare Jesus' comments in Matt 7:21–23).

Intercession was integral to prophecy. The first person for whom "prophet" is the dominant designation is Samuel. When the people are the object of his prophetic rebuke, their instinctive reaction is to ask him to pray for them, and his response includes the assurance that he would view it as a sin against Yahweh if he stopped doing so (1 Sam 12:19, 23). Amos 7 well illustrates the point that being a prophet involves being an intercessor, as Amos instinctively asks for the suspending of the very punishments that he announces. In Amos's case, before we are assured that he indeed confronted people with Yahweh's warnings (Amos 7:10–17) we meet with a prophet who takes for granted that his job is to confront God when given pictures of calamity, to query whether punishment should be implemented (Amos 7:1–6). Admittedly Amos does not confront Yahweh's third and fourth pictures (Amos 7:7–9; 8:1–3), which may imply that there is a time when prayer can be answered and a time when it cannot.

Moses is also called a prophet, and he too is an intercessor, though Ps 99:6 perhaps assumes that Moses prays as priest; the Aaronic priesthood interceded for the people in presenting their offerings. The conversations between Moses and Yahweh in Exod 32–34 illustrate the same dynamics as those involving Abraham and Samuel. Yahweh declares the intention to annihilate the people. Moses responds with a number of reasons why Yahweh should not do so: it is inconsistent with the activity of bringing them out of Egypt, it will make a fool of Yahweh in the eyes of the Egyptians, and it conflicts with the undertakings given to Israel's ancestors. Yahweh is convinced and has a change of mind (Exod 32:7–14). When we intervene in some context to speak on someone's behalf, we may well be concerned to commend them as worth acting on behalf of. This is also a feature of intercession. In thanksgiving the intercessor draws attention to what God has already achieved in a person's life, which is a reason for God's work in them to be taken further (cf. Phil 1:3–5).

Human beings fulfill their prophetic/priestly intercessory vocation when they query whether God's intentions regarding calamity should be implemented. A remark of God's to Ezekiel makes the point sharply. Among the ills of the household of Israel, including its prophets, is that "I sought for someone from among them as a repairer of the wall and one who would stand in the breach before me on behalf of the land, so that I would not destroy it; but I did not find anyone" (Ezek 22:30). Isaiah 62:6–7 offers a variant on the same picture. God has made and announced certain decisions regarding Jerusalem-Zion's restoration, decisions that might have seemed slow to be implemented. Now God recalls having also made sure that there were people who would press for this implementation. God appoints God's own reminders, people to trouble God. Jeremiah's story proves the rule as the prophet is forbidden to intercede in order to get a decision changed and thus to fulfill the normal God-appointed role of a prophet by advocating alternative actions to those Yahweh announces. The reason is that the people's punishment is now irrevocable

(Jer 14–15). It is not explicit whether Jeremiah is to take this as Yahweh's final word, in keeping with the second pair of Amos's visions, or whether it is an implicit invitation to another form of intercession.

These examples of prophetic intercession suggest that special significance attaches to intercession as a means of seeing that people do not pay the penalty for their failures. Praying for mercy and forgiveness for people is of decisive importance to what happens to them. The comprehensive failure of Jonah as prophet not surprisingly includes a failure here as intercessor. When he ought to have been praying in the ship, he was fast asleep (Jonah 1), and when he ought to have been concerned for Nineveh, he was concerned only about his parasol plant (Jonah 4). Yet the story also shows that God need not be constrained by the failures of intercessors.

Intercession is part of a prophet's role for the same reason that prophecy is part of a prophet's role. It arises from a prophet's being admitted to Yahweh's cabinet (Jer 23:18). As members of this cabinet, prophets know about its decisions and are therefore in a position to prophesy but also in a position to take part in its deliberations, and in particular to question plans announced by Yahweh. Prophets urge God to take mercy seriously as they urge people to take wrath seriously. As individuals identified with both parties and with neither, their role is thus uncomfortable and isolated.

There is a long Christian tradition of praying to the saints or asking the saints for their prayers. This practice does not appear within either Testament. Yet, angels belong with prophets in Yahweh's cabinet, and thus they, too, take part in its deliberations by interceding for us and for the world. The vision of this in Zech 3 also portrays a heavenly being interceding against us, a heavenly adversary or accuser (cf. Job 1–2; the Hebrew word *hassatan* means "the adversary"). There is a hint that this figure has a role as His Majesty's loyal opposition but fulfills his adversarial role misguidedly or too enthusiastically. Perhaps it might be possible to redeem him by appealing to him to fulfill his proper vocation by intervening against the wicked who ought to be the objects of his hostile intervention. Appeal to the Adversary would thus be a way of appealing for justice to be done.

3. Intercession Presupposes That God Is Like the Rector

If God invites human beings in general, and prophets and intercessors in particular, to take a share in the making of decisions concerning what happens in the world, this implies a markedly different understanding of God and of God's relationship with the world from the one implicit in much Christian theology and piety. That often thinks of God as like a king, and a king who exercises a sovereignty more like absolute power than anything we see in a Western monarchy. It is when this picture is combined with that of God as a father who obviously wants what is best for his children that difficulties are generated for an understanding of how things are in the world or the church. Those pictures are scriptural ones, but they mislead if they are taken as the whole truth. The Bible also implies another picture that needs combining with those. God is also like a (half-decent) rector or senior pastor. A rector does not decide alone on parish policies and implement them but involves the people of the parish in the process of decision making and implementation. The rector does not act in isolation but collaboratively. Likewise God does not act alone but collaboratively.

It is in keeping with this inclination that God involves people such as prophets in decision making. Prophets are God's assistant ministers, troubling God as assistant ministers trouble rectors (as my rector used to tell me). The story told in the Christian Bible as a whole and the story of the church and the nations also illustrates the way God declines to act alone and monarchically. Those stories show God not generally imposing a will on people but seeking to draw people into the fulfillment of the divine purpose, though usually failing. So the rector reflects God's way of setting about the implementing of a purpose. Perhaps God's purpose embraces the process as well as the result, because the process reflects something of what God wants to achieve, something of the aim; it requires the involvement of people. Intercession is one way we are involved and take part in the process whereby decisions are taken and implemented.

Of course the rector will have some aims for the church with regard to areas such as service, evangelism, and worship, will keep working at those, and ultimately will not compromise over them or give up on them. But the way those aims are pursued and the timing of attempts to fulfill them may be endlessly negotiable, because the process is part of the aim. The kind of community the rector is committed to building has to be involved in the fulfillment of the aims; otherwise the rector's very aims would not be being fulfilled. In a parallel way, God has some ultimate aims: that people should come to know God and that right should come to prevail in the world. Our prayer needs to accord with God's will in the sense of matching those aims. But because of that concern for process and the building of a community, God is willing to be tirelessly flexible about the fulfillment of these aims.

To intercede, then, is to urge that certain decisions get taken and implemented on the basis of their consistency with the aims. No doubt it needs to be accompanied by a commitment on the intercessors' part to the implementation of the aims, but it loses its intrinsic meaning if it is transformed into a form of prayer whose real significance is to change the people who pray. It is about the taking of decisions regarding what is to happen, and if people do not take part in the urging of certain decisions, the decisions may not get taken in the way they might have urged. The discussions are real and issue in real change. In the same way it is not necessarily appropriate for intercessors to want to know specifically what God wants before they themselves pray. Their prayer needs to accord with God's policies, but often it plays a part in the determining of God's will rather than merely asking for that will to be implemented.

At least it may do so, if our urging wins its way in the debate. There is no mystery about the fact that many of our contributions to the debate, many of our urgings, do not win assent. As can happen with any item on an agenda, there may be other insights and other factors that overcome our urgings this time. Perhaps another time this will not be so; it is worth keeping making our point, because its moment may come. So we persist in prayer and repeat our prayers. And when we intervene with an "Amen" in the midst of someone's prayer, it is like saying yes or nodding our head when someone makes a contribution to a debate. It adds to the force of the argument. Likewise when Christians pray in Jesus' name, we are claiming that the point we make is in conformity with Jesus' priorities; that too adds to the force of the argument (see, for instance, John 14:13–14; 15:7, 16; 16:23–24).

When the rector as chair proposes a course of action, this is a proposal, not a decision. It is a matter for people to debate, and the debate may lead to a different course of action from the one proposed. In light of the debate the rector will be as free as anyone else to have a change of mind about what should be done, even if this implies no change of mind about ultimate aims. To change one's mind in that context is a sign of strength. In the same way, the Bible takes for granted that God is free to have a change of mind in the course of equivalent discussions. As we have seen, in the Bible, intercession is characteristically designed to change the chair's mind about a decision concerning the world (Gen 18) or concerning the people of God (e.g., Exod 32–34).

In a single context the First Testament can declare that God does have a change of mind and that God does no such thing, or at least not as a human being does (1 Sam 15:11, 29; cf. Num 23:19). Put alongside each other the second of these safeguards the first by affirming that Yahweh's changes of mind do not indicate inconsistency or fickleness or capriciousness, but it must not be allowed to emasculate the earlier statement as if were a trivial figure of speech. It is an important expression of the standard biblical picture of God living in real relationship with human beings in history and thus acting both by initiative and response.[2]

4. Intercession Involves Intervening on Behalf of People

It is characteristic of group deliberations of the kind we have been considering that people speak urgently and fervently on behalf of groups they represent. At least, it should be so, and it is so with intercession. To intercede involves standing in the place of people who need to have their position represented and speaking from that place. Hebrews 13:3 urges its hearers to remember people who are in prison or who are being tortured "as though you were in prison with them . . . as though you yourselves were being tortured." Prayer happens "as though." It puts itself in the place of those for whom we pray.

The scriptures' own manual of praises and prayers, the Psalms, includes little that we would recognize as intercession. Psalm 72 is an exception that perhaps proves the rule by making one wonder whether it is really in part a veiled exhortation rather than a prayer. That and other such psalms for the king (e.g., Ps 20) may also be seen as veiled supplications, because the king's blessing is also the people's blessing. But examples such as Jeremiah's suggest that the psalms of lament were designed to be prayed not merely by the afflicted themselves but by others who

---

[2]See further chapter 3 above.

prayed with them and on behalf of them. They are prayers prayed for people oppressed or hurting, prayed by people who identify with them and urge their need
on God, even in a way they may not be able to do for themselves. These psalms are
then intercessions as much as petitions. They point us to the fact that in intercession we identify with those for whom we pray, and we pray not for them but for us,
as happens in the prayers in Jer 14. This may fit with some instances of the way in
which the prayers of the Psalms move between "we/I" and "they" as the intercessor oscillates between identification and distinction. While that may reflect the
dynamic of Ps 20 whereby "we" pray for the king because his blessing matters to us,
it may sometimes indicate a more altruistic prayer in which I can think of myself
as interceding for "them" or for "us."

This motif of identification fits with a linguistic fact. There is a rare Hebrew
word that is translated "intercede," *paga'* (e.g., Isa 53:12; Jer 7:16; 15:11). In ordinary
speech it means to "meet" or to "intervene" (cf. Gen 23:8, NRSV "entreat"; Ruth 1:16,
NRSV "press"; Isa 59:16). An intercessor is one who intervenes on someone's behalf
and has a meeting with another person on their behalf. The equivalent New Testament words *[hyper]entunchano* are also rare; they have the same meaning, though
the verbs are not used of human intercession (the noun appears in 1 Tim 2:1).

Elsewhere in the New Testament, Rom 8:26–27 sees the Spirit as our intercessor, while Rom 8:34 and Heb 7:25 see Christ as our intercessor in the manner of an
Israelite priest when offering sacrifice or of Moses as covenant mediator (figures
who may lie behind the servant "interceding" in Isa 53:12). The implication is that
the Spirit or Christ is the one who makes meetings between us and God possible.
Christ does that objectively. Because of our behavior we had forfeited our right to
membership of the group where decisions get taken, but because Christ died for
us we have the right to rejoin the meeting and to speak there. Herein lies another
significance of our interceding "in the name of Jesus": we speak because Jesus
brought us back into the cabinet. He makes meetings between us and God possible objectively. The Spirit makes these meetings possible subjectively, giving us
the confidence to speak to God, the ideas and words to speak, and the instinct to
speak what is in accordance with God's nature.

But those technical words for intercession are rare in scripture. It more often
uses more ordinary words when it wants to speak about intercession, especially
the everyday expression "ask on behalf of" somebody. The Bible tends not to use
special religious words for our religious activities; it links our religious life with our
everyday life. So instead of talking about praying, it talks about asking. And using
the same words for asking for things on behalf of others again draws our attention
to the fact that intercession is the same as supplication or praying for oneself. We
pray as if we were doing it for ourselves when we are doing it for someone else. So
however we pray for ourselves, in intercession we do that with other people in mind.
In his book *Prayer*, Otto Hallesby[3] sees prayer as starting from our helplessness and
giving God access to our needs in the manner encouraged by the picture in Rev 3:20,
where Christ stands seeking access to the community's heart or life. In intercession

---

[3](Reprint ed.; London: IVF, 1959).

we identify with others' helplessness and give God access to their needs, opening the door of their lives on their behalf and asking God to enter.

Intervening and arguing a case may well involve effort and persistence. The New Testament also speaks of a need for effort and persistence in prayer (e.g., Rom 12:12; Col 4:2) and implies it requires self-discipline, hard work, and doggedness. In this sense there may be no special or modern reason why Christians are tempted to give up prayer. If the analogy holds between prayer and the confrontational arguing of a case, this may help to indicate why prayer often seems hard work and potentially seems to require perseverance and the refusal to give up a task before it is completed.

Paul indeed speaks of prayer as engaging in a fight (Rom 15:30; Col 2:1; 4:12). For people such as Abraham when he prays for Sodom, and Moses at Sinai praying for Israel, the battle of prayer is a struggle with God, a battle to change God's mind. For Moses in Exod 17, when the Israelites are fighting the Amalekites and he is lifting up his hand directing the heavenly forces, it is a matter of exercising authority over forces that themselves battle against God's people; in Eph 6, too, it is a battle against other powers (cf. the battle in Rev 13). In battling to change God's mind we assume that there is another side to God to appeal to. In battling against other powers we assume that we can appeal to God as the chair of the group.

Another way of expressing what I have described as the objective and subjective aspects to making intercession possible is to see it as involving the work of both priest and prophet. The priest makes it possible by helping to restore people's relationship with Yahweh, and the prophet puts this potential into effect by interceding. If the church has Abraham as its example, inherits the priesthood of Christ, and is filled by the Spirit of prophecy, it receives the responsibility of taking its part in the process of heavenly decision making and representation undertaken by people such as Abraham, Moses, and some prophets by being involved in intercession. If all believers may prophesy and may approach God's presence, it follows that all may individually share in this involvement. Indeed, for them not to do so has the same snags as when some people never take part in a discussion in a meeting. At the same time, if some have a special gift of prophecy or a special position as priests, it follows that some have a special gift or responsibility for intercession. Thus Paul's intercession is an aspect of his exercise of a priestly ministry. Part of his responsibility for the churches in his care was to present them to Christ whole, holy, and mature, when Christ appears (e.g., Rom 15:15–16). So intercession for his people is an aspect of his ministry to his people.

It is a characteristic expression of God's instinctive self-humbling to share with us the making of decisions in the world; and we do this by intercession.

15

What Is Israel's Place in God's Purpose?

As the adopted offspring of Abraham and Sarah, Christians stand in perennial need of a theological understanding of the Jewish people, the descendants of Abraham and Sarah who do not recognize Jesus. Present generations stand in particular historical need of such a theological understanding of the Jewish people's place in the world because of the events of the past century or so, especially the exponential growth of the Jewish community in Palestine, the cataclysm of the Holocaust, the establishment of the State of Israel, and the ongoing conflict between Israel and the Palestinian people, all these events being in part attributable to the action or indifference of European powers and the United States. Yet precisely because of these events, an understanding that does justice to the complex exegetical, historical, political, theological, and moral issues is more difficult than it has ever been. Grief and anger at the suffering Zionism has brought to the Palestinian people, and joy and wonder at God's ancient people finding a home for itself again in its promised land, stand in strong tension. But both are biblical responses to events.[1]

My attempt to do justice to such tensions is structured around four polemical theses.

1. The Jewish People Is Still God's People but Is Destined to Come to Recognize Jesus

Is it really the case that the Jewish people has a special theological significance such as does not attach to the Chinese, the British, the Arabs, or the U.S.A.?[2] Many nations bolster their self-esteem by thinking that God attaches special significance to them.

Christians, at least, can hardly view the idea of God attaching special significance to the Jewish people as a myth. The New Testament presents Jesus to us as a Jew whose story continues and brings to a climax the history of God's purpose

---

[1] This chapter combines material first published as "The Christian Church and Israel," in *Theological Renewal* 23 (1983): 4–19; "The Jews, the Land, and the Kingdom," in *Anvil* 4 (1987): 9–22; "Modern Israel and Biblical Prophecy," in *Third Way* 6/4 (1983): 6–8; and "Palestine and the Prophets," in *Third Way* 2/7 (1978): 3–6.

[2] On this question, see further chapter 16 below, § 1.

with Israel and who can only be understood in connection with that story. Further, finding we hear God's word out of Jewish scriptures (the New Testament being a Jewish book as essentially as the First Testament is), writings that emerged from the life and history of the Jewish people, carries implications regarding the specialness of the Jewish people in the purpose of God.

But if the Jews were once of special significance in God's purpose, are they still so? Jesus spoke of his fellow Jews killing the vineyard owner's son and having the kingdom of God taken away from them to be given to others (Matt 21:43), and Paul can speak of his fellow Jews in very negative terms (Phil 3:2; 1 Thess 2:15–16). In line with this, the New Testament applies to the church many First Testament designations of Israel (e.g., 1 Pet 2:9–10). The people who belong to Christ are the offspring of Abraham; they are the real circumcision (Gal 3:29; Phil 3:3). Has the church taken over the position Israel lost because of its failure to respond to Jesus? Ephesians describes the people of God as now a single new humanity in which the distinction between Jew and Gentile has been abolished (Eph 2:15). It often seems to Jews that Christians describe the superiority of their Christian faith in such a way as to encourage anti-Semitism; phrases such as "the Jews crucified Christ" especially have this effect. Has God given up any special relationship with the Jewish people, in response to its turning away expressed in its spurning of its Messiah?

The way the New Testament story continues after Jesus' crucifixion suggests this is not so. Acts emphasizes that the Jews are the first to be invited to renew their place in the kingdom and that very many of them respond.[3] The terrible "prayer," "his blood be on us," has found its adequate counter-prayer in Jesus' "Father, forgive them."[4] Jesus' warnings, taken up by Paul, need to be understood by analogy with those of the prophets, whose warnings that their contemporaries were in imminent danger of forfeiting their destiny (and who did so) did not mean that the ultimate destiny of that people to which God had made a commitment in Abraham was endangered. This is not surprising. God had, after all, made a pledge to a permanent covenant with Israel. As is the case in the First Testament, Jesus' word of judgment that sounds so final is followed by the undeserved word of grace. The Israel of any particular generation, like the church of any generation, can be threatened with rejection and can be cast off. But God will still keep a commitment to the seed of Jacob as an entity. Israel is still the people of God, even though no longer its sole embodiment, and even though its rejection of Jesus puts it largely into a state of suspended animation. And therefore it will come to acknowledge Jesus. This is not so much a prediction as a promise that God will keep issuing the invitation to it to respond as God's elect should, until it does so.

Paul notes that there are severe theological and spiritual difficulties about the idea that God could terminate commitment to Israel, even in response to acts on Israel's part that could quite justify such a response. This is expressed in the New Testament's most systematic attempt to theologize about the Jewish people, in Rom 9–11.

---

[3] See Jacob Jervell, *Luke and the People of God* (Minneapolis: Augsburg, 1972), 44–46.
[4] David Pawson, *The Church, Britain, the World, and Israel* (taped address; Bromley: Prayer for Israel, 1981).

These chapters form no digression extrinsic to the main argument of Romans. They constitute a climax within it, perhaps even *the* climax.[5] The question of Israel's destiny first appears near the opening of the letter, but it is set aside as Paul attempts to establish that his gospel of salvation by faith is a good Jewish gospel. He does so by showing it corresponds to Abraham's experience, that its effects parallel the effects of Adam's sin, and that it leads to the fulfilling rather than the frustrating of the law's essential purpose (Rom 4–8). But he also has to establish the logic of his claim that Israel's unfaithfulness and turning away from the gospel do not nullify God's faithfulness (so Rom 3:3–4), since this possibility constitutes another powerful objection to his gospel. He thus points out that God's faithfulness has ensured that a remnant of the Jewish people has responded, which was often all that happened in First Testament times (Rom 9:6–29); that responsibility for not responding rests with the Jewish people itself, since it has had opportunity to respond (Rom 9:30–10:21); but that after its failure has found positive fruit in leading to a concentration on mission to the Gentiles, it will be restored (Rom 11:1–32).

"And so all Israel will be saved" (Rom 11:26). Presumably this will come about by the same means as the salvation of Gentiles, by the Spirit opening Israel's eyes to the significance of Jesus (there are not two ways of salvation). But Paul is silent on that; perhaps he has told us all he felt clear about. He has shown that his gospel is Jewish and biblical. It establishes the Jewish people's vocation as the people of God in a new and undreamed-of way, rather than annulling it. It is still God's people, and God still intends to save it.

John Calvin believed that when Paul declares that "all Israel will be saved," "Israel" refers not to the Jewish people but to the "new Israel," the church.[6] If we understand this to denote the church as opposed to Israel, the context of the statement undermines this interpretation. It would bring Paul's whole argument to a limp conclusion. This argument at least requires that the Jewish people be included in this "Israel" (as Calvin, indeed, assumed); otherwise Paul's demonstration of God's faithfulness to the Jewish people collapses. Further, "Israel" appears ten times elsewhere in these chapters, and each time it refers to the Jewish people; there is no indication that it has a different sense in Rom 11:26. There is no point in the New Testament where "Israel" denotes the church. Although the New Testament uses terms to describe the church that the First Testament uses to describe Israel, it does not describe the church as "Israel" or the "new Israel" or the "true Israel." The transference of such terms from the Jewish people to the church begins with Justin Martyr, when the tension over the Jewish people's position that is maintained in the New Testament is lost and the church is distancing itself over against Judaism.[7] In

---

[5] So Krister Stendahl, *Paul among Jews and Gentiles and Other Essays* (Philadelphia: Fortress, 1976), 4.

[6] See *The Epistles of Paul the Apostle to the Romans and to the Thessalonians* (Edinburgh: Oliver and Boyd, 1961), on the passage.

[7] On this process, see P. Richardson, *Israel in the Apostolic Church* (London / New York: Cambridge University Press, 1969); his treatment of Gal 6:16 presents the most plausible understanding of the verse as (in keeping with Rom 9–11) seeking God's mercy on Israel as well as on believers in Christ.

the New Testament, "Israel" means "Israel." The New Testament does not describe even Jesus as Israel, the true Israel, or the new Israel. The Jewish-Gentile church comes to share in Israel's privileges and can be understood by means of images that the First Testament uses to describe Israel, but this does not mean that the church has replaced Israel.

If "all Israel" refers to the Jewish people, does it denote the sum total of believing Israel throughout the generations,[8] or rather the people as a whole turning to Christ at the end?[9] The latter view brings into focus the important expectation that God's faithfulness will bring a large-scale acknowledgment of Jesus on the part of the Jewish people, the former avoids the danger of this vision becoming a piece of distant eschatology without direct application to the present. In any case we must see Paul's argument and hope in the context of his own ministry and experience;[10] in this context, there might be little difference between these two alternatives. Paul hoped that he himself would see the Gentile world, and thus the Jewish people, too, turn to Jesus. It was this hope that energized his ministry, as happened again when this understanding of Paul was recovered by the Puritans.[11]

When one considers how to relate the two perspectives (Israel's rejection and its security) within the New Testament, Rom 9–11 provides the most comprehensive horizon for an understanding: it embraces the theme of Israel's rejection, which is acknowledged but seen as ultimately subordinate to its acceptance. These chapters themselves show that the application to Gentiles of Hosea's "not-my-people" becoming "my people" (1 Pet 2:10) need not imply that the description "my people" is simply transferred to the church and no longer applies to the Jewish people. Paul quotes this passage from Hosea (see Rom 9:22–26) in the context of an argument that ultimately asserts that the Jewish people does still belong to God. The church comes to share its historic privileges and is described in terms that historically described it, but this does not imply that those descriptions no longer apply to the Jewish people. Gentiles come to be fellow heirs with Jews, not replacements of them.

If the New Testament has a concept of a new Israel, while not using the expression, the New Israel is that body that comprises the Jewish people as a whole plus Gentiles who in Christ become adopted children of Abraham, a vision that corresponds to the one in Isa 2. As with the covenant, the new takes up and transforms the old, it does not set it aside; otherwise, God would hardly be faithful and self-consistent. The resistance of most Jews short-circuits the process of bringing the new Israel into being and makes this new Israel still the object of faith and hope; the largely Gentile church with a vacuum at its center can hardly comprise the ultimate new Israel. Meanwhile, the true Israel includes Gentile believers by adoption, but it explicitly comprises the remnant of Jews that does recognize Jesus

---

[8] So, e.g., William Hendriksen, *Israel and the Bible* (Grand Rapids: Baker, 1968).

[9] So, e.g., C. E. B. Cranfield, *The Epistle to the Romans Volume II* (Edinburgh: Clark, 1979), on the passage.

[10] See G. C. Berkouwer, *Studies in Dogmatics: The Return of Christ* (Grand Rapids: Eerdmans, 1972), 346–52.

[11] See I. H. Murray, *The Puritan Hope: A Study in Revival and the Interpretation of Prophecy* (London: Banner of Truth, 1971), esp. 42.

(so Rom 2:28–29; 9:6).[12] At the same time, alongside the one new humanity of which Ephesians speaks, the original embodiment of God's covenant people continues to exist, as something of an anomaly indeed, pending its recognizing Jesus and finding its rightful place in that new humanity that is so truncated without it.

God's continuing commitment to the Jewish people does not imply they are all right without recognizing Jesus, that it does not matter if they do not acknowledge him. One way to put that view is to suggest that God has two covenants, a covenant with the Jews that goes back to Abraham, then one with Gentiles that depends on Jesus. But a universal significance attaches to Jesus, a significance for Jews as well as Gentiles. The idea that Jews are perfectly all right without acknowledging the Jewish Messiah seems an odd one and can hardly be reconciled with the argument of Rom 9–11, as some "two covenants" theologians recognize. Paul assumes that God's commitment to Israel means it will indeed come to recognize Jesus; it does not mean it has no need to do so. In heaven I expect to meet Jews who have not recognized Jesus: not only Jews from First Testament times but also Jews who have lived since Jesus' day, people who have perhaps been prevented from recognizing him by the church's failure to reflect him. They will be there by God's electing grace, as I will be, and they will be there because Jesus lived, died, and rose for them, as he did for me (even if it is only then that they recognize that this was so), and they will be there because they have put their trust in God and God's grace, as I will be (not because they have done their best; no one will be there on that basis). There is only one covenant. All God's promises find their yes in Christ (2 Cor 1:20).

If God is still committed to the Jewish people but they do need to come to recognize Jesus as their Messiah (and God promises that they will), what is their continuing theological significance? The fundamental point derives from the simple fact that they continue to exist. This has often been seen as a powerful argument for believing in the existence of God; the argument has the more force after Hitler. Whether or not it should convince an agnostic of God's existence, for the believer (Rom 9–11 implies) it certainly witnesses to the faithfulness of God, for it reflects the fact that God long ago made a commitment to them. If God had not kept this commitment, what grounds would one have for believing that God would keep any other commitments? Precisely by its continuing existence despite its resistance to the gospel, the Jewish people witnesses to the faithfulness of God, to the grace of God, to the fact that salvation stems from grace and is based on election and on God's word of promise and not on human deserve, to the mercy of God that continues to love them despite their refusing to acknowledge Jesus, and to the power of God that continues to use them as God's witnesses. At the same time, it witnesses to the sinfulness of humanity, to the judgment that sinfulness deserves, and to the particular sinfulness of the people of God. To the Jewish people belong the covenants and the promises; yet it refuses Jesus. How necessary, then, Jesus (and specifically as the suffering Messiah) was. The Jewish people's failure and rejection warn the church against a false confidence in its relationship

---

[12]Cf. H. Berkhof, "Israel as a Theological Problem in the Christian Church," *JEcS* 6 (1969): 329–47 (335).

to God. If Israel could be given so much and fail, let those who think they stand take heed lest they fall.[13]

Once the church cut itself off from its Jewish roots, Israel came to have further theological significance for it. James Parkes summarizes the features of the Sinai revelation as the acceptance of a life that looks outward to the world because it looks upward to God, that is viewed as a unity because secular and religious are not divided, that involves life in community, and that is based on the law of God faithfully but boldly reinterpreted in each generation. The tragedy of a Christianity that has polarized over against Judaism and embraced Hellenism instead is that it has cut itself loose from its Jewish roots and thus developed unbiblically. H. Berkhof adds the Jewish people's having to live with the hiddenness of God, its insistence that the world is not yet redeemed, and its calling nevertheless to live by God's faithfulness in an unredeemed world.[14]

The Jewish people still belongs to God, and Jesus belonged to it; recognizing him is thus its privilege, responsibility, and calling. It still needs what the first sermons in Acts speak of: to find forgiveness and the gift of the Holy Spirit by turning from waywardness and acknowledging the crucified one as the one whom God has made both Lord and Messiah. It needs this no more than Gentiles do (it is not uniquely sinful), but no less than they (even though it already belongs to the God who offers these gifts to it).

Indeed, its need to recognize Jesus is more pressing than it was in New Testament times. There is no adequate theology of the Holocaust, but there can be none except via thinking through the relationship of the crucifixion of the Jewish people and the crucifixion of Jesus. "If its faith in the faithfulness of God and in the integrity of his covenant is to survive, Israel cannot continue to hold apart the God in whom it believes and the enormity of its own suffering and hurt but must surely allow them to come together in the very heart of its trust in the living God. And how is that to come about except through the cross of Jesus Christ?"[15]

A Christian writer observes that "ultimately Romans 9–11 ends on a conversionist note that is unacceptable."[16] That view is itself unacceptable. Yet two millennia of church history make it more difficult to express what it is a Christian thinks a Jew is called to. "Conversion" has a different meaning in our world from the one it had in Acts, and Romans does not refer to the conversion of the Jewish people. We cannot easily talk of a Jew becoming a Christian or joining the church, because

---

[13]On Rom 9–11 see further Karl Barth's sustained theological exposition in *Church Dogmatics* II/2 (Edinburgh: Clark, 1957), 195–305.

[14]J. W. Parkes, *Judaism and Christianity* (Chicago: University of Chicago Press, 1948), 27–28, summarized in J. T. Pawlikowski, "The Church and Judaism," *JEcS* 6 (1969): 573–97 (588–89); cf. H. H. Harcourt, "Psychology, Reality, and Zionism," *JEcS* 7 (1970): 324–31 (325); Berkhof, "Israel as a Theological Problem in the Christian Church," 338, 346; also Hans Küng and Pinchas Lapide, "Is Jesus a Bond or Barrier?" *JEcS* 14 (1977): 466–83, on the Jewishness of Jesus.

[15]T. F. Torrance, "The Divine Vocation and Destiny of Israel in World History," in *The Witness of the Jews to God* (ed. D. W. Torrance; Edinburgh: Handsel, 1982), 85–104 (95).

[16]J. T. Pawlikowski, "The Contemporary Jewish-Christian Theological Dialogue Agenda," *JEcS* 11 (1974): 599–616 (602).

"church" stands over against "synagogue," and joining the church implies leaving the Jewish community, while becoming a Christian means "ceasing to be a Jew." This was not the case in the early years of Christianity, and one cannot necessarily fault Jews who come to believe in Jesus today for hesitating to use terms such as "Christian" and "church." Alternative terms such as "messianic assembly" are etymological equivalents, but they have not been subjected to centuries of reinterpretation that have given them essentially Gentile connotations. Even the Jewish rite of baptism became the supreme sign of leaving the Jewish community and reneging on one's Jewish faith (perhaps at the command of the sword), so that one may sometimes hesitate today to hurry a Jewish believer into baptism. Jewish believers still have to fight to establish within Judaism and within the church the conviction that believing in Jesus is a Jewish thing to do, that it is not a denial of their Jewishness but makes them "completed Jews," not ex-Jews. There could in theory be some danger here of the emergence of a new Christian Judaism. The challenge to messianic Jews and to the church is for the church to let messianic Jews help it recover something of its Jewish heritage. The particular challenge in Israel is the continuing development of a believing community that embraces Jews and Arabs.

Further, one has to acknowledge that calling Jesus Messiah may require an even greater leap of faith today than it did in A.D. 35. The Messiah is, after all, the one who brings about the reign of peace and justice. Two millennia of history leave the world no more full of peace and justice than it was. It is difficult to claim that matters are better in areas where the Christian church is strong, and it is understandable that Jews who have experienced manifold Christian persecution, harassment, or neglect are especially skeptical when they are told that the Messiah came long ago. Indeed, should we cease claiming that Jesus was the Messiah? After all, recognition as Messiah seemed to be the last thing Jesus himself sought. At least we have to recognize that like calling him Lord, calling Jesus Messiah is a statement of our faith, hope, and commitment; it is not what can actually be seen.[17] Yet we know that Jesus will fulfill the messianic dream because he *was* the one who lived, died, and rose from the dead for us. And that commitment continues to make its demand of Jews, too.

2. The Jewish People Still Has a Claim to a Homeland in Palestine

Thinking that God has abandoned the Jewish people or never chose them would naturally bring in its train the conviction that a Jewish claim to land in Palestine or anywhere else and an attaching of theological and moral significance to the State of Israel should be considered on the same basis as would apply to any other people or state. Two-covenant theology, in contrast, as well as implying that Jewish evange-

---

[17] See J. Cott, "The Problem of Christian Messianism," *JEcS* 16 (1979): 496–514; Pawlikowski, "The Contemporary Jewish-Christian Theological Dialogue Agenda," 603–5; C. Klein, "Catholics and Jews—Ten Years after Vatican II," *JEcS* 12 (1975): 471–84 (480–82); M. Hellwig, "Christian Theology and the Covenant of Israel," *JEcS* 7 (1970): 37–51 (49–50).

lism is unnecessary and wrong, will naturally go along with a positive view of the relationship between Jews and the land and a positive view of the establishment of the State of Israel. People who believe that God is still committed to the Jewish people but that they are destined to recognize Jesus are inclined to share that positive view.

In speaking of the theological entity "Israel," I have so far mostly referred to it as "the Jewish people" because "Israel" is also the name of the modern state. The Jewish people as a whole numbers some thirteen million, an average size for a modern people, perhaps, and a far larger size than it was in biblical times, despite crusade, inquisition, pogrom, Holocaust, and the running toll of assimilation. Nearly half of the thirteen million live in the United States. Nearly five million live in Israel. The rest are spread through Europe, South America, and elsewhere.[18] Yet for the Jewish people and for Gentiles, the State of Israel has an importance out of all proportion to its numbers. Does it have a distinctive theological significance? What sort of claim does Israel have to territory in the Middle East?

Israel can argue a claim to land in Palestine on historical, legal, and moral grounds. Israelites and Jews have lived there for more than three thousand years. When Zionist pioneers began to increase the number of Jews in Palestine just over a century ago, they generally acquired land legally or reclaimed land that was uncultivated. Their achievement in making swamp, desert, and barren hillside bloom is remarkable. After the Second World War, they accepted the United Nations plan to partition Palestine. Their subsequent territorial gains have been won in wars that arguably were all defensive: in particular, East Jerusalem and the West Bank were occupied only after Jordan had initiated attacks on West Jerusalem in 1967. Israel's right to land and nationhood in Palestine is as secure as, for instance, the United States' right to New Mexico or the rest of the territory the U.S.A. occupies or Britain's to the Falklands.

Israel's claim to Palestine is buttressed, however, in the mind of many Christians and Jews by theological considerations parallel to those relating to the Jewish people's special theological significance. God gave the land of Canaan to Israel, and a commitment to give Israel this land still stands. It goes back to God's original promise to Abraham, and it is thus intrinsic to the very beginning of God's commitment to Abraham's descendants (Gen 12:1–7; 15:1–21); it is not a relatively late theme like the promises concerning David and concerning the temple. It recurs in the account of God's second solemnizing of a covenant with Abraham, where possession of the land is to be as lasting as is the covenant itself (Gen 17:7–8; cf. Ps 105:7–11). There are various ways of understanding "all the land of Canaan" (Gen 17:8), but it is hard to think of it omitting what is now East Jerusalem and the West Bank.

Does such a promise still hold after the coming of Christ, in whom all God's promises find their yes (2 Cor 1:20)? Hebrews 3–4 sees the "rest" that the land embodied, the inheritance it symbolized, as now enjoyed in Jesus (cf. 1 Pet 1:4). Has the literal promise of land had its day?[19]

---

[18] See http://www.simpletoremember.com/vitals/world-jewish-population.htm.

[19] For discussion, see, e.g., Walter Brueggemann, *The Land* (Philadelphia: Fortress, 1977 / London: SPCK, 1978); W. D. Davies, *The Gospel and the Land* (Berkeley / London: University

Until the 1970s, Christian theological study of the First Testament paid little attention to the land of Israel and its theological significance. Indeed, examining how the theme of the land is handled provides one litmus test for evaluating a work on Old Testament theology.[20] If it fails to handle this theme, whatever the value of its treatment of other themes, the work as a whole cannot be expected to offer a guide to the First Testament's theological implications as a whole. The land is one of the handful of key themes in the First Testament; any claim to do justice to its theological concerns, any attempt to write Old Testament theology has to give this theme considerable prominence.

If the land is so prominent in the First Testament, why was it often ignored by works on Old Testament theology? It has commonly been the case that the Christian faith of scholars has had a narrowing influence on Old Testament theological study undertaken by Christians. In the New Testament there is very little allusion to the theme of the land. The aspects of Israel's story to which it makes most appeal concern Israel's experience before becoming a landed people, and then God's promise to David. Abraham and the exodus, David and the temple, come into greater focus than Joshua and the entering of the land. Linked with this is the way the New Testament emphasizes salvation as an otherworldly matter. It urges Christians not to be attached to the things of this world. It even has Abraham seeking a better country than his earthly one, seeking a heavenly country (Heb 11:13–16). Matthew 5:5 does have Jesus affirming the promise that the meek will possess the land (Ps 37:11), but English translations assume that Jesus here destines his followers to inherit the world, presumably in a sense that coheres with the world focus that appears elsewhere in the New Testament. It asserts Jesus' lordship over the whole world and his commission to spread the gospel through the whole world. This would naturally make it relatively uninterested theologically in the land of Israel in particular. When most Jews rejected the gospel, this encouraged the development of a worldwide perspective.

Judaism's rejection of the gospel also transformed expectations regarding how God's rule would be manifested in the world. The means of this manifestation turn out to be not Israel with Gentiles holding onto its coat sleeves but a Gentile Christian church fulfilling what was supposed to be Israel's role. We have noted already, however, that the significance of this largely Gentile church could be expounded only by means of the stories and symbols of First Testament Israel (see, for instance, 1 Cor 10:1–13). It is in this connection that the land comes to feature in the New Testament. Where it appears as a theologically significant theme, it is usually as metaphor rather than as material reality. Jesus is the "inheritance" of the community of faith; it is in him that it finds its "rest"; the "blessing" that counts is the blessing in the heavenly places that it receives in Christ (1 Pet 1:4; Heb 3–4; Eph 1:3).

---

of California Press, 1974); H.-R. Weber, "The Promise of the Land: Biblical Interpretation and the Present Situation in the Middle East," *SE/16* in *StudyEncounter* 7 (1971).

[20] For instance, Brevard S. Childs, *Old Testament Theology in a Canonical Context* (London: SCM, 1985 / Philadelphia: Fortress, 1986), ignores it.

The New Testament's concern with land, with space, is thus broadened to embrace the world, narrowed to center on Jesus, and refocused to work via the largely Gentile church. Theologically, the New Testament does not have room for the notion of sacred space (as it does not have room for other aspects of the sacred) or of a holy land, because of its emphasis on the whole world being God's and because Jesus takes the place of this central image in Judaism. This is partly because he takes the central place once occupied by the people of Israel, the notion of land being tied to that of people. "To be 'in Christ' . . . has replaced being 'in the land' as the ideal life"[21] as Christ is also the locus of that rule of God that the First Testament associates with the land of Israel.

That would imply that the theme of the land itself is dispensable. Indeed, W. D. Davies has asked whether the theme is dispensable to Judaism.[22] The promise, the covenant, and the law, after all, had their origins outside the land, and the experience of exile arguably affected the faith expressed in the First Testament more profoundly than the experience of the land itself did, as dispersion experience has decisively shaped Judaism. Judaism could survive without the land; it transcends the land. So how important is the land to Jews or to Christians? The other systematic Christian treatment of this theme from the 1970s is Walter Brueggemann's pioneering study (that seems the right image).[23] He attempts to maximize indications that the New Testament is concerned with this theme in the literal sense, but he is less convincing than Davies, who grants that in the New Testament land is not an overt interest.

In these two works, the scholars' exegetical study is surely affected by their theological agenda. While the land can indeed function for Jews as a metaphor for hope, I doubt whether Judaism can be deterritorialized, as Davies believes.[24] Neither is Brueggemann's attempt to territorialize the New Testament persuasive; further, for him the particularity of the land of Israel rather disappears. While he is aware of his study's significance for Jewish-Christian dialogue,[25] it is land as a theme for all peoples from which he starts and which the theme of land in the First Testament seems especially to suggest to him.

Brueggemann does, however, thus draw our attention to an important feature of the First Testament, its materialism. A faith based on the New Testament alone risks a false otherworldliness; this-worldly concerns are less prominent in the New Testament. Yet even the New Testament is concerned not to free people from living

---

[21] Davies, *The Gospel and the Land*, 217.

[22] See his "Reflections on the Territorial Dimension of Judaism," in *Jewish and Pauline Studies* (Philadelphia: Fortress / London: SPCK, 1984), 49–71; his *The Territorial Dimension of Judaism* (Berkeley: University of California Press, 1982) is an expansion of this article.

[23] *The Land.*

[24] Contrast, for instance, A. Hertzberg, "Judaism and the Land of Israel," *Judaism* 19 (1970): 423–34 = Jacob Neusner, ed., *Understanding Jewish Theology* (New York: Ktav, 1973), 75–88.

[25] "Christians cannot speak seriously to Jews unless we acknowledge land to be the central agenda" (*The Land*, 190).

their lives in this world but to free them to live this life, in light of the age to come. Further, New Testament faith itself bars the way to otherworldliness by its belief in incarnation, its conviction that in Jesus God himself becomes material reality. In this sense the First Testament's stress on the land is in keeping with the New Testament's beliefs about Jesus (or rather, vice versa), and the theme of the land is of importance to Christian theology partly because it affirms parallel theological convictions to those of the doctrine of the incarnation.

Indeed, if Jesus and Paul see God as still committed to Israel, they thereby imply a concern with the land of Israel. The notion of land is intrinsic to the notion of peoplehood; exceptions (the Jews, the Armenians, the Romanies) only prove the rule. The New Testament would perhaps have needed to make it explicit if it had not assumed that God's promise of land to Israel still held. Any people's identity is rooted in land (the metaphor of "roots" is a telling one). Secure possession of a home you can call your own is built into what it means to be a person, a family, or a nation. Unless people willingly renounce these for some reason, lacking them means lacking a fundamental element in what it means to be human. Possessing land is bound up with being a people. This is true for the Jews as it is for any other people. Taking seriously God's commitment regarding the land is involved in taking seriously any divine commitment to Israel. It is an aspect of having a real, rather than a docetic, view of Israel.[26]

The New Testament's silence on the theme of the land of Israel may thus imply that this theme should be taken for granted, not that it should be rejected. Of course the notion of Israel presupposes the notion of land, the dispersion notwithstanding. It is still to the physical Jerusalem that dispersion Jews pilgrimage (cf. Acts 2). Israel's independence is an issue the New Testament touches on, because it is an issue of the day. Israel's landed-ness is an uncontroversial question. The New Testament makes explicit that in Christ the temple and the sacrificial system lose their literal significance. If it had meant to suggest that this happens with the promise of the land, it would have had to make this explicit, too. But while it once or twice applies the rest/inheritance motif to Jesus, it never directly suggests that the First Testament promise regarding the land is fulfilled in him. We might infer that this promise is one to which God says yes in Jesus not in the sense that his coming fulfills it but in the sense that his coming confirms it, guarantees that like all other promises it will be fulfilled. It could naturally follow that the positive purpose of God lies behind the Jews regaining a home for themselves in Palestine. God's commitment to Israel had to find expression in seeing it has a home; otherwise it is not a commitment at all. The New Testament's concern with the being of the Jewish people cannot but imply a concern with the land of Israel.

Although we cannot interpret First Testament promises as if Christ had not yet come, this does not mean that the New Testament's reapplication of First Testament motifs decides the only meaning these motifs have. The New Testament's use of the

---

[26]See Torrance, "The Divine Vocation and Destiny of Israel in World History," 103; H. Siegman, "A Decade of Catholic-Jewish Relations: A Re-Assessment," *JEcS* 15 (1978): 243–60 (252–53).

First Testament generally has a specific concern with how the First Testament can be used to illumine the significance of the Christ event. It is not designed to interpret the First Testament in its own right, and how we do that has to be determined on broader grounds. It often spiritualizes First Testament references to this-worldly realities such as life, health, love, land, peace, and justice, because it is concerned to interpret Christ's significance for our inner relationship with God. But we have noted that even the New Testament is ultimately concerned not to free people from this life but to free them to live this life in light of the age to come. It thus leads us back to the this-worldly realities of life, health, love, land, peace, and justice that are the First Testament's direct concern.

The question whether biblical faith means being interested in material realities such as land is part of the broader question of how biblical faith deals with differences between the Testaments. If we are to be biblical people, the agenda for Christian theology, ethics, and preaching is to be set by the two Testaments jointly and not by the New alone. In other words, much depends on whether the First Testament has "revelatory significance" in its own right, and in what sense we have to read it in the light of the New.[27] In discussing the land, Brueggemann can give the impression that Christians' theological agenda is rightly set by the New Testament, so that if it is not concerned about the land, then biblical theology cannot be (though in many subsequent writings he makes clear that he does not make this assumption). The New Testament itself does not imply that it is itself an adequate guide for an understanding of Christian faith. Its own assumption is that the First Testament must contribute very significantly to the agenda for Christian theology, ethics, and preaching. Of course, when the first Christian writings came into being, the New Testament did not yet exist. The First Testament was the Bible for people of New Testament times. The New Testament presupposes an understanding of God and God's concerns that comes from the First Testament and frequently refers the reader to it as its own source of authoritative teaching. What the New Testament says is not a complete exposition of Christian faith. It assumes people also need the First Testament for that. So whatever we find in the First Testament has to be taken seriously theologically. If we find that the two Testaments take a different view (for instance, over the land, in the sense that the subject is not a focus in the New), we view their different perspectives as complementary; we do not look at one through the other and emasculate it.

Thus Christians have to take the materialism of the First Testament seriously. This will draw us not into a wholly materialistic and this-worldly faith but into holding onto the conviction that God is concerned with this world along with the conviction that God is concerned with the new age and with the other world, with resurrection life, and with relationships with God. Both are present in both Testaments, but it is easy to simplify the First Testament to the one and the New Testament to the other, to let the latter have theological priority over the former, and thereby to end up with an oversimplified and unbiblical faith.

---

[27] Weber, "The Promise of the Land," 11.

3. Commitment to the Jewish People Does Not Imply Commitment to the State of Israel

The promise of the land still stands. This is presupposed by the kind of Christian attitude to the question of the State of Israel and the land of Israel expressed in dozens of paperbacks that assume God indeed fulfilled First Testament promises concerning the land in the events of the late nineteenth century and the period since the Second World War. This view appears in a more sophisticated form in Torrance's words:

> The intense actualization, once again, of God's covenanted communion with the people of Israel within the land of promise, now called Israel, brings home to us in a new way not only the fact that the people and the land are woven indivisibly together in the fabric of Israel's vicarious mission and destiny among the peoples and nations of the earth, but also the fact that in this unitary spiritual and physical form Israel constitutes God's sign-post in the history of world-events, pointing ahead to a culmination in his saving interaction with mankind in space and time. . . . When God acts, he always takes us by surprise in breathtaking events. The startling reintegration of Jerusalem and Israel in our day, after nearly two millennia, is just one of these events.[28]

The implication is that the contemporary Israeli state is the fulfillment of God's promise to Abraham.[29]

One reason why this is too unequivocal a stance is that it ignores the moral aspect to the relationship between Israel and the land. When God promised the land to Abraham, the promise's fulfillment was delayed for "four generations" to avoid being unfair to its Canaanite inhabitants, because their waywardness did not in Abraham's day justify their being thrown out of the land (Gen 15:16). When Israel occupied Canaan, it did so as the agent of God's punishment of a people that are not Israel's own enemies but that can by then be described as godless and immoral (Deut 9:4–5). Israel was also itself warned that possessing this land placed religious and moral demands upon it. If it failed to meet them, the same logic that had brought it into the land would eject it from it; and so, with the exile, it turned out. The withholding and the fulfilling of God's promise of land to Israel in First Testament times was tied up with how it and other nations involved with it stood before God and before standards of right and wrong. One may assume that this is still the case.

The point is inherent in the Christian attitude to Israel that is hostile to Zionism, which appears white-hot in Lucas Grollenberg's *Palestine Comes First*,[30] and in more moderate form in Colin Chapman's *Whose Promised Land?*[31] and in the British Council of Churches report *Towards Understanding the Arab/Israeli Conflict.*[32] Grollenberg and Chapman both worked for some years in Arab areas, but

---

[28]"The Divine Vocation and Destiny of Israel in World History," 104.

[29]So, for instance, L. Lambert, *Till the Day Dawns* (Eastbourne: Kingsway, 1982); Pawson, *The Church, Britain, the World, and Israel.*

[30](London: SCM, 1980).

[31](Tring, U.K.: Lion, 1983).

[32](London: British Council of Churches, 1982).

they would want their work to be considered on theological grounds, not to be dismissed as mere expressions of a particular political stance. Both emphasize a different side to prophecy from the one dominant in the paperbacks just referred to: prophecy's "remorseless condemnation of religion, temple and state when they are used wrongly,"[33] its "passionate concern for justice" that calls us to a concern for every individual and community in the Middle East.[34] The land was to be the place where the just judgment of the God of Israel was embodied. It was not merely a possession but a vocation and a moral destiny. "According to Deuteronomy no self-sufficient and self-glorifying possession of the land is possible. . . . According to the prophets [the] future relation between the people of Israel and [the land of] Palestine must serve the nations."[35]

A related consideration is the Palestinian Arabs' historical, legal, and moral claim to the land of Canaan, which is as strong as that of the Israeli Jews; they have a theological claim too, as equally the sons of Abraham with Israel. They had been the majority inhabitants of Palestine for centuries: Jewish settlers did not return to an empty land but to one with a native population of a million people. The Balfour Declaration said that "nothing should be done to prejudice the civil and religious rights of the existing non-Jewish communities in Palestine." But the Jewish people have regained the land at the cost of displacing another people whose main crime was the misfortune of being in the wrong place. It is no more a solution for them to resettle in another Arab country than it would be for a displaced Englishman to settle in another European country or for the Jews to settle in Uganda (as Britain once proposed). The tragedy of Palestine is that two peoples make irreconcilable claims on the same strip of land. There is thus an ambiguity and a pathos about both the Jewish and the Palestinian destiny.[36] The Jewish return to the land raises moral questions that mean it cannot be unequivocally affirmed as the fulfillment of God's purpose.

It also raises religious questions. We have noted that from a Christian perspective one can understand, or at least cope with, the Holocaust only in light of the cross of Christ. A Jew attempting to reflect on the Holocaust may observe, "At least the Holocaust was followed by (led to?) the founding of the State of Israel." Thus "for us Jews Israel is our Jesus."[37] Freedom to enjoy a happy and secure life in Palestine is a part of God's commitment to the Jewish people, and its present freedom to live there comprises a partial fulfillment of that commitment. For deep and compelling reasons the State of Israel is thus a key religious focus for Jews. But it could thus become an idol, a substitute Messiah that becomes an anti-Messiah, especially in connection with the uncritical commitment to Israel often expected of U.S. Jews.[38]

---

[33] Grollenberg, *Palestine Comes First*, 139.

[34] Chapman, *Whose Promised Land?* 175, 221.

[35] Weber, "The Promise of the Land," 3, 11.

[36] See Kenneth Cragg, *This Year in Jerusalem* (London: DLT, 1982); also *Towards Understanding the Arab/Israeli Conflict*, and Grollenberg, *Palestine Comes First*.

[37] Quoted in Pawlikowski, "The Contemporary Jewish-Christian Theological Dialogue Agenda," 599.

[38] See B. Krasner (with P. Chapman), "A Jewish-Christian Dialogue," *JEcS* 9 (1972): 104–11 (see 109); cf. E. S. Shapiro, "American Jewry and the State of Israel," *JEcS* 14 (1977): 1–16.

When Christians similarly commit themselves unreservedly and uncritically to Israel, then, they may be helping to make sure that an idol does not fall over.

There is another moving aspect to the significance of that promise to Abraham and its relationship to two peoples' attachment to Palestine. We have suggested that God's commitment to Abraham included the promise of land because land is intrinsic to peoplehood; the promise of land was part of the promise to make Abraham into a nation. But why was God bothering to make Abraham into a nation? God's ultimate aim was that all the families of the earth should pray to be blessed as Abraham would be blessed (Gen 12:3 NEB). Genesis 1–11 has related how God's blessing was originally given to but imperiled by humanity. God's commitment to Abraham begins the story of how the blessing will be restored. God will so bless Abraham that his blessing will become the standard of blessing, modeling what God can do with one landless, childless person. God's promise is thus given not only for Abraham and Sarah's sake but for the world's. It is not to be spiritualized, but nor is it to be confined to Israel. It is to be universalized.

The restoration of Israel will thus be a restoration to being a means of God's blessing the nations. The First Testament declares that the Jewish people is of key significance to God's purpose in history. Purely geographical consideration may make it difficult for Israel to avoid being the crossroads of history. Within the Eastern Hemisphere, it stands at the point of meeting (or point of conflict) of north and south, east and west. Its geographical location matches the theological significance given to the Jewish people by God's irrevocable choice of it to be the means of fulfilling a purpose in the world; perhaps God gave Israel this land because it would symbolize and facilitate its ministry to the world. That purpose declared in the First Testament (for instance, Gen 12:1–3 and Isa 2:1–4) is reaffirmed in the New Testament (see especially Rom 9–11). A consequence of mistakenly describing the church as "the new Israel" is to obscure God's continuing intention that the Jews should be the central nucleus of the worldwide people that recognizes Jesus as Lord, a worldwide people that must include the Palestinians.

There might be various ways this could come about. While God's commitment to Israel does entail its enjoying the land of Canaan, it need not entail it having exclusive possession of it, certainly not to the *a priori* exclusion of fellow descendants of Abraham, some of whom believe that Jesus is the Messiah. For centuries Jews who were Zionist in the sense that they wanted to live in their historic homeland, but not Zionist in the sense of claiming exclusive sovereign possession of the land, shared it reasonably happily with Arab Muslims and Christians.[39]

Nor need God's promise entail Jews occupying the land as a state. During the first three millennia or so of its existence, only for a few hundred years (from Saul to the exile and then for a century after the deliverance from Antiochus Epiphanes) was the people a sovereign state with a central government, like others.[40] At the beginning, Israel's ancestors had some freedom to enjoy life in the land of prom-

---

[39] Cf. H. H. Harcourt, "The Perils of Psychologizing Anti-Zionism," *JEcS* 7 (1969): 634–40 (637).

[40] On the contents of this paragraph, see further chapter 7 above.

ise, though they had no independent statehood there. From Joshua to Samuel the descendants of Abraham enjoyed something like independent nationhood in the land of Israel, but without the kind of state government that other peoples had. Yahweh was their king; their earthly rulers had none of the permanent institutional authority possessed by other peoples' kings. That might look like God's ideal arrangement; but its result seemed to be that Israel found it increasingly difficult to live a viable national life, to live in politics, and a time came when Israel insisted on having the kind of government that other nations had. While recognizing this as an act of rebellion against Yahweh's own kingship, Yahweh acceded to their plea and got involved in the choice of the human king who would have a kingdom in Israel. Henceforth the kingship of Yahweh is exercised from the throne of David. Yahweh then takes on the idea that this should be so not only within Israel but in relation to the world as a whole: God's purpose was to realize rule over the world through the same Davidic king who ruled over Israel (see Ps 2). The story of Israel's experience of statehood, however, which lasted only those few centuries from Saul to the exile, is a discouraging one. By and large, Israel's governments by no means implement Yahweh's government. God's kingdom and Israel's kingdom look two quite different things, and Israel comes to realize that an ordinary earthly king will never lead Israel that way. Its hopes of a king who will do so come to attach themselves to a future king who will have to be a special gift from God, not merely the next young Davidide to accede to the throne in Jerusalem. The exile brings the end of the Davidic monarchy, and the postexilic period brings no constitutional revival of it. This experience encourages hopes of an anointed one, a Messiah, to come, but it also brings the emergence or reassertion of other attitudes to statehood and monarchy, to kingship and kingdom. Daniel talks about the kingdom of God being given by God to Nebuchadnezzar, though Daniel also sees the successive Middle Eastern empires as no more worthy vice regents of the God of Israel than David and his successors had been, so that in due course the kingship is given to the enigmatic human-like figure of Dan 7. Perhaps he in some way represents Israel as a whole; he is not simply a messianic figure. In the chapters of Isaiah that relate to the exile, the anointed king, the Messiah, through whom God's worldwide purpose is to be put into effect is the Persian Cyrus (Isa 45:1).

The Balfour Declaration spoke only of a Jewish homeland in Palestine and maintained a shrewd silence on the question of statehood. Theologically, statehood is not involved in the promise to Abraham, and whatever God's using Israel as a way of reaching and blessing the nations is to mean, it hardly requires Israel to become their political head as the world's superpower. Indeed, the First Testament story of Israel's experience of statehood that took it to exile is hardly an encouraging precedent for the revival of such statehood.

Unlike the question of land, the question of Israel's independent sovereign statehood is explicitly raised in the New Testament (though not clearly resolved), especially in Luke-Acts.[41] It surfaces at the beginning of Luke's story, where Jesus' birth is heralded as the means of Israel's deliverance both from the power of its

---

[41] See E. Franklin, *Christ the Lord* (London: SPCK, 1975), 13, 95–96, 102, 130.

enemies and from the power of its sins (e.g., Luke 2:68–79). It appears at the end of the Gospel, where Jesus speaks of Jerusalem being trodden down by the Gentiles until their times are fulfilled (Luke 21:24). The natural inference is that the Jews will then once again enjoy being able to live in Jerusalem, though Jesus does not explicitly say so. At the beginning of Acts, the apostles ask whether Jesus is now going to "restore the kingdom to Israel"; he rebukes them for asking when this will happen but not for the idea itself (Acts 1:6–8). It is at this point that Luke-Acts leaves the ends untied. Jesus diverts the apostles' attention to the task of witnessing to the world, the focus of the rest of Acts. It is not quite clear whether or not the New Testament sees the restoration of Israel's sovereign independence as within the purpose of God. Nor is it clear how the sovereign independence of Israel relates to that rule of God that Jesus comes to proclaim and to inaugurate. If it is by its witness to the nations that (religiously) the kingdom is restored to Israel,[42] one might have expected the point to be more explicit. More likely the restoration of Israel's sovereign freedom is assumed to be within God's purpose but is set aside because it is to be left to God.

It seems to be an implication that the Jews should have freedom to enjoy the land of Palestine, but that in principle or in theory this freedom need not take the form of an Israeli state. To affirm that the land of Israel is still the destiny of the Jewish people is thus not in itself to imply a theological judgment about the State of Israel. Being able to enjoy the land and possessing independent sovereign statehood are separable questions; for most of history they have been. A commitment to and a longing for Zion as an essential symbol of God's covenant with Israel and Israel's relationship with God need not imply a commitment to Israel's possessing this land as a nation-state.

4. Israel's Destiny Is Secure, but Its Present Is Dependent on Its Decisions

There is a famous controversy about how to define a Jew, but perhaps we can say about the Jews corporately that they are a people, with an ethnic awareness and a common sense of history and tradition. They are not a religious community; in this connection, "Jews" is a word more like "Hispanics" or "Arabs" than a word like "Christians" or "Muslims." To count as a Jew, a person does not have to believe anything or to take on any particular practices or to live in Israel. The average Israeli is hardly more likely to have religious convictions or to attend religious services than the average Briton. In the dispersion, where most Jews live, in the long run the pressure of assimilation may have a more devastating effect on the Jewish community than the Holocaust did. There are naturally differences of opinion over whether this situation is made worse or better by the fact that large numbers of Jews have come to believe in Jesus over the past fifteen years, mostly in the United States.

---

[42] Cf. Jervell, *Luke and the People of God*, 51–53, 81–82.

Related to the need to be wary of defining the Jews in religious terms is the fact that the return of Jews to Palestine over the last century or so, which made the foundation of the State of Israel possible, is part of the story of the development of the modern world, and it can only be understood when it is seen as part of that story. Many of the instincts that led to it and the factors that made it possible are identical to or parallel to ones that lay behind the formation of the other European, Asian, and African states, most of which did not exist a century ago in the form that we know them. That Israel as a nation had a right to exist parallel to the right of other nations was first argued by Rabbi Liva ben Bezalel in the sixteenth century.[43] But Israel has its state at the cost of most Palestinian Arabs losing their homeland. It is not surprising that they feel a sense of grief and anger at the suffering that Zionism has brought to Palestine. This suffering has taken Arabs and Jews from coexistence to a history of mutual terrorist attacks and wars that independent parties have condemned.

Zionism, that love for Palestine that led to Jews wanting to return there at the end of the nineteenth century, was based on high ideals. It was concerned for justice, for equality, for the development of the land (often neglected), and for a right use of it. Israel has been immensely courageous in caring for Jewish people all over the world. The foundation of the state reflected a determination on the part of its founders that Jews should possess somewhere where they had the same kind of national security and control of their destiny as any other people. In other words, Israel wanted to be a state like any other. And Israel has the profound political, social, and economic problems that many states have. Becoming a state like others risks a collective assimilation to the ways of the Gentiles as dangerous as the individual assimilation of the dispersion.[44]

The Torah and the Prophets expect that God's morality and justice should be practiced in the world. They are a challenge to Israelis and Palestinians, to Jews and Arabs elsewhere, as well as to powers such as the United States and Britain. Torah and Prophets confront Israel about its moral life, reassert the moral and just nature of its God, and reassert God's righteous demands. When Jesus speaks of fulfilling the Torah and the Prophets (Matt 5:17–20), it would be reasonable to reckon that he is committed to obeying and furthering the purpose of God's commands in the Torah and the Prophets, as well as confirm and bring into reality God's promises there. In a parallel way, for modern Israel to be the fulfillment of biblical prophecy would involve its embodying the moral concerns of prophecy.

In certain ways it has sought to do so. There was a moral earnestness about the pioneers of the Zionist movement that reflected the righteous earnestness of the prophets. But many Jews inside and outside Israel now declare sadly that that day is over. Perhaps the Gentile/Christian world is too guilty for the way it has treated the Jewish people in the past, especially in the twentieth century, to have the moral

---

[43] So Martin Buber, *On Zion: The History of an Idea* (repr., Edinburgh: Clark, 1985), 77–89.

[44] D. Marmur, *Beyond Survival: Reflections on the Future of Judaism* (London: DLT, 1982), 170–71.

right to express an opinion or a judgment on that question. But the implication of these Jewish opinions is that Israel's treatment of the Palestinians has taken modern Israel several steps further away from being the fulfillment of this central message of biblical prophecy.

The moral aspect to prophecy also means that Israel's present possession of the land of Palestine is not bound to be a permanency; its leaving the land again is not theologically inconceivable. Despite God's gift of the land to Abraham's descendants, they lost substantial possession of it in 721, in 587, in the Second Temple period, in 135, and on various other occasions (to judge from the Psalms). David Pawson speaks of the threat it would be to his faith if Israel lost the land again.[45] The argument of Rom 9–11 does suggest that if the Jewish people ceased to exist, this would be a severe threat to one's faith. But to anchor that faith to the people's possession of the land at a particular moment is to give it false security. The people who lost the land in biblical times possessed promises that they would never lose the land, but they did lose it because they did not give the God of the promise the allegiance that the promise relationship demanded. The final security of the Jewish people and its freedom to live securely in the land is sure, but whether any individual generation enjoys God's blessing and enjoys possession of the land depends on its relationship to God. There is no reason to make the present generation of the Jewish people an exception.

This is not to imply that if Israel were to lose the land, it must be because of its sin. Arguments such as these have been used to enable Christians to shrug their shoulders over the Holocaust. The working of God's moral purpose in the world is commonly too ambiguous for one to be able to make clear judgments of that kind. If Israel were to lose the land, this might, like the Holocaust, reflect Gentile indifference rather than Jewish sin. My point is that one cannot assume that Israel will continue to possess the land, as if God's commitment regarding the land had no religious and moral implications. God's promises always make such demands upon us, and how we respond to them makes a difference to whether and how they are fulfilled.

God's commitment to the Jewish people also does not mean that the friends of Israel are committed to supporting its every action in an uncritical way. After various countries yielded to pressure to move their embassies from Jerusalem to Tel Aviv, a group of mainly expatriate Christians in Israel opened an International Christian Embassy in Jerusalem "to comfort Zion and to render practical service to modern-day Israel." They believe that the calling of Christians is to comfort and support Israel, not to attempt to criticize or evangelize her.

Perhaps they chose the wrong moment to make an imaginative move, for unfortunately the embassy's best publicized act was its unequivocal statements of support for Israel's invasion of Lebanon in 1982. Comfort is sometimes God's word to the people, but at other times God's word is more judgmental. It may not be our business to criticize Israel, but the right alternative is not uncritical support, lest we are offering comfort at a time when it needs confrontation, even if not from us.

---

[45] Pawson, *The Church, Britain, the World, and Israel.*

Likewise, the forswearing of Christian witness to Jesus in relation to Israel or the Jewish people seems a doubtfully loving act, even if more foreign missionaries is the last thing the Israeli state or the Israeli church needs.

It is a plausible view that the return of many Jews to the land in our day is part of God's fulfilling a purpose for the world, for the Jews, and for the church. As long as the Jews exist as a people, it is natural for their focus to be there, and the fact that the salvation story was played out there also makes this natural. Thus the fact that this return has happened is, for Christians, reason for praise and for hope. At the same time, an invariable accompaniment of our thinking about the Jews has to be penitence before our God for the history of crusades, inquisition, pogroms, and Holocaust over the centuries; and not least for the toll for the Jewish people and for other Middle Eastern peoples of twentieth-century political decisions or lack of decisions taken by Britain and, more recently, by the United States. If it is hardly the case that God could have purposed to give Palestine to the modern Jews in a way that overrode the rights of Palestinian Arabs, then in the Palestinians' loss (even though it may have been in part caused and then aggravated by mistaken policies on their part) Christians should be weeping and grieving with them—many of them being our brothers and sisters in Christ.

It is nice but sad to romance about other forms that fulfillment of Yahweh's promise might have taken. There was a time in the first half of the twentieth century when the Balfour Declaration's schizophrenic vision of a Jewish national home that did not trample on Palestinian rights might have been fulfilled, a time when Palestine might have developed into a Jewish-Arab independent state. But practical politics has to accept the fact that the State of Israel does exist. There was a time more recently when one might have dreamed of an internationalized Jerusalem, or of Jerusalem as a Jewish-Arab condominium, but the events just before and just after 2000 make that also now difficult to imagine, even though some Palestinian thinkers contemplate abandoning the two-state solution and campaigning for a single, bi-national state.

The church is called to stand with both Israelis and Palestinians in prayer, rejoicing with those who rejoice and weeping with those who weep, seeking to share and to bring before God their suffering, their fear, their insecurity, their needs, and their temptations. Each of the longer prophetic books addresses the experience of exile and thus concerns itself with how people cope with the suffering it brings. Jeremiah seeks to prepare people for exile and speaks of his own suffering in that connection, Ezekiel does the same even while experiencing the anticipatory 597 exile, and Isa 40–55 takes it as its background as it seeks to rebuild a demoralized people with news of a God who reigns but whose purpose finds fulfillment through the suffering of the servant of Isa 53.

One cannot blame Jews for declining to carry on accepting the role of the suffering servant in exile, which the Gentile/Christian world has imposed on them. But the role of the suffering servant, fulfilled by Jesus yet not exhausted by him, keeps haunting the story of the Middle Eastern peoples and the church. Until we (or they) have discovered its positive implications for them (and us), we will not have plumbed the depths of what it means for prophecy to be fulfilled there.

"What does it mean, Lord, when now two people pray, 'next year in Jerusa-lem!'?" asks Barbara Krasner.[46] We pray for the peace of Jerusalem (Ps 122:6), aware that this is a prayer for peace for all those who love Jerusalem, including both Jew and Arab, and that with this prayer more than most we have to expect (and rejoice) that the manner of its answering will probably be quite different from what any of us who pray it quite envisage.

---

[46]B. Krasner with M. Roache, "Relationship Dynamics and Our View of the Middle East," *JEcS* 12 (1975): 257–60 (260). Compare Cragg's portrait of the tragedy of both Jews and Palestinians in *This Year in Jerusalem*.

16

Is Election Fair?

In any discussion of the First Testament's theological value and values, the annihilation of the Canaanites comes up sooner rather than later. It seems that Yahweh's liberation of the Israelites to freedom in Canaan is also Yahweh's oppression of the Canaanites. For all the rationale of Deut 9:4–6 with its statement about their waywardness, they did not deserve this experience more than other peoples. Their annihilation was an act sitting in tension with the commitment to justice that Yahweh claims and expects of Israel. Rolf P. Knierim has suggested that we have to choose between the theology of exclusionary election and the theology of inclusive justice and must surely then choose the latter as the more comprehensive framework for Old Testament theology.[1] Is Yahweh fair? Is election fair?[2]

1. Election in a Theological Context

There is a more formal and a more substantial aspect to the question. The formal aspect is that Israel's distinctive election is a central and pervasive theme in the First Testament. Throughout its narrative framework, in Genesis to Kings and in Ezra-Nehemiah and Chronicles, for instance, the Israelites are the special people of Yahweh in a way that the Canaanites, for instance, are not. Thus H. D. Preuss made the theme of election the organizing principle for his *Old Testament Theology*.[3] Even if Israel's distinctive election is a mistaken concept, one cannot realistically suggest it is an unbiblical concept. "God did not specially elect Israel from among other peoples" is no more a statement that can appear in an Old Testament theology than is "God does not exist" or "Yahweh is not God."

---

[1] See Rolf P. Knierim, *The Task of Old Testament Theology* (Grand Rapids: Eerdmans, 1995), e.g., 450–52; further, Robert Allan Warrior, "Canaanites, Cowboys, and Indians," *Christianity and Crisis* 49 (1989–90): 261–65 and often anthologized; the comments by D. Jobling and C. Rose on "Canaanite Readings" of the First Testament in "Reading as a Philistine," *Ethnicity and the Bible* (ed. M. Brett; Leiden / New York: Brill, 1996), 381–417 (see 381); more systematically, Michael Prior, *The Bible and Colonialism* (Sheffield: Sheffield Academic Press, 1997); from the Palestinian angle, Naim S. Ateek, *Justice, and Only Justice* (Maryknoll, N.Y.: Orbis, 1989).

[2] First published as "Justice and Salvation for Israel and Canaan," in *Reading the Hebrew Bible for a New Millennium* (ed. Wonil Kim et al.; 2 vols.; Harrisburg, Pa.: Trinity Press International, 2000), 1:169–87.

[3] (2 vols.; Louisville: Westminster John Knox, 1995, 1996).

The more substantial aspect to the problem heightens the stakes on the question whether the idea of Israel's distinctive election is mistaken. Abandoning this idea significantly affects (I would say skews) not only the content of First Testament theology but also that of New Testament theology, of Christian theology, and of Jewish theology. Thus, whereas J. D. Levenson attributes Knierim's slant to his Christian commitment,[4] R. K. Soulen's study of *The God of Israel and Christian Theology*[5] points to a forceful critique of it from a Christian angle. If the existence of the Jewish people is a matter of indifference to the God of Israel, this "introduces a note of incoherence into the heart of Christian reflection about God."[6] He notes that there have been two periods when the status of Israel has forced itself on Christian theological reflection, the original separating of the church from Israel and the recent events of the Holocaust and the establishment of the State of Israel. The period in between was the period of Christendom, which Soulen sees as characterized not only by triumphalism in relation to the Jewish people but also by "a latently gnostic assessment of God's engagement in the realm of public history."[7]

Knierim does not take the classic Christian position of supersessionism, the view that the church replaced Israel in God's purpose. He abjures anti-Semitism and knows that we have to do theology in the light of the Holocaust.[8] But his position does resemble the one Soulen associates with Immanuel Kant and Friedrich Schleiermacher: that God never had entered into a special relationship with the Jewish people, so that its continuing existence became a matter of theological indifference. Kant believed that the Jewish people's conviction of its own exclusive election was one of the features of its faith that made it unable to function as a universal moral religion.[9] There is thus a Jewish affirmation of Knierim's position; in due course we will note another, Judith Plaskow's.

There is also more Jewish critique of it. Soulen does his work in dialogue with that of Michael Wyschogrod, in particular *The Body of Faith: God in the People Israel*.[10] The foundation of Wyschogrod's theology is not, for instance, the Torah but "his affirmation of God's free, irrevocable election of Israel as the people of God."[11] Despite its exclusiveness, for Wyschogrod that election expresses God's affirmation of humanity in its fullness. "God confirms the human creature as it was created to live in the material cosmos."[12] Israel is "the carnal anchor that God has sunk into the soil of creation."[13]

---

[4] See his review in *RelSRev* 24 (1998): 39–42.
[5] (Minneapolis: Fortress, 1996).
[6] *The God of Israel and Christian Theology*, 4.
[7] Ibid., x.
[8] *The Task of Old Testament Theology*, 311, 452.
[9] See, e.g., *Religion within the Limits of Reason Alone* (New York: Harper, 1960), 117; quoted by Soulen, *The God of Israel and Christian Theology*, 64. Cf. Levenson's comments on "Enlightenment rationalism" (*RelSRev* 24:41) and F. Crüsemann's comments on "human solidarity and ethnic identity" in *Ethnicity and the Bible*, 57–76 (see 57–58).
[10] (San Francisco: Harper, 1983).
[11] Soulen, *The God of Israel and Christian Theology*, 5.
[12] Ibid., 6.
[13] *The Body of Faith*, 256.

"But why should God be God of election at all? Does not God love all persons equally?"[14] Wyschogrod's answer is that "undifferentiated love" cannot be love that meets individuals in their individuality; that kind of love requires exclusivity.[15] By electing Abraham and his seed, God has chosen in favor of genuine encounter with human creatures in their concreteness. "The distinction between Jew and Gentile—far from indicating a limit or imperfection of God's love—testifies to God's willingness to engage all creation on the basis of divine passion."[16] A friend recently wrote to my wife and me and ended "with all my love." This might seem hard on her husband and sons. Yet there can be something about love that makes it not necessarily exhaust itself when given wholly to one person; it can mysteriously self-regenerate and multiply in the giving so that it pours out over others than the original object.

Perhaps something like this is presupposed by a comment in Sifre on Deuteronomy, chapter 40. God cares for the land of Israel (Deut 11:12). Does this mean God does not care for other lands? Job 38:26–27 excludes this. So Deuteronomy implies that God cares not only for this land, "but because of His care for it He cares for all the other lands along with it." Similarly God "keeps" Israel; and Job 12:10 sets all nations in God's keeping. So God keeps not only Israel, "but because He keeps them He keeps every other nation along with them."[17] Wyschogrod sees this as implicit in Gen 12:1–3. And he sees God's plan to some degree to have worked. Nations have come to experience humanity and history (and justice and righteousness, to revert to Knierim's concerns) with Jewish categories, as an outworking of God's distinctive love for Israel and God's love for other peoples.

In principle, then, the particularistic election of Israel and a concern for universal justice and righteousness can work together. There is no inherent tension between them. First Testament theology does not have to choose between them.

2. *Mishpat Usedaqah*

The same point emerges from a consideration of the use of *mishpat usedaqah* in the First Testament, which indeed becomes an alternative way of making the same statement.

Expressions such as "justice and righteousness" have become standard English equivalents to the hendiadys *mishpat usedaqah*, but they are unsatisfactory equivalents. Both "justice" and "righteousness" are abstract nouns; *mishpat* and *sedaqah* are not. Set over against each other, "justice" suggests something about equal relationships in society, while "righteousness" suggests personal right living. This

---

[14] Soulen, *The God of Israel and Christian Theology*, 7.

[15] *The Body of Faith*, 61; Soulen, *The God of Israel and Christian Theology*, 7–8.

[16] Soulen, *The God of Israel and Christian Theology*, 8, summarizing Wyschogrod, *The Body of Faith*, 63–65.

[17] *Sifre: A Tannaitic Commentary on the Book of Deuteronomy* (New Haven, Conn. / London: Yale University Press, 1986), 79; cf. Soulen, *The God of Israel and Christian Theology*, 129.

bears inadequate correspondence to the Hebrew expression. Set alongside each other and understood as a hendiadys denoting "social justice," the words suggest the combination of fairness that treats everyone alike and conformity to some norm of rightness. This bears little more relationship to the Hebrew expression. Whatever *mishpat usedaqah* means, it is not "justice and righteousness."

"Just judgment"[18] is a better equivalent, though the "judgment" is not confined to judicial decisions. Whereas "social justice" is an abstract expression, *mishpat* and *sedaqah* are both commonly used as concrete nouns. One cannot "do [a] social justice" as one can "do a *mishpat*" or "do a *sedaqah*." Characteristically, *mishpat* suggests the declaring and implementing of a decisive judgment, while *sedaqah* denotes the quality of some act, the way it fits into a worldview and a set of relationships that possess among other things some moral and social order. Together *mishpat* and *sedaqah* thus form a powerful combination. They point to an exercise of authority that has a certain relational and social commitment and to a certain relational and social vision that expresses itself in decisive action. While they operate in the court, they also operate in government and in community relationships. Neither refers directly either to justice or to righteousness.

Whereas righteousness suggests conformity to a norm or standard, then, *sedaqah* is a relationship word. That is implicit in its first appearance in scripture. Abraham manifests a strange willingness to trust Yahweh's word against the odds, though with a little evidence from the events of which we have read in the previous three chapters. And Yahweh counts this as *sedaqah* (Gen 15:6). This is not a legal fiction whereby he is treated as if he had lived by the norms of right living when he had not. Rather, it is Yahweh's declaration that such trust counts as *sedaqah*.[19] This fits Klaus Koch's contention that *sedaqah* is closely related to faithfulness and loyalty, especially faithfulness and loyalty that go beyond the call of duty.[20] Believing Yahweh's outrageous word is the expression of such faithfulness and loyalty that Yahweh approves. In Yahweh's own case, terms parallel to *saddiq* are *khannun* and *khasid*.[21] Conversely, in Rom 9:14 Paul bases his denial that God manifests *adikia* on the fact that God has carried on showing mercy and compassion to Israel. If that involved unfairness to Esau or to Pharaoh, this is irrelevant to the question whether God is *dikaios*.[22] Being *dikaios* is a matter of being faithful. Likewise Tamar's status as relatively *sadeq* (Gen 38:26) is intelligible on the basis of an understanding of *sedaqah* that links it with relationships in the community rather than directly with moral norms.

In contrast to *sedaqah*, *mishpat* is more inherently a matter of the exercise of power or authority. It does presuppose a concern for harmony and order in the

---

[18] Knierim, *The Task of Old Testament Theology*, 121.

[19] It is not clear whether Yahweh or Abraham does the counting; if the latter, then Abraham is taking Yahweh's word as a commitment to *sedaqah*. My point here is not affected.

[20] See Ernst Jenni and Claus Westermann, eds., *Theological Lexicon of the Old Testament* (3 vols.; Peabody, Mass.: Hendrickson, 1997), 1046–62.

[21] K. Koch, "צדק *sdq* to be communally faithful, beneficial," *Theological Lexicon of the Old Testament*, 1057.

[22] See James D. G. Dunn, *Romans 9–16* (Dallas: Word, 1988), 551.

community; the use of the word "judgment" in English to denote wisdom and insight parallels the way a word for giving authority can presuppose that authority is exercised properly. Thus *mishpat* used on its own can imply "just judgment" (see Isa 1:17; 32:7; 59:8; 61:8; Jer 7:5; 10:24; 17:11; Mic 3:9; Prov 12:5; 13:23; 16:8, 11). The First Testament can similarly use the verb *shapat* to speak of judging the needy and the oppressed, in the sense of taking fair action on their behalf (e.g., Isa 1:17, 23; Pss 10:18; 72:4; 82:3). Yet in itself *shapat* means "govern," "rule," or "exercise authority," as *mishpat* signifies authority in action; it often appears alongside words such as *hoq* and *miswah* (law, command). Thus the connotation "just judgment" is usually made explicit through the pairing of *mishpat* with some other word such as *sedaqah.* This specifies that the exercise of such authoritative judgment recognizes that the problem in the community was not merely an individual wrong but a breakdown in the harmonious order of the community and that it is designed to restore this. The word *din*, similarly, can require the adjective *yatom* (Jer 5:28) or can in itself suggest not merely legal judgment but fair legal judgment (Isa 10:2).

The fact that *mishpat* refers inherently to decisive action more than to just action is further reflected in Leviticus's talk of *mishpat* being exercised in a way that reflects *'awlah*, wrong not right. That comes about when those who are involved in *mishpat* favor either poor people or important people (Lev 19:15; cf. Prov 24:23; the verb in Mic 3:11; Ps 58:2 [1]) or when they cheat in business (Lev 19:35). The striking prohibition on favoring the poor suggests that the stress elsewhere on judgment for the poor implies a concern for them to get their rights, not an arbitrariness about law. Elsewhere, the positive comment regarding the king is that he does not trespass in *mishpat* (Prov 16:10), though this is a statement of hope; in practice, when he exercises *mishpat*, he may do so in a way that involves trespass. Judges will certainly exercise *mishpat*, but it is an open question whether this will be *mishpat-sedeq*, to use the interesting construct phrase in Deut 16:18 (cf. Ps 119:160; also Ps 119:7, 62, 106, 164 in the plural).[23] There are related verbal expressions in Deut 1:16, Isa 11:4, and Prov 31:9, while the similar phrase *mishpat 'emet*, true judgment, appears in Ezek 18:8 and Zech 7:9. Instead of exercising such just *mishpat*, judges may rather bend or twist *mishpat* (Deut 16:19; cf. Hab 1:4; Prov 17:23; 18:5). It is a sign of degeneration when *mishpat* springs up like poisonous weed (Hos 10:4).[24] It is *sedeq* alone that the community is to pursue when it exercises *mishpat* (Deut 16:20). No tautology is involved in declaring that Yahweh's *mishpatim* have the quality of being *sadeq* (Pss 19:9 [10]; 119:75); one could not speak of *sedaqah* being exercised in a way that reflects *'awlah*.

So *mishpat* refers directly not to justice but to the exercise of authority or power or capacity or willingness to make decisions or to take decisive action. The point

---

[23] Cf. Knierim, *The Task of Old Testament Theology*, 118–19. Moshe Weinfeld, *Social Justice in Ancient Israel and in the Ancient Near East* (Jerusalem: Magnes / Minneapolis: Fortress, 1995), 33–34, says that *mishpat sedeq* ("a righteous judgment") is to be distinguished from *mishpat usedaqah*, which signifies "social justice."

[24] G. Fohrer's brisk emendation to *mispah* (cf. Isa 5:7) is a sign that there is a problem here with the assumption that *mishpat* means "justice"; see "Der Vertrag zwischen König und Volk in Israel," *ZAW* 71 (1959): 1–22 (see 17).

is further illustrated by the Torah's four references to Yahweh's *mishpatim* in Egypt. Twice the focus is on *mishpatim* on behalf of Israel (Exod 6:6; 7:4). Twice the focus is on *mishpatim* upon Egypt's gods (Exod 12:12; Num 33:4). In none of these passages is the notion of justice present. The idea is that Yahweh will act decisively for or against bringing freedom or exposure.

Apart from this, neither the Torah nor Joshua ever use *mishpat* or *sedaqah* or related words in connection with the Israelites' deliverance from Egypt or their occupation of Canaan, even though a passage such as Exod 3 does see Israel's deliverance as a response to its *se'aqah* ("outcry"). The language of *mishpat* and *sedaqah* is applied to Israel first in connection with the deliverance of Israelite clans from their oppressors in the book called *shopetim*, Judges. Deborah's expression for such acts of deliverance is *sidqot*, though these can be described as Yahweh's or as Israel's (Judg 5:11). Samuel picks up the word (1 Sam 12:7) and in his elaboration does include reference to the exodus, though intriguingly here it is not Yahweh at all who delivers Israel; Yahweh sends Moses and Aaron and they bring Israel out of Egypt and into Canaan, despite being dead for the latter event.

It is in the aforementioned Deut 9:4–6 that the Torah comes closest to declaring that Israel's occupation of Canaan is an act of *sedaqah*, though even here it does not say this. On the one hand, Israel's possession of the land does not issue from its *sedaqah*. On the other, it does issue from the other nations' *resha'*, the antonym of *sedaqah*, and it reflects Yahweh's faithfulness to the promise given to Abraham (which would make it an expression of *sedaqah*). In what way it relates to the nations' *resha'* is unstated. Elsewhere the Canaanites' wickedness is in itself the cause of their loss of their land (see, e.g., Lev 18:24–30), but the context in Deut 9 more likely implies that the wickedness of the Canaanites leads to their being removed lest they mislead Israel.[25]

As Joshua makes clear, the Israelites did not annihilate the Canaanites; furthermore, these statements in Deuteronomy were formulated some centuries after Moses' and Joshua's day, though it is hazardous to base any arguments on any view regarding their actual origin. Nevertheless we can be sure enough that they come from a period when their audience had no prospects of annihilating the Canaanites (if Canaanites existed) in the way Deuteronomy enjoins. While the mere question whether Joshua is fact or fiction may make little difference to the theological significance or status of its stories about annihilation, the vision that the factual or fictional narrative sets before its audience will vary according to their circumstances. In the late sixth century, for instance (when orthodox critical theory dated the bulk of Deuteronomy), Israel as represented by the people led by King Josiah is a tiny community with little prospect of playing a significant part in Middle Eastern history, while in the late sixth or fifth century (when the Torah reached the form we have it) the community that appears in Isa 56–66, Haggai, Zechariah, Malachi, Ezra, and Nehemiah is even more embattled over against its context. This community's much-despised ethnocentricity looks very different when one belongs to a marginal ethnic group struggling for survival than it looks to secure, mainstream members of

---

[25] See Knierim, *The Task of Old Testament Theology*, 98.

a liberal society, and it is to be evaluated differently on the part of minority groups trying to maintain identity than it is on the part of groups with power.[26] Conversely, "when Jews have known relative freedom . . . they have found it easy to express broadly and comprehensively the world-wide dream of their people. The literature of ancient Alexandria and the Moslem-Jewish symbiosis gives ample evidence of that," as does modern Judaism.[27]

3. So Is Yahweh Fair?

The Canaanites may have been *resha'im*, but hardly more so than many other peoples, and it is therefore difficult to maintain that Yahweh's judgment is just in the sense of treating all peoples alike in the way that Yahweh's own commands require of Israel. Is it the case that "an interpretation of the conquest that ignores the cry of the Canaanites for help, a cry not represented in the Old Testament because it pleads only Israel's case, is in fundamental conflict with the Old Testament understanding of God as the just and merciful judge"?[28]

The Torah does raise the question whether Yahweh's treatment of other peoples is always fair. While it does not refer to Yahweh's acts of *mishpat* or *sedaqah* in relation to Israel, it includes an intriguing reference to Yahweh's *sedaqah umishpat* in relation to Sodom. Genesis 18 is as suggestive for theological reflection as for prayer.[29] It might aid theological reflection on Yahweh's dealings with Israel, but it more overtly does that in relation to Yahweh's dealings with other peoples, and specifically with the earlier inhabitants of Abraham's promised land. Here in its first appearance in the First Testament *sedaqah umishpat* is related to Yahweh's promise to Abraham and to the intention that Abraham's blessing be significant for all nations. Abraham is responsible for *sedaqah umishpat*. This is not a surprising suggestion, for we have already heard of Abraham's *sedaqah* (Gen 15:6), the word's first occurrence in scripture. The passage was also the first time we were taken inside Abraham's mind and told something other than what he did. Confronted by Yahweh's promise of progeny, Abraham trusted Yahweh, and Yahweh counted this as *sedaqah*.[30]

In Gen 18, Abraham and his family are to put *sedaqah umishpat* into effect and thus keep Yahweh's way, which implies Yahweh's claim that *sedaqah umishpat* are Yahweh's way. The nouns come in the reverse of the usual order, suggesting "rightness that is expressed in decisive action" rather than "decisive action that expresses

---

[26] See M. Brett, "Interpreting Ethnicity," *in Ethnicity and the Bible*, 3–22 (see 16–20), with his references. Cf. D. L. Smith-Christopher's comments in the same volume, "Between Ezra and Isaiah," 117–42 (see 122–23).

[27] E. B. Borowitz, "The Dialectic of Jewish Particularity," *JEcS* 8 (1971): 560–74 (see 564).

[28] Knierim, *The Task of Old Testament Theology*, 318.

[29] Indeed, Walter Brueggemann has posited that it was intended thus: see *Genesis* (Philadelphia: Westminster Press, 1982), 162–77.

[30] The point would need re-expressing on the alternative understanding of Gen 15:6 noted above, but it would still hold.

rightness," but I have not been able to see any significance in this (cf. Ps 33:5; Prov 21:3; Hos 2:21 [19]; Pss 89:15 [14]; 97:2 have *sedeq umishpat*, Ps 103:6 *sedaqot umishpatim*).

Doing *sedaqah umishpat* is here associated with the promise that Abraham's family will become a great and powerful nation and that all the nations of the earth will "bless themselves by him" (Gen 18:18). The verb *barak* is niphal as in 12:3; 28:14, not hitpael as in 22:18; 26:4. This might imply that the meaning is passive rather than reflexive, which would strengthen the argument that follows, but I am content to suppose that the two verb forms are rhetorical variants and that the meaning is reflexive. The nations are to "pray to be blessed as he is blessed" (NEB) rather than explicitly "to be blessed" (NRSV, TNIV). The promise that Abraham will become a standard for blessing puts the emphasis on the magnitude of blessing for Abraham rather than directly on hope for other peoples. Nevertheless the promise implies that a prayer for Abraham-like blessing would be a reasonable prayer for a nation to pray, a prayer to which Yahweh might be expected to respond positively. If Yahweh were instead to respond by questioning whether the dogs can have the children's food, a Canaanite woman will be able to suggest an answer (see Mark 7:24–30).

The expectation that Yahweh might be expected to respond positively to such a prayer is supported by the context on both sides of Gen 18:18–19. On one hand, Gen 1–11 has been concerned with God's blessing of all peoples and with the question whether that blessing will ever find realization, and the first statement of Yahweh's promise to Abraham in Gen 12:1–3 follows directly on those chapters. Yahweh's promise to Abraham presupposes a concern for the whole world. Then on the other hand, the very prayer for Sodom that follows in Gen 18:1–21 presupposes an interest in all peoples.[31] Even if Sodom becomes a figure for Jerusalem (Isa 1:9–10), perhaps like Jonah's Nineveh,[32] it is hardly merely that.

The story speaks of a particularly loud outcry against Sodom (Gen 18:21; 19:13). Such an outcry (*se'aqah*) is the opposite of what is right (*sedaqah*); compare Isa 5:7. So Yahweh will take action against Sodom and thus deliver those it oppressed. Abraham's question is then whether this is a way Yahweh can go about being a *shopet*, a person in authority. "Shall not the *shopet* of all the earth do *mishpat*?" he asks (Gen 18:25). It is a strikingly formulated question, though commentators seem not to have noticed, and translators let the reader off the hook by having Abraham ask whether the judge of all the earth must not do justice; we then read it as if Abraham had asked whether the judge must not do *sedaqah*.

From Abraham's angle, it might seem that the last thing Yahweh needs is a challenge to do *mishpat* if that indeed means merely "decisive action"; God is already on the way to being decisive, and this is what worries Abraham. More likely "do *mishpat*" indeed has its common implication "take action on behalf of the righteous or needy" (see, e.g., 1 Kgs 3:28; Ps 9:17 [16]). Thus *mishpat* does here imply judgment that reflects *sedaqah*. Whereas elsewhere the point is often explicit through

---

[31] Cf. Knierim, *The Task of Old Testament Theology*, 319–20.
[32] See R. E. Clements, "The Purpose of the Book of Jonah," *Congress Volume: Edinburgh 1974* (VTSup 28; Leiden: Brill, 1975), 16–28.

the addition of the word *sedaqah* to *mishpat*, on other occasions it is made explicit through mention of the objects or beneficiaries of the action, and here they have just been mentioned. Abraham's point is then, "You have to take action that reflects concern for the righteous in Sodom as well as for the oppressed elsewhere."

So what would Abraham say about the Canaanites? He knows that Yahweh's giving the land of Canaan to Israel is part of a purpose designed to benefit other nations as well as Israel; in Gen 18 Yahweh recognizes the need to maintain a concern for the righteous within a wicked nation. Genesis 15:16 contains a more overt response. Yahweh intends to keep the promise regarding giving the land of Canaan to Abraham's descendants, but not until the *'awon* of the Amorites is full. Do Genesis and Deuteronomy imply a conviction that the Canaanites' waywardness was greater than that of other peoples? Such knowledge as we have from other sources does not suggest that they were more depraved than other contemporary peoples or the present inhabitants of southern California. But we are familiar with the way peoples do demonize each other, especially if they need to justify their own attacks on them. J. D. Levenson makes this point in asking "Is There a Counterpart in the Hebrew Bible to New Testament Antisemitism?"[33] He sees such a counterpart in the way the Hebrew Bible "caricatures" the Canaanites in order to justify Israel's displacement of them. Judith Plaskow offers a parallel Jewish feminist critique of Wyschogrod and of election theology in general.[34] The feminist vision for diversity without hierarchy parallels Knierim's vision for the particular without particularism. Plaskow associates Jewish election theology with patriarchalism; election is a "fundamentally hierarchical" notion.[35]

Yet Plaskow also notes that election and exclusiveness need not belong together. Judaism has not spoken or behaved as if its election made it feel superior to the rest of the world. It has been the victim of such views rather than the subject of them. The Torah's explicit emphases make it not surprising if Judaism lacks a sense of superiority, for the context of Deuteronomy's statement about Canaanite wickedness is a denial of Israelite superiority. Something indefinable attracted Yahweh to Israel. Whatever this was, it was neither Israel's numerousness nor its *sedaqah* (Deut 7:7–8; 9:4–6); rather the opposite (see 9:7–8 and the passage that follows). Further, the idea that the notion of superiority and domination is key to Israel's understanding of its relationship with Canaan is difficult to fit with its explicit understanding of the annihilation of the Canaanites as a dedication of them to Yahweh (*kherem*). If the latter is some kind of veil for the former, it is one that subverts it.

Additional significance attaches to those statements in Deut 7–9 given that a handful of passages in that context (Deut 4:37; 7:6, 7; 10:15; 14:2) are the only ones in Genesis-Joshua that refer to Yahweh's choice of Israel (cf. later 1 Kgs 3:8; Neh 9:7). Even if this is a presupposition of the books, the language is exceptional; it does not even come in Deut 9.

---

[33] *JEcS* 22 (1985): 242–60, esp. 248–52. See also "The Universal Horizon of Biblical Particularism" in *Ethnicity and the Bible*, 143–69.

[34] See *Standing Again at Sinai* (San Francisco: Harper, 1990), esp. 75–120.

[35] Ibid., 99.

The theme of election can indeed be present when the word is not. NRSV presupposes this in rendering the verb *yada'* by "choose" at Gen 18:19. It might have done the same in rendering Jeremiah's account of his "call" (another construct that we import into the Bible) where he speaks of Yahweh acknowledging him, distinguishing him, and then appointing him to a task (Jer 1:5). In Isa 40–55 it is the verb *qara'* (call/summons) that more often denotes what theology refers to as election. This language underlines the fact that Yahweh's choosing Israel as much resembles a master's summoning a slave or a cook's choosing which pan to use as it does a woman's choosing a man on whom to bestow her love.

It is doubtful whether in Isa 40–55 or anywhere else (except Isa 66:19?) we should speak of Israel's being called to a "mission" to the nations (yet another construct from outside the Bible). The suggestion that Israel is elected for service is also too easy an oversimplification, for Israel remains God's chosen even when it fails to serve, while conversely serving Yahweh does not make one a member of Israel.[36] Yet if Israel is indeed called, summoned, or chosen by Yahweh (e.g., Isa 41:9), then it is as a servant.

We thus need to be wary of reading into the books all that we might mean by the notion of election when their own language works in a different way and points to an idea with different dynamics. This is the more so when we take account of the theological point that is made by explicit talk in terms of choice here and elsewhere. In Deut 7:6–7, for instance, the point is not at all to encourage Israelite superiority but to underline a demand for a distinctive Israelite commitment to Yahweh (cf. Deut 10:15; 14:2). In 1 Kgs 3:8 it is to underline the demand that leadership lays on the king. In Isa 40–55 it is to encourage a people oppressed by a much more powerful overlord. Of a piece with this is the conviction that an awareness of being especially loved by its God (knowing itself chosen) has played a key role in keeping the Jewish people going over subsequent millennia; even Israel's sin will not cancel out its election, because Israel's righteousness was not the basis of its election in the first place.[37]

Perhaps Plaskow is right that election is an inherently particularist notion, and that is one significance of the First Testament's restraint in explicit use of this language even though it talks more broadly about Israel's special relationship with Yahweh. But we need also to note that election talk's openness to ideological misuse does not in itself establish that there is a question mark about the actual notion of election. Practically everything is open to ideological misuse.[38] Plaskow instances the call to obey the Torah, which can encourage "empty legalism,"[39] even as a stress on God's grace can encourage antinomianism (see Rom 6; cf. Jas 2). Regina Schwartz has emphasized monotheism's potential to encourage the same violent exclusivism as election, though it is not clear why polytheism would be less

---

[36] Cf. Levenson, *Ethnicity and the Bible*, 155–57.

[37] See Wyschogrod, *The Body of Faith*, 12, 24–25, 213.

[38] Cf. the remarks of Daniel Boyarin, *A Radical Jew* (Berkeley / London: University of California Press, 1994), 247–48.

[39] *Standing Again at Sinai*, 217.

open to this temptation.[40] The counter to bad election theology need not be no election theology but the good election theology that Knierim approves, election theology that links election with inclusiveness not exclusiveness, with responsive commitment and a desire to share.

Another instance of election thinking that does not utilize the actual word is the use of the notion of Yahweh's unexplained favor (*khen*: e.g., Gen 6:8). J. M. G. Barclay has suggested that "Paul partially deconstructs his own Christological exclusivism by his pervasive appeal to the grace of God."[41] If "finding favor with Yahweh" is another way of speaking of election, then it is striking that the Torah never refers to Yahweh's favor to Israel but does refer to Yahweh's favor to Noah. Along with its assertion that Yahweh's favor is exercised at Yahweh's discretion (Exod 33:19), the Torah similarly deconstructs any exclusivism it implies.

4. The Harnessing of Unfairness

The fact that peoples do demonize and caricature each other is not in itself evidence that Israel did so and that the Israelite account of the Canaanites is wrong, and it may be that the latter's religion and life incorporated a distinctively appalling combination of features such as the sacrifice of children, the ritualization of sexual activity, and oppressiveness in the society. But let us suppose that the Canaanites were only averagely wicked. What happens to them is not fair compared with what happens to other people. Yet what happens to them is only a spectacular example of a phenomenon that recurs in the First Testament and in life. There is a randomness about whether people get their comeuppance. If you are in the wrong place at the wrong time, you experience the disaster you deserve (or do not deserve). If you are lucky, you do not. Most generations of Canaanites, indeed, were not annihilated by the Israelites, in fact or fiction. Most generations of Judean leadership did not get transported to Babylon, even though they may have deserved it quite as much as the generation of Jehoiachin and Zedekiah.

The experience of nations in general often seems unfair, as the experience of individual human beings seems unfair. This was as much so for Israel as for any other people: it "has endured its history much more than it has shaped it."[42] This had been the case with Israel before the exodus, and it would in due course seem to be almost systematically so, in such a way as to raise the question whether Israel's election was an election to suffering. In general, different peoples and different individuals have different degrees of giftedness and resources and different degrees of oppression and hurt. While much of that unfairness can be traced to human agencies, much of it cannot, and the implication seems to be that God either is not very interested in fairness or is not in a position to ensure it. What happens in the

---

[40] See *The Curse of Cain* (Chicago / London: University of Chicago Press, 1997), with Miroslav Volf's review in *Christianity Today*, April 27, 1998, 32–35.

[41] "'Neither Jew nor Greek,'" in *Ethnicity and the Bible*, 197–214 (see 213).

[42] Preuss, *Old Testament Theology* (2 vols.; Louisville: Westminster John Knox, 1995, 1996), 1:294.

story in Joshua, then, is that Yahweh utilizes history in its unfairness, getting hands dirty rather than stay unsullied in a heavenly environment in which there would be no accusation of unfairness but also nothing achieved. Admittedly such theological comments are modern observations regarding an issue that does not seem to have been a problem for authors in either Testament. There is very little evidence that any of them were embarrassed by the story in Joshua. The New Testament speaks only positively about him and about the Israelites' taking of the land (see Acts 7; Heb 11).[43] The point is related to the distinctively modern and Western nature of our preoccupation with theodicy. While other cultures have assumed that life should be fair (Israel indeed did), the nature and extent of our preoccupation with the questions raised by its unfairness is a modern and Western one.

To put it another way, acceptance of (at least a story of) the annihilation of the Canaanites is an instance of the First Testament's living with the penultimate.[44] But the notion of living with the penultimate presupposes that we believe in the ultimate. The First Testament lives with a tension between what was designed from creation and what is possible given the obduracy of the human will, and with the same tension between what will be at the end and what is possible now given that obduracy.

Indeed, Yahweh makes history's unfairness the means of putting *mishpat usedaqah* into effect. First, although Joshua does not describe Israel's entering into possession of the land of Canaan as an act of *mishpat usedaqah*, it could have done so. Exodus-Joshua imply "that Israel's oppression of the Canaanite nations and Israel's liberation from Egyptian oppression are equally just." They justify both liberation of and oppression by the same people. "Justice is what serves Israel's election by and covenant with Yahweh rather than and regardless of a principle of justice that is the same for all nations."[45] Exodus 3:7–8 makes the point vividly. In this connection *mishpat usedaqah* are thus not universalizable principles. But Yahweh is also said to exercise *mishpat usedaqah* elsewhere than in the story of Israel. All Yahweh's work is done in faithfulness, Yahweh loves *sedaqah umishpat*, and the world is full of Yahweh's *khesed*. Psalm 33 follows up these observations with a look back to creation, but even without this its statements have universalized Yahweh's *mishpat usedaqah*. Yahweh is committed to decisive action in the context of a relationship that means doing right by the other party and is committed in this respect to the whole world. Yahweh decides for the world with *sedeq* (Ps 9:9 [8], cf. Ps 98:9; the verb is *shapat*). The foundation of Yahweh's throne, the throne from which Yahweh rules all the world, is *sedeq umishpat*, and the heavens proclaim Yahweh's *sedeq* (Ps 97:2).

Following H. H. Schmid, M. Weinfeld saw this exercise of *mishpat usedaqah* as the imposition of order on the cosmos,[46] but this formulation understates the re-

---

[43] See M. Walzer, "The Idea of Holy War in Ancient Israel," *The Journal of Religious Ethics* 20 (1992–93): 215–28 (see 215), against D. Jacobson, *The Story of Stories* (New York: Harper, 1982), 37 (cf. Wyschogrod, *The Body of Faith*, 218).

[44] Knierim, *The Task of Old Testament Theology*, 107, 129–30.

[45] Ibid., 97.

[46] *Social Justice in Ancient Israel and in the Ancient Near East*, 20, referring to H. H. Schmid, *Gerechtigkeit als Weltordnung* (Tübingen: Mohr, 1968). Cf. Knierim, *The Task of Old Testament Theology*, e.g., 15.

lational implications of *mishpat usedaqah*. However, Weinfeld usefully emphasizes three moments of Yahweh's imposition of *mishpat usedaqah* in the First Testament, creation, the origins of Israel, and the final judgment.[47] One would expect there to be some coherence about these acts of *mishpat usedaqah*. If they must be moments when Yahweh acts decisively to do right by those to whom Yahweh is committed, that has to apply to the world and not just to Israel.

A second way the unfairness of history is harnessed to *mishpat usedaqah* is then that Israel's occupation of Canaan forms part of a story about the blessing of the world and about Yahweh's bringing *torah* and *mishpat* to the world (Isa 2:2–4). Paul hints at this point in his midrash on the First Testament in Rom 9–11, where he includes some discussion of God's fairness. He, too, assumes that God has always been concerned for the blessing of the whole world and that the people of Israel is the means of this intention finding realization. The pharaoh of the exodus then acts as a kind of necessary foil to Israel in the story of how that realization comes about. Gentile salvation is thus achieved only through Gentile loss.

The Canaanites might be looked at the same way. Genesis assumes that for the world to regain blessing it is necessary for Israel to flourish. Deuteronomy assumes that for Israel to flourish it is necessary for the Canaanites to be removed. Knierim suggests that Deuteronomy should have trusted in the inherent power of Israel's theological convictions. If they cannot withstand such pressures, are they worth annihilating for? In the long run they showed themselves able to do this, but perhaps Deuteronomy was only being realistic in recognizing the power of Canaanite temptation when Israelite faith in Yahweh was a relatively newly-budded flower.

The fate of Canaan is subordinate to the promise to Israel. But the promise to Israel is in turn subordinate to the fate of the whole world. A temporary unfairness that discriminates for Israel and against Canaan is designed to give way to a broader fairness. Election is exclusive in the short term but designed in due course to benefit others than its short-term beneficiaries. This does not imply that Israel ever ceases to be God's first love, but it could imply that other peoples can be equally loved in their own way.

---

[47] *Social Justice in Ancient Israel and in the Ancient Near East*, 5, 21.

17

WHAT IS THE RELATIONSHIP BETWEEN CREATION AND SALVATION?

There is a wide divergence between the treatment of God, humanity, and the world generally characteristic of the First Testament's narratives and the prophets and that which characterizes Job, Psalms, Proverbs, Ecclesiastes, and the Song of Songs. The former assume that God and God's purpose were known especially to Israel in the course of a particular series of historical events through which that purpose, in which Israel as God's special people had a key place, was put into effect. Motifs such as exodus, covenant, and prophecy are central here. In contrast, the poetic books refer rarely to specific historical events, to an unfolding purpose, or to a particular people; indeed, outside some psalms they do not do so at all. They concentrate more on the world and on everyday life than on history, more on the regular than on the once-for-all, more on individuals (though not outside their social relationships) than on the nation, more on personal insight and experience than on sacred tradition. How may these two approaches interrelate theologically?[1]

1. Salvation History Emphasized and Subjected to Critique

The former of those two sets of emphases has often been described as the salvation-history approach. During the middle third of the twentieth century it was overemphasized, and the theological significance of the approach that focuses on God's involvement in the regularities of life was neglected. More recently, interest in the latter has increased, while the emphasis on salvation history has been subject to a wide-ranging critique. Its reference is ambiguous; was it really salvation that Israel found in history, and was it really history that brought Israel salvation? Its importance had been overstated; it could not provide the comprehensive framework for understanding the First Testament that had been attributed to it, and even the salvation events themselves could not reveal God's purpose without the word of interpretation that explained their meaning. Its basis seemed uncertain; both tradition historians and theologians questioned whether the events of salvation

---

[1] First published as "A Unifying Approach to 'Creation' and 'Salvation' in the Old Testament," in *Theological Diversity and the Authority of the Old Testament* (Grand Rapids: Eerdmans, 1986; Carlisle: Paternoster, 1995), 200–39.

history had actually happened. Its relevance no longer seemed self-evident; what meaning attaches today to the claim that God is "the God who acts"? Its uniqueness (compared with other religions) was questioned: did not all nations, after all, believe that their gods were active in their history?[2]

To say "goodbye to *Heilsgeschichte*"[3] would be an overreaction. While not omnipresent, the salvation-history approach outlined above is very prominent in the Bible. The first half of each Testament comprises narrative works that, while pre-critical rather than modern history, offer a series of connected interpretations of events of the past that were regarded as significant for the time of their writers; they assume that certain historical events in the life of one people were of key significance for the unveiling and effecting of the ultimate saving purpose of God. The same assumption is explicit in most of the non-narrative works (the prophets and the epistles) that follow; and it is not absent from some of the other remaining books (e.g., Psalms, Revelation).

The emphasis on salvation history drew attention to the fact that in both Testaments faith is not characteristically a system of abstract truths but a message related to certain concrete events. The events become meaningful only as they are understood within a context of interpretation or are accompanied by words of interpretation, but the propositional truth itself is characteristically expressed in the form of comments on historical events.

It is expressed, in fact, as a story. It is not a story like a children's tale or a western, which gives fictional embodiment to what we hope life is like (the good guys win in the end). It is an interpretation, but an interpretation of factual events: these things come to pass so that you will know that Yahweh is God; if Christ is not raised, then our faith is vain. The story is valid only if the events it relates actually took place. Thus, even if talk of "the God who acts" raises problems, it is too prominent in the Bible for it to be sidestepped in biblical study. Indeed, while this way of speaking can be paralleled elsewhere, no other people's literature gives the central place to their gods' involvement in their history that the Bible does. Middle Eastern religions, Gnosticism, and existentialism and other philosophies in the contemporary world have all offered worldviews that did not give prominence to once-for-all historical events; they thus contrast with the Bible's perspective.

Nevertheless, the notion of salvation history was long used uncritically in theological study and allowed to overshadow other biblical themes.

2. Nature, Blessing, and Wisdom
Overshadowed and Re-acknowledged

Nature as a realm in which God was involved was underplayed in the classic mid-twentieth-century works on Old Testament theology by Walther Eichrodt

---

[2] See, e.g., Brevard S. Childs, *Biblical Theology in Crisis* (Philadelphia: Westminster Press, 1970), 13–87, 223–39; Antonius H. J. Gunneweg, *Understanding the Old Testament* (London: SCM / Philadelphia: Westminster Press, 1978), 173–217, and their references.

[3] See Franz Hesse, *Abschied von der Heilsgeschichte* (Zürich: EVZ, 1971).

and Gerhard von Rad.[4] Various reasons may underlie this neglect. "Nature" as a self-contained structure with inherent creative power is hardly a First Testament idea; in First Testament thinking, the unity and dynamic of "natural" phenomena derive from their dependence on Yahweh. Second, when the First Testament does refer to Yahweh's lordship over the natural realm, it generally links this lordship with the theme of redemption (so, e.g., Genesis; Amos; Isa 40–55; and such Psalms as 33; 74; 89; 136; 148). Even Hosea and Deuteronomy, where the question of lordship in nature is a point at issue, do not appeal to Yahweh's creative activity in isolation from Yahweh's redemptive activity. Appeal to nature in isolation from history may be reckoned historically late and theologically secondary. Third, the alien character of such a religious interest in nature may be of theological significance. It was the nature religions that focused on it, and Hosea's polemic reveals where such an interest leads. Authentically First Testament faith historicized the farmer's instinctive involvement with the cycle of nature, subordinating the agricultural significance of the farmer's festivals to a relationship with the salvation events whereby Israel came into possession of the land, and thus encouraging in them a faith absolutely different from that of Canaanite religion.[5]

The German-speaking theology of the Eichrodt-von Rad era was also encouraged to emphasize the negative aspect to a religious interest in nature by seeing the faith of the "German Christians" as a nature religion from which theologians who identified with the Confessing Church dissociated themselves in stressing the particularity of what God did with the Jews.[6] Embarrassment with the clash between Gen 1 and Darwinian science perhaps also encouraged the focusing of attention on other aspects of the First Testament, though if so the clash between the First Testament's view of history (or the role attributed to history by First Testament theological study) and the critical historian's view of First Testament history now provokes at least equal embarrassment.

Even before the ecological awareness of the 1960s some scholars who affirmed the primary significance of salvation history wrote as if they partially recognized the imbalance of this emphasis. After all, Israelites had to reflect on Yahweh's relationship to nature, because they came to be involved with land and agriculture and had to face the question whether Yahweh was the source of fertility for them, not least in light of their contemporaries' convictions regarding the link between their gods and nature. This is part of the significance of Gen 1–2, as well as of Hosea, Deuteronomy, and Psalms such as 47, 65, 67, 93,

---

[4] Walther Eichrodt, *Theology of the Old Testament* (2 vols.; London: SCM / Philadelphia: Westminster Press, 1961, 1967); Gerhard von Rad, *Old Testament Theology* (2 vols.; Edinburgh: Oliver and Boyd / New York: Harper, 1962, 1965).

[5] For these reasons, see, e.g., von Rad, *The Problem of the Hexateuch and Other Essays* (Edinburgh: Oliver and Boyd / New York: McGraw-Hill, 1966), 131–43, 152; *Old Testament Theology*, 1:136–39, 426, 2:103–4; H. Wheeler Robinson, *Inspiration and Revelation in the Old Testament* (Oxford / New York: Oxford University Press, 1946), 1.

[6] See, e.g., Norman Young, *Creator, Creation, and Faith* (London: Collins / Philadelphia: Westminster Press, 1976), 17–20.

and 96–99.[7] While asserting that Yahweh is lord of the material world and the source of its life, Israel recognized that this world is a unity characterized by recurrence and regularity, with a life of its own, and although this is not a view of nature as a system possessing an inherent dynamic, it is a view of nature;[8] it is both interesting to compare with the Western metaphysical view of nature that underlies the use of metaphor from nature in poetry and instructive for our formulating an attitude toward God and natural resources.[9]

Some of the First Testament's own interest in nature (notably in Proverbs and the Song of Songs) has a practical concern, with learning from it about human life, but elsewhere its joy in the specifics and in the total wonder of nature seems less pragmatic (e.g., Pss 145; 147). Both in its order and in its wonder creation reflects something of its creator, declares the creator's glory (Pss 19; 24; Isa 6:4), and fulfills the creator's will, even when becoming a means of chastisement and not just of blessing for human beings (Gen 3; Deut 28; Joel 3:3–4 [2:30–31]). It thus shares life with humanity, yet it enjoys God's blessing independently of human beings and can be set over against them. The fullest First Testament review of nature in its mysterious detail, in Job 38–39, is given neither to explain everything to him nor ultimately to confound Job but to reassure him that the mystery of God that lies behind the mystery of nature is one that can be accepted as nature itself can be.[10] Israel's "reticence about creation in her early traditions"[11] should not be exaggerated.

Blessing is a motif that suggests God's involvement in the regular and the everyday affairs of birth and death, marriage and the family, work and society, which are essential to human life. To concentrate exclusively on the once-for-all acts whereby God effects a purpose in history also involves neglecting God's involvement in these everyday affairs. Salvation is treated as effectively coextensive with acts of deliverance, and the theme of blessing in everyday life is missed.[12] The overshadowing of this theme appears also in the longstanding neglect of the Song of Songs' overt concern with sexual love. It is still illustrated in Barth's extensive treatment, where the Song is seen as written on the basis of the nature of God's love for Israel; the covenant between Yahweh and Israel is the original of which the relationship between men and women is a copy.[13]

As is the case with the theme of nature, even the apologetic concern that has emphasized the First Testament's interest in history (because it has seen the cutting

---

[7] See, e.g., Walter Harrelson, *From Fertility Cult to Worship* (repr., Garden City, N.Y.: Doubleday, 1970), 12–18; John W. Rogerson, "The Old Testament View of Nature," in *Instruction and Interpretation* (*OtSt* 20, 1977): 67–84.

[8] Cf. Robinson, *Inspiration and Revelation in the Old Testament*, 1–48 (with his references esp. to Genesis and Job); Rogerson, "The Old Testament View of Nature," 69–73.

[9] Cf. Brian Wicker, *The Story-Shaped World* (London: Athlone / Notre Dame, Ind.: University of Notre Dame, 1975), 1–8, 50–70; J. Gerald Janzen, "Modes of Power and Divine Relativity," *Encounter* (Indianapolis) 36 (1975): 379–406 (385).

[10] Robinson, *Inspiration and Revelation in the Old Testament*, 6–8.

[11] Bernhard W. Anderson, *Creation versus Chaos* (New York: Association, 1967), 52.

[12] See especially Claus Westermann, *Blessing in the Bible and in the Life of the Church* (Philadelphia: Fortress, 1978), 15–17.

[13] *Church Dogmatics* iii/1 (Edinburgh: Clark, 1958), 311–29.

edge of the First Testament's significance for our own day to lie here) ought to be motivated also to emphasize the First Testament's interest in blessing, with its concern for concrete personal experience and feelings; Yahwism must have a relevance to everyday human life.[14] Yahweh is involved in the contingencies of the individual's personal history as well as in those of the history of the nations, involved in the blessings of life itself, of fertility, success, happiness, good health, prosperity, honor, and of peace in the community, of all the good that comes from having Yahweh with you. This is illustrated by the stories of people such as Ruth, Saul, and David, but (again like the theme of nature) it becomes a focus in the Psalms and Job. In the praise and lament of the Psalms all the positive and negative experiences of everyday life are treated as part of people's relationship with Yahweh,[15] while Job focuses on the experience of calamity in everyday life, of blessing becoming curse. Of the narrative works, Genesis has most to say about blessing. The concrete blessings given to all humanity and the struggle between blessing and curse are a key motif in Gen 1–11, while Gen 12–50 is structured by the theme of blessing promised, sought after, imperiled, sacrificed, bought and sold, fought over, but always vouchsafed and, at least in part, experienced. Blessing is also a central theme in Deuteronomy, where it is set before Israel as a prospect to enjoy in the promised land (e.g., Deut 7:13–14; 28:3–6; 30:19); it is prominent in the prophets' vision of a future state of salvation;[16] and it is the gift that God gives people in Christ.[17]

Wisdom is both the way to blessing and the embodiment of blessing. In Proverbs and Job, the person of insight is the one who can see how to live the blessed life: how to find peace, prosperity, success, and happiness. The blessed person is then the one who can give wise counsel and formulate a wise purpose.[18]

The wisdom writings are the books of the First Testament most like parallel writings of other peoples, and their understanding of God and humanity reflects the common theology of Mesopotamia, Palestine, and Egypt. This is one reason for the overshadowing of wisdom by history and prophecy. Indeed, God might seem to be dispensable from wisdom's understanding of reality, and wisdom might seem to be an essentially intra-worldly, humanity-centered, non-authoritarian, self-sufficient, pragmatic approach to life, picturing events working out in accordance with cause-effect forces built into them. The occupational hazard of the wise is to walk by calculation rather than by faith.[19] The prophets are thus as rude about Israel's wise as they are about the wise of other peoples (see Isa 19:11–13; 29:14; 31:1–3).

Yet Proverbs and the other wisdom books are committed to taking Yahweh into account (e.g., Prov 16:1, 9; 21:30–31). Admittedly, they reveal that their resources do not quite enable them to answer the questions they ask. Proverbs assumes that

---

[14]Cf. Janzen, "Modes of Power and Divine Relativity," 385.

[15]Cf. Claus Westermann, *What Does the Old Testament Say about God?* (London: SPCK / Atlanta: John Knox, 1979), 69, 71.

[16]See Westermann, *Blessing in the Bible and in the Life of the Church*, 8–11, 33–34, 63–64, 81.

[17]Ibid., 24–26, 64–101.

[18]Cf. ibid., 37–40.

[19]See, e.g., William McKane, *Prophets and Wise Men* (London: SCM / Naperville, Ill.: Allenson, 1965).

facts must always be preferred to theories. Even though it is concerned to wrest order from the chaos of experience, such order cannot be forced to emerge when it is not really present, and Job's friends have to ignore Proverbs' nuances and qualifications in order to generate the dogmatic confidence of wise men who think they know everything (also derided by Ecclesiastes). The book of Job avoids skepticism by working toward an unexpected climax, a theophany, a special revelation, without which the story of Job would come to a stop rather than an end. This event brings no new data for the resolution of the book's theological question, but it brings Job to a trustful submission to Yahweh through the experience of being personally confronted by Yahweh. Such a device, however, has no place in a true wisdom book; theophany is a distinctly non-rational, non-generalizable, non-everyday phenomenon. So the book solves the problem it examines only by looking outside the wisdom tradition, and it does not offer an intellectual solution to the intellectual problem of theodicy but a religious solution to the religious problem of how one relates to God.[20]

Ecclesiastes has a more negative final atmosphere than Job, because the author refuses to introduce what he might call a *deus ex machina*. Ecclesiastes is Job without the theophany. It is both more rigorous in and earns more admiration for its unremitting insistence on a verifiable worldview, and in the end more wrong, if taken as the whole truth. It takes the wisdom approach to its logical conclusion and proves this to be a dead end. It too shows that there is no escape from theological impasse within the wisdom tradition itself.[21] Wisdom records "an unfinished and even unfinishable dialogue about man and world";[22] it can operate only on the basis of an epistemological consensus and with the assumption of an order brought into creation at the beginning, and it cannot deal with a recurrent threat to that order or with a questioning of that consensus.[23]

Renewed interest in wisdom in the last decades of the twentieth century was encouraged by factors in theology and society. The wisdom tradition is decidedly world-affirming in its attitude to life and learning, and such features that had seemed shortcomings now became assets.

3. The Polarity of God's Involvement in the Regularities of Life (Creation) and God's Acts of Deliverance (Redemption)

The First Testament embraces both God's acts of deliverance in the history of Israel and God's involvement in the regularities of life that makes it possible for the

---

[20] Cf. J. Coert Rylaarsdam, *Revelation in Jewish Wisdom Literature* (repr., Chicago: University of Chicago Press, 1976), 74–90.

[21] Cf. James L. Crenshaw, "Popular Questioning of the Justice of God in Ancient Israel," *ZAW* 82 (1970): 380–95 (389–90).

[22] Gerhard von Rad, *Wisdom in Israel* (Nashville: Abingdon / London: SCM, 1972), 318.

[23] Cf. Hans-Jürgen Hermisson, "Observations on the Creation Theology in Wisdom," in *Israelite Wisdom* (ed. John G. Gammie et al.; S. Terrien Festschrift; Missoula, Mont.: Scholars Press, 1978), 43–57 (47–54), and Walter Brueggemann, "The Epistemological Crisis of Israel's Two Histories," in the same volume, 85–105 (86). See further chapter 5 above.

natural world to be a place of blessing if it is approached in wisdom. How do these two themes relate to each other?

W. Zimmerli observed that "wisdom thinks resolutely within the framework of a theology of creation."[24] The comment is an exaggeration, but a theology of creation, which emphasizes God's ongoing involvement in the regularities of the world that God created and maintains in existence, does underlie wisdom, as it underlies an emphasis on God's blessing in everyday experience and an emphasis on God's involvement in nature. This suggests that we may speak of the two themes in terms of the theological expressions creation and redemption. Whereas one or other of these is commonly seen as ultimately more significant than the other, more likely their relationship is thoroughly dialectical. The First Testament itself both interconnects them (in the Hexateuch) and sets them side by side (if one considers the broad sweep of the narrative and prophetic books and that of the poetic books over against each other), without clearly making one subordinate to the other. It speaks both of God's everyday involvement in the ongoing life of nature and cosmos, of nation and individual, with the insights that emerge from an empirical study of these realities, and of God's once-for-all acts of deliverance on behalf of the particular people Israel, with the specific insights given in association with those acts, and raises the question for us how we may correlate them without subordinating one to the other.

Both seek to bring order (continuity, generalization) to the specific and concrete or to allow such order to emerge from it. Both presuppose a trust in Yahweh as one whose actions are an embodiment of wisdom, ordered, not random, yet free, a trust based on experience of God's ways. Both require insight as well as trust; an openness to an intra-worldly way of looking at events and their interconnections as well as a sensitivity to God's activity. Both contrast with myth in offering paradigms of the relative, changing, temporal nature of all human experience. Wisdom and other ways of thinking that link with the creation trajectory develop in history and find links with history in the person of Solomon and in the ministry of prophets such as Amos and Isaiah; historical thinking depends on assumptions about God's regular activity and is put into writing by "wise men."[25]

Creation and redemption are not to be set in too sharp a disjunction. But neither are God's universal involvement in life's regularities and God's particular redemptive acts in Israel's history simply to be assimilated to each other. Although the First Testament can see redemption as an act of creation, it does not systematically integrate statements about creation into the acting of God in history, and it does not see creation itself as an act of liberation in the way other peoples did.[26] The

---

[24] "The Place and Limit of the Wisdom in the Framework of the Old Testament Theology," *SJT* 17 (1964): 16–58 (148).

[25] See, e.g., John J. Collins, "The 'Historical' Nature of the Old Testament in Recent Biblical Theology," *Catholic Biblical Quarterly* 41 (1979): 185–204; John L. McKenzie, "Reflections on Wisdom," *JBL* 86 (1967): 1–9; Hans-Jürgen Hermisson, "Weisheit und Geschichte," in *Probleme biblischer Theologie* (ed. Hans Walter Wolff; G. von Rad Festschrift; Munich: Kaiser, 1971), 136–54.

[26] As Burton Cooper notes ("How Does God Act in Our Time?" *Union Seminary Quarterly Review* 32 [1976–77]: 25–35), this raises problems for liberation theology's approach to

polarity we are concerned with is not to be dissolved by assimilating the two poles any more than by subordinating one to the other. Our concern is to tease out the various ways in which the two poles relate to each other, preserving the tension between them. I shall consider four facets of the relationship between creation and redemption that emerge from the First Testament material.

4. The World God Redeems Is the World of God's Creation

The two ideas, creation and redemption, correspond to two aspects of our position in the world. Although the First Testament sometimes relates these to each other as a chronological sequence (humanity was first created, then redeemed), even Genesis recognizes that the world does not cease to be God's ordered creation when humanity is in a state of rebellion and in need of redemption. The redemptive revelation presupposes an existent relationship of the world and humanity with the creator. Creation is not only the preparation for redemption but also its permanent horizon; the total view of created reality expressed in Gen 1–2 continues to take precedence over the narrower concern with a particular redeemed people that follows.[27]

The creationwide perspective of Gen 1 appears also in many psalms, especially the hymns, which respond directly to the wonder of God's handiwork still perceptible in God's world and call the whole cosmos to praise God. Like Genesis, the poetic books sometimes refer to creation as a historical event, but characteristically they stress God's ongoing activity in creation. To suggest that they think in terms of continuous creation would be anachronistic, but they emphasize that as well as giving life at the beginning, God ever gives life to the world and to humanity; as well as establishing order in the world at the beginning, in creative power God goes on maintaining the world's order and restrains forces that oppose it.[28] In the poetic books, humanity is not just lost and the world is not just the sphere of Satan's activity. Humanity in the world is given life by God, each individual being formed as once Adam was (e.g., Ps 139:13–16), and humanity is in continuing dependence on God for the breath of life, as originally Adam was (Job 34:14–15). Before God as creator, sustainer, and savior, humanity is invited to enjoy life fully, to live it responsibly, to master it actively, to understand it intelligently.[29]

An understanding of God, humanity, and the world that comes from creation, reason, and human experience to human beings as human beings will not

---

creation as expressed (e.g.) in Gustavo Gutiérrez, *A Theology of Liberation* (Maryknoll, N.Y.: Orbis, 1973 / London: SCM, 1974), 153, paraphrasing von Rad.

[27] Cf. Rolf P. Knierim, "Cosmos and History in Israel's Theology," *HBT* 3 (1981): 59–123 (82–89, 122 n. 60).

[28] See, e.g., Hermisson's comments in "Observations on the Creation Theology in Wisdom," 48–51, on Pss 84; 93; 104.

[29] Cf. Roland E. Murphy's comments on the stimulus here toward "theological anthropology" ("The Interpretation of Old Testament Wisdom Literature," *Int* 23 [1969]: 289–301 [292]).

be confined to the particular people on whom the salvation history focuses. It is based on principles common to humanity at large. There is therefore a theological rationale for its manifesting parallels to and being overtly open to the thought of other peoples (e.g., Prov 22:17–23:11; 30:1, 31:1; Job). It encourages us to be open to what there is to learn from all of human endeavor and insight, without abandoning the conviction that there is something distinctive about the biblical tradition.

Conversely, God's creation relationship with human beings as human beings implies a concern about all human beings; this concern is not limited to people within the stream of salvation history. "By me kings reign," says the Wisdom inherent in creation (Prov 8:15–16), drawing attention to God's universal revelation of how to live successfully, while Gen 1–11 indicates that "the so-called salvation-history can . . . never be seen apart from the universal acting of God."[30] Indeed, God's concern is not only with humanity but with the whole cosmos in its own right, with which Genesis begins and to which God directs Job in warning him against thinking that the universe revolves around him.

Humanity's life as God's creatures has its ethical norms, and creation morality is similar in content to the covenant expectations emphasized by salvation history and is just as authoritative as these.[31] Its basis, framework, and motivation, however, lie elsewhere, in the ordered nature of the world, human beings' assumed inherent moral awareness, their experience of life, and their reasoning about it.

Convictions about the ordered nature of the world and life suggest a confidence in the world's trustworthiness that in the First Testament reflects a confidence in God—or, as the First Testament itself more often puts it, a reverence for God, and more specifically a reverence for Yahweh (rather than Baal, for instance). It also suggests a mutuality between experiences of the world and experiences of God.[32] Among the poetic books the Psalms, of course, take an overtly religious approach to creation. This is inherent in their form; if people were not responding to creation in a theistic way, it would not be psalms that they wrote. The opposite is true about the form of the wisdom books and the Song of Songs, which are intrinsically experiential and rational, focused on humanity and on everyday life. These features are not felt to be in tension with a religious perspective. For Israel "everyday" did not mean secular or secularist, humanity-centered denoted a starting point but not necessarily a total perspective, experiential included experience of God, and rational did not mean rationalist; it included an intuitive aspect. It is doubtful whether the poetic books—even apart from Psalms—are less religious than the histories.

Indeed, the insight that people receive from the created world is divinely given insight; created things teach, declare, recount, make known (Job 12:7–9).[33] As well as speaking to God in praise, creation speaks to humanity in wisdom. It speaks in grace: it does not use that word, but it reveals the creator as the great giver, en-

---

[30] Claus Westermann, "Creation and History in the Old Testament," in *The Gospel and Human Destiny* (ed. Vilmos Vajta; Minneapolis: Augsburg, 1971), 11–38 (17).

[31] E.g., Berend Gemser, *Adhuc Loquitur* (Leiden: Brill, 1978), 144–49.

[32] Cf. von Rad, *Wisdom in Israel*, 62; cf. 190–94, 307, 317–18.

[33] E.g., ibid., 162–63, 301–3.

trusting life with all its wondrous joys to humanity and not giving up on human beings despite their abusing that ongoing trust. "Creation is grace."[34] In creation God reaches out in grace to all people, and in living in an ordered, created universe humanity has the prior contact with God and God's ways upon which conversation about the possibility of redemption can build.

Not that there is any inevitability about wisdom's revelation reaching humanity; it needs a human teacher to speak for it. Indeed, "revelation" may be a misleading category to apply to creation. First, the concept emphasizes divine initiative and human receptiveness, whereas learning from creation involves human initiative, even if one sees the task as that of opening oneself to the cosmic, moral, and social order that is present in the world by God's creation. Discovering and living in accordance with the cosmic order are hard work; they are not simply given. They are a "response to God" in the form of a "striving after knowledge."[35]

Second, the concept of revelation suggests an extraordinary activity on God's part, an unveiling of what otherwise conceals itself, whereas the notion of learning from creation presupposes that there is a resource of insight permanently available in creation, not one that manifests itself only occasionally.

Third, "revelation" suggests the manifest and inescapable unveiling of something otherwise hidden, whereas the wisdom books suggest rather that reality is divided between matters of clear meaning (no revelation being required in order to see them) and matters of such deep mystery that they cannot be grasped (no revelation being given in order to grasp them). One may sense their mystery but not enter into it. For Job, being confronted by this perspective is ultimately reassuring; Ecclesiastes, however, makes a vice out of the necessity that the mystery of meaning is beyond the grasp of human beings.

Part of what creation reveals, or of what creatures discover, is that God is active in the regular, interrelated features of the world, as well as the irregular, the "miraculous," the "acts of God" that "break natural laws." God is the God of the normal chain of cause and effect, involved in every historical event. Indeed, a belief in such a presence of God in the mysterious depths of reality as a whole (an understanding that holds together faith, reason, and experience) is the presupposition of faith in a divine activity in particular historical events. It is because the whole of history can be seen as the act of God that particular events can be seen as God's acts of special significance for humanity's salvation.[36] It is on the basis of being the creator that Yahweh can be expected to act in history (cf. 1 Sam 2:8; 2 Kgs 19:15–19), both to judge the people (1 Sam 12:17; the doxologies in Amos) and to save them (Josh 10:12–13; Isa 40:12–31).

In the New Testament, the creation revelation of God is treated directly by Paul in Rom 1:18–20, though his point is that the revelation fails to achieve its goal. The

---

[34] Karl Barth, *Dogmatics in Outline* (London: SCM / New York: Philosophical Library, 1949), 54 (cf. Young, *Creator, Creation, and Faith*, 90).

[35] Von Rad, *Old Testament Theology*, 1:365.

[36] Cf. Wolfhart Pannenberg's comments on von Rad in "Glaube und Wirklichkeit im Denken Gerhards von Rad," in *Gerhard von Rad* (ed. Hans Walter Wolff et al.; Munich: Kaiser, 1973), 37–54, 57–58 (51).

Paul of Acts appeals to what people can know as creatures (and to the limitations of that knowledge) to pave the way for his proclamation of Christ. Jesus' own treatment of this theme is less explicitly theological but in the end more far-reaching. It is he who appeals to God's concern for the world as its creator, to the rain falling on the just and the unjust, to nature's embodiment of the ways of God and humanity (see especially the parables), assuming that those whose eyes are open to the world will also be open to God.[37]

5. The World God Created Is a World That Needed to Be Redeemed

As God's creatures, human beings have to accept certain limits.[38] They are not God, and part of their submission to God is to accept the limits God places upon them. The First Testament narrative expresses this in terms of a prohibition of access to the tree of the knowledge of good and evil, a prohibition issued at the moment of creation.

Proverbs recognizes its limits by declaring that in principle a grasp of wisdom depends on a prior commitment to Yahweh (Prov 1:7) and then by acknowledging that we cannot by thinking, observation, and analysis solve all the questions and problems that our experience of life raises. There remains an element of ambiguity and unpredictability about life, before which the wise person can only acknowledge the hand of God, the "act of God" (e.g., Prov 16:1, 9). "The future is largely determined by our present decisions so we should act responsibly," but "in spite of our best planning there is an inscrutable mystery about our experience that we cannot master or manipulate."[39] The wise do seek to bring order to the manifold nature of human experience, but they also recognize the limitations of what they can achieve in this venture.[40] Trust in Yahweh or reverence for Yahweh replaces confidence in order; as long as limitations continue to be recognized and trust continues to be the wise person's stance, there is no need for the crisis brought about when dogma devoid of contact with experienced reality causes doubt or skepticism to replace trust in order. True wisdom involves an unfinished dialogue rather than the construction of a comprehensive system.[41]

The tension between the search for order and the acknowledgment of limits is heightened by Job and Ecclesiastes. Job's friends take their stand on the dogma of order, though they are not rationalists: their world "is surrounded by the insurmountable wall of the inexplicable."[42] Job agonizes for an overall perspective that

---

[37] Cf. Charles E. Carlston, "Proverbs, Maxims, and the Historical Jesus," *JBL* 99 (1980): 87–105 (105).

[38] See von Rad, *Wisdom in Israel*, 97–110.

[39] Walter Brueggemann, *In Man We Trust* (Richmond: John Knox, 1972), 60.

[40] Murphy repeatedly emphasizes this point: e.g., "The Interpretation of Old Testament Wisdom Literature," 294.

[41] E.g., von Rad, *Wisdom in Israel*, 318–19.

[42] Ibid., 293.

can do justice to his experience, and Eliphaz accuses him of wanting to know too much (Job 15:8). But early on, Job acknowledges that God the creator can neither be resisted nor comprehended (9:4–14), and he returns to this theme near the end of the dialogues (26:7–14); it is expounded in the wisdom poem (Job 28) and taken further by Yahweh in person in responding to Job (Job 38–39). Ecclesiastes, too, sets the question of a total understanding in the center of his work and has to acknowledge more grudgingly that he cannot reach the tree; a human being cannot come to any deep comprehension of what God is doing (Eccles 3:10–11).[43] Ecclesiastes is thus the frontier guard who leads wisdom back to an awareness of the limitations of its empirical approach—or is himself a danger signal on a dangerous road.[44] Whatever of the ways of God can be perceived in God's world, something beyond the witness of nature, reason, or everyday experience is needed if one is to perceive creation's deepest mystery or the creator's identity.[45]

The barring of access to the tree of the knowledge of good and evil suggests limitations that are behavioral as well as cognitive. Human beings are not given total freedom. In Genesis, their power over the created world is given positive direction and is also negatively hedged. There is a certain ambiguity about their position: they are sent into a world that they will have to tame, deprived of access to what looks like a potential key resource, and subject to the blandishment of at least one rather wily fellow member of God's creation.

The negative aspect of life in God's world is alluded to in material such as the Psalms that focuses on the world as God's good creation. Psalm 104 contrasts with Gen 2–3 in portraying creation not as a quality of life now diminished or lost but as a present attribute of the natural world.[46] Yet even Ps 104 is aware of the dark side to the created world: the need for the waters to be restrained, hinting at the experienced threat of their bursting their bounds, the darkness of night itself, Leviathan albeit reduced to the Loch Ness Monster, the suffering and death that follow the mysterious turning away of Yahweh's face and the taking away of Yahweh's breath, the trembling of the earth despite its allegedly secure foundation, the presence in the world of moral evil yet unpunished (Ps 104:6–9, 20, 26, 29, 32, 35). Psalm 93 affirms that Yahweh reigns and that the world stands immovably firm, yet does so in the context of acknowledging that the floods hurl themselves against Yahweh's order. Psalm 113 makes similar affirmations in the context of acknowledging the existence of the poor, the downtrodden, and the barren.

The dark side to life appears also in the background of the thanksgiving psalms, which look back on some experience of that dark side. Proverbs recognizes it when it acknowledges or presupposes the inequalities of life and when it portrays us

---

[43] Cf. James L. Crenshaw, in *Studies in Ancient Israelite Wisdom* (ed. James L. Crenshaw; New York: Ktav, 1976), 28–30.

[44] So, respectively, Zimmerli, "The Place and Limit of the Wisdom in the Framework of the Old Testament Theology," 158; von Rad, *Wisdom in Israel*, 235, 315–16.

[45] Cf. Knierim, "Cosmos and History in Israel's Theology," 91–92.

[46] Odil Hannes Steck, *World and Environment* (Nashville: Abingdon / London: SCM, 1980), 79.

wooed not only by Ms. Wisdom but also by Ms. Folly, so that the "organizing voice" of wisdom can be lost if it is not heeded, with catastrophic consequences.[47]

In Genesis, the negative aspect of life becomes more prominent in Gen 3. Humanity's response to hedges is to tear them down (cf. also Ezek 28). Human beings' need of redemption now arises not merely from the intrinsic limitations of their creatureliness but also from the added limitations of their waywardness, climaxing in personal death and cosmic destruction. Their inclination to use power in whatever godless way they like is now not merely possible but actual, in the story of Cain and Abel, in the violence that leads to the flood, and in the instincts expressed in building a tower that will reach heaven. A hedging of human power by God's words is therefore reinforced by God's chastisements.[48] The confidence about life in its Gen 1–2 aspect, which also predominates in the psalms of praise, Proverbs, and the Song of Songs, thus gives way to a more somber perspective in Gen 3–11.

There is, however, an ambiguity about Gen 3–11, the reverse of the ambiguity that appears in Gen 1–2. Life east of Eden is not a reversion to total disorder. When human beings overstep their limits, they are not thereby deprived of God's effective blessing, nor indeed of God's saving acts. Even Cain in his deserved vulnerability is saved by the mark Yahweh puts on him. Even the profoundly violent humanity and the profoundly spoiled world are saved by the preserving of a human and animal remnant and the ebbing of a flood. After that event, furthermore, the permanent preservation and blessing of the world is promised and covenanted (Gen 8:15–9:17).[49] There is nothing wrong with the realm of creation in itself. The cosmos was created whole and secure and remains so (Gen 1) even if humanity and history have put themselves out of joint in relation to it, and even if it becomes God's means of chastising humanity (Gen 3, Deut 28). It still serves God's will; it is not spoiled in itself. The world is established and cannot be moved (Ps 93:1). If the First Testament comes to promise a new creation it is because humanity's rebellion makes human beings experience the present cosmos as a locus of disorder, but it is thus history that is the real locus of disorder.[50]

The Gen 3–11 aspect of life is the focus of the psalms of lament, Job, and Ecclesiastes. In a lament, sometimes a renewed confidence about life in its Gen 1–2 aspect may appear, so that a lament becomes a psalm of trust or confidence; but alternatively, any residual such confidence may dissolve, so that the afflicted person's eyes focus exclusively on the experience of suffering, isolation, and abandonment, never to be raised again (so Ps 88). The entire books of Job and Ecclesiastes concern how one copes with the experiential and intellectual consequences of life east of Eden, where the creator's revelation seems invisible and the creator's grace obscured. Job (by including the friends' speeches and by ending the way it does) and Ecclesiastes (by including much proverbial material) acknowledge the truth

---

[47] See James L. Crenshaw, "In Search of Divine Presence," *Review and Expositor* 74 (1977): 353–69 (366); cf. von Rad, *Wisdom in Israel,* 161.

[48] George W. Coats, "The God of Death," *Int* 29 (1975): 227–39 (233–34).

[49] Cf. Claus Westermann, *Creation* (Philadelphia: Fortress / London: SPCK, 1974), 120–21.

[50] Knierim, "Cosmos and History in Israel's Theology," 80–81, 94–97, 119–20.

in the more positive teaching of Proverbs—there is an ambiguity here, too—but they insist it is not absolutized, as if we could still live in Gen 1–2. When understanding faces the ultimate questions of reality, it may well feel that it encounters a "merciless darkness."[51]

The poetic books and the histories offer different strategies for coping with humanity's situation thus conceived. The poetic books explore the redemptive potential of the creation order itself. As creation is an ongoing activity of God and a present human experience, so is redemption. Salvation comes to humanity through "factors inherent in creation itself"; "creation theology has a soteriological character."[52]

The psalms of praise, Proverbs, and the Song of Songs still focus more on life in its Gen 1–2 aspect, the psalms of lament, Job, and Ecclesiastes more on life in its Gen 3–4 aspect, but both seek to overcome the limitations imposed in Gen 3–4, if not those of Gen 1–2. In Song of Songs 8:6–7, "love is represented as a force that is able to overcome the negative forces that threaten the very existence of world and mankind. Love gains the victory over chaos and creates wholesome order and life."[53] In this new paradise-garden with its fruit trees (Song 4:12–13) the tension of Gen 2–3's garden is gone. "No serpent bruises the heel of female or male"; love's lyrics are redeemed and redemptive.[54]

Once more, however, there is an ambiguity in the picture. Ecclesiastes, too, recreates the outer form of paradise-garden with its fruit trees but acknowledges that it has not recreated the inner reality (Eccles 2:5, 11). The Song of Songs is aware of the point: even here death, shame, separation, and domination are still realities of experience, and perhaps the rareness with which the positive note struck in the Song is heard in the First Testament (and is echoed in the Song's interpretation) reflects the need to see the topic in light of the limits of life east of Eden.[55]

A comparable recognition that creation theology's resources cannot solve all the problems it can perceive may be implied by the building of bridges with the histories' approach to creation and redemption. Psalm 19 and Job 28 suggest that the voice of God cannot be properly heard in creation and that the secret of the universe cannot be found; they go on to express the conviction that one may better understand the cosmos and God's involvement with it, if one understands Israel and God's involvement with them.[56]

---

[51] Ibid., 91–92, quoting von Rad, *The Problem of the Hexateuch and Other Essays*, 159 (the published English translation there has "hopeless gloom").

[52] Hans Heinrich Schmid, "Schöpfung, Gerechtigkeit, und Heil," *Zeitschrift für Theologie und Kirche* 70 (1973): 1–19 (8); cf. von Rad, *Wisdom in Israel*, 314.

[53] Nicolas J. Tromp, "Wisdom and the Canticle," in *La sagesse de l'Ancien Testament* (ed. Maurice Gilbert; Gembloux: Duculot, 1979), 88–95 (94).

[54] Phyllis Trible, *God and the Rhetoric of Sexuality* (Philadelphia: Fortress, 1978), ch. 5 and p. 156.

[55] Cf. Francis Landy, "The Song of Songs and the Garden of Eden," *JBL* 98 (1979): 513–28 (524).

[56] Cf. von Rad, *The Problem of the Hexateuch*, 156–63. Von Rad also considers Prov 8 (where, however, it seems to me that a concern to relate creation wisdom and redemption revelation is less marked), and Sir 24.

Genesis also seeks to relate these two understandings but from the opposite direction, setting Israel against the background of an understanding of the world. After its gloomy portrayal of the intrinsic limitations of human creatureliness and the added deprivations of human rebelliousness, it reaches a turning point when God takes hold of Abraham and his family and declares the intention to make him a model of blessing and thus a means of blessing to the world. The ambiguity between the two aspects of human existence, which it portrays as arising in history was—or has begun to be—solved in a particular sequence of events beginning with Abraham and Moses. This sequence of events offers a resolution of the twofold need suggested by Gen 1–11.

One need is of a revelation concerning the mystery of humanity's place in the world and the meaning of reality as a whole. The wisdom books recognize this mystery and do not expect to resolve it; the historians are confident that they can see the heart of its meaning.[57]

The other need is of a release from the bondage into which the human longing for freedom had taken humanity. So alienation from God is replaced by a covenant with God, family disruption (Gen 4; 9:20–27) by a family relationship with God, insecurity by a place to possess, violence and oppression by liberation and a concern for justice. This begins to take place through the once-for-all historical events of the call of Abraham, the exodus, the meeting at Sinai, and the occupation of Canaan. Henceforth the power of creation is enjoyed only through the explicit celebration of the events of God's salvation for the people in their history. They cannot relate to and appropriate the power of creation "directly"; order is not allowed to triumph over liberation.[58]

The difference between the poetic books' approach to redemption and that of the histories should not be drawn too sharply. Psalm 19 and Job 28 build bridges between the two from one side. The stories of Saul, David, and Solomon do so from the other side, for they take the wisdom approach and challenge people to follow David's way and avoid Solomon's. Admittedly even they raise the question whether this call can be heeded, whether human beings inevitably fail to live up to the trust placed in them. Even David is, after all, an ideal type; the historical David betrayed trust and misused power.[59] Nevertheless, the histories assume that it is the God of creation who redeems in history, it is the God who is lord of all history who exercises lordship in particular in Israel's history, redemption as well as creation is an embodiment of the creator's wisdom, and redemption history serves creation by taking steps toward its restoration.

---

[57] Cf. von Rad, *Wisdom in Israel*, 292–94. Von Rad also suggests that, whereas wisdom teaching was in need of legitimation, for the histories legitimation was superfluous (291–92). Surely both wisdom and history found their legitimation in the same place, in the factuality of concrete experiences? It is such experiences, concrete historical events, that the histories relate; their legitimation is contained within them, in their factuality and meaningfulness.

[58] Cf. Coats, "The God of Death," 238; Walter Brueggemann, "Trajectories in Old Testament Literature and the Sociology of Ancient Israel," *JBL* 98 (1979): 161–85 (172–74).

[59] Cf. Brueggemann, *In Man We Trust*, 64–77, with Coats's comments, "The God of Death," 236.

The creation that history serves also becomes the instrument of history, as Yahweh uses creation (flood and storm, earthquake and plague) as a means of salvation and judgment. The events of Israel's history were of unique significance for the granting of insight into God's ways and for the achieving of humanity's redemption; these events were not merely one manifestation of the creative power that forms the world but a universally important expression of it.[60] Thus the creation perspective of the poetic books provides the presuppositions for the redemption story, but the poetic books themselves are set in the context of a whole that is shaped by the salvation-history approach.

Such conclusions are confirmed by the New Testament, where wisdom appears in several contexts that are reminiscent of the First Testament. In the synoptic tradition Jesus proclaims a wisdom designed for life in the last days, its basis modified by the fact that the rule of God is at hand;[61] further, Q's collection of the wise teaching of Jesus is grounded in salvation history by being incorporated in a Gospel. In John 1, the notion of the Word takes up ideas and terms from the wisdom tradition as well as from Gen 1 but reconnects them with salvation history in declaring that "the word became flesh." Romans asserts that the disorder of sin and guilt is replaced because of the Christ event by the order of righteousness and forgiveness.[62] First Corinthians both utilizes and attacks a concern with knowledge, as Isaiah both utilizes and opposes the wisdom approach, while Col 1 reflects the "foundational significance" of wisdom theology outside the area where First Testament influence was inevitable and brings together creation and redemption, wisdom and cross.[63] Blessing becomes a motif expressing what God has done in Christ, fulfilling in him the promise made to Abraham (Gal 3:8–9, 14; cf. also Acts 3:25–26) and bestowing on us in him every spiritual blessing (Eph 1:3). God's involvement in the regularities of life and God's acts of deliverance in Israel's history intersect in the life and achievement of Jesus.

In the context of reaffirmation of the significance of creation theology, one needs to note how central to the Bible is its stress on particular once-for-all events that are God's means of bringing salvation to the world. It does encourage us to learn from creation, from reason, and from experience, but its understanding of how salvation came goes beyond this, and if this understanding raises difficulties for us, it nevertheless remains part of the stumbling block of its message that as such requires close attention.[64]

This is not, however, to resolve the creation-redemption polarity in favor of the latter, for this would be to miss the object of redemption itself.

---

[60] Cf. Steck, *World and Environment*, 125–26; Knierim, "Cosmos and History in Israel's Theology," 197–98.

[61] Cf. Richard A. Edwards, *A Theology of Q* (Philadelphia: Fortress, 1978), 78; Hartmut Gese, "Wisdom, Son of Man, and the Origins of Christology," *HBT* 3 (1981): 23–57 (40–45).

[62] Cf. Schmid, "Schöpfung, Gerechtigkeit, und Heil," 12–14.

[63] Cf. Gese, "Wisdom, Son of Man, and the Origins of Christology," 47–50.

[64] Cf. Oscar Cullmann's comments on Rudolf Bultmann in *Salvation in History* (London: SCM / New York: Harper, 1967), 11–12, 19–28.

6. Human Beings Are Redeemed to Live Again Their Created Life before God

The object of redemption is the restoration of creation. Human beings are redeemed so as to live again their created life before God.

Most people do not live at a moment when one of the great redemptive events occurs; they have to live their lives before God nevertheless. Even the generation that does live at such a moment has to make the transition from that experience to ongoing life. The climax of salvation history is thus only the beginning of our history, and salvation history's concern with once-for-all redemptive events achieved by God is its strength but also its limitation. The salvation-history tradition cannot stand on its own; the events it speaks of have to be grounded and applied and their consequences for ordinary life worked out. We have to live historically in Pannenberg's sense, to live in light of those once-for-all past historical events that shape the possibilities of life in the present. We also have to live historically in Bultmann's sense, to make the decisions pressed upon us by our own historicality; and to live historically in Beardslee's sense, to live in time as the "little history" in accordance with the continuities of our existence from day to day and from year to year.[65]

In the First Testament, creation is not a mere subordinate preamble to history; history's purpose is to fulfill the purpose of creation. The First Testament is as concerned with the mythicizing of history (the elucidating of history's permanent significance for ordered life) as it is with the historicizing of myth, as concerned with the cyclization of history (salvation history's fulfillment in the blessing of the ongoing agrarian life cycle) as it is with a turning away from cyclic to linear history.[66]

This is reflected in the structure of the Pentateuch itself. Exodus (the salvation event) has Genesis (creation and its blessing) behind it; it also has Deuteronomy (renewed blessing in living the created life) after it. The promise to Israel's ancestors is of blessing in the form of increase and of land; the object of the occupation of the land is then life in the land. The promises of God are fulfilled, the Day of Yahweh's blessing is here, Israel has entered into its inheritance and begun to enjoy Yahweh's rest, it has begun the life of love and rejoicing that can be its privilege to the end of the age. The manna, the bread of saving, is now replaced by the produce of Canaan, the bread of blessing (Josh 5:12), as the God of salvation history becomes also the God of fertility.[67]

---

[65] William A. Beardslee, "The Wisdom Tradition and the Synoptic Gospels," *Journal of the American Academy of Religion* 35 (1967): 231–40 (240); cf. Rudolf Bultmann's remarks, *Theology of the New Testament* (New York: Scribner's / London: SCM, 1951), 1:25. Cf. also Bultmann's understanding of statements about God as creator as confessions of one's dependence on God (e.g., *Existence and Faith* [New York: Meridian, 1960 / London: SCM, 1961], 171–82, 206–25) with Young's comment that the doctrine of creation thus refers to humanity's historicity, not the origin of the cosmos (*Creator, Creation, and Faith*, 130).

[66] Cf. Schmid, "Schöpfung, Gerechtigkeit, und Heil," 8–10; Knierim, "Cosmos and History in Israel's Theology," 99.

[67] Cf. Westermann, *Blessing in the Bible and in the Life of the Church*, 30; *What Does the Old Testament Say about God?* 46; Gerhard von Rad, *Das Gottesvolk im Deuteronomium* (Stuttgart: Kohlhammer, 1929), 61–64.

Deuteronomy holds together Yahweh's special acts of deliverance and Yahweh's involvement in the regularities of life in a variety of ways. It portrays Israel at the transition point from the one kind of experience to the other, celebrating their arrival in the settled, agrarian existence of their "rest" in the land of their secure possession, an existence embedded in "the structure of the cosmic space and its cyclic time," the life in the presence of the order of God's creation that was salvation history's goal (cf. 26:1–11).[68] A life of blessing in this land thus becomes part of the covenant relationship with its focus on the historical relationship between Yahweh and Israel. The covenant relationship in turn makes blessing in the regularities of life dependent on obedience to Yahweh; failing this, Israel will experience God's curse and once again stand in need of Yahweh's act of deliverance.[69] The instruction that Yahweh gave in history is also an embodiment of wisdom that the nations will recognize (Deut 4:6).[70] Israel's regulations for worship introduce it to living in accordance with the orders of creation in the realm of time (especially annual festivals, months, and days), food, and sex; "Israel's arrival in this seasonal-cyclic life is celebrated as the fulfillment of Yahweh's salvation-history with Israel," and it now participates in the creation rest of God.[71]

Creation order is also implemented in the life of Yahweh's redeemed people in a practice of justice and steadfast love in society. Justice and steadfast love constitute the essence of Yahweh's moral character as the holy one (see Isa 5:16; Hos 11:9) and therefore the essential character of the created world as Yahweh purposes it to be (see Ps 33:4–5 leading into the treatment of creation and history that follows; also Pss 85:11–14 [10–13]; 89:10–15 [9–14]).[72] Salvation history frees Israel to provide history with a paradigm of this creation order in its social life. If it does not (and often it does not), the creation order itself can be called to witness against it. It is the natural world that is the context of Israel's little history, blessing that is God's ongoing gift that brings it to its fulfillment, and wisdom that shows Israel the way to grasp that gift and to live the life of God's redeemed creatures in God's created world. The "worldliness" of the First Testament as a whole reflects its conviction that humanity's redemption by God releases us to live life in the world that God created, not out of that world.

It is perhaps Israel's brief subsequent experience of ruling other peoples in the time of David and Solomon that leads it to ask questions about the cosmos as a whole and Yahweh's relationship to it. While Israel's significance, and the significance of salvation history, can be more fully appreciated only in light of creation, by a feedback process creation is more fully appreciated only in light of Israel and of salvation history.[73] This involvement with the nature of the whole creation connects also with an awareness that the fulfillment of creation's purpose involves

---

[68] Knierim, "Cosmos and History in Israel's Theology," 99.

[69] Cf. Westermann, *Blessing in the Bible and in the Life of the Church*, 47–49.

[70] See Moshe Weinfeld's study of links between Deuteronomy and wisdom, *Deuteronomy and the Deuteronomic School* (Oxford / New York: Oxford University Press, 1972), 244–319.

[71] Knierim, "Cosmos and History in Israel's Theology," 84, 103.

[72] Cf. ibid., 87–88, 96, 99–100, also Schmid's thesis in "Schöpfung, Gerechtigkeit, und Heil" that *sedeq* = Egyptian *ma'at* or "order."

[73] Steck, *World and Environment*, 125.

not just Israel but the world. Even if traditio-historically the primeval history is secondary to salvation history, and even if it is added to aid an understanding of Israel's significance, this does not establish that the object of the creation of the world is the existence of Israel rather than that the object of Israel's existence is to stand in service of God's creation of the world.[74] Salvation history finds its context in creation theology and is the context for it.

Thus the creation approach of the poetic books is the presupposition for the histories; yet the poetic books belong within the life of the redeemed people. This is rarely explicit in the way they speak, except in some psalms. Elsewhere it appears in the use of the divine name Yahweh, though that is not universal. But a wisdom literature is given a distinctive flavor by its own cultural stream, so that "every wisdom has its own history"; it is only people who know the Yahweh who became involved in Israel's history who experience and describe life and the world as Proverbs and Psalms do.[75]

Historically, of course, these books belong in the life of the redeemed people in that they were composed or adopted here. In the First Testament itself, they follow the salvation story; they do not precede it.[76] The Psalms, then, are the praises and prayers of the redeemed people of God, whether or not they refer to events such as the exodus; Proverbs teaches this people how to live before God the everyday life of redeemed creatures; the Song of Songs models for them what it means to love and be loved; Job pictures for them a human being coping with suffering; and Ecclesiastes reveals the believer wrestling with the doubt that can affect even those who have been on the receiving end of God's saving acts.

Further, salvation history itself is fully grasped only in light of the approach of wisdom. To see Israel's histories as actually deposits of wisdom thinking may be an exaggeration, but these histories do emerge from an interaction between an awareness or conviction about certain once-for-all events and a set of assumptions or questions that are similar to those of wisdom. Wisdom is thus the means of analyzing, understanding, and testing salvation history. It will refuse to let salvation history keep its head in the clouds and insist on clear thinking even in the area of faith's response to the acts of God.

The New Testament is not as worldly as the First Testament, yet it too sees that people have to live their everyday life even when they have been redeemed. It portrays Jesus blessing children, blessing bread, and blessing those he leaves with a peace that will stay with them.[77] It develops the parenesis in Paul's letters (sometimes, as in Romans, manifestly the working out of salvation history's implications for ongoing life). It preserves Q (albeit in its new narrative context), formulates the "new law"

---

[74]Cf. Knierim, "Cosmos and History in Israel's Theology," 69.

[75]Hans Heinrich Schmid, *Wesen und Geschichte der Weisheit* (Berlin: Töpelmann, 1966), 198; cf. Steck, *World and Environment*, 178.

[76]Cf. Roland E. Murphy, "Wisdom and Yahwism," in *No Famine in the Land* (ed. James W. Flanagan and Anita Weisbrod Robinson; J. L. McKenzie Festschrift; Missoula, Mont.: Scholars Press, 1976), 117–26 (123–24).

[77]Cf. Westermann, *Blessing in the Bible and in the Life of the Church*, 83–91.

of Matthew, and accepts James as a "compendium of wisdom"[78] despite its lack of specific redemption content. It was natural, perhaps, for Luther, at a moment when the Pauline gospel came to life again, to inveigh against James, but life—Christian, redeemed, but created life—has to go on. The cross of Christ is God's wisdom, but Christ's concern with creation theology, as with law, is not to destroy but to fulfill it.[79]

7. The Redeemed Humanity Still Looks for a Final Act of Redemption/Re-creation

We have noted that created humanity needed some further act on God's part because of the limits placed on human understanding and because of the bondage imposed on human beings as a result of their rebellion against the creator. God's redemptive acts might be expected to deal with these two needs, but they do so only partially.

We find further reasons why we cannot foreclose discussion of the relationship between creation and redemption by simply declaring that salvation history has solved the problem described by Gen 3–11. The ambiguity of human life remains after Abraham, Moses, Joshua, and David, and after Christ.[80] Genesis 12 to Revelation is as ambiguous in its way as Gen 1–2 and 3–11 are in theirs. Something of the tension between Gen 1–2 and Gen 3–11, the psalms of praise and the psalms of lament, Proverbs/Song of Songs and Job/Ecclesiastes continues. The inherent limitations and pressures of the created order remain; the added bondages of the rebellious order are not wholly overcome. We live as children of two ages, of this age and of the age to come, or of this age and of the age that is lost.

Still living east of Eden, human beings continue to experience limits; sage or philosophical theologian is still unable to formulate satisfying answers to fundamental questions. Indeed, it is God's redeemed people, invited to live full lives in the created world, who most urgently discover the absence of God from their history. It is often in such a situation that an appeal to God's activity in creation becomes particularly forceful, as in Job and in Isa 40–55.[81] God the creator is, of course, central also to Ecclesiastes. "YHWH the Name, has disappeared for Koheleth. Only Elohim remains, but perhaps when one enjoys life and light, the Name, the Presence will reappear."[82] Certainty and doubt, recognition and puzzlement, coexist in the believer's mind.[83]

---

[78] David A. Hubbard, "The Wisdom Movement and Israel's Covenant Faith," *TynB* 17 (1966): 3–34 (23).

[79] Hermisson, "Observations on the Creation Theology in Wisdom," 55.

[80] Claus Westermann, *Beginning and End in the Bible* (Philadelphia: Fortress, 1972), 34.

[81] Cf. Brueggemann, "Trajectories in Old Testament Literature and the Sociology of Ancient Israel," 176–79; F. M. Cross Jr., *Canaanite Myth and Hebrew Epic* (Cambridge, Mass.: Harvard University Press, 1973), 343–46; Steck, *World and Environment*, 209–13.

[82] James G. Williams, "What Does It Profit a Man?" in *Studies in Ancient Israelite Wisdom*, 375–89 (387), following Kornelis H. Miskotte, *When the Gods Are Silent* (London: Collins / New York: Harper, 1967), 450–60.

[83] Cf. J. Lévêque, "Le contrepoint théologique apporté par la reflexion sapientielle," in *Questions disputées d'Ancien Testament* (ed. C. Brekelmans; Gembloux: Ducolot, 1974), 183–202 (200).

There is a sense in which Christ provides the "answer" to Job and Ecclesiastes.[84] Questions about the relationship between humanity and God, especially as they are raised by the experience of suffering, cannot be the same after the cross, and questions about death cannot be the same after the empty tomb. Nevertheless, Christians can and do find themselves in the same position in relation to the tradition of their salvation events as some Jews evidently did in relation to theirs. These events come to seem rather remote (historically they are very remote). Christians can then find that Job and Ecclesiastes speak as powerfully today as they presumably did in postexilic times. The questioning of Job and Ecclesiastes and the reading of earlier parts of the canon through wisdom's eyes may still facilitate a survival of faith that would otherwise be impossible.[85] Israelites experience suffering, defeat, and death, and then a renewed saving activity of God in which God's creation power is reasserted (e.g., Ps 18), yet such experiences are never final, and thus they look for a future climactic experience of this same creative-redeeming activity (e.g., Pss 74; 77).[86]

The ambiguity about Israel's position arises not only out of what happens to them but also out of their own life. Rebellion against God is not merely a general human phenomenon that made salvation history necessary. It is also and more strikingly a consistent feature of Israel's own relationship with God, from the very moment of the sealing of that relationship (Exod 32–34).[87] Saving acts of God in history were needed because the insights and energy of the created order itself were insufficient to solve the problems caused by humanity within the created order, but even the saving acts of God in history do not solve these problems. The works written for the redeemed people (instructions, wisdom teaching, narrative, prophetic books) have that people's continuing waywardness as a key focus.

In the end, Israel had to give up mythologizing history. It seems to be a good means of bringing judgment but an ineffective way of implementing creation order. Even Israel's own history does not offer the paradigmatic implementation of Yahweh's creation order on earth that it was meant to be; still less can it take the place of Yahweh's creation and sustaining of the world as a whole. Indeed, Israel's existence and form in history easily becomes an end in itself rather than the means of Yahweh's presence in the world, and when this happens, Yahweh has to be the one who imperils that very history in order to preserve an inverted form of witness to the priority of Yahweh's creation purpose. The aim in choosing Israel and becoming involved in its history, the aim of thereby taking steps toward the restoring of creation order in the lives of all nations remains unfulfilled except in this Pickwickian form.[88] History is then both the locus of Yahweh's activity and of Yahweh's hiddenness from Israel. History itself is not unequivocally revelatory; there is a plan of

[84]Cf. G. Campbell Morgan, *The Answers of Jesus to Job* (London: Marschall, 1934 / New York: Revell, 1935); Aarre Lauha, *Kohelet* (Neukirchen: Neukirchener, 1978), v, 24, 37, 60.

[85]Cf. Harvey H. Guthrie, *Wisdom and Canon* (Evanston: Seabury-Western Seminary, 1966).

[86]Young, *Creator, Creation, and Faith*, 66–67.

[87]Cf. Westermann, *What Does the Old Testament Say about God?* 55.

[88]Cf. Knierim, "Cosmos and History in Israel's Theology," 61–62, 97, 100–101, 108–9, with his reference to von Rad, *Old Testament Theology*, 2:374–82, on the hiddenness of God.

God being implemented in history (cf. Isa 8:9–10; 14:14–27), but it is a plan that cannot be perceived by human wisdom (cf. Isa 28:21; 29:14).[89]

As well as continuing divine mystery and continuing human sin, a third factor makes for dissatisfaction with the redeemed order: continuing worldly mortality. To compare humanity with grass that springs up in the morning but fades and withers by evening (Ps 90:7 [6]; cf. Isa 40:6) is explicitly gloomy about humanity but also implicitly gloomy about the world around us that mirrors this sad experience. Conversely, to contrast Yahweh's eternity with the perishable, aging, throwaway nature of Yahweh's creation (Ps 102:27 [26]) explicitly exalts Yahweh but implicitly downgrades it.

The story of God's involvement with the people in the First Testament (and in the New Testament) is thus one that comes to no final resolution; it continues to drive forward. It cannot merely be seen as a "study in crisis intervention" designed episodically to "re-establish a 'steady-state' universe"[90] (fullness of blessing in the created order). It must have its goal in some fuller realization of God's purpose than history has yet seen. Thus some in Israel came to look for a new world, more intelligible, more just, more lasting, more fulfilled than the present one. Gerhard von Rad begins his treatment of prophecy in his *Old Testament Theology* with the exilic Isaiah's exhortation, "Remember not the former things nor consider the things of old. For behold I purpose to do a new thing" (Isa 43:18–19). The words are at least open to referring beyond Israel's history to the event of creation, and forward beyond Israel's history to a new creation, as they do in Isa 65:17.

Such hopes cluster in the book of Isaiah, though they do appear in other prophets and take up aspects of poetic oracles and other promises of blessing in the Torah (e.g., Gen 12–13; 49; Exod 3; Num 22–24; Deut 33).[91] No doubt they reflect the diversity of the book's origins, which is matched by their own diversity of portrayal; yet they surface in most of the various parts of the book and give its whole a particular cast. Here Israel's royal ideal is explicitly projected onto the future Davidic ruler people hope for, and the ideal keeps the notes of wisdom, peace, justice, and harmony in nature; nature will now contain no threat to humanity, and the whole world will be full of the knowledge of Yahweh (Isa 9:5–6 [6–7]; 11:1–9; cf. Jer 23:5–6). Isaiah 24–27 portrays final judgment as an act of de-creation affecting both the inhabitants of the world and the powers of the heavens (24:1–23); it also portrays a scene of final blessing and feasting that includes the abolition of death itself (25:6–8), that first undoing of God's creation that Genesis sees as the result of humanity's first rebellion. The further picture of restoration in Isa 35 portrays a blossoming of nature that turns desert into joyful abundance, human disability into joyful strength and wholeness, and human danger, sin, and folly into joyful security, holiness, and freedom.

Isaiah 40–55 relates overtly to a specific historical context, and these chapters provide evidence for the view that a concern with creation serves a concern with

---

[89] Cf. Walther Zimmerli, "Wahrheit und Geschichte in der alttestamentliche Schriftprophetie," in *Congress Volume: Göttingen 1977* (VTSup 29; Leiden: Brill, 1978), 1–15 (7–9).

[90] Dale Patrick, *The Rendering of God in the Old Testament* (Philadelphia: Fortress, 1981), 101.

[91] Cf. Westermann, *Blessing in the Bible and in the Life of the Church*, 32–34.

history. Transformation of nature is a means of Yahweh's purpose being effected in history (40:3–4; 43:19–20) or a metaphor for it (41:17–20; 44:3–4) or a sign of it (55:12–13). This last, however, also implies that renewed experience of creation blessing (progeny, land, peace, justice, security) is the object of God's activity in history (cf. 54:1–17).

In several ways, the final chapters of the book of Isaiah go beyond this. They, too, relate specifically to Israel; even the existence of a new cosmic order serves its needs and is part of the transformation of historical experience that it will enjoy (60:19–20). The new creation is embodied in the new Jerusalem (65:17–25). The security of that new heavens and new earth is also the security of Yahweh's people (66:22). At the same time, however, the new life that is here promised is the new life of a new creation; the best that can be promised to Yahweh's people is that they will enjoy long life and security, live in the homes they build, work and eat the fruit of their labor (65:17–25). Paradise is regained. In this sense what the book of Isaiah finally envisages is a restoration of creation order and a reintegration of human history into that order.[92]

In Christ all the promises of God find their yes (2 Cor 1:20). That assertion must include the promise of a new creation. What is true of all those promises is especially clear with this one, that this yes means not that in him they are all (yet) kept but that in him they are all confirmed.[93] As the one in whom the whole creation holds together and in whom God's wisdom is embodied, and as the resurrected one, he brings new creation now to those who belong to God (2 Cor 5:17); he also guarantees that there will be a new heavens and a new earth (see especially Revelation). The Gospel of John begins as the First Testament begins; the Revelation of John and thus the New Testament itself ends as the First Testament (in its Greek/English shaping) ends.

In his study of *Creator, Creation, and Faith*, Norman Young considers four theological approaches to his theme: the ontological (Tillich), the transcendentalist (Barth), the existentialist (Bultmann), and the eschatological (Moltmann).[94] The categorization is similar to the four approaches to creation and redemption that we have been considering, though coincidentally so (I did not discover Young's book until after drafting this chapter). The sharpest contrast, once one considers the content of the theologians' work that Young studies, appears in his chapter on Moltmann, for here the prospect of a new creation becomes centrally a stimulus to Christian action "designed to overcome the gap between what God has promised and what remains to be fulfilled."[95] There are hints of such an understanding in

---

[92] See further Knierim, "Cosmos and History in Israel's Theology," 104–8; Knierim also discusses the alternation between consummation of creation and new creation in Isaiah.

[93] Cf. Wilhelm Vischer, *The Witness of the Old Testament to Christ* (London: Lutterworth, 1949), 1:24, referring to Karl Barth, "Verheissung, Zeit-Erfüllung," *Münchner Neueste Nachrichten*, 23.12.1930.

[94] Young deals with Barth first.

[95] Young, *Creator, Creation, and Faith*, 154; see, e.g., Jürgen Moltmann, *Theology of Hope* (London: SCM / New York: Harper, 1967), 19–22, 329–38. The theology of liberation takes a related approach to creation theology more generally: see, e.g., Gutiérrez, *Theology of Liberation*, 155–60.

the New Testament (notably in 2 Pet 3). Generally, however, the point of creation language is precisely to emphasize the transcendent origin of what God has done, is doing, or will do. The praxis Moltmann desires may be right, but its ideology lies elsewhere.

The biblical material on creation and redemption invites the reader to a highly paradoxical perspective. Each of the four facets of the mutual relationship of these two poles is in tension not only in itself but also with the other facets. The temptation is to opt for one rather than another.[96] The challenge of First Testament theology is to hold them together as the varied facets of the dialectic or complementarity or counterpoint suggested by the First Testament's treatment of God's involvement in the regularities of our lives and God's acts of deliverance in history, so that the whole can be fruitful for our own faith and living.

---

[96] Cf. Knierim, "Cosmos and History in Israel's Theology," 107, on P and Isa 56–66.

18

HOW DOES THE FIRST TESTAMENT
LOOK AT OTHER RELIGIONS?

What attitude does the First Testament suggest to religious plurality? Different parts of the First Testament suggest a variety of perspectives on this question. Two insights then emerge from the First Testament as a whole. One is that it is possible to recognize foreign religions as reflecting truth about God from which Israel itself may even be able to learn; the other is that nevertheless the First Testament sees these religions as always in need of the illumination that can come only from knowing what Yahweh has done with Israel. So the First Testament does not suggest one should take a radically exclusivist attitude to other religions, as if they were simply misguided, simply the fruits of human sin or inspired by demonic spirits. Yet one cannot affirm them as if they are just as valid as First Testament faith itself. The closing sections of this chapter suggest why this is so, pointing to the narrative nature of First Testament faith as key to understanding its attitude to this question. The First Testament is not simply a collection of religious traditions parallel to those of other peoples, though that is one aspect of its significance. In the story of Israel that led to the story of Jesus Christ, God was doing something of decisive importance for the whole world. The First Testament's religious tradition is therefore of unique and decisive importance to all peoples because it is part of the Christian story.[1]

1. Perspectives from Creation: Humanity's Awareness of God and Distance from God

Genesis 1–11 assumes that human beings are created in God's image and are aware of God. Their disobedience and their expulsion from God's garden did not remove the image or the awareness; this is presupposed by their religious observances in act and word (e.g., Gen 4:1, 3, 26). The God they refer to in connection

---

[1] An expansion and revision of a paper written for the Tyndale Fellowship Conference on Religious Pluralism in 1991, itself revised in light of comments by Christopher J. H. Wright as respondent and published under both our names as "Yahweh Our God Yahweh One" in *One God, One Lord in a World of Religious Pluralism* (ed. Andrew D. Clarke and Bruce W. Winter; Cambridge: Tyndale House, 1991), 34–52 (2nd ed.; Carlisle, UK: Paternoster / Grand Rapids: Baker, 1992), 43–62.

with these observances is identified as Yahweh, though on the usual understanding of Exod 6 this identification is a theological interpretation of their practice rather than an indication of the name for God they would themselves have used. They acknowledge God as creator, giver of blessing, judge, and protector and respond to God in offering, plea, and proclamation. The chapters imply an understanding of the religious awareness of human beings in general that corresponds to the understanding of the ethical awareness of human beings expressed in Amos 1–2, and they imply a universal lordship and involvement of Yahweh among all peoples corresponding to that stated in Amos 9:7.

This understanding also bears comparison with that of Proverbs, Ecclesiastes, Job, and the Song of Songs. These works have particularly clear parallels with others from ancient Mesopotamia and Egypt. Sometimes the relationship with these involves direct dependence, as is the case with the Thirty Sayings in Prov 22–24. Sometimes the parallels are matters of theme, form, emphasis, and mode of treatment, which as such apply also to features of proverbial, skeptical, philosophical, dramatic, and erotic literature from other times and areas. In either case non-Israelite insight is set in a new context within the religion of Yahweh (cf. Prov 1:7), but the implication of the parallels is that pagan thought has its own insight. The First Testament pictures God's wisdom involved and reflected in creation (Prov 3:19–20; 8:22–31) and pictures God's breath infused into human beings by virtue of their creation (e.g., Job 32:8). Both ideas suggest a theological rationale for expecting that the nature of the created world and the experience, thought, culture, and religion of the human creation will reflect something of God's truth. The wisdom literature is thus evidence of the ability of Yahwistic faith to incorporate the insights of other cultures, recognizing its value while removing from it idolatrous or polytheistic elements. We might thus reflect on the significance of the wisdom tradition as a starting point for cross-cultural communication of biblical faith and interreligious dialogue.[2]

The picture of all humanity as made in God's image might seem to point in the same direction, though the First Testament itself does not develop this idea. Its not referring to this motif in Gen 1 (as to other aspects of Gen 1–3) can puzzle Christians, for whom these chapters are of key theological significance. Exegetically the meaning of "the image of God" is much disputed.[3] Further, despite the universal form of the expression, originally its point may have been to reassure Israelites of their human significance as much as directly to make a comment on humanity as a whole. So we may say that the First Testament indeed presupposes that all humanity was made by God and has some insight into the significance of human life, but it does not use the idea of being made in God's image to express the point.

From the time of Noah, human beings in general are seen as in a form of covenant relationship with God (Gen 6:18; 9:8–17; cf. the covenants of Isa 24:5; Amos 1:9?). This Noah covenant undergirds the providential preservation of life on earth. The fundamental idea of covenant in Hebrew as in English is that of a formalized

---

[2] See John Eaton, *The Contemplative Face of Old Testament Wisdom in the Context of World Religions* (London: SCM / Philadelphia: Trinity Press International, 1989).

[3] See the introduction to chapter 4 above.

commitment in relationship; the commitment may be one-sided or may be more mutual. It would not have raised our eyebrows if the relationship between God and humanity in Gen 1–2 had been described as covenantal, and it has often been interpreted as implicitly so. The absence of the term "covenant" in Gen 1–2 perhaps suggests that a covenanted relationship is by definition one that needs special protection or undergirding because of known pressures on commitment such as the human shortcomings that come to expression in Gen 3–6. It is only when sin has become a reality that commitments need to be the subject of a covenant. It is in any case striking that God enters into such a committed relationship with humanity after the Flood on the basis of their shortcomings having clearly emerged (cf. the explicit argument of Gen 8:21).[4]

This is not, however, the kind of special redemptive covenant relationship that Israel later enjoys, with its more explicit committed mutual relationship (which itself turned out to be insufficient to solve the problems unveiled in Gen 1–11). The human beings in the covenant relationship initiated with Noah are not readmitted to God's garden, and they tend to resist the fulfillment of their human destiny. Indeed, the events that follow on the covenant making of Gen 9 underline the moral and religious shortcomings of Noah's descendants and give Gen 1–11 as a whole a rather gloomy cast. The chapters are a background to the necessary story of restoration that follows.

Both sides to Gen 1–11 have implications for attitudes to the religions of our own day. On one hand, the religions reflect humanity's being made in God's image and being in a form of covenant relationship with God. Books such as Proverbs, too, point us toward an attitude to other cultures (of which their religions are part) that looks at them as sources of insight and not merely as expressions of lostness. On the other hand, Gen 1–11 suggests that the religions, like all human activity, belong in the context of a world that needs restoration to the destiny and the relationship with God that were intended for them, which God purposed to bring about through the covenant with Israel that culminated in the mission and accomplishment of Jesus. Similarly, books such as Proverbs, Job, Ecclesiastes, and the Song of Songs illustrate the limitations of what can be said on the basis of human experience outside of Yahweh's special involvement with Israel.

The religions can thus be viewed both positively and negatively. They are not inherently demonic or merely sinful human attempts to reach God. We can learn from them. Yet they are not equally valid insights into the truth about God. They may provide a starting point and certain areas of common ground but not a finishing point. They cannot tell us about the special and vital activity of God in Israel that came to a climax in Christ; and further, all human religion is not only inevitably tainted by our wayward life in this earth but also can be the very means we use to keep at arm's length the God we choose not to obey. Religion can express our rebellion as well as our response. This, of course, is as true for Israelite religion, as the prophets pointed out, and for Christian religion as for any other faith. Religion always has this duality or ambiguity, a simultaneous seeking after God our creator and fleeing from God our judge.

---

[4]TNIV's "although" obscures this point. On "covenant," see chapter 9 above.

2. Perspectives from the Stories of Israel's Ancestors: The Possibility and Limitations of "Ecumenical Bonhomie"[5]

The stories in Gen 12–50, following the book's opening exposition of the world's createdness and its turning away from God, speak of special acts and words in relation to Israel's ancestors in connection with a special purpose God has for them. In a sense these later chapters are thus moving from a more inclusive to a more exclusive attitude, but this purpose is one intended to benefit the whole world. Further, the ancestors' words and deeds do not imply the belief that other peoples in Canaan have no knowledge of God, though the ancestors do seem to establish their own places of worship, near those of the Canaanites, rather than making use of Canaanite sanctuaries. Like some other peoples in the Middle East, Israel's ancestors enjoy a particular awareness of God as the God of the head of the family, a God who enters into a special relationship with their leader and through him guides them in their lives.

In keeping with Gen 1–11, Gen 12–50 presupposes that this God is the one whom later Israel worships as Yahweh. It also speak of this God as El, commonly in compound with other expressions in phrases such as El Elyon (El Most High; 14:18–22), El Roi (El Who Sees Me; 16:13), El Shaddai (?El Almighty; 17:1; 28:3; 35:11; 43:14; 48:3), and El Olam (El Eternal; 21:33). Like its equivalent in other Semitic languages, *'il,* Hebrew *'el* can be both a term for deity, like *'elohim* (e.g., Exod 15:2; 20:5), and an actual name for God. It is thus sometimes properly transliterated El, sometimes properly translated "God" or "god."

Its background as a Canaanite name for "the god par excellence, the head of the pantheon"[6] lies near the surface in Gen 14, where Melchizedek, the priest-king of Salem, blesses Abram in the name of his god, "El Elyon, owner of heaven and earth" (Gen 14:19). Abram in turn takes an oath in the name of "Yahweh, El Elyon, owner of heaven and earth" (Gen 14:22). Apparently Abram and Genesis itself recognize that Melchizedek (and presumably other people in Canaan who worship El under one manifestation or another) serves the true God but does not know all there is to know about that God. It is in keeping with this that in due course Israel, having taken over Melchizedek's city of Salem, locates Yahweh's own chief sanctuary there. "Yahweh roars from Zion" (Amos 1:2); indeed, "El, God, Yahweh" shines forth from Zion (Ps 50:1). A similar implication emerges from Abraham's calling on God as Yahweh El Olam in Gen 18:33. El Olam appears only here, as a designation of Yahweh, but comparable phrases come elsewhere to designate Canaanite deities. Such Canaanite texts also more broadly refer to El as one who blesses, promises offspring, heals, and guides in war, like Yahweh. Joseph and Pharaoh, too, seem to work on the basis that the God they serve is the same God (see Gen 41:16, 39; and compare

---

[5] Gordon J. Wenham's phrase in "The Religion of the Patriarchs," in *Essays on the Patriarchal Narratives* (ed. A. R. Millard and D. J. Wiseman; Leicester: IVP, 1980 / Winona Lake, Ind.: Eisenbrauns, 1983), ch. 6.

[6] F. M. Cross Jr., *Canaanite Myth and Hebrew Epic* (Cambridge, Mass. / London: Harvard University Press, 1973), 13.

Pharaoh's giving and Joseph's accepting an Egyptian theophoric name and a wife who was a priest's daughter, 41:45).

So there are a number of correspondences between Yahweh and El as the Canaanites know him, but these correspondences do not constitute identity. They do not indicate that Canaanite and Israelite faith are identical, or equally valid alternatives depending on where you happen to live. From the perspective of the historical development of religions, it might be feasible to see Yahwism as a mutation from Middle Eastern religion, as Christianity was a mutation from Judaism, but this does not imply that the mutation is of similar status to its parent; rather the opposite. Canaanite religion had its insight and limited validity, but what God began to do with Abram was something of far-reaching significance, even for the Canaanites themselves. The process was not merely syncretistic in a natural development of human religious insights. In dealing with the ancestors of Israel, the living God, later disclosed as Yahweh, made an accommodation to the names and forms of deity then known in their cultural setting. This does not thereby endorse every aspect of Canaanite El worship. The purpose of God's particular action in the history of Israel is ultimately that God, as the saving and covenantal God Yahweh, should be known fully and worshiped exclusively by those who as yet imperfectly know God as El. The end result of what God began to do through Abram was of significance for the Canaanites precisely because it critiqued and rejected Canaanite religion.

It has been suggested that biblical faith emerged in a context of multiple religious options. That is too Californian a way to put it. People did not think in terms of options, and these options were not multiple. Abraham lived in a context of one faith in Babylon and another in Canaan. He was summoned out of the first in order to begin a different narrative. He is then content to live that narrative alongside Canaanites such as Melchizedek who live their own narrative. What to do with the difference between these narratives is God's business.

In the context of premodernity, people had one religious option which they recognized was the truth but accepted that other people lived by other narratives. In the context of modernity, people did not allow others to live by different religious options. In the context of postmodernity, everybody has a story and all stories are equally valid.

3. Perspectives from Exodus and Sinai: The Distinctive Importance of Yahweh's Acts of Redemption

The distinctive foundation of Israelite faith is that the true God, El Most High, the creator of heaven and earth, eternal and almighty, has acted in a specially significant way in relation to Israel. God gives concrete expression to the relationship with and guiding of the particular people whose story Gen 12–50 tells, by bringing them out of service to Egypt and into service of Yahweh and renegotiating the covenant with them at Sinai. This God goes on to give them the whole land of Canaan as a secure home. All this happens in fulfillment of specific promises made to their ancestors long before. That gives new content to the understanding of the God they share with the Canaanites, new content anticipated in this God's self-revelation to Moses as Yahweh (even if some form of that name was already known, perhaps even as an epithet of El) and reflected in the centrality of the name Yahweh henceforth. The God of these other religions is now more fully known in Israel, ultimately so that this God may be more fully known among other peoples, too. The creator's victory over Sea, of which Canaanite stories told, has been won in history.[7] El's decrees and judgments are delivered on earth at Sinai.

It is still the God worshiped within these other religions who is more fully known here, and the First Testament apparently assumes that Israel can still learn from these other religions. Many religious observances and concepts in Israel correspond to those of other Middle Eastern peoples, and for that matter to those of traditional religions elsewhere. Parallels with traditional religions remind us that at a number of points Israelite and other religions developed independently in parallel ways. Since priesthood and sacrifice are common human institutions we need not imagine Israel borrowing these ideas from Canaan, though other cases apparently did involve adaptation from contemporary cultures. Perhaps it makes little theological difference which of these routes applies in different instances; in either way, God expects Israel to utilize human instincts in order to think of Yahweh and to worship Yahweh.

Thus the significance of the exodus is brought out by the reuse of motifs from Canaanite myth expressed in terms of a victory over Sea. The Mesha stone with its reference to "devoting" things by destroying them suggests that Israel's theology and practice of war making overlap with the pattern and theology of war elsewhere in Palestine. The wilderness sanctuary of Exod 25–40 follows Canaanite models for a dwelling of El, in its framework construction, its curtains embroidered with cherubim, and its throne flanked by cherubim. Such adapting continues with the building of the temple, the religion of the Psalter, and the ideology of kingship (divine and human). It continues in the oracles of the prophets, whose admission to the council of Yahweh is an admission to the council of El (cf. Ps 82), where they overhear El giving judgment, and in the visionary symbolism of the apocalypses. Occasional specific texts indicate concrete dependence (see Ps 104?). This is not to say that these institutions, ideas, or texts are unchanged when they feature within Yahwism but that it was able to reach its own mature expression with their aid.

We have noted that the First Testament treats worship of El offered by Israelites and non-Israelites as worship of the true God. The story of Jonah presupposes that Yahweh alone is God, but it does not initially picture the Ninevites or the sailors consciously relating to Yahweh, as Jonah does. Yet when Jonah tells his story, the sailors do call on Yahweh (as Jonah does not!), and subsequently the Ninevites' fasting and crying to God (*'elohim*) meets with a response from the one whom Jonah can call *'elohim*, Yahweh, and El.

Indeed, Deuteronomy suggests that worship of other deities by non-Israelites is ordained by God (see Deut 4:19; cf. 32:8–9).[8] This may be an example of the way

---

[7] Ibid., 87–88.
[8] See, e.g., NRSV and TNIV mg, following the Qumran ms and LXX.

the First Testament attributes to Yahweh as sole cause phenomena that we tend to attribute to secondary human volition. If Israelites observed that other nations worshiped their own deities, and if Yahweh was sovereign high God over all, then Yahweh must in some way be responsible for the fact. However, seeing Yahweh as bearing responsibility for all events still leaves a theological question unresolved (and cf. Ezek 20:25?). There remains a tension between the stance of these Deuteronomic texts and the expectation commonly expressed in the Psalms that all peoples should or will come to acknowledge Yahweh as Lord of the whole world. Perhaps the first is an interim acceptance, while the second is God's ultimate purpose.

Such interim acceptance has to be interpreted, however, in the light of the later fuller awareness of the inadequacy of such religion. The Bible does not hint that in finally coming to acknowledge Yahweh, these peoples' own religion finds its fulfillment. Rather, the acknowledgment of Yahweh exposes the inadequacy of any earlier religious understandings. Once the fullness of Yahweh's self-revelation is earthed in Israel, the way is open to a critique of other gods and religions and to the expectation that one day all peoples will acknowledge that truth and salvation are to be found in Yahweh alone. They will then either join Israel in worshiping and obeying Yahweh or face a destiny of judgment and destruction. The progress of history thus does change things. Joshua's renewal of the covenant (Josh 24) implies that, whatever kinds of polytheistic worship may have been part of Israel's ancestry, polytheism was no longer appropriate in light of Yahweh's great redemptive achievements in relation to Israel. Fresh choices had to be made "today." This seems consistent with Paul's affirmation of God's apparently differential attitude to human religion at different stages of either history or awareness, in Acts 17:27–31. The knowledge of Christ requires repentance even from things God had previously overlooked.

However, the First Testament does not explicitly base its condemnations of other peoples on the grounds that they believe in the wrong gods. Condemnation of the nations, where reasons are given, is usually based on their moral and social behavior (see the pronouncements about the nations, e.g., Amos 1–2; Isa 13–23). Condemnation of religious deficiency is reserved for the people of God (cf. Amos 2). The gods of the nations are regarded as simply impotent. Worship of them is not so much culpable as futile. They cannot save. So, whether Jonah's sailors or the Ninevites pray to Yahweh consciously or to whomever they recognize as God, it is Yahweh who saves them. The whole point of much of the mockery of other gods, by Elijah, but even more so in Isa 40–55, is that when the crunch comes, they are ridiculously powerless to save. Worse, they are an encumbrance to their worshipers. It is Yahweh alone who saves.

Deuteronomy 32 not merely allocates the worship of other deities to the different peoples. Yahweh allocates the peoples to these deities. These are not merely figments of the peoples' imagination. They are actual entities under Yahweh's sovereignty. Admittedly they do not always submit to that sovereignty (cf. Ps 82). Further, whether they do so or not, they have no power of their own; they are merely Yahweh's underlings.

In First Testament terms, then, the question whether there is salvation in other religions is a non-question. There is salvation in no religion because religions do not save. Not even Israel's religion saved them. It was at best a response to Yahweh, the living God who had saved them. And only this God can save. When the nations come over to Israel, in the prophet's vision, it will not be to say, "Now we realize that your religion is the best one," but to acknowledge, "In Yahweh alone is salvation" (Isa 45:14, 24). When people such as Jethro or Rahab come to acknowledge Yahweh, it is on the basis of a realization that the story they have been told about Yahweh demonstrates this. It would be an exaggeration to say that First Testament faith was not ethnic; it was to an ethnic group that Yahweh reached out. But belonging to the right ethnic group was not enough; the members of this ethnic group needed to make their response to Yahweh. And not belonging to this ethnic group was no bar to making its story one's own and thus being adopted into it.

On the part of Israelites themselves the First Testament rejects worship of any deity alongside the true God (e.g., Exod 20:3). Their confession is, "Yahweh our God Yahweh one" (Deut 6:4): Yahweh is the object of their entire commitment. The worship of El need not contravene this commitment because it is a form of worship of Yahweh. The worship of deities distinguishable from Yahweh does contravene it.

We might then regard adherence to, for instance, an African traditional religion as a God-given starting point for people on their way to recognizing that the definitive acts of God are found in the story of Israel that comes to a climax in Jesus. It might be possible to take the same stance in relation to a religion such as Islam or to British folk religion or to American new age religion, though here the question is complicated by the fact that these are at least in a formal sense post-Christian religions that explicitly or implicitly presuppose a conscious rejection of the gospel.

4. Perspectives from Life in the Land: The Shortcomings of Baal Religion

While the First Testament can be implicitly open to other peoples' understandings of deity, it is by no means consistently so. There is a conflictual dimension to its view of other religions, which also needs to be seen in its context. While Joseph and the pharaoh of his day presuppose that they serve the same God, the pharaoh of Moses' day has notoriously forgotten Joseph and refuses to acknowledge the God of Israel. Thus while Moses can accept the identification of Yahweh and El, he must represent the opposition of Yahweh to the Egyptian gods served by Pharaoh. The exodus signifies the former's victory over and judgment on the latter (see Exod 12:12). The basis for Yahweh's action here is both a commitment to the descendants of Abraham and a commitment to compassion; Pharaoh and his gods are opposed to both. A major subplot of the exodus narrative seeks to show the stages by which Pharaoh is forced to acknowledge Yahweh (the train of thought runs through Exod 5:2, 7:5, 17, 8:10, 22, 9:16, 30; 14:18, 25). No matter how positively we view the openness to other people's experience and worship of God, there are circumstances that demand a conflictual stance. In this case it was because of rival claims to deity, resistance to God's redemptive work in history, and manifest, unrepentant oppression and injustice.

The worship of Baal, who apparently displaced El as the most prominent god among Israel's neighbors, and the worship of other gods and goddesses also has a different status within the First Testament from the worship of El. Admittedly there are hints that at certain stages Yahweh could have been worshiped under the name Baal. Baal is an ordinary noun meaning "owner" and could have been used, like *'adon* ("master"), to acknowledge the authority of Yahweh (cf. Hos 2:16 [18]). Behind the biblical text there may be what F. M. Cross calls a conflation of El and Baal in the person of Yahweh.[9] In the First Testament itself, however, the worship of Yahweh utilizing the word Baal is never accepted. Even a name such as Eshbaal (man of Baal; 1 Chr 8:33) is altered to Ishbosheth (man of shame; 2 Sam 2:8). Baal religion is seen as a negative influence on Israelite religion. Baal sanctuaries are to be destroyed rather than adapted (Deut 7; 12). The Baalistic influence on Israel's religion introduced by Solomon is a perversion. Thus worship of God as El is affirmed; worship of God as Baal is repudiated. Israel does not have to choose between Yahweh and El but does have to choose between Yahweh and Baal (1 Kgs 18:21; cf. Josh 24:14–15).[10]

The First Testament is not explicit on the basis for this contrast in attitudes to the religion of El and that of Baal. Perhaps the high god El could more easily become the sole God Yahweh than the subordinate Baal could; worship of Baal implied worship of other gods than Yahweh, rather than worship of Yahweh as Baal. The historical power of El was that shown in Israel's key experiences of exodus from Egypt and conquest of Palestine, even if the nature of El, not least as one failing to exercise real control in heaven, would need redefining in the light of those experiences. Baal, too, is involved with war, but his additional involvement with fertility might make it more important for Yahweh to be distanced from Baal lest questions of fertility become too important within Yahwism and lest the way they are approached within Baalism affects Yahwism. Israel's history recalled the way Baal worship led the wilderness generation into sexual immorality (Num 25:13), and Hosea attacks the way Israel let itself be influenced by this aspect of Canaanite religion. Yet the nature of Yahweh also gained in definition under the influence of Baalism as Yahweh was more explicitly declared to be lord of the crops and was portrayed as Israel's own lover. In coming to describe the relationship between Yahweh and Israel in marriage terms, Hosea thus adopts language and imagery from Canaan even while attacking the theology that the Canaanites expressed by means of it.[11]

If we reflect on the contexts in which the conflict between Yahweh and the gods of Egypt and the Baals of Canaan is characteristically presented, it becomes clear that it had a moral dimension that provides some help for our own evaluation of human religions and cultures.

---

[9] Cross, *Canaanite Myth and Hebrew Epic*, 163.

[10] I refer here and elsewhere in this chapter to the First Testament's own stance to such questions. Both the biblical text and archeological discoveries suggest that in its practice Israelite religion was much more open-minded.

[11] Cf. Board for Mission and Unity of the General Synod of the Church of England, *Towards a Theology for Inter-Faith Dialogue* (London: CIO, 1984), § 28. See also D. Senior and C. Stuhlmueller, *The Biblical Foundations for Mission* (London: SCM, 1983), chs. 1–5.

The presenting cause of Yahweh's hostility to Pharaoh (god himself and representative of the gods of Egypt) is his oppression of the Hebrews. There is no such conflict and hostility in the narratives of Genesis when first Joseph and then his brothers have their long interaction with Egypt. On the contrary, there is a recognition of the God of Joseph by the then pharaoh (e.g., Gen 41) in a way echoed later in Daniel. But the exodus pharaoh, having initiated a state policy of oppression that has political, economic, social, and spiritual aspects, refuses to acknowledge the God of Moses (Exod 5:2). It is this that arouses Yahweh to action—faithful action in the biblical sense of acting against the oppressor and rescuing the oppressed. The destruction of Pharaoh is thus a declaration of Yahweh's opposition to a religion that sanctions a social order that in turn sanctions inhumanity and oppression.

The more protracted struggle with Baalism lasting from the very emergence of Israel in Canaan through the ministries of all the pre-exilic prophets has similar features. From the specific condemnations of it in the Torah (e.g., Lev 18; 20; Deut 7) to its characterization in prophetic material such as Hosea and Jeremiah, it is seen as including practices that were degrading or destructive or both, such as sexual rites and child sacrifice, as well as occult arts. The First Testament implicitly argues that these were prevalent at the time of Israel's emergence in Canaan in a way that had not been the case in the era of Israel's ancestors. The less conflictual attitude to Canaanite religion in Genesis goes along with the statement that "the iniquity of the Amorites is not yet full" (Gen 15:16), whereas the wrongdoing of the later inhabitants of the land is enough to make the land itself vomit them out (Lev 18:24–28).

In other words, we can discern again a differential response to other religions related to the kind of social and moral characteristics they foster among their adherents.[12] What Elijah (and Yahweh) so vehemently opposed was not merely the worship of the wrong God (or rather of a no-god), as focused on Mount Carmel, but the hijacking of the whole social, economic and legal ethos of Israel by the religious vandalism of Jezebel's Phoenician Baalism, as focused in the Naboth incident (1 Kgs 21). The struggle was not simply over what was the right religion but over what was a right and just society for Naboth to live in. Baal religion undergirded, or at least imposed no restraint on, the way Ahab and Jezebel treated Naboth. It could be argued, therefore, that the moral, social, and cultural effects of a major religious tradition do give us some grounds for a discriminating response to it, though this can be as uncomfortable an argument in connection with Christianity as a cultural religion as in connection with any other.

We have noted that the First Testament is ambivalent about Israel's own means of worship. Sacrifice and temple are accepted, along with monarchy and priesthood, as human instincts rather than originally divine initiatives. But women priests are

---

[12] Cf. the discussion of this point in Christopher J. H. Wright, *Living as the People of God* (Leicester: Inter-Varsity Press, 1983) = *An Eye for an Eye* (Downers Grove, Ill.: InterVarsity Press, 1983), ch. 8; also "The Authority of Scripture in an Age of Relativism: Old Testament Perspectives," in *The Gospel in the Modern World: A Tribute to John Stott* (ed. M. Eden and David F. Wells; Leicester: Inter-Varsity Press, 1991), 31–48; and now *Old Testament Ethics for the People of God* (Downers Grove, Ill.: InterVarsity Press, 2004).

not accepted, and neither is worship by means of an image of God. This last is a distinctive important feature of the religion of the First Testament. In popular Christian thinking the reason for prohibiting images has been the essentially nonphysical nature of God, but the First Testament does not make this point, and arguably both the idea of humanity's being in God's image and the idea of incarnation are difficult to reconcile with it. The Decalogue juxtaposes and interweaves the prohibition on worshiping Yahweh by means of an image with the prohibition on worshiping other gods, and it may imply the conviction that the one easily slides into the other: an image could as easily be of Yahweh or of Baal, so we will be wise to avoid images as part of avoiding Baalism. The argument of Deut 4 is that a silent, static image cannot represent the essentially dynamic speaking and acting nature of Yahweh, and this fits the polemic of Isa 44 and Isa 46 against both domestic images and national images. But 2 Sam 7 uses parallel arguments against the building of a temple and then allows it. Christian history certainly illustrates the way images can be a snare, but the Orthodox icon tradition also illustrates how they can be a means of true worship.

Perhaps openness to the influence of other religions can be an enrichment or a perversion according to whether it allows a religion to come to full flowering as Yahweh's nature is more clearly grasped and Yahweh's lordship more fully acknowledged or whether it turns it into something other than itself and leads to the ignoring of Yahweh's nature and expectations. But we have to come to terms with the fact that we do not know the rationale for a number of God's requirements of Israel in religious affairs and that a number of these requirements may be culture-relative or arbitrary. In deciding about the adapting or avoiding of different humanly devised forms of worship, it seems likely that a significant part is played by tactical considerations regarding what may do more harm than good. Another factor often underlying Yahweh's requirements of Israel is the desire that they should look and behave differently, as a means of advertising to them and to other peoples that they are different in the sense of having a distinctive place in God's purpose. The Cornelius story marks the termination of the period when God operates by this principle, though the new period it introduces is not one in which differences between one religion and another can now be ignored but rather one in which they can now be confronted rather than avoided.

5. Perspectives from the Babylonian and Persian Periods: The Interrelation of Universalism and Exclusivism

The stances taken in the literature that relates to the Babylonian and Persian periods offer further pointers regarding the contextual nature of attitudes to other religions and their adherents. Prophecies in Isa 40–55 take a polemical stance over against the Babylonian gods Bel and Nebo, the equivalents of El and Baal. Either Yahweh is God, or they are gods; the possibility of seeing Bel as the name under which the Babylonians worship the one God is not entertained. Yahweh alone is creator, Yahweh alone rules in heaven, Yahweh alone acts in world events, Yahweh alone reveals the significance of those events (see Isa 40:12–26; 41:1–7, 21–9;

42:5–9; 46; and cf. Jer 10). Babylon and its religion will be put down. The affirmation that Yahweh creates both light and darkness and is responsible for both prosperity and disaster (Isa 45:7) perhaps sets itself over against the dualism of other religions.

In its mono-Yahwism and its affirmation of Yahweh's commitment to Israel, Isa 40–55 might be seen as the most exclusivist and nationalist section of the First Testament. Yet alongside this aspect of its stance is a conviction that Yahweh's relationship with Israel is of significance for the whole world, a conviction that has often made these chapters seem the most universalist in the First Testament; the same two-stranded attitude continues in Isa 56–66. Perhaps one implication is that Yahweh offers people alternative scenarios: on the basis of what they see Yahweh doing with Israel the nations will come to acknowledge that Yahweh alone is God, but they choose whether they do so willingly and joyously or unwillingly and profitlessly.

In contrast to Isa 40–55, Ezra-Nehemiah and Daniel identify Yahweh as the God of heaven, a title that other peoples within the Persian empire could give to their chief god (see Ezra 1:2; 5:11–12; 6:9–10; 7:12, 21, 23; Neh 1:4–5; 2:4, 20; Dan 2:18–19, 37, 44; in 5:23, "the Lord of heaven"). Daniel, Ezra, and Nehemiah are involved in the service of the Persian court, and like Joseph, Daniel and his friends accept a courtly education and foreign names, with their religious implications. At the same time Ezra and Nehemiah insist on keeping the people of Yahweh separate from the peoples around and their religions, while Daniel insists on the importance of Jews maintaining their distinctive faithfulness to their God and their purity (Dan 1) and their distinctive worship (Dan 3) and piety (Dan 6).

It is an oversimplification to suggest that the separatist strand to Ezra-Nehemiah characterizes the Second Temple period as a whole and contrasts with a more inclusive attitude earlier. We have noted that Ezra-Nehemiah is capable of expressing its theology with the help of the terms of the surrounding culture and religion, as Exodus and Hosea do. Exodus, Deuteronomy, and Hosea are separatist in a parallel sense to the one that applies to Ezra-Nehemiah. Isaiah 19 belongs among a number of passages in the prophets that are usually listed as especially inclusivist and that are usually dated during the Second Temple period. We have noted that Isa 40–55, often reckoned the universalist high point of the First Testament, includes the First Testament's most scathing treatment of other religions. The stance the First Testament takes to other religions apparently varies not only with the nature of the religion but also with the nature of the power and the pressure exercised by its adherents, but both openness and guardedness seem to feature in all contexts.[13]

6. Perspectives from the Greek Period: The Creativity of Exclusiveness

Similar considerations arise from the closing scene of the period covered by the First Testament, related in the visions in Daniel. Like Daniel (see Dan 5:23), the

---

[13] The often-quoted Mal 1:11 is of such uncertain significance it seems unwise to argue from it.

Syrian king, Antiochus, seems to have presupposed that Yahweh could be identified with "the Lord of Heaven," the Syrian high god. In some sense or in some periods one might have expected Jews to accept this assumption, but the visions in Daniel presuppose that the two are incompatible. To accede to the religious prescriptions of the king would be to abandon one's commitment to the God of Israel. Once more the First Testament suggests that there is a time or a case for openness to other religions and a time for recognizing that this risks the survival of Israelite religion and the Israelite people.

It is simplistic and misleading for the Anglican document *Towards a Theology for Inter-Faith Dialogue* to say that it is "when Israel is most open to others that she is most creative" while "exclusiveness and isolation . . . have an impoverishing effect."[14] Out of a context of "exclusiveness and isolation" Daniel is rather a creative book. The pluralistic context of Israel's life suggests that Israel's ways of relating to other religions ought to be a resource for us in a situation that is now more like postexilic Israel's than the Western church has experienced for some time. But to affirm "openness not isolation"[15] is only to simplify down a characteristic scriptural dialectic in the opposite direction to the one that the report elsewhere deplores when it does not match its own instincts.[16]

7. The Narrative Nature of Biblical Faith

If other religions make a starting point in relating to God but not a finishing point, the fundamental reason lies in the nature of the gospel.

Now Maurice Wiles, for example, offers what he intends as an uncontroversial summary of the essential nature of the Christian faith in terms of convictions about the reality and nature of God (e.g., as love).[17] If one understands scriptural faith to focus on such eternal truths about God, then it may be difficult to identify the essential shortcoming in a religion. A religion may have a secure grasp of such truths. There are, after all, other ancient and modern religions that include belief in a God who is just and loving, creator, committed to one's own people, and who expects a response from people in prayer, worship, obedience, and concern for justice. Likewise, one may see the essential nature of Christian faith as involving profound religious experiences—a friend of mine thus speaks of (say) a U2 concert as "church." If so, this will again suggest other criteria for comparing different faiths. In the First Testament, sacred institutions such as sacrifice, priesthood, monarchy, and temple are pictured as devised by human beings, harnessed with partial success to God's purpose but inclined to contribute to the paganization of Israel. Some of

---

[14] *Towards a Theology for Inter-Faith Dialogue* § 30.

[15] Ibid., § 31.

[16] Ibid., § 46. It is significantly ironic, too, that *Towards a Theology of Inter-Faith Dialogue* is capable of what now seems a rather old-fashionedly anti-Jewish tone in the way it downgrades Second Temple Judaism in order to commend the New Testament (see §§ 33, 35, 36).

[17] M. Wiles, *Explorations in Theology* 4 (London, SCM 1979), 61.

these institutions may have distinctive theological meaning within Israelite religion, but it would be precarious to base the decisive significance of Israel's faith on its having features of such a kind.

The significance of Israelite religion does not lie in itself or in the number of distinctive features we can chalk up for it in comparison with other religions (always a risky business, because parallels elsewhere then have a way of emerging). Israel's significance lay in its status as witness to the deeds of the living, active, saving God. This is the repeated thrust of Isa 40–55: written in the context of overbearing religious plurality, the prophet did not encourage Israel to compare its religion with the Babylonians' and feel superior, but he directed their thoughts to the acts of Yahweh in its actual history and declared, "You are Yahweh's witnesses."

The framework of First Testament faith, like that of New Testament faith, takes narrative form. It is a declaration about things God has done. It is good news, not a good idea. It states that in the history of Israel and of Jesus, God has acted in love to restore humanity to God and to its destiny. The gospel is the news that God created the world, stayed involved with it when it went wrong, became involved with Israel in order to put it right, commissioned God's son to become a Jew himself, let him die, and raised him to a transformed life. Christian faith involves the conviction that this story offers the central key to relating to God and to what it means to be human.

It is the narrative nature of this gospel that binds together the First Testament and the New Testament and gives the First Testament a distinctive place in relation to the Christian gospel. In this sense there cannot be other First Testaments for people with a background in other religions. There is a distinctive sense in which Jesus came as the climax to the story of Israel. This is not to imply that God was absent from these other people's stories. Walter Moberly speaks of the story of Israel's ancestors as "the Old Testament of the Old Testament"; it leads into Israel's story as Israel's story leads into the story of Jesus and the church.[18] One might then see Gen 1–11 as "the Old Testament of the Old Testament of the Old Testament"; the story of the world leads into the story of Israel's ancestors. And we might see the stories of other peoples and other religions as testimonies to God's involvement with them and as declarations of the significance of their stories, analogous to the story of God's involvement with the nations in Gen 1–11. But the First Testament itself is still *the* First Testament.

It is sometimes argued that translation is a fundamentally impossible enterprise. A mediating view on this question is the suggestion that narrative is fundamentally translatable in a way that many other genres are not. Poetry loses in translation, which means the wisdom books, the Psalms, and the prophets lose. Paul's discursive theology also takes considerable translation, because it takes considerable interpretation; it is very dense because of its use of metaphor, and very contextual. But a story is another matter. Stories lose less in translation. There is then some irony in the fact that while Paul kept in touch with the narrative nature of the gospel, in their discursive theological work subsequent church fathers had a harder time doing so. One fateful development of their centuries was the reworking of the gospel into Greek terms, which is often called a translation into Greek

---

[18] R. W. L. Moberly, *The Old Testament of the Old Testament* (Minneapolis: Fortress, 1992).

concepts, but it was more than translation. The reworking involved the effective abandonment of the narrative dynamic of Christian faith.

It is as well that the principle of translatability applies especially to narrative, because of that fact that the Bible is dominated by narrative for the reason just suggested. This is not merely a statistical fact but one that reflects the nature of scriptural faith, as not a collection of concepts, even declarations such as "Yahweh is God" or "Jesus is Lord," but a story, a piece of news, a gospel. The scriptural narrative becomes a gospel again when its implications are worked out in a context, as happens in different ways within scripture and then in many subsequent different contexts. Mother-tongue scriptures make the articulation of the gospel possible because they make it possible to work out how that narrative is gospel in a context. It would not be surprising if other religions possess narratives that illustrate the significance of the biblical narrative and illumine the nature of the gospel. They will thus bring blessing to people who share the gospel with people of this culture and make it possible for them as storytellers to respond to that gospel. But they are not the gospel story.

The process of contextualizing the gospel story may also lead to loss of understanding. The Christian church in the West learned to tell that story in a predominantly legal framework. God is judge, human wrongdoing is the breaking of the law, Jesus pays the legal penalty for sin, and that enables believers to be acquitted. This is only a marginally biblical framework for understanding the gospel. It came to be prominent in the Western church in a particular cultural context but then came to have a life of its own. In present Western culture such a legal way of looking at the relationship of God and humanity has less power than it had a millennium ago, but the church has a hard time escaping from this way of telling the scriptural story into a more relational way of explaining the gospel's significance.

In a context of religious plurality, the nature of the gospel is worked out afresh as the biblical story is set alongside another religion's story, or its non-story nature. This means that the people who tell the story appreciate it afresh, as happens when a Ghanaian Christian comes to see Jesus as ancestor or elder brother. It also means that the people who hear the story for the first time see how the story is good news for them in their particularity. It is specifically the context of the biblical narrative that constitutes the context that readers enter in order to participate in its world of meaning and experience. I think I have heard it suggested that non-Western cultures have retained an awareness of the importance of narrative that modernity encouraged Western cultures to lose (in the rarified form in which one meets them in theology and philosophy). So communicating the gospel is aided by the fact that the gospel takes narrative form.

8. The Narrative Nature of Biblical Faith and Religious Dialogue

Awareness of the narrative nature of the gospel thus gives us a point of contact with people living in other religious contexts. But it also distances us from them, because it makes the claim that this narrative is of unique importance. This is so not because of its nature as revelation but because it tells of the key events that determine the way God relates to the world. As a matter of fact, God created the world as a place that was good and not half-finished, to contradict a common modern narrative. When humanity then flouted God's word, God determined to "carry" its wrongdoing (the literal meaning of the Hebrew word routinely translated "forgive"). God determined to put up with it, not to be put off by it, to pay the price for it in God's own being in order to keep the relationship going. God did that through Israel's story in a way that came to a climax in the cross, where God went so far as to let Jewish and Gentile humanity do the last thing it could possibly do by way of rejection, by putting God to death, and God carried that too, and thereby frustrated it. God declined to be overcome by it, in either sense of "overcome." God did not give up on the relationship, nor did God agree to stay dead. Jesus' resurrection and his appearing to his disciples is the indication that he declines both these.

This story is a revelation of the nature of God, but it is that because it is more fundamentally an account of something God did once for all. In other religions (as in Hollywood movies) there might be promises of this story, or prophecies of it, or metaphors for it, or even revelations of it, but there cannot be regular narratives of it, because these narratives need to come from the people who experienced these events and who in the scriptures give their testimony to them.

Religious plurality involves competing narratives. Israel's neighbors had very different narratives about the origin of the world from Israel's, and Gen 1, at least, seems to have been written to counter these by giving a very different narrative account of deity, the world, and humanity. The New Testament story is intolerant and exclusive in its claim that cross and resurrection are the final and effective expression of God's resistance to being overcome by humanity. The Holy Spirit may indeed be involved in enabling different peoples to perceive and respond to insights about God and about life in the context of many ways of living religiously, but all such possible insights need to be brought into the context of the gospel expressed in the biblical narrative.

In the church in Southern California, for instance, at least in the Anglo-American church, I am particularly aware of two influential narratives. One is the narrative of "my individual spiritual journey." A local church I know routinely welcomes people to worship "wherever you are on your journey of faith." Individual students at Fuller Theological Seminary keep spiritual journals, implying the conviction that their journey matters. They have individual spiritual directors, guides on this journey. The other narrative is the story of the United States, its finding of its own freedom (July Fourth, Independence Day, is a very big event; it seems odd that the world's great superpower should make such an issue of its independence) and its receiving a vocation from God to bring democracy to the world.

In relation to the first of these narratives, the church assumes that I and my personal relationship with God is the key to understanding the significance of Christian faith, not noticing that if this were so, one would expect the Bible to be more like a book on spirituality. In relation to the second narrative, the church often accepts the identification of church and nation that is a paradoxical feature of the United States. It formally keeps church and state separate but substantially intertwines them in a way that does not obtain in countries where there is still a church-state connection but where church and culture are more overtly separate.

So churches commonly affirm one or other or both of those two narratives and do not set them in the context of the gospel narrative to let it test them, broaden them, or refute them. Our situation is thus rather similar to that which obtains in the First Testament story. There, one way of describing the dynamic of Israelite religion as (for instance) Jeremiah sees it would be to say that the Canaanites' narrative, expressed (for instance) in the stories of Baal and Anat, often influenced Israel more than the story of the exodus and Sinai. Israel did not consciously abandon this story, but it lived as if the true story was that other one with its direct potential for understanding the crucial processes whereby the crops grew each year.

Instead, we are called to invite people to tell their story and then see how that illumines the gospel and how the gospel illumines it, sets it in a new context, and relativizes it. It is when another narrative threatens to overwhelm the scriptural narrative that we must stand against it. It is then that it becomes demonic.

Both the First Testament and the New Testament are exclusivist in the sense that they believe in the supreme importance of the history that begins with the promise to Israel's ancestors and the exodus. Both are universalist in the sense that they believe that this history is designed to embrace all peoples; its benefits are not simply for Israel or the church. Thus a passage such as Isa 2:2–4 shares God's dream that at the end all peoples will come to learn from Yahweh in Jerusalem. The situation in Gen 1–2 is more than restored.

The shortcoming of other religions is that they cannot and thus do not focus on this story. Humanity's problem was not merely lack of knowledge concerning the nature of God and humanity but the need for a restoration of the relationship between these two so that humanity may realize its destiny. We needed redemption, not merely revelation. Whatever insight other religions may have on the nature of God and humanity, they lack the key to the restoration of the relationship and the realization of the destiny, because this lies in what God did in Israel and in Christ. Biblical religion is not primarily another set of religious teachings about God but a witness to what God did to save creation. That witness does generate insights about God and creation, some of which are so fundamental to the reality of the way things are that they are held in common with the religious understandings of other groups of human beings made in God's image. But merely listing the common beliefs between biblical faith and other religions (like drawing parallels between movies and the gospel) does not dissolve the significance of the Bible as witness to the unique events by which God has acted to restore creation.[19]

Claiming to be witnesses to the one sequence of deeds whereby God acted to redeem the world inevitably smacks of arrogance, as well as being unpostmodern. We can only ask people to look in the direction we are pointing and make their judgment *a posteriori*, not *a priori*. Our problem then will be that the Christian religion has also often proved itself incapable of encompassing the gospel or reflecting it, so that the response of someone who belongs to another religion can under-

---

[19] Cf. R. R. De Ridder, *Discipling the Nations* (Grand Rapids: Baker, 1971).

standably be that even if Christianity has rightly diagnosed the human problem, it has still not identified the solution.

In *Uncompleted Mission: Christianity and Exclusivism*,[20] Kwesi A. Dickson notes that there are "exclusivist" and "open" strands within the First Testament's attitude to other religions and cultures. He sees the New Testament as taking up the first rather than the second, regrets that modern Christian mission has followed (partly through its involvement with imperialist expansionism), and argues for the opposite stance. I have argued that there are good theological reasons why the First Testament has both exclusivist and open strands and that we should follow.

---

[20](Maryknoll, N.Y.: Orbis, 1991).

19

Is Leadership Biblical?

I once did a search on my seminary's website on "leader(s)/leadership," and it yielded 1916 hits. Leadership is really important to us. All three schools in the seminary offer courses on leadership—indeed, whole degree programs. They indicate a deep desire for the church's leadership to be shaped by biblical principles. Students on the way to the pastorate want their own leadership to be so shaped. Why is leadership such an important focus of people's thinking? It is a distinctive marker of U.S. culture, one of the features of the U.S. psyche that has generated the country's monumental achievements in the modern world. It reflects a part of the U.S. genome. The kind of men and women who have come to the United States over the centuries will have been people of above-average drive and initiative, people with leadership instincts. As is the case with other cultural traits, the church then mirrors the culture in its concern with leadership. It is also a distinctive marker of the church in the United States. This will link with the monumental achievements of the U.S. church, for instance in church building and in foreign missions. In turn, the seminary mirrors the church which mirrors the culture.[1]

1. "Leaders" in Scripture

It is then striking that the words "leader" and "leadership" are rather rare in the Bible. Two Hebrew words traditionally translated "leader" are *nasi'* and *sar*; both usually refer to people in an official position of leadership (they are also translated by words such as "ruler" and "officer"). Among other Hebrew words, some recent translations have illuminatingly used "leader," "lead," and "leadership" in connection with the *shopetim*, conventionally the "judges." These were people who led without being in an official position. In the New Testament, the word most commonly translated "leader," *archon*, likewise suggests someone in an official position, but etymologically the verb *hegeomai* (see especially Luke 22:26) is similar to "lead" in the way it works as a metaphor. But there are not words in Hebrew and Greek that correspond to "lead" and "leader."

Now the fact that a language lacks a word does not mean the culture lacks the concept that the word refers to. Yet alongside that fact about U.S. culture, this

---

[1] Not previously published. But see also John Goldingay, *Authority and Ministry* (Bramcote, U.K.: Grove, 1976).

linguistic phenomenon puts us on the track of the fact that leadership as such is not something the Bible focuses on. Leadership resembles topics such as the rights of women or peacemaking. They are topics that we think important, and in connection with them we can seek scriptural material to resource us in pursuing our interest, but they are not topics scripture itself directly focuses on. There are indeed many people in scripture who in our terms act as leaders, people such as Moses, Deborah, Gideon, David, Esther, Peter, and Paul, not to say Jesus. Yet the scriptures do not have a term for them; they do not seem to see them as belonging to one category. Among the deuterocanonical writings, Sir 44–45 does so: such figures are *endoxoi*, people held in honor. Like our term "leaders," that is a generic expression that reflects its culture. This offers food for thought. While the scriptures' inclusion of so many stories that refer to the activity of "leaders" means we can use their stories to speak to our agenda, it is our agenda. We might also be interested in discovering what scripture suggests is God's agenda, and in conforming our agenda to that.

There is another caveat suggested by scripture's way of speaking of leaders. U.S. Christians often assume that the main significance of the stories of people such as Moses or Deborah or Gideon is to give us models for our life of faith and obedience, and specifically role models for leadership. The First Testament does not give the slightest impression that Israelites or Israelite leaders were supposed to take these people as their models. Even Heb 11, which offers them as models of faith, does not take them as models of leadership, though Hebrews is the letter that talks most about "leaders," in Heb 13. This reflects the fact that in general the Bible is about God. It is about what God has done, more than about what human beings have done. When God created the world, the idea was that humanity should be active in it, serving God's purpose in the world. But this did not work, and God had to get involved in the world to put things right. The Bible is the story of God's doing so.

Accepting this does not come easily to humanity. Again, it is especially a U.S. trait. We want to fix things. We want to make a difference. We read the stories of Moses and Deborah and Gideon as people who made a difference and who can therefore inspire us.

The Bible implies different significance in their stories. Moses, for instance, was a headstrong and unwilling draftee who never showed leadership ability. He was the feeblest man on earth (Num 12:3). The word used of him, *'anaw*, usually means "poor" or "weak," and there is no basis for translating it "meek" except the presupposition that the story could not be describing Moses as weak. Fortunately it did not matter that Moses was weak; he did not need any leadership qualities, because he did not have to do anything except tell Pharaoh and the Israelites what God said.

2. Visionary Ideal and Inspired Compromise

If "the first responsibility of a leader is to define reality,"[2] this will include defining the reality of leadership. In a Christian context, such a definition will need to be a biblical theological one. I suggest that leadership as we understand it is a

---

[2] Max De Pree, *Leadership Is an Art* (repr., New York: Dell, 1990), 11.

subset of patriarchy and that a biblical theology of leadership is a subset of the biblical doctrine of sin. It is therefore not surprising that scripture has little positive interest in leadership.

At the beginning, God did make leadership part of the way the world was created. Leadership was going to be needed if the world was to be subdued and made into a place that worked by peace and order, and the agents made responsible for this leadership were the human beings God created (Gen 1:26–28). In the second creation story, likewise God planted a garden, formed a gardener, put him in the garden to "keep" it (literally, to "serve" it), and then provided him with a co-worker but did not tell Adam to exercise headship over Eve. In both stories, it was humanity as a whole that was commissioned to subdue the world and serve the garden. There was no leadership of one human being over others, only leadership of the world by humanity as a whole. As Bob Dylan put it in "Gates of Eden" (on the album *Bringing It All Back Home*), "There are no kings inside the Gates of Eden."

Or as Jesus put it, "from the beginning of creation" it was not so (Mark 10:6; cf. Matt 19:8). Jesus provides his disciples with a crucial hermeneutical clue for understanding the scriptures. From either Testament you can justify male headship or slavery or war because much of the Bible is written "because of your hardness of heart" (Mark 10:5). Jesus' particular concern at this point is the legitimacy of divorce. There is no doubt that the scriptures allow it, yet divorce stands in tension with the way God created man and woman (Mark 10:6–9; cf. Gen 1–2). The scriptures are not simply a collection of visionary ideals, though they are that. They are also a collection of timely compromises.

This does not mean they cease to be God's word; Jesus takes the regular Jewish attitude to the impeachable authority of the scriptures. No one ever accused him of any other attitude. Rather, he points to the realization that part of their marvelous inspiration is their combining eternal ideal and timely compromise. If we had only the timely compromise, nothing would pull us toward the eternal ideal. If we had only the eternal ideal, nothing would help us live in the everyday world. Their being this combination is a magnificent expression of God's grace. So when lifelong monogamous heterosexual marriage yielded to all sorts of other patterns of relationship, the Torah regulated some of these to safeguard against gross disorder and to protect the weak. Outside the garden, humanity's serving the earth met with the earth's resistance, harvests failed, and people had to sell their labor to their peers. The Torah regulates that by allowing indentured labor to last long enough for people to get on their feet, without their employers being able to turn them into permanent slaves. (Employment, which to us seems natural, is thus another variant on making things work east of Eden, but "from the beginning it was not so"—we were not designed to sell our labor.) When we seek to shape our lives by these scriptures, we learn from the way they expound eternal ideals and from the way they make needed compromises. One of the significances of the Sermon on the Mount (where a briefer version of the comment on divorce recurs, in Matt 5:31–32) is that Jesus here calls his disciples to live by creation's standard. The disciples are, of course, appalled (Matt 19:10), and Acts and the Epistles show that the New Testament churches did not do so.

3. Theology of Leadership as a Subset of the Doctrine of Sin

The practice of leadership within humanity rather than by humanity is another aspect of the way sin came to spoil human life. The distortion of leadership began with the activity of the serpent, who was supposed to be led but was clever enough to be the first leader in scripture apart from God. After it has succeeded in its leadership, God declares that the result will be to damage not only marriage and work but also human partnership. Henceforth one human being will rule over another. Leadership is thus "toxic" in its origin, and is generally portrayed as toxic through scripture.[3] Hosea 10:3–4 uses this image in describing *mishpat* (the noun from that word *shopet*, "leader") as "springing up like poisonous weeds." The *shopetim* and the kings (that is, both nonofficial and official leaders in Israel) illustrate this well, as do prophets, priests, and sages. Hosea 13:9–11 thus takes up a comment on the community's desire for kings and *shopetim* and sees God's involvement in the rise and fall of such leaders as an expression of divine wrath.

"All kings is mostly rapscallions" (Huckleberry Finn)[4]—and presidents and CEOs, not to say quite a few senior pastors and seminary presidents. Again because the church is part of the culture, it is not surprising that Christian leadership in state and church continues to be toxic. We experience this regularly in church life. In political life, at the time of writing it seems possible that the United Kingdom and the United States have got themselves into a moral and strategic mess in Iraq, and if they have, this has not issued directly from the British and American peoples but from their leaders, most of whom are committed Christians—from the politicians who made the decisions and the pastors who taught them, preached to them, and supported them.

Initially a theology of leadership is a subset of the doctrine of sin because it has its origin in sin; instead of exercising leadership over the creation, humanity let itself be led by creation. It is a subset of the doctrine of sin because the work of a leader is spoiled by the leader's sin (see Moses' story). It is so because the necessity of leadership issues from the fact of sin in the community (see Judges and the development of leadership in New Testament and post-New Testament churches). It is so because the desire to be a leader is an expression of sin (see Abimelech's story, and many others). It is so because the desire to have leadership is an expression of sin (see the story of the introduction of the monarchy). It is so because a leader has opportunity to be much more sinful than ordinary people (see David's story). It is so because leaders have opportunity to lead their community in sin (see the stories of many priests and prophets). Continuing the pattern in scripture, Christian history provides many stories of Christian leadership being a main means of expressing and encouraging sin.

Now Christians who think about leadership are aware of that and seek to take account of it. They do so by emphasizing, for instance, that we need to pay

---

[3] On the notion of toxic leadership, see, e.g., Jean Lipman-Blumen, *The Allure of Toxic Leaders* (Oxford / New York: Oxford University Press, 2005).

[4] Mark Twain, *Adventures of Huckleberry Finn* (repr., Mineola, N.Y.: Dover, 1994), 116.

attention to the spiritual and moral formation of the leader. But this is to fail to take the theological point seriously, in at least two senses. First, it is equivalent to saying that because they are sinners, human beings in general need to work harder at being good. The total depravity of humanity means this cannot work, and the total depravity of humanity means not only that it cannot work for leaders either but also that the consequences of leaders' sin will be much greater. Second, attention to the dynamics of redemption suggests that the church can no more settle down for accepting leadership as one of our givens than it can accept the subordination of women, slavery, or war. These two theological points are of course in tension with each other. Sin means we must avoid having leadership; sin means we must have leadership. It is the same tension that Jesus identified.

4. So Where Do We Go from Here?

In light of this, what would be a pastor's vision for his or her leadership? And in what direction would he or she like to see the church grow in its leadership, maybe in the medium or long term?

First, while scripture rarely describes people as leaders, it often describes someone we would call a leader as a servant of God; Moses is the great example, though the point applies to many others. Contemporary interest in the designation "servant" contrasts with our preference for "leader" (a search on my seminary's website for servant(s)/servanthood generated 206 hits). Further, even if we do think in terms of service, we likely think in terms of serving other people. Scripture itself does relate the forming of Adam to serve the garden and does record the advice given to Rehoboam about service in 1 Kgs 12:7, though this may point to servant leadership as a ploy. But that preferred designation in scripture presupposes that being a servant means serving God. People such as Moses are God's servants, not their people's servants.

It is still the case that there are no grounds for reckoning that Moses as servant of God is an example for us. The point about Moses is that he had a unique role, and the significance of calling him "servant of God" is not to frame our imitation of him but to encourage us to take seriously what he said and did. Yet the designation does suggest a further reframing of the question about leadership that we especially need in our culture. It links with the fact that scripturally considered, the art of leadership is part of Wisdom, part of the way we find insight on life from the life that we live, in our culture. That is Wisdom's strength and its limitation. When scripture takes on the insights of other people's wisdom, it recognizes the need to subject them to the reframing of faith and ethics (Prov 1:1–7). In this case, that reframing would mean we stop talking about leadership and start talking about servanthood (and let's have less weasel talk of "servant leaders," please). Of course describing yourself as a servant can be ideological and has been another way of facilitating sin.

Second, New Testament congregations were never led by individuals but only by groups, which suggests a pattern for all congregations. The church did feel the need to develop the "monarchic episcopate" (that is, the position of senior pastor), but subsequent history makes clear that this is as capable of encouraging sin as reducing it, like the introduction of the monarchy in Israel. Leadership by a group can safeguard against the toxic leadership of individuals, though one might end up with toxic leadership by a group. Nations such as the United States with powerful individual leadership may achieve more than nations such as the United Kingdom, which do not have presidential-style leadership, but that also risks their making bigger moral mistakes.

Third, the church's calling is to imagine our way back into the garden, as it is with other matters such as relations between the sexes, in light of what God has done for us in Christ and does in the Holy Spirit. That would imply seeking to do without leadership. A church could delegate responsibility to a group it elects, without there being any standing for election. The group could make decisions by consensus. A different person could chair its meetings each year. We would achieve less, but we might also sin less. If this worked, it would be an aspect of the modeling of an alternative reality that is the church's vocation, instead of the church simply baptizing the culture.

When the prophets reflected on the fact that God had brought the monarchy to an end, some responded by promising that God would restore it, and this subsequently gave the first Christians a way to think about the significance of Jesus. But Second Isaiah saw God having the kind of covenant relationship with the people as a whole that God had once had with David, in keeping with God's earlier intention that Israel as a whole should be a kingdom of priests and a holy nation (Isa 55:3–5; Exod 19:5–6). It is odd that the church has left the Jewish community to live by that vision better than the church has.

In the world we will continue to need leadership. But the church's job is to be an alternative community that embodies God's vision for the whole world.

20

IS GOD IN THE CITY?

In an address at the 1978 Lambeth Conference of the bishops of the Anglican Communion, the Archbishop of York, Stuart Blanch (previously Bishop of Liverpool), told a story about a Church of Scotland minister who was moving to a new parish. On the eve of his move he overhears his small son saying his goodnight prayers: "Well, goodbye God, we're going to Glasgow." Is God there in a city such as Glasgow or Liverpool, or Pittsburgh or Birmingham? How are we to understand the city? Such an understanding involves theology as well as sociology, history, and economics. A theology of the city is both desirable and possible. It is desirable, because changing the world depends on understanding it—understanding it before God and understanding God's purpose for it. And it is possible, not least because there is a rich strand of material in the Bible concerning the city. That can help us to identify what might be called "theological middle axioms," which can be resources for people in their particular contexts as they seek to discover more precisely what the gospel is for them.[1]

Like other themes, the city surfaces in the Bible in widely varying forms of material. These forms are not part of the Bible's throwaway wrapping; they are essential to what it is and to what it does. The Bible tells stories about the city, makes laws for the city, speaks of the city's future in prophecy and apocalypse, and brings the city into its praise and prayer. My concern here is to consider something of the significance of each of these.

1. Enoch: and Laws for the City

The Bible's first city is named after Adam's grandson Enoch (Gen 4:17). Cain has killed his brother and been sentenced to wander the earth as a fugitive. Away from Yahweh's presence, east of Eden in the land of Wandering, Cain marries a wife, they start a family, and Cain builds a city, which he names after his son. The city begins as a refuge from the insecurity of an open and hostile world. The city will in due course become a metaphor for community, but archaeological work in Palestine also draws attention to this more primary facet of its significance. The

---

[1] First published as "The Bible in the City," in *Theology* 92 (1989): 5–15.

dominant architectural feature of the Israelite city is its walls. It is first and foremost a stronghold, a refuge from enemies (compare the way the metaphor is used in Pss 46 and 48).[2] But Cain's insecurity had been willed by God. The story priest of the city has an inauspicious beginning.

The end of the story in Gen 4 is also inauspicious. First there is the proud violence of Lamech, hinting at the fact that the city is a place where violence flourishes, not least family violence. Then we discover that while Cain is starting his family, Adam and Eve are rebuilding theirs. God gives them a son to replace Abel, and "at that time people began to call upon the name of Yahweh" (Gen 4:26). This has been seen as the beginning of the story of the church, of the line of redemption. This is the line in which Yahweh is active and known. The line of Cain stands for the world, sinful and under judgment, desperately seeking to shape a life without God; and the city is one of the devices whereby it attempts to do so.

But Gen 4:17–24 is more ambivalent about the city than that. It tells us that the development of the city is the context in which families grow (Enoch, Irad, Mehujael, Methushael, Lamech) before it is the context in which the God-given order of marriage becomes imperiled when Lamech takes two wives. The city is the context in which art and technology begin to develop (the invention of harp and flute, the forging of bronze and iron tools) even though the first recorded use of such discoveries is in the glorifying of human violence (in Lamech's proud verses about the execution of his wrath on an enemy) as the city becomes a place where vengeance has to be subjected to constraint, where the created order is imperiled and has to be protected.[3] There are of course huge differences between preindustrial cities and the vast cities of the industrial era, but also common features, and these include the fact that both facilitate the development of art and technology. They are thus the context where specialized activities and crafts evolve, though the underside of this latter is the emergence of a class structure in society. They are also the context where writing develops: if there had been no city, it seems there would have been no history, no theology, no science, no Bible.

The negative aspects to the city hinted in Gen 4 are also factors underlying the formulating of the Torah in Israel. It is therefore illuminating to consider the First Testament's regulations for the city in light of its stories about the city, and specifically to look at Deuteronomy, the most urban of the First Testament's bodies of instruction. In its literary context it is the teaching given to Israel on the edge of the promised land, and thus on the edge of life in an urban setting which Israel will share as it takes over Canaanite cities (cf. Deut 6:10) or builds its own towns. In the perspective of source-critical theory, the material in Deuteronomy belongs to urban Jerusalem. It reflects a more developed state than that of the regulations in Exodus and a more "everyday life" set of concerns than that of the priestly material

---

[2] Cf. F. S. Frick, *The City in Ancient Israel* (Missoula, Mont.: Scholars Press, 1977), 81. Illuminating broad background to the development and place of the city in the ancient world appears also in H. Frankfort, *The Birth of Civilization in the Near East* (repr., Garden City, N.Y.: Doubleday Anchor 1956), and L. Mumford, *The City in History* (repr. Harmondsworth, U.K.: Penguin, 1966).

[3] So Walter Brueggemann, *Genesis* (Atlanta: John Knox, 1982), 66.

represented by Leviticus, which may presuppose the collapse of urban life in Jerusalem in 587. There is also a possibility that much of the material in Deuteronomy was formulated in light of stories in Genesis, its stories about the city among them: they are instructions that safeguard against any repetition of unacceptable events in Genesis.[4]

There runs through Deuteronomy a series of concerns that are illuminated by the awareness that this is teaching for an urban culture.[5] First, it emphasizes honesty and truth in society. There is to be no swindling of customers by merchants (Deut 25:13–16). There is to be machinery for handling tricky legal cases in a fair way (Deut 17:8–13). The same law is to apply to rich and poor. That is not how it feels to many inner-city people, particularly when race is factored in. Deuteronomy 19 includes a law to limit the taking of vengeance, by establishing places where a person guilty of accidental homicide may find refuge from the vengeance of his victim's family. Second, the teaching is concerned for the needy, in particular for groups whom we might call the underclass, the people who have fallen out of the regular support systems of society. In Israel these comprise especially people who have no land by which to support themselves (we might see being without land as the Israelite equivalent to being without a job). They include Levites, widows, orphans, immigrants, poor people generally, and people whom debt has taken into servitude (e.g., Deut 14–15).

Connected with that, third, is Deuteronomy's stress on brotherhood.[6] When it seeks to motivate people to take action on behalf of those needy groups, it keeps reminding them that such people are their brothers (e.g., Deut 15). It reminds people in government not to forget that they are the brothers of those they govern (e.g., Deut 17:14–20). As an institution, the city combats the more natural division of humanity by families and clans: where people live now counts as much as to whom they are related. As Deuteronomy sees it, the community needs to be the family writ large. It might be saying retrospectively to Cain and Abel, "Come on, you're brothers." Fourth, as if to anticipate the charge of being sexist in its stress on brotherhood, it adds a concern for womanhood. Its teaching repeatedly mentions attitudes to mothers, wives, and daughters, and their rights and responsibilities, as well as those of fathers, husbands, and sons (e.g., Deut 15; 18). It points to the fact that women need protecting in the city. In *The Origin of the Family, Private Property, and the State*,[7] Friedrich Engels traced the subjugation and oppression of women to the breakup of the communal kin group and the transformation of the nuclear family into the basic economic unit of society, because this turned women's work into a private service for their husbands. It was thus an urban phenomenon.

---

[4]So Calum M. Carmichael, e.g., *The Laws of Deuteronomy* (Ithaca, N.Y.: Cornell University Press, 1974).

[5]I have analyzed these concerns in *Theological Diversity and the Authority of the Old Testament* (Grand Rapids: Eerdmans, 1987; Carlisle: Paternoster, 1995), ch. 5, though not in relation to the city.

[6]Cf. chapter 12 above.

[7](repr., New York: International, 1942).

Related to this concern for womanhood in Deuteronomy, fifth, is a concern about family order and sexual relations (e.g., Deut 22). Sex easily goes wrong in the city. Sixth, and most strikingly, a recurrent theme in Deuteronomy is happiness. Only in Psalms and in Proverbs among the First Testament books does the verb "rejoice" occur more than it does in Deuteronomy. Its teaching keeps returning to the joy of festivals and the joy of food and perhaps invites us to see the joys of the city as God-given and its unhappiness as to be fought in the name of the God of joy.

The reason why these ideals come to expression in Deuteronomy is that they are not embodied in Israel's urban life. Another noteworthy feature of Deuteronomy, given our present concern, is that it starts where society is. Its vision can seem insufficiently radical by the standards of some parts of both Testaments, but one reason is that in seeking to pull society toward ideals it ought to affirm, Deuteronomy manifests a practical concern that begins from society as it is in its sinfulness or "hard-heartedness" (Mark 10:5). Politics and social policy combine ideals and the art of the possible. Paul Wilding has protested at the notion of the "politics of imperfection," in the name of a politics of perfection, of possibilities, of vision, of transcendence.[8] Deuteronomy implies that we should both be realistic about how things and people are but also be visionary about the ideals we affirm and then specific in the way we bring the two together. That is the vocation of society's lawmakers, economists, and planners. People concerned about the city often pay their respects to the First Testament by nodding toward the eighth-century prophets, but the Deuteronomists provide at least as suggestive a role model for practical involvement in society. If we as the church want to play a part in the shaping of urban policy, we need to do that by nurturing the economists, lawyers, planners, and civil servants in our midst—in the midst of the suburban church more than of the inner-city church, in all likelihood. This is a key way for the suburbs to partner with the inner city with a view to seeking to implement the concerns of the prophets.

One further feature of Deuteronomy that deserves consideration is that it is not just a legal or ethical work but fundamentally a theological one, built on the fact that Israel is Yahweh's people and Yahweh is Israel's God. This, among other factors, underlies its concern about right and wrong forms of worship in the sanctuary that Yahweh chooses. In a culture in which palace and temple stood together at the apex of the city, this urban document could not ignore religious issues. It is easy for city and religion to be interwoven to the exclusion of God, a theme which also emerges in Genesis.

2. Babel: and a Vision for the City

Apart from the telling note in Gen 10:8–12 about Nimrod, the mighty warrior who was the great city builder (which permits Jacques Ellul to observe how the city

---

[8] "Christian Theology and the Politics of Imperfection," *The Modern Churchman* 27/2 (1985): 3–12.

and war go together),[9] the Bible's second major city is Babel. People decide to settle in Shinar, which becomes "the cradle of urban civilization."[10] They build themselves a city there, with a tower that would reach to the heavens, so that they would not be scattered all over the world. Again the city is a refuge from the insecurity of an open world and from the destiny willed for them by God. They were supposed to fill the world, and the previous chapter has described the scattering of peoples as part of humanity's filling the world after the flood; but these people resist that destiny. They want to stop in one place and find a unity grounded in fear and excluding God, though not excluding religion. Indeed, they seek to make use of religion, as a government may expect to use an established church and as politicians do in the United States. The city is a place to reach for heaven. There are echoes of the Babylonian ziggurat and a reflection of the fact that a characteristic feature of a city is the presence of monumental buildings, which urban economics make possible. One aim of the whole project is for the builders to make a name for themselves: the phrase may sound negative, though it can be used in the First Testament in a positive way (see 2 Sam 8:13). The city represents human ambition and pride, which can be positive as well as negative attributes.

Again, it may be that we are to see this city as a monument to human creativity and inventiveness, as its builders work out how to use manufactured brick in the absence of natural stone.[11] Or it may be that Genesis speaks with some irony, because "brick" means mud shaped and dried in the sun, a common enough building material for private houses but inferior to the stone hewn from a quarry which the story's hearers would know was preferred for important buildings. Further, the builders lacked proper cement and had to fix their mud bricks together with tar, so that their edifice must have been a little reminiscent of those 1960s apartment blocks that were the pride of the city as they were being built but turned out to be makeshift.[12] There is an ambiguity about Genesis's portrayal of the city, which perhaps corresponds to the ambiguity of Israel's experience of the city, and of ours.

Building a city was also a dangerous enterprise, as God saw it. "Who knows where else it may lead?" God asks. The city builders threaten to become like gods. So those who were afraid of being scattered are scattered by God, and they give up building the city. It becomes a place of non-communication. One is reminded of the issues that nuclear weapons place before us as the human beings whom God has allowed to acquire the power to destroy ourselves, and who might be wise to invite God to come down and confuse their language again; and of the possibility that world peace and the success of the United Nations would more likely be demonic in effect than divine.

The scattering was an act of judgment, but it was one that opened up the possibility of God's own purpose being realized in the filling of the world rather than

---

[9] *The Meaning of the City* (Grand Rapids: Eerdmans, 1970), 13.
[10] Ibid., 14.
[11] Claus Westermann, *Genesis 1–11* (Minneapolis: Augsburg / London: SPCK, 1984), 546.
[12] Derek Kidner, *Genesis* (London: IVP / Downers Grove, Ill.: InterVarsity Press, 1967), 110.

people stopping in one place.[13] The act of judgment plays a part in the implementing of God's vision for humanity. It thus points us toward the prophets and their vision of judgment on the city. There has been a longstanding debate about whether the prophet's calling was fundamentally to declare that inevitable calamity was about to fall upon Israel or whether it was to challenge Israel about its life and to call it to repentance so that calamity might be averted. In seeking to apply the Bible to their society, people naturally presuppose the second understanding, which looks more immediately promising, but the first is at least as plausible. The prophets were people who lived in the midst of calamity, in vision or in reality. Their vocation was to prepare people for calamity, to interpret it, and to respond to it.

They did not behave like social reformers. Historically, classical prophecy begins with the appearance of the Assyrians on Israel's northern horizon and with the need for Israel to discover what God was doing with the nation in this context. The first of the prophetic books opens by presupposing that disaster has overtaken the cities of Judah: Isaiah's aim is to try to explain it and to help Judah learn the lesson (see Isa 1). Prophets do call for repentance, but too hasty a desire to link them to programs for social reform may obscure their significance in a way that reduces their importance for us in the long term. Isaiah focuses on declaring to the people of God the fact and the significance of the judgment that hangs over their city. The city of David which became Yahweh's city, the holy city, is now the bloody city, and Isaiah declares that "Yahweh Armies has a day in store for all the proud and lofty, for all that is exalted . . . ; for every high tower and every fortified wall" (Isa 2:12, 15). It is a warning rather than a program for reform.

A prophetic ministry involves drawing attention to facts and threats, to make it difficult for government or nation to ignore clouds that can be seen on the horizon. The task of propounding alternative policies, I have suggested above, is more the job of lawmakers and economists than of prophets. It is easy to take up a role that is halfway between prophet and social reformer and risk being less effective at either. Prophets took part in public debate by trying to make people face facts.

It might be wondered whether this prophetic ministry applies only to Israel and cannot be extended to the secular city; but another prophet was sent to tell a huge foreign city, a bloody city notorious for double-dealing, greed, and aggressiveness, that it was about to be overturned (Jonah 3:1–3). He did not invite Nineveh to repent, but to his disgust it did so, and his awful fear was fulfilled. God relented. "Am I not allowed to care about this great city with its hundred and twenty thousand people who do not know their right hand from their left," he asks; "let alone the cows?" The story of Jonah suggests that pagan cities can be saved as well as Israelite ones, though they do need to repent, not just be reformed.

Nor does this approach apply only to individual cities. In Isa 24, there is a nightmarish portrayal of a ruined city that stands not for a particular place but for the world's urban civilization, high and lofty but defiled and desolated. It is a portrayal of a fortified town turned into a heap of rubble never to be rebuilt. Its memorial is those lifeless tells that scatter the Palestinian landscape, mute

---

[13] Brueggemann, *Genesis*, 99.

witnesses to the collapse of an urban civilization (cf. Isa 25:2; 26:5). The ruined city is a symbol of humanity under judgment. Nor is this perspective an exclusively First Testament one. Jesus denounced urbanized Galilee, Corazin, Bethsaida, and lofty Capernaum and declared God's woe on them, in the manner of a prophet. Unlike Nineveh, they were cities that failed to repent when confronted by his ministry (Matt 11:20–24). Near the end of the New Testament there is Revelation's terrible tirade against the great city of Babylon, the byword for trade, achievement, entertainment, civic pride, power, prosperity, craftsmanship, and culture. Here the city has also become the embodiment of demonic contempt for God and aggression against God's people, so that the proper stance in relation to the city is abandonment (Rev 18). "In order to have 'staying power' [for its mission to the city], the church must withdraw regularly 'into the desert,' to be free and detached from the city's power."[14]

Those negatives are not all there is to the Bible's vision for the city. Isaiah 1 closes with a transition from the city under judgment to the city transformed. Again, encouragingly, the judgment is itself the means of transformation. "Afterwards you will be called 'Justice City,' 'Faithful City'" (Isa 1:26). This Zion will be raised on high by God, not by human will. Such promises are to be spurs to human action (cf. Isa 2:5), but to demythologize them into merely veiled exhortations regarding what we are to achieve is a besetting temptation that Christian social activists must resist. They are promises of what God purposes to achieve, causing this Zion to attract the world as a place where it may discover the keys to truth and peace (Isa 2:2–4; a significant promise when the news from Jerusalem is persistently disheartening).

This hope for the city recurs throughout the book of Isaiah (e.g., 26:1; 45:13; 52:1) and then reappears at the end of the Bible. Revelation's attack on Babylon is not its last word on the city. It closes with "the Holy City, the new Jerusalem, coming down out of heaven from God." The city is affirmed as a place of splendor, strength, community, provision, security, generosity, healing, and holiness, accessible to all as a place where God is known in glory and love and grace (Rev 21:1–22:5). Whereas the Bible began in a garden from which humanity was soon excluded, and might have been expected to conclude in the garden, it ends in the city, or in a place with the virtues of both, a garden city watered by a life-giving river and nurtured by fruiting trees. The city is one of a series of human devices such as sacrifice, monarchy, and temple, which are taken up by God, even though they did not arise from God's initiative, and are worked into God's purpose so graciously that we would not be able to conceive of worship or of Jesus or of the fulfillment of God's final purpose without them. "Almost in line with contemporary urbanization, the Scriptures begin in a garden and end in a city."[15]

There are profound grounds for hope in this vision of the city, and the bringing of hope is a key aspect of the church's calling, not least in the city, often a place of despair. It is a hope that does not derive from what we ourselves may be able to

---

[14] D. S. Lim, "The City in the Bible," *Evangelical Review of Theology* 12 (1988), 138–56 (154).
[15] B. Tonna, *A Gospel for the City* (Maryknoll, N.Y.: Orbis, 1982), 121.

do but from what God is committed to doing, so that our actions are worthwhile because and insofar as they mesh with God's purpose. First Testament prophets and visionaries suggest that God has a dream for the city, so that the church's calling is to declare in its preaching and in its life that there is reason for hope even when there is no scope for action and when justice looks utterly defeated. The church's prophetic ministry involves not only making public proclamations about government policies (proclamations that can easily have a moralistic tone to them) but also telling the city that God has a vision for it and for us, which the most determined policies or neglects of governments will not frustrate. This takes us back once more to Genesis.

3. Sodom: and Prayer for the City

The Bible's third city is Sodom. On its first appearance, Sodom is characterized as a place of wickedness (Gen 13:13). Genesis 19 portrays Sodom as a perverted city, a place where society is sick, but it does not suggest that its sexual twistedness is its fundamental sickness. Sodom's wickedness is the subject of outcry to God (Gen 18:20–21; 19:13), and "outcry" is the word used of Abel's blood crying out from the ground to God (Gen 4:10) and of the Israelites crying out because of their suffering in Egypt (e.g., Exod 2:23; 3:7, 9; see also Isa 5:7; 42:2). This suggests that Sodom's wickedness consists in its being a place of oppression. That is in keeping with the rationale that Genesis gives for Yahweh's revealing to Abraham what is to happen to Sodom, that Abraham's vocation is to do with *sedaqah umishpat* (Gen 18:19), the exercise of power in a way that does right by the people in one's community, the classic double priority to which the prophets keep returning.[16] The oppression Sodom practices is also the aspect of its wickedness that is taken up when Judah is compared with the city of Sodom in Isa 1:10 and Ezek 16:46–50. Perhaps the reference is not to the affliction practiced by one citizen on another (otherwise it would not be the entire community that deserved to be judged); it is to the relationship that existed between the city and the surrounding countryside. In principle the relationship between city and country can be one of harmony and cooperation. The country provides the city with food, and the city provides the country with specialized services and manufactured goods.[17] But the city as a whole easily ends up being parasitic on the country, exacting tribute and taxes, attracting resources and wealth, and enjoying luxury and indulgence, while the countryside lives at a much lower standard.

God hears the plaintive, hurt lament of the people around Sodom and Gomorrah and decides to discover if what they say is true, declaring the intention, if it is, to act in judgment on their behalf. But first, God listens to another cry and

---

[16] See J. P. Miranda, *Marx and the Bible* (Maryknoll, N.Y.: Orbis, 1974 / London: SCM, 1977), 88–97; and chapter 16 above.

[17] Cf. R. R. Wilson, "The City in the Old Testament," in *Civitas: Religious Interpretations of the City* (ed. P. S. Hawkins; Atlanta: Scholars Press, 1986), 3–13 (8–9).

responds to that. Indeed, he draws Abraham into crying out on behalf of Sodom, telling Abraham of the intention to act in judgment, then waiting, while two aides go to check things out there, to see if Abraham wants to say anything. There follows the extraordinary barter in which Abraham sees how far God would go in order to reprieve the city. Abraham is to be a means of blessing to the world (Gen 18:18); the way he puts that into effect is by praying for the world. At one level, Abraham's plea for Sodom may be seen as much as a discussion as a prayer, a tutorial on the subject of whether everything is predetermined or whether God is capable of acting in a different way from the one that seems inevitable. Will God let mercy triumph over deserve? The man or woman of God becomes a blessing to the city by praying for it, in the conviction that its destiny is open, even at the point where it looks most closed.[18]

Historically, praying the Psalms was a consistent part of Christian worship and devotion, but in the twentieth century it largely lost that place. In particular, the psalms of lament and protest largely disappeared from the church's worship. One way in which praying these makes sense is that many people in congregations need to be able to give expression to the hurts in their lives to God, but another is that people who do not have such hurts to express pray them for those who do, pray them as part of a suffering people. It is an aspect of weeping with those who weep, as in praying psalms of praise we rejoice with those who rejoice. Praying from the position of the people whose need we take into our heart is the way the Psalms go about intercession. And the pain, suffering, and oppression the Psalms lament are often those of the city (compare also Lamentations). "Lord, swallow up, divide their speech, because I see violence and contention in the city. Day and night they go round it, on its walls. Harm and troublemaking are within it, destruction is within it. Injury and deceit do not leave its square" (Ps 55:9, 11 [10, 12]). The city is supposed to be a place of refuge, of safety, but it is not; so the Psalms challenge God to do something about that. Conversely, when the Psalms are rejoicing, it is often a joy in the city. The city is the gift of God (Ps 107:36). Jerusalem "is built as a city that is joined together to itself.... Ask for well-being for Jerusalem: 'May people be at ease who are dedicated to you'" (Ps 122:6). "If Yahweh himself does not guard a city, in vain will the guard have been wakeful" (Ps 127:1); the reminder appears in abbreviated form on the coat of arms of the City of Edinburgh (cf. also Ps 48). The Bible does not tell us to pray for the city; it shows us how to do so.

Prayer and praise are the vital accompaniment to story and law and prophecy. They are the distinctive gift that the church alone can bring to the efforts of social and community workers, politicians, and civil servants, on behalf of the city. They are the church exercising its indispensible ministry on behalf of the city. If it abandons these, it falls short at the crucial point; we are then simply activists alongside other activists who may fail because we neglect to lay hold on the resources for the city that lie in God. The Psalms do not point us toward the horizontal kind of prayer

---

[18]Cf. Westermann, *Genesis 1–11*, 291; Brueggemann, *Genesis*, 168; G. von Rad, *Genesis* (rev. ed.; London: SCM / Philadelphia: Westminster Press, 1963), 209; and see further chapter 14 above.

in which we exhort ourselves to play our part in bringing in the reign of God, nor even just the semi-vertical kind of prayer that asks God to enable us to fulfill our commitment to justice and peace, nor the kind of prayer that assumes God is real enough but is sitting in the gallery watching what goes on, keenly interested but not active in the arena itself. The Psalms point us toward the disinterested kind of prayer that begins from human helplessness and lays hold on divine mercy because that is all there is; at many points in the city that *is* all there is. They also point us toward the disinterested kind of praise that gives God the glory for the joys of the city and for the wonder of that new Jerusalem which is perhaps even now coming out of heaven from God.

I recall one All Saints Day, in the inner-city church in England to which I belonged, realizing as we read the New Testament lection from Rev 7 that this little congregation formed a microcosm of the heavenly multitude that no one could number, of a kind that I had known nowhere else. It included Caucasian, Afro-Caribbean, and Asian people, babies, children, teenagers, young adults, middle-aged, and old, women and men, working-class, underclass, and middle-class people. The church is called to be, and can sometimes be seen to be, a microcosm of heaven, an anticipatory embodiment of that new Jerusalem. The life of the church is a key part of its proclamation. And it is when it is engaged in praise and prayer that it can most faithfully anticipate the heavenly city. That, too, is something we are responsible for, while being at the same time something God must bring about, so that we seek it from God.

21

DOES GOD CARE ABOUT ANIMALS?

The most interesting, creative, illuminating, dangerous, and misleading exercises in reading the First Testament happen when people study it in light of some new question or conviction that they bring to the text. This question or conviction may open a new window that enables us to see aspects of the text that we had missed or may constitute a mirror that means we do not see the text but see only ourselves reflected. One can watch this kind of study happening in Matthew's reading of Isaiah, or St. Bernard's reading of the Song of Songs, or Luther's reading of Romans, or Wellhausen's reading of the Pentateuch, or feminism's reading of Genesis. In practice, all ventures in interpretation create both windows and mirrors. It is thus a further exercise in interpretation to reflect on this process to try to discern where a question or conviction is functioning as a mirror and where as a window. This second exercise ideally requires the participation of readers who are open-minded but a little less committed than the first set of readers. They need to be people who are open to seeing through new windows but are not so committed that they may fail to recognize mirrors.[1]

Study of the First Testament in light of a concern for the earth, the natural world, the animal world, is an example. Are God and the human world in a covenant relationship with the animal world, which ought to affect the way we live in the world? Does that question open up a window on the First Testament itself, or is it an idea alien to it? My conclusion is that it is somewhere in between.

1. Animals in Genesis

The First Testament opens with two creation stories that characteristically both raise searching questions within themselves and suggest contrasting perspectives when we read them alongside each other. They do this in their treatment of the animal world. In Gen 1 the created world apart from humanity, including the animal world, has great prominence in its own right and is wholly good. Human beings are put in control of the animal world, including birds, sea creatures, reptiles, and

---

[1] First published as "Covenants and Nature," in *Covenant Theology* (ed. M. J. Cartledge and D. Mills; Carlisle: Paternoster, 2001), 21–32, as a response to a paper by Stephen Clark.

wild animals (Gen 1:26–28). The control does not imply a gentle pastoral picture. The verb *radah* (NRSV "have dominion") always denotes hard-won dominance or domination like that of an emperor or an oppressor; it presupposes resistance rather than cooperation (e.g., Lev 26:17; Isa 14:6; Ps 110:2; Neh 9:28). The same is true of the verb *kabas* (NRSV "subdue": e.g. Josh 18:1; Jer 34:11; Zech 9:15; 2 Chr 28:10). It denotes rape in Esth 7:28.

All this suggests that on the basis of words alone, there was plausibility in the claim that Gen 1 encouraged human spoiling of the earth, though the fact that serious spoiling of this kind began only in the modern period suggests it was not the key factor. Indeed, it is significant that after the giving of control to human beings, by implication they are not supposed to eat animals, nor are animals to eat animals. What kind of control do animals need if they are not to be eaten? Or is the question what kind of control would be needed to stop them eating each other?

The apparent tensions within Gen 1 reflect the fact that its concerns lie elsewhere than ours. The chapter is the beginning of a Priestly account of Israel's history. It is one that has a direct relationship with the material in Leviticus enjoining which animals may be eaten and which may not, detailing the sacrifices that involve their being cooked and eaten, and describing the festivals at which they are eaten with particular celebration.

A major point about Gen 1 is to establish the framework for these aspects of Israel's religious life. The emphasis on the structuring of life by the sun and moon and the seasons relates to its significance for Israel's worship life. Similarly, the emphasis on the animals multiplying "according to their kinds" relates to the Priestly emphasis on orderliness in nature that reflects and encourages orderliness within Israel and between Israel and the world. The patterning of what may be eaten at the beginning, after Noah, and after Sinai is part of the patterning of the Torah as a whole. It may be simply a patterning, one no more offering historical information or instructional norms than does the picture of God's doing the work of creation over six days. To require vegetarianism on the basis of Gen 1 would then be a similar mistake to the requiring of belief in a six-day creation or to the opposing of evolution because it conflicts with belief in God's creating animals "according to their kinds." This conclusion would fit with the fact that other creation stories than Genesis also describe humanity as originally vegetarian. An Egyptian hymn hundreds of years older than the time of Moses addresses Amon-Re as "the one who made grass for the cattle and the fruit-tree for humankind."[2] Nor is that understanding only a Middle Eastern phenomenon.[3]

Yet this may nevertheless reflect a human unease about killing and eating animals, to which traditional cultures lived closer than people in modern cultures, a feeling now reviving in Europe and to a lesser extent in the United States. Admittedly, if there was an unease, it did not affect people's lives a great deal. The texts associate vegetarianism with a long-gone time to which we do not belong.

---

[2] Column 6; see *ANET*, 366.
[3] See Claus Westermann, *Genesis 1–11* (Minneapolis: Augsburg / London: SPCK, 1984), 162–65.

Vegetarians are then like naturists. Yet in other respects we assume that God's purpose in Christ was to restore creation and get behind the mess that issued from human disobedience, and this might imply that vegetarians are not so wrong. At least we may be glad that some people insist on witnessing in this way to that unease about killing and eating animals.

In Gen 2–3 the animals are formed as potential helpers and partners for the sake of the first human being. The exercising of the power to name them then suggests a controlling relationship that limits the sense in which they can be helpers and partners. They are thus explicitly distinct from and subordinate to human beings and not adequate as companions for the man. They are not described as good, and one of them leads Adam and Eve astray. In Gen 4, furthermore, one of Adam and Eve's sons gets God's acceptance by killing one of the sheep he looks after and burning (?part of) it as an offering to God, while the son who offers a non-animal sacrifice does not please God. By the time of the flood, the eating of animals is accepted, for God tells Noah to take with him seven pairs of the animals that will be open to being eaten in Israel, but only one pair of animals which cannot be eaten. After the flood, God's covenant with Noah[4] is different from the Abrahamic and Mosaic covenants in its explicit inclusion of all the beings created on the sixth day, animal as well as human. This makes the Noah story paradoxical, because it also explicitly legitimates the eating of meat. That raises the question whether even the inclusion of animals in this covenant is for humanity's sake.

2. Animals in Exodus–Deuteronomy

Exodus, Leviticus, and Deuteronomy include exhortations that require a number of actions serving the interests of animals. Why is this? It is surely for God's sake that livestock, like human beings, observe the sabbath (Exod 20:10). Notwithstanding Mark 2:27, Gen 1, at least, does not imply that the sabbath was made for human beings or animals (for instance, because we need rest), except in the sense that it acts as a reminder for them that the week belongs to God. The sabbath was made for God. It is also thus incidental that wild animals benefit from the sabbath year's fallowing (Exod 23:10–11): that is simply a fortunate consequence of this way of recognizing that the years and the produce of the land belong to God. The rules in Exod 21:33–22:4 [3], in turn, relate to animals purely as human property. Even the requirement to have mercy on your enemy's ox or donkey may have as its main concern the limiting of the human enmity that destroys community life. It is a way of loving your enemy by being concerned about your enemy's property, at least as much as a way of loving animals.

Looking back to the exhortation not to muzzle the ox when it is treading out the grain (Deut 25:4), Paul asks whether God is concerned about oxen or whether Deuteronomy is speaking entirely for the sake of human readers of Deuteronomy like himself (1 Cor 9:9). Paul's rhetorical question is designed to elicit the answer

---

[4] See chapter 9 above.

"No, God is entirely concerned about us." But preachers sometimes find that the trouble with rhetorical questions is that people may answer them, and that they are susceptible to an answer that the questioner did not intend. This may apply even to inspired rhetorical questions. Paul gives a hostage to fortune by his question. One of the most creative (which is not the same as being compelling or right) contemporary interpreters of the Torah does argue that its context shows Deut 25:4 to be not really about animals at all. It indeed expresses God's concern for human beings. The ox stands for an Israelite, for the context suggests that the prohibition relates not to the support of the ministry (the topic to which Paul relates it) but to the need not to deny an Israelite his portion in the land. That is the aim of the requirement about brothers-in-law, which follows. In Deut 22:10, the argument also suggests, the ox again stands for the Israelite, who should not marry a non-Israelite.[5] Animals do commonly symbolize or represent humanity in the First Testament: they provide "food for thought."[6] The point about references to them may then lie in the varied senses in which they are relevant to human beings. Israel appears "in the mirror of nature"; animals may regularly then be referred to not in their own right but because of their usefulness in this connection. Christianity's abandonment of animal sacrifice is then a sign of its moving to a new root metaphor (that of the human body) in an urban rather than an agricultural context.

Leviticus 1–7 is dominated by accounts of how to kill animals so that they can be burned or eaten in the course of worship. Whereas the First Testament disapproves of human sacrifice, while recognizing that it was practiced from time to time in Israel as elsewhere, it shows no sign of disapproving of animal sacrifice. Andrew Linzey has taken up the argument that animal sacrifice might have been acceptable because it was a way of enabling a creature to find its end in its return to its maker, and thus find its happiness in God and for God's glory.[7] Yet the same might be argued with regard to killing human beings for God's glory. It does not provide a rationale for killing animals and not killing human beings in worship.

Several of the prophets disapprove of animal sacrifices, but they give no hint that this relates to a concern for the animals involved. Whether or not they imply a root-and-branch opposition to sacrifice, they make it explicit that disapproval derives from the way the people's worship is not accompanied by right behavior in relation to other human beings. God's disapproval applies to the whole of worship, including prayer, praise, and offerings of other things than animals (for instance, bread). And in the last of the books in the prophetic canon, God's disapproval concerns the fact that the animals are blind, lame, or sick and that people fail to bring the best of their flocks for sacrifice (see Mal 1).

---

[5] Calum M. Carmichael, *The Laws of Deuteronomy* (Ithaca, N.Y. / London: Cornell University Press, 1974), 238–40, also 159–63.

[6] Howard Eilberg-Schwartz, *The Savage in Judaism* (Bloomington: Indiana University Press, 1990), 115–40, whom the rest of this paragraph summarizes.

[7] *Animal Theology* (Urbana: University of Illinois Press, 1995), 103–4. He attributes the argument to Eugène Masure as cited by E. L. Mascall, *Corpus Christi* (repr., London: Longmans, 1965), 92.

3. Animals in the Prophets and the Writings

The vision for a New Day expressed in Zech 14:21 includes continuing animal sacrifice. Isaiah 25:6 similarly envisages a feast on this New Day that will include rich, well-marrowed food. And if animal sacrifice becomes redundant after Christ's death, this in itself constitutes no comment on whether it is disapproved of for the animals' sake. The New Testament contains no pointers in this direction; indeed, the death of Christ and the giving of the Spirit explicitly mean that more meat eating is now possible (see Acts 10).

As in many traditional societies, the eating of meat was much less common in Israel than in modern Western societies; one may note the prevalence of reference to grain and fruit in passages such as Deut 8:7–10, Hos 2:22 [24], and Amos 9:13–14. One implication of the rules about sacrifice is that eating meat takes place in a religious context; it is not a purely domestic affair. Paradoxically, the practice of sacrifice may indeed have the effect of constraining meat eating, though this is hardly its design. Deuteronomy 12 does permit people to kill animals for meat in a nonreligious setting, because they live a long distance from the shrine. KJV speaks here and elsewhere of the people "lusting after" meat, but the word in question applies elsewhere to God's "desire" and should surely be understood neutrally. It denotes illicit desire in Num 11, but this illicit desire is for fish, cucumbers, melons, leeks, onions, and garlic, as well as meat; though I would go a long way with anyone who recognized that onions and garlic are key to cooking. Israelites enjoyed eating meat; that is treated as a morally neutral fact. What is important is that they should not eat meat in an apostate way.

Psalm 104 rejoices in the way God established the earth securely and provides for it day by day. This includes giving drink to wild animals and making grass grow for cattle, providing trees for birds to nest in and remote mountains for wild goats and coneys, making the night as a time for lions to seek their food from God, and providing the creatures of the sea with their food. Animals, like human beings, are inbreathed by God's spirit/breath. God's address to Job in Job 38–39 also emphasizes the independent significance of the animal world, along with many other aspects of the creation such as desert areas that are empty of even animal life. The wild donkey, the wild ox, the ostrich, the horse, and the hawk show that the world does not circulate around a human being like Job. These things indeed "exist 'for their own sake,' because God wishes just those things to be"; "they aren't simply 'for us.'"[8] In Job 38:39–41, God implicitly provides the lion with its prey, and explicitly does so for the raven, and of course God does that by enabling lion and raven to catch, kill, and eat other creatures. The same point will be implicit in Ps 104 (compare Ps. 147:9).

Isaiah 11:6–8, in contrast, pictures wolf and lamb, leopard and kid goat lying down together, and lion becoming vegetarian. We might ask of this passage an equivalent to Paul's question, "Is it for lambs and goats that God is concerned?" First, God will apparently need to turn some of these animals into something other

---

[8] So Eilberg-Schwartz, *The Savage in Judaism*, 115–40.

than themselves; wolves, leopards, and lions that live like this have ceased to be wolves, leopards, and lions. Perhaps Isa 11 is thus picturing God as involved in an act of new creation that improves on the first creation or implements its original design. But the general context in Isaiah does not make one expect discussion of the destiny of the animal world here. Further, the narrow context in Isa 11:1–5 and 9 suggests that Isa 11:6–8 uses talk of unnatural or supernatural harmony in the animal world as a metaphor for harmony in the human world. Strong and powerful people will live together with the weak and powerless because the latter can believe that the former are no longer seeking to devour them. The book called Isaiah indeed opened by using animals to stand for human beings (Isa 1:3), in connection with the question of knowledge, as in Isa 11:9. So they do in Isa 11:6–8.

Whether that is correct or not, it provides a parable for the allusions to the animal world in the First Testament as a whole. It is not a topic of interest in its own right. It is of interest insofar as it relates to the human world. This is paradoxically so even in Job 38–39, which refers to the animal world only to make a point about the human world. The independent significance of the animal world is mentioned only because of its significance for the human world. As Paul puts it, "Is it for oxen that God is concerned? Or does he not speak entirely for our sake?" The answer is, Yes, God speaks entirely for our sake. This would cohere with the fact that the vision of a New Day in Ezek 34:25–28 assumes that wild animals retain their instincts to eat living things and promises the community's protection by devices other than changing the animals' nature. The same assumption may underlie Hos 2:18 [20], where the arrangements for "that day" include a covenant whereby humanity will be protected from the varying threats posed by the animal world.[9]

4. Feedback

And yet . . . I began by noting that people who read the First Testament in light of modern questions often see things there that have been missed, even if they also run the risk of reading modern concerns into the text. The First Testament does not directly assert that women and men have equal status in the world, or that all races are equal before God and must treat each other on equal terms, or that all human beings are equal before God and therefore must not enslave one another, or that human beings must not make war on each other because they are all made in God's image, or that humanity is to look after the earth rather then exploit it. Indeed, the First Testament contains material that can be read either way on each question.

New insight on scripture often comes through people starting from secular premises rather than from traditional Christian ones that have made Christians read scripture according to a certain slant. The dynamics of this process can be seen clearly with regard to the position of women. New premises have enabled people to see things that were always there but were invisible. They then may enable people to

---

[9]See Francis I. Andersen and David Noel Freedman, *Hosea* (Anchor Bible; New York: Doubleday, 1980), 279–81.

read scripture in a way that produces a picture doing better justice to the whole. It will not be surprising if unbelievers are the people who spot truths of God's which everyone needs to take note of and which they can see because they have the advantage as well as the disadvantage of standing outside our tradition of interpretation.

I have suggested that even the author of Job was unconcerned about animals in their own right. Yet by a feedback mechanism, the book's appeal to the significance of animals in their own right means it is implying that they are important in their own right. If the care of shepherds for sheep can be used as a theological illustration, then Ezekiel implicitly recognizes the appropriateness of a caring rather than an exploitative stance in relation to animals, which would exclude their being treated as if they were machines or their being reared in the inhumane conditions in which we do raise animals for food.

We need to continue having the discussion over whether, for instance, the acceptance of sacrificing animals in the First Testament and of meat eating in the New is a point at which the Bible has not worked out the logic of its own presuppositions or whether they put a question mark by the claim that the Bible points toward universal vegetarianism.

22

WHAT IS A FAMILY?

1. Definitions

We are used to distinguishing between the nuclear family and the extended family.[1] The First Testament makes an overlapping distinction between the *bet* (or *bet-ab*) and the *mishpahah*.[2] Both words can be translated "family," though more often *bet/bet-ab* is translated "house[hold]/father's house." So if we want to know what the First Testament says about the family, passages in the English Bible that speak of the "house[hold]" are at least as significant as passages that speak of the "family." Here I will use the words "household" and "kin group" as equivalents for the Hebrew words for the family in these two senses.

A household might in theory comprise up to four generations: middle-aged and/or elderly parents, their grown-up/married children, and their dependents (plus servants, if any). Such a household might well have to spread itself over several of the kind of Israelite dwellings that can be seen in significant numbers in towns such as Beersheba and in the villages where most people lived. Within any one such community (a village or town) a further number of the houses would presumably then be occupied by other households from the same kin group. But the fact that Israelites referred to this entity as a household points to these people all occupying one house, which would reflect the harsh realities of life. Factors such as short life expectancy would mean that in practice one household would be the kind of number that could live together in this way. The Ruth story illustrates the way tragedy could decimate a potentially large household.

In theory, then, a household was what we might see as an extended family, but in practice the relationship between a household and a kin group might be comparable to that between a nuclear and an extended family. The arrangement differs from that in Western societies in that the households would more often live close by each other. But this is not invariably the case; in the Ruth story, again, Elimelech's household moves away from the rest of the kin group for economic reasons, as happens in the modern world.

---

[1] Not previously published.

[2] See Norman K. Gottwald, *The Tribes of Yahweh* (Maryknoll, N.Y.: Orbis, 1979 / London: SCM, 1980), 285–92; J. R. Porter, *The Extended Family in the Old Testament* (London: Edutext, 1967).

The Ruth story also illustrates how there can be more than one household/kin group pattern, as it pictures two women living together for a period, while in the English Bible the next story (1 Sam 1) concerns a family comprising one man, two women, and in due course the children of both, while the daughters of Zelophehad are allowed in effect to become a family so that they are in a position to inherit their father's property when he has no sons (Num 27). These provide illustrations of the assumption that there is a usual pattern of family structuring involving a man and woman and their children, but that this does not have to be maintained dogmatically.[3] Although Gen 1 makes both the subduing of the world and the growth of the family both men's and women's business, the story of Hannah and Samuel assumes that in Israelite culture, as traditionally in ours, the early upbringing of children is their mother's work (cf. Exod 2:1–10).

In terms of its theological or moral significance, the family occupies a place midway between marriage and the state. On one hand, the creation stories offer an account of the origin of marriage and declare God's blessing on it, which they do not do for the family or the state. On the other, 1 Samuel offers an account of the origin of the monarchic state that is much more critical of it, on the grounds that monarchy threatens God's position as Israel's leader; there is no such fundamental critique of marriage or the family. In between these, the family is neither blessed nor critiqued but taken for granted. Biblical stories then illustrate how it can work for good or ill. This might fit with a tendency in the New Testament to declare judgment on the state in the light of an assertion that God rules in Jesus, to continue to affirm the position of marriage, and to put the family in its place, along with other structures that depend on blood ties such as the distinctive position of Israel.

2. The Family in Israel's Story

The words for "family" appear most often in passages such as Num 1–4, Num 26, and Josh 13–22. For Israel as for us, the family is often chiefly an administrative convenience, useful for the purpose of the ancient equivalents to assessing the community charge, though also for the distributing of land. In contrast, words for family do not appear in Gen 1–6; indeed, the only allusion to kin groups in Gen 1–9 is a reference to the animals leaving the ark by kin groups in Gen 8:19. All this goes to show that one cannot do theology with a concordance, because the unnamed family is central to the story of the world's origins. Genesis 1–2 doubtless presupposes that the blessing of procreation will work itself out in families, for that was the experience of the tellers and hearers of the story. It is more explicit that the curse of death works itself out in families. Eve is warned about the pain of motherhood, not merely the pain of giving birth but the pain of family strife such as the next chapter describes, where the Bible's first domestic scene is one that combines worship and murder.

---

[3] Cf. A. Brenner, "Female Social Behaviour," *VT* 36 (1986): 257–73 = *A Feminist Companion to Genesis* (ed. A. Brenner; Sheffield: Sheffield Academic Press, 1993), 204–21.

It is as a household (Gen 7:1) that Mr. and Ms. Noah and their sons with their wives (no children are mentioned) find escape from world judgment, and as a family that they then demonstrate that this was not because they were better than anyone else. The opening scenes that follow the first creation (Gen 4) and the renewal of creation (Gen 9:20–27) thus open up a theme that runs through the First Testament and through contemporary experience, that the family is regularly the locus of strife and immorality.

The ambiguity of the family is clear in the stories of Abram and Sarai. Finding God's blessing involves leaving kin group and household (Gen 12:2), but in a sense to start a new one. The family continues to be the natural structure through which God's blessing finds fruition. More specifically, it is the structure through which the vulnerable find protection. After his father's death, Lot becomes his grandfather's responsibility, and on his grandfather's death becomes the responsibility of Abram as his eldest uncle: within Terah's kin group, Lot belongs to the household of Haran, then to that of Terah himself, then to that of Abram (Gen 11–12). He is never on his own until he is big and powerful enough to make this both possible and necessary (Gen 13), and even then Abram is morally obliged to intervene on his behalf when he gets into trouble (Gen 14).

The promise of blessing presupposes the natural human instinct to have children. In Abram and Sarai's case that leads to surrogate parenthood and to unhappiness throughout the family (Abram, Sarai, Hagar, Ishmael). Lot's story in due course adds further family sexual immorality to this story of family strife (Gen 19).

The most elaborate account of the reality of family strife in Genesis is the story of Jacob's sons, true sons of their father in his own relationship with his twin brother. Jacob's favoritism for his next-to-youngest son Joseph colludes with Joseph's dream of being in a position of power over his brothers, which generates deeper resentment in them but no intervention from Jacob. The failure to grasp the nettle in the family exacts a terrible price, the situation being made worse by complicated relationships within the family that issue from the children having the same father but different mothers; something of the dynamic parallels the complications in Western society when divorce and remarriage generate complex sets of interweaving families whose children may have mothers and fathers, stepmothers and stepfathers, and possibly brothers/sisters, half-brothers/sisters, and/or stepbrothers/stepsisters. Joseph in due course has opportunity to exact a price from his brothers, but eventually the family is reunited, though realistically the scars remain, and once Jacob is dead the brothers are not sure the reconciliation will stick. And the whole story is set in the context of the purpose of God, who is not said to have inspired the dream but does seem to make it come true and uses the conflicts in the family to preserve the family and fulfill a purpose for it and through it.

In the family of David, both sex and strife are problems. Belonging to David's household does not mean everyone living together; Absalom lives separately from David and Amnon. David is capable of feeling angry when his son Amnon rapes his half-sister, but like Jacob he does nothing; the overall comment regarding his parenting of another son is that he had never antagonized him by criticizing him (1 Kgs 1:6). One key to the portrayal of David is that his story interweaves decisiveness in the realm of politics with feebleness in the private realm that often also spells disaster in the public realm.[4] When Absalom has Amnon killed, David weeps. When Absalom then flees, David mourns and later allows him to return to Jerusalem but will not see him. When David allows him to foment revolt, Absalom lets Ahitophel try to kill David, and when Absalom dies, David is grieved. David knows how to fight but not how to relate to people—men, women, or family.

The First Testament story matter-of-factly recognizes the family's potential for both blessing and abuse. It contains no shred of romanticism about the family; with hindsight, we can see it had the potential to preserve us from failing to expect family life within the church to be characterized by sexual abuse and other forms of violence and strife. It prohibits us from naïveté about what family life within the church will be like behind the curtains. It suggests no assumption that the cycle of abuse and violence can be broken. It does suggest that God can set limits to its death-dealing work (Cain and Abel), stand by the victims and rework the divine scheme of things so that they have a place within it (Hagar and Ishmael), work miracles in individual broken families (Jacob and Esau), bring good out of what human beings intend as evil (Joseph), or at least stay with it and move on (David).

3. The Family in Israel's Rule of Life

In several senses the rule of life expressed in what we call Israel's laws follows from its story. One of the senses in which this is so is that this rule of life is concerned to try to set limits to the rule of strife and immorality that the stories recognize is the reality of human life inside the people of God as well as outside it.

Thus the community needs a rule of life for the family that recognizes the reality of sexual immorality within it. Leviticus 18 and Lev 20 systematically prohibit many forms of sexual relations within the kin group. There are doubtless a number of socio-economic, anthropological, and theological reasons for these prohibitions,[5] but these include a desire to safeguard family order, the structured arrangement of marriage and family. Another potential role of the prohibitions is to signal the outlawing of various relationships in which abuse takes place.

Other imperatives urge the responsibilities of children for parents and offer safeguards against the instinct for strife and selfishness in the family (e.g., Exod 20:12; Lev 20:9; Deut 27:16; cf. Prov 19:26; 23:22–25; 28:24). The main corresponding imperative regarding the responsibility of parents for children is the repeated reminder to teach them about the gospel and its demands (Deut 4:9; 6:7, 20–25; 11:19; 32:46). There are few practical imperatives regarding the obligations of parents (see Deut 21:15–17). This may reflect the fact that it is parents who draw up the

---

[4] K. R. R. Gros Louis, "The Difficulty of Ruling Well: King David of Israel," *Semeia* 8 (1977): 15–33, reprinted in *Literary Interpretations of Biblical Narratives* (ed. K. R. R. Gros Louis; 2 vols.; Nashville: Abingdon, 1982), 2:204–19.

[5] See, e.g., A. Brenner, "On Incest," in *A Feminist Companion to Exodus to Deuteronomy* (ed. A. Brenner; Sheffield: Sheffield Academic Press, 1994), 113–38; C. Pressler, "Sexual Violence and Deuteronomic Law," in the same volume, 102–12.

instructions (cf. Deut 21:18–21!), though the balance will also reflect the temptation for grown-up children to cease to look after their parents when they need this, a temptation with which Western society is familiar.

While the family can easily be the means whereby people are led astray religiously (Deut 13:6–11), it also has the potential to be the social structure of festivity before Yahweh (Deut 12:7; 14:26; 15:20). The Ruth story illustrates how the kin group provides a structure of responsibility or a safety net when families break down. Leviticus's dream of a periodic year when debts are cancelled and transactions reversed is concerned for the restoration of the familial status quo (Lev 25:10, 41); it also presupposes the assumption that underlies the Ruth story, that the members of a person's kin group have a moral obligation to take practical action on their behalf when, for instance, they are overtaken by debt.

The assumption that the family cares for its members no doubt underlies the way the family becomes Deuteronomy's model for the working of society.[6] Deuteronomy is very fond of referring to people's fellow Israelites as their brothers: it encourages people to see Israel as the family writ large.[7] The fact that other members of the community are your brothers is a fact to take into account when they have financial difficulties or are due to be released from indentured labor or are liable for punishment—or are guilty of perjury (Deut 15:1–12; 25:4; 19:18–19). The fact that other members of the community are the brothers of Israel's judges, kings, Levites, and prophets (Deut 1:18; 17:14–20; 18:1–18) needs to affect both their attitude to the people they lead and the people's attitude to their needs.[8] Israel's rule of life thus makes explicit a need implicit in its stories, that the presence of abuse within family life means that the community has to establish practical policies to safeguard the weak. At the same time, the fact that the family becomes a model for life in society indicates that it could be a place where people experienced love.

4. The Family in Israel's Nightmares and Visions

For the prophets, too, the family can be a model for the community of faith. Ezekiel is especially fond of seeing Israel as a family, a household, "the household of Israel"; a rebellious household (Ezek 2; 3; 12). In Ezek 16 and 23 relations within the family provide the metaphor for portraying the people's history (cf. also Isa 1:2). In Hos 1–3, relations within the family provide the metaphor for portraying the people's coming destiny.

This metaphor is used in the context of the patriarchal family (patriarchal over against egalitarian, not over against matriarchal or fratriarchal). The use of the family metaphor in this way risks incidentally degrading the women and children

---

[6]See John Goldingay, *Theological Diversity and the Authority of the Old Testament* (Grand Rapids: Eerdmans, 1987), 134–66.

[7]The point is not so clear in NRSV and TNIV because of their commitment to gender-inclusive translation.

[8]See Hans Walter Wolff, *Anthropology of the Old Testament* (London: SCM / Philadelphia: Fortress, 1974), 196–97.

who appear in the metaphor and further imperiling their position in the family and everywhere else.[9] Apparently God was prepared to take that risk in seeking to get through to the men who led Israel in its waywardness.

The degradation of women and children is a matter of literal reality as well as metaphor. The prophets in particular recognize the way the sins of fathers are visited on their (wives and) children, which happens in their day as it does in ours, as the children also enjoy the positive fruit of the fathers' lives and work if they are more fortunate. Children (and wives) are bound up in the bundle of life with the fathers, for good and for ill. When a man is wayward, his wife and his children share the trouble that comes to him (e.g., Amos 7:17), partly because a family tends to be involved with its "head" in his wrongdoing as well as in its fruits (Jer 3:25; 11:10; 31:29).

The good news is that if the family of Israel is to be destroyed, it is also destined to be rebuilt (Ezek 37:11 and the context; 39:11). And fortunately the prophetic nightmare that threatens to further the oppressiveness of the patriarchal family is accompanied by a prophetic vision that subverts the patriarchal hierarchy of the family. Children will be able to escape the influence of their parents, so they will no longer follow their parents in sin and die (Jer 31:29–30). Both Yahweh's sons and Yahweh's daughters will be brought back from the ends of the earth; all of them are called by Yahweh's name and created for Yahweh's glory, purposefully and individually shaped and made by Yahweh (Isa 43:6–7). Women share with men in the fullness of a family relationship with Yahweh in the present, and they will thus share in the future in the fullness of Yahweh's ingathering. Both sons and daughters are to prophesy, and ageism and classism are also subverted (Joel 2:28–29 [3:1–2]). The strife between parents and children (cf. Mic 7:6) is to be brought to an end (Mal 4:6 [3:24]). That is promise, not demand, but it puts children into a position of responsibility to do their own turning rather than making their membership of a family an excuse for having no control of their destiny, for casting themselves into the role of victim (Ezek 18).

The prophetic vision offers empowerment to the victims of the patriarchal family.

5. The Family in Israel's Life Experience

The life and experience of the ordinary family feature in Proverbs, the Song of Songs, Job, and the Psalms.

In Proverbs, the family is the place of learning. Although its opening verse speaks of Proverbs' wisdom as Solomon's and might thus imply that education is the business of the state, the king soon disappears and mother and father are the source of insight for their children (e.g., Prov 1:8, 10; 2:1; 3:1, 11, 21). Specifically

---

[9]See, e.g., T. D. Setel, "Prophets and Pornography: Female Sexual Imagery in Hosea," in *Feminist Interpretation of the Bible* (ed. Letty M. Russell; Philadelphia: Westminster Press, 1985), 86–95; Renita J. Weems, "Gomer: Victim of Violence or Victim of Metaphor?" in *Interpretation for Liberation* (ed. Katie G. Cannon and Elisabeth Schüssler Fiorenza; *Semeia* 47, 1989), 87–104.

they are the source of insight for their sons, which raises the question where the mothers and the other discerning women who appear in the book gained their insight and how insight came to be personified as a woman (e.g., Prov 1:20–33). Perhaps it is intuitive; only men have to be told. Or perhaps the explicit concern with sons reflects Proverbs' links with education for community leadership that was largely confined to men. This would suggest that there is an element of metaphor in the address to sons but that the metaphor presupposes such a literal reality in the background. Or women could work in the civil service as scribes and messengers,[10] so Proverbs would have been relevant to them and needed by them, and the reference to sons may not be designed to exclude daughters.

Consideration of training for leadership draws attention again to the fact that whenever the First Testament refers to sons and daughters, it likely has adults in mind. In light of the First Testament's experience and ours that the family is the locus of sex and violence, it is striking that the first topic in Proverbs is violence and that the dominant one in the chapters that follow is sex; money is also a recurrent theme. The parents who reckon to offer their children advice on these topics will need to heed it themselves if their advice is not to be sham. That need will be reinforced by the fact that teaching on violence, sex, and money is set in the context of teaching on relationships with God. Family learning on one of these areas cannot be divorced from family learning on the other, because the realities themselves interweave in the way God makes life work.

The other side of the coin of the parental anxiety in Prov 1–9 is the need reflected in the Song of Songs for a young man and woman to have space as they find a new brother and sister in each other. The sense that your parents or your siblings are always looking over your shoulder is not likely to keep you out of trouble and is quite likely to alienate you from them.

In Job, the family is the place of pain. Perhaps this is so under the surface in Proverbs; its anxious fantasies about the young man yielding to the blandishments of teenage rogues or a beguiling woman or easy money suggest the nightmares of parents as their children grow beyond the years when they are under parental control. Sons can be a source of sorrow, grief, and bitterness as well as joy (Prov 10:1; 15:20; 17:25). Job is the story of a man who does his absolute best for his family; the height of the description is the fact that Job is a person who prays for his children continually. It is precisely for that reason that he has to watch it all fall apart. His children grow up and all get on famously with each other, unlike Jacob's or David's. While they are doing so they are all killed. When Job himself is overcome by affliction, his wife can take it no longer. Job is left alone with God.

At the end of the story, his family is rebuilt. We will not be able to see how ten more children can truly compensate for the loss of the first ten, nor in what state all this left Ms. Job (who was old enough to have ten grown-up children before she started on the next ten), but an important point is made by the fairy-tale "so they all lived happily ever after" ending. The fiction embodies the promise that somehow

---

[10] See S. A. Meier, "Women and Communication in the Ancient Near East," *Journal of the American Oriental Society* 111 (1991): 540–47.

God does make things work out aright and that this promise applies to families, even if we cannot see how this can be possible.

That the family is a place of healing is a more inferential point.[11] The Psalms presuppose that people in pain have contexts in which they can articulate their physical, emotional, or spiritual need and in which other people can then minister God's healing to them or simply stay with them in their pain. The context of that prayer ministry is sometimes the institutional ministry of temple or other sanctuary, as classically in the story of Hannah in 1 Sam 1. But that story located at the annual pilgrimage festival implicitly shows how such ministry cannot cope with people's all-year-round needs. What happened for the other fifty-one weeks of the year? The family may again have been the answer. The kin group would be the natural body to offer support and prayer and to facilitate a person's restoration to society, of which it was the most immediate embodiment. First Testament faith, like ours, then presupposed that involvement with a small group complemented involvement with the corporate worship of the large congregation, if one's kin group constituted a person's small group. It is a form of family therapy, though in Israel's case not one presupposing that it is the family that is ill.

As one might expect, it is the poetic books with their experiential base that most directly address everyday life issues as these affect the family, though they only do directly what appears less directly in story, rule of life, and nightmare and vision. Together these four ways of speaking acknowledge the realities of family life, indicate agenda for it, and suggest hopes for it.

---

[11] See E. Gerstenberger, *Der bittende Mensch* (Neukirchen: Neuchirchener, 1980), conveniently summarized in Patrick D. Miller, *Interpreting the Psalms* (Philadelphia: Fortress, 1986), 6–7.

23

WHAT DOES THE BIBLE SAY
ABOUT WOMEN AND MEN?

1. Women and Men in the First Testament

We may begin with the opening chapters of scripture, because sexuality is an important theme in both creation stories. This is rather striking. One would hardly have expected either a religious text or an account of the origins of the world to have been so interested so soon in the significance of humanity's maleness and femaleness.[1]

Genesis 1 comes to its first climax with the creation of a God-like humanity (its second climax is God's ceasing work). The verses are allusive over wherein the God-likeness consists.[2] Indeed, much is allusive in Gen 1–3, not least over matters to do with sexuality, and we have tended to build too much doctrine and ethics on these chapters too easily and need to be a bit more reticent in our handling of them. There is no suggestion that humanity's God-likeness consists in its reasoning power or spiritual nature. Insofar as the context offers any guidance, it consists in (or perhaps rather implies) humanity's being put in control of other creatures (1:26) and in its being created male and female (1:27); only this second gloss on God-likeness is mentioned when the formula reappears later (5:1–2). Humanity is present only in this combination of male and female, and thus the God-likeness of humanity is present only in the combination. In this context, 'adam does not

---

[1] Sections 1 and 3 first published as "The Bible and Sexuality," in *SJT* 39 (1986): 175–88; section 2 not previously published. As well as sources referred to in the notes, I am aware of having used A. Berlin, "Characterisation in Biblical Narrative: David's Wives," *JSOT* 23 (1982): 69–85; P. A. Bird, "Male and Female He Created Them," *Harvard Theological Review* 74 (1981): 129–59; A. Brenner, *The Israelite Woman* (Sheffield: JSOT, 1985); P. D. Hanson, "Masculine Metaphors for God and Sex Discrimination in the Old Testament," *Ecumenical Review* 4 (1975): 316–24 = Hanson, *The Diversity of Scripture* (Philadelphia: Fortress, 1982), 136–47; J. H. Otwell, *And Sarah Laughed* (Philadelphia: Fortress, 1977); W. E. Phipps, "Adam's Rib," *ThT* 33 (1976–77): 263–73; T. R. Preston, "The Heroism of Saul," *JSOT* 24 (1982): 27–46; Katharine Doob Sakenfeld, "The Bible and Women: Bane or Blessing?" *ThT* 32 (1975–76): 222–33; A. Tilby, "How the Virgin Birth Attracts Hostility," *The* [London] *Times*, November 28, 1981; J. G. Williams, *Women Recounted: Narrative Thinking and the God of Israel* (Sheffield: Almond, 1982).

[2] See further the introduction to chapter 4 above.

refer to the male; it is a word like "mankind" or "humanity" or *homo sapiens*. It is then further defined as "male and female." There is about humanity both a unity and a plurality, both a unity and a diversity. Genesis 1 thus immediately subverts the suggestion that the male is the natural human being, the female being a deviant type. Only man and woman together make real humanity. Together they hear God's word, receiving God's blessing and commission to multiply as families, to exercise power in the world, and to enjoy its produce. Genesis indicates no differentiation of role in the fulfillment of this commission or any internal hierarchy within humanity.

Not least in light of Gen 1, Gen 2 may be read in a similar egalitarian way. Here, too, God forms "a human being": *'adam* again, but not a collective, and the context here stresses the link between *'adam* and the *'adamah* from which it was made.[3] In the first part of the story, effectively the creature is sexually undifferentiated. When differentiation appears, a divine awareness of the being's incompleteness appears with it. God thus forms another human being as a companion for the first, one who stands over against the first. KJV's "help meet for him" has misled people. "Helper" does not suggest a subordinate; God himself is often people's "helper" in the First Testament. The image of the Holy Spirit as the one who comes alongside to be our helper and companion (John 14) may contribute to our getting the right impression in Gen 2.

The identity of being that is shared by these two people is expressed by the picture of one of them being built up from a part of the other. Their equality may also be suggested by the part being a rib: the woman is not made from man's head, to rule him, or from his feet, to be treated as his servant, but from his side, to stand alongside him "in a partnership of love."[4] It is when she stands alongside him that the man becomes aware of himself as a man, in the company of a woman (*'ish*, *'ishshah*). He addresses her as a person over against himself (he does not name her, as if he were in control of her, in the way he did the animals). The aloneness of the sole human being need not imply loneliness, but it does imply that he faces a monumental task on his own, and a task that a man cannot accomplish, because he cannot bear children. His aloneness is overcome through the gift of another in whom he recognizes identity, yet also the differentiation of sexuality, which is a means of their communion and their procreating.

The idyll is soon spoiled. It is not explicit in the story that cynicism and disobedience gain access to human experience through some distinctive female weakness. The weakness of the male, so strangely silent even though apparently present through the exchanges between serpent and Eve, is as clear as that of the female. The story does not indicate why it was the woman that the serpent approached. (I shall hint at a religio-historical understanding of this element in the story when we consider women in Proverbs.) The woman fails by her words, the man by his silence, and both by their deeds.

---

[3] Hence Phyllis Trible, on whom much of this section depends, translates "earth-creature": see *God and the Rhetoric of Sexuality* (Philadelphia: Fortress, 1978).

[4] Peter Lombard, *Sentences* II, 18/2.

Consequences follow in the area of sexuality, as in other areas. Whereas in Gen 1 there is no suggestion that man and woman are responsible respectively for home and family, world and work, is it significant that these realms are now assumed to be divided between the sexes (3:16–19)? Certainly both realms are spoiled. But the pain of motherhood (3:16) is more likely the inner pain of parenthood, of watching your sons kill each other, for instance (Gen 4:8), rather than merely the physical pain of giving birth; elsewhere, the word has a reference of this kind, and it fits the context. It is a pain Adam will also feel, though Genesis is explicit that he feels it in relation to this work (3:17). As a result of turning from God's way the couple become aware of their nakedness (3:7; this has usually been taken to indicate a negative awareness of their sexuality, though it may rather denote an awareness if their weakness and indigence). Less disputably, it is as a result of this turning that a hierarchical relationship between a man and his wife comes into being. "To love and to cherish" becomes "to desire and to dominate" (3:16).[5]

What next shall I say? For time will fail me to tell of Gideon, Barak, Jephthah, Samuel, and various other interesting males, let alone Jephthah's daughter.[6] I will say something about Samson, the other figure who receives only bare mention in Heb 11.[7] He illustrates well how "to love and to cherish" is turned into "to desire and to dominate." His story focuses on desire and domination, woman and violence. He is the First Testament's most macho "hero," the Bible's James Bond. Yet the comparison is superficial. James Bond is usually the successful ladies' man. If hearts are broken, it will not usually be his. He rides off into the sunset with a sequence of attractive girls.

Four women feature in Samson's story. The first is his mother, one of those archetypal Israelite women who for years tried and hoped and prayed in vain for a child, then bore one in fulfillment of God's promise, a son out of whose eyes the sun shone (his name, Samson, resembles the word for "sun"). The picture of this woman and her husband (Judg 13) contrasts sadly with those of the woman he marries because he fancies her (Judg 14–15) and of the woman he picks up to spend a night with because he feels like it (Judg 16:1–3). Then there is the woman he falls in love with. It is a tale of unrequited love. Delilah is interested only in being the woman who can find out for the Philistines the secret of Samson's strength, for thirty silver pieces. The Philistines are able to seize him, gouge out his eyes, and take him back as a trophy to Gaza. There, bound in bronze chains, he grinds at the mill in the prison (Judg 16:4–20).

Samson is a tragic hero because of the contrast between his actual life and his divine calling. He was destined to use the strength of his manliness to deliver God's people from their enemies, but he did not know how to be a real man either with that strength or in his relationships with women, which were directly his downfall.

---

[5] Derek Kidner, *Genesis* (London: Inter-Varsity Press, 1967), on the passage.

[6] Phyllis Trible considers her in *Texts of Terror* (Philadelphia: Fortress, 1984), along with some other women not mentioned in Heb 11.

[7] See James L. Crenshaw, *Samson* (London: SPCK, 1979).

Inside most of us there is a little James Bond, a little Samson (or a little Deli-lah?); the James Bond film appeals to those fantasies. The Bible's James Bond, how-ever, lives in the real world, where sex and violence rebound on you. It insists that we live in this real world, not in a celluloid one, a real world in which, because there is something of Samson and Delilah inside us, something of their tragedy also in-evitably appears in our lives. We make a mess of what we do with our maleness and our femaleness, as many other films outside the Bond genre recognize. What the Bible adds is that making a mess of your life, your relationships, and your calling need not be the end of the story. Samson's failures cannot be undone, but eyeless in Gaza he prays, and his manly strength knows one final, terribly fruitful moment of violence (Judg 16:30).

Samson appears once more in Scripture, in that list of the heroes of faith in Heb 11. Even Samson is there, among the cloud of witnesses. If there is room for him, there is room for anyone else who makes a mess of being a man or of being a woman.

The First Testament's next, and greatest, study in maleness is David.[8] Violence and sex are prominent in his story, too. Each of the first four chapters in which he appears (1 Sam 16–19) emphasizes his significance as a warrior. Saul kills in thou-sands, David in ten thousands. David has sex with many women but is never said to love one. The only relationship about which he expresses any feelings is that with Jonathan, and it is only after Jonathan dies that he clearly does that, in his moving lament at the deaths of Jonathan and his father (2 Sam 1). The story of David and Jonathan emphasizes Jonathan's love for David, which prevented Jonathan's com-peting with David for his father's throne. One does not have to be too cynical to see the preserving of David's lament as designed to indicate that he is not rejoicing in the death of the king and the person whom many Israelites would view as heir to the throne. The political significance of David's relationships with women is even clearer (e.g., 1 Sam 18:26; 2 Sam 3:12–16). Ironically, however, it is through letting a Samson-like fancy for a woman get the better of him that he sows the seeds of destruction for his regime as well as for his family life (2 Sam 11). His handling of his family in succeeding years consistently betrays a weakness that contrasts with the decisiveness he manifests in affairs of state and inevitably carries implications for the latter; he loves those who hate him and hates those who love him (2 Sam 19:6). The end result of all this is the mirroring of the sexual feebleness of his last days and the political feebleness that still cannot grasp the nettle with regard to designating his successor.

We are taken much further inside the character of the man himself than we are in the case of Samson, though in the end this leaves his character a deeper enigma. Sometimes he seems to be the man who walks in God's way, seeking God's guid-ance, honoring those who deserve honor, making merry before Yahweh no matter

---

[8] See Robert Alter, *The Art of Biblical Narrative* (New York: Basic, 1981), 114–30; K. R. R. Gros Louis, "The Difficulty of Ruling Well: King David of Israel," *Semeia* 8 (1977): 15–33, reprinted in *Literary Interpretations of Biblical Narratives* (ed. K. R. R. Gros Louis; 2 vols.; Nashville: Abingdon, 1982); D. M. Gunn, *The Story of King David* (Sheffield, JSOT, 1978).

who is watching (2 Sam 2:1–7; 6:1–19); and he is the man Yahweh loves and blesses (5:10, 12; 7:1–16). He can equally be portrayed as the man with the knack of falling on his feet as rivals to the throne one by one disappear from the reckoning and the man with an eye for the main chance (e.g., 3:13–14; 9:1–13?). Rarely are his motives stated, even (indeed notably) in the Bathsheba story and its unpleasant aftermath, so that the narrative leaves us with a deep ambiguity over his character.[9]

Between the stories of Samson and of David, in the order in the English Bible, there appear Ruth and Hannah, whose stories manifest a different form of ambiguity. Elsewhere in the First Testament, a number of Israelite women make their mark in political and military roles (Deborah, Jael, Esther), though without moving quite outside female frameworks (Deborah is "a mother in Israel," Jael uses her role as hostess, Esther hers as consort). Ruth's and Hannah's stories stay well within those frameworks.

Both stories assume a patriarchal structuring of society. Ruth begins with Elimelech in charge of Naomi and with their sons "taking wives" (1:1–4). When all three women are widowed, Naomi assumes that Ruth and Orpah have no alternative but to find security in the house of a husband (1:9), while Naomi's own future—and, in the end, Ruth's, when she insists on accompanying Naomi—will depend upon a male guardian figure or "restorer" (*go'el*; evv kinsman/redeemer) fulfilling his moral obligations (2:1; 3:1–2). When the restorer, Boaz, meets Ruth, he asks who (that is, which man) she belongs to (2:5). When Naomi sends Ruth to court him, she assumes that the man will tell Ruth what to do (3:4). When the legal position turns out to be more complicated than we thought, the destiny of the two women has to be determined by two male parties in the presence of ten of the city's male elders (4:1–12). When agreement is reached, it involves the man buying the woman in order to preserve the name of another man (4:10). When the story ends, it is with a list of the male line to which Ruth's son belongs (4:17–22).

Hannah's life, in turn, is substantially shaped and given its significance by the stereotypes of a patriarchal society (see 1 Sam 1–2). She, too, is presented to us as a man's wife, under his lordship, an appendage to him. She has to share even that status with someone else and bear the hurt that follows from this. Her significance or worth is determined first by her not having and then by her having a child (rather, a son). While Hannah's story does work within these stereotypes, it also works against them. Hannah is a woman open with her emotions, direct in her words, forthright with her husband, bold in her promises, courageous in her acceptance of Yahweh's promise, and vindicated in her trust in Yahweh. She seems to have found a form of freedom within stereotypes that were hallowed by nothing but tradition but which she could hardly demolish.

In Ruth, a questioning of customary attitudes is first hinted by Ruth's "clinging" to Naomi and her plea not to be forced to "leave" her: they are the expressions used of the man and woman in Gen 2:24. Back in Bethlehem, the two women begin with

---

[9] See P. D. Miscall, *The Workings of Old Testament Narratives* (Philadelphia: Fortress, 1983); L. G. Perdue, "'Is There Anyone Left of the House of Saul . . . ?': Ambiguity and the Characterization of David in the Succession Narrative," *JSOT* 30 (1984): 67–84.

initiative and move on to manipulating if not propositioning Boaz; despite the talk of Boaz telling Ruth what to do, it is the other way round (Ruth 3:7–9; what exactly Ruth did and what she invited is left allusive). When Boaz marries Ruth, the Bethlehem women see their child not as Elimelech's, and certainly not as the child of Boaz and Ruth (I remember reflecting when we got married that it did not really seem to be our occasion but our parents', and for Ruth and Boaz even the birth of their baby was not their own); "a son has been born to *Naomi*," they declare. Naomi, Ruth, and the Bethlehem women bear their own burdens and work out their own salvation in a man's world; "they are women in culture, women against culture, and women transforming culture."[10]

There are, then, a number of First Testament stories that imply reflection, or at least stimulate reflection, on what it means to be a man and what it means to be a woman. Once we leave Gen 1–3, however, there seems to be little in these stories that looks on the two together in relationship to each other. We do find such reflection, offered or encouraged, in Proverbs and the Song of Songs.

It is one of the major themes of the collected aphorisms that dominate Prov 10–31, and one of the two topics that dominate the sermons in doggerel verse that occupy the bulk of Prov 1–9. By nature, Proverbs does not systematize its reflection; it characteristically offers the reader individually encapsulated insights. These often look unbalanced in isolation; if one takes particular aphorisms such as the cartoons of the nagging wife out of the context of the rest of the book, Proverbs seems narrow and chauvinistic. Illuminating insights on what makes a marriage work emerge from bringing together the varied material in Proverbs on male and female roles and temptations and allowing the aphorisms and sermons to confront each other.

To a man, Proverbs says, "Love, don't wander." Keep alive a vision for a relationship that remains full of joyful delight, of enthusiastic affection, even when it is decades old (5:18–19). The will, not just autonomic feelings, is assumed to be involved. You commit yourself to loving her, to focusing on what attracts you to her rather than on what annoys you (cf. 10:12). Loving her must be wary of setting itself to changing her, though love does have a nurturing, transforming effect. It also nurtures the relationship itself, because of the loving response it draws from its object. The converse point is that marital unfaithfulness is both wrong and stupid (5:16–17, 20; 6:28–29). Proverbs 1–9 lays great emphasis on this point, probably because it sees a parallel between how husbands and wives relate and how God and Israel relate: marital faithfulness is a parable of religious faithfulness. This metaphor may have been further encouraged by the role that women ministers played in contemporary religions. The women that Proverbs warns men against are at one level these female religious functionaries. And this may be the reason the creation story pictures sin entering the garden through the *woman* yielding to the blandishments of the serpent, a fertility-cult symbol.

The twofold exhortation to men, "Love, don't wander," the positive with its negative corollary, may be paralleled by a twofold exhortation to women, "Do, don't nag." When a woman nags (19:13; 21:9, 19; cf. 15:17: 17:1), her complaints overtly

---

[10]Trible, *God and the Rhetoric of Sexuality*, 166, 198.

concern peccadilloes, shortcomings that look trivial yet that she is unable to ignore. If he loved her, she might be able to ignore them; it is one of the senses in which love hides a multitude of faults (10:12). A woman who is loved is unlikely to nag. But a woman who nags is not loved; it is a vicious circle.

A woman's nagging may also be a displaced way of giving expression to a general dissatisfaction with her lot in life. Here the positive exhortation is important. "Do [that is, achieve], don't nag." Proverbs closes with a sometimes derided portrait of an achieving woman (31:10–31). Home is still assumed to be the arena of what she does, though a man's work in that culture would also be more home-based than is the case in ours. But she is clearly a woman who is achieving and who is expected and trusted by her husband to achieve. This woman is surely less likely to be a nag.

Even when it is being positive, Proverbs is predominantly problem-centered in its treatment of sex, as of other topics. The Song of Songs offers a marked contrast. It is not even merely a manual of teaching about sexuality but a celebration of it.[11]

It has commonly not been read that way. In his book on the *Signs of Glory* in John's Gospel,[12] Richard Holloway notes how the first of these signs, at Cana, relates to two areas of life that easily go wrong, sex and drink. Enthusiasm for each can be a form of idolatry, because they offer ersatz versions of the love and joy that are to be found in God alone. The church has therefore often attempted to outlaw both sex and drink, but when it has sought to do so, it has had difficulty in living with Scripture, either with a story about Jesus facilitating drinking at a wedding or with poems about sexual love, which it rendered harmless by means of typology and allegory. (I recently heard an allegorical exposition of the enthusiasm for strong drink and male make-up in Ps 104:15, too.)

The Song of Songs no doubt assumes a context in faith and morality; certainly this is the context in which it is set, by virtue of appearing in scripture. But it has little or no overt concern with ethics or religion; it does not talk about what you ought to do, and it makes no mention of God. It does not mention marriage as the context of sexual activity, or children as its purpose, though again its context in scripture will imply that these are respectively its context and part of its purpose. But in itself the Song is a multifaceted expression of the feelings of two people in love: enthusiasm, excitement, longing, happiness, wonder, fulfillment, acceptance, delight, anticipation, joy.

A "garden" is a key image in the poems (e.g., Song 4:12–5:1; 6:1–12). Karl Barth treated the Song of Songs as an extended commentary on Gen 2:18–25.[13] It is almost as if in their love the woman and the man recover Paradise lost. As Irving Berlin put it, "Heaven, I'm in heaven. . . ." But only "almost." "In the Song, Paradise is limited by the fallen world; Death is undefeated, society imposes shame on the lovers, time inevitably separates them. . . . The ideal harmony of 'I am my beloved's and my beloved is mine' disappears on the last appearance of the formula: 'I am my beloved's and his desire is for me'" (Song 7:10, echoing Gen

---

[11] See further chapter 24 below.
[12] (London: DLT, 1982).
[13] See *Church Dogmatics* iii/1 and 2 (Edinburgh: Clark, 1958, 1960).

3:16).[14] As the warnings of Proverbs are accompanied by some positive statements about sex, so the celebration of the Song is accompanied by indications that it has not surrendered to romanticism.

2. Models for Women and Men in Ministry in the First Testament

"Models" here means not so much examples to follow as illustrations of people coping with questions and issues that may be like ours. Like us, they have to deal with the reality of ministering in a patriarchal society and of the need to find ways through that. Their way of doing so provides us with stories to set against our own experiences so that we can understand our own experiences. They can then encourage us to dream of ways we might operate in our very different cultural context (they are inspired, and therefore inspiring). And they can function as checks on our dreams (they have the authority of the word of God).

First, there is Miriam and her little brothers. If it had not been for Miriam, there would have been no Moses, at least no Moses as the person he became (Exod 2:1–10). She is then the first Israelite to be called a prophet in scripture, leading in praise, music, dancing, and theological reflection. Was the song that Moses and the Israelites sang (Exod 15:1a) a song that Miriam composed (Exod 15:20–21)? If so, she has been marginalized in the story but not squeezed out.

Miriam and Aaron's criticism of Moses for marrying an African (Num 12) may illustrate the tensions that can arise when men and women work together.[15] Marriage complicates ministry. The pastor's wife may come to have excessive significance in the ministry. Miriam and Aaron could feel crowded out, even if mistakenly. Miriam pays a price for that feeling, though Moses prays for her and she is healed.[16]

It would be nice to feel that if Moses had written the Pentateuch, he would have given more prominence to his sister. . . .

Second, there is Deborah and Barak. Deborah is the first prophet in the promised land. It is as a prophet, too, that she leads in singing, intercession, and theological reflection (Judg 5). But before that she is Israel's greatest leader in the story from Joshua to Saul (Judg 4; English translations use the word "judge," but "leader" gives a better idea of that word's significance).

Deborah helped people make decisions about disputes in the community (Judg 4:5); she evidently had the kind of wisdom Solomon had, the discernment of good and evil (1 Kgs 3:9). She commissioned Barak to go and take on the Canaanites, but he was unwilling to do so unless she came with him. She therefore agreed to

---

[14] Francis Landy, "The Song of Songs and the Garden of Eden," *JBL* 98 (1979): 513–28 (524); see further Landy, *Paradoxes of Paradise: Identity and Difference in the Song of Songs* (Sheffield: Almond, 1983).

[15] Admittedly, the central issue in Num 12 is likely the relationship of Torah, prophecy, and priesthood, for which Moses, Miriam, and Aaron respectively stand.

[16] On this story, see Renita J. Weems, *Just a Sister Away* (San Diego: LuraMedia, 1988).

do so but pointed out that a woman was therefore going to get the credit for how things turned out. Deborah and Jael evidently have more macho temperaments than Barak. As a man he prefers operating as number two to being number one. He likes the security of women's headship.

Then there is Isaiah, Ms. Isaiah, Second Isaiah, and Ms. Second Isaiah. While Mr. Isaiah is eventually described as a prophet in the book called Isaiah (Isa 37:2; 38:1; 39:3), he does not call himself a prophet. The only person Mr. Isaiah describes as a prophet is Ms. Isaiah (Isa 8:3). Yet the only ministry we are told she exercises is having children. It turns out to be the means of bringing a powerful message (Isa 8:3–4).

A different ball game is played in Isa 40–55. Second Isaiah seems to be a man; at least he has a beard (Isa 50:6). But a woman's voice makes itself heard in Isa 40–55 more clearly than anywhere else in scripture. Second Isaiah speaks like someone who knows what it is like to be a wife, someone unable to have children, a mother, someone abandoned by her husband, a divorcée, and a widow, and also perhaps someone who has been raped. Awareness of these experiences decisively shapes the way he thinks of God and God's relationship with the people and the way he thinks of the people of God and their experience. Presumably no one woman has personally shared all these experiences with him, even Ms. Second Isaiah, but he has apparently learned about them from her and from other women, and they have thus decisively shaped the theology of the chapters that many people see as the high point of the First Testament.

Fourth, there are Josiah, Hilkiah, Huldah, and Jeremiah. When King Josiah's workers find a Torah book behind the air-conditioning system while they are remodeling in the temple, Josiah knows he had better ask prophetic advice about what to do in response to its scary contents. The person for whom Hilkiah and Josiah's aides make a beeline is Huldah (2 Kgs 22). Were they scared to ask Jeremiah, who should have been available at the time? If so, they get more than they bargain for from Huldah. "Tell the man who sent you to me . . .": no exaggerated respect for manhood or monarchy here. Huldah tells it extremely straight to the king but also promises that Yahweh has heard the way he responded when he read Yahweh's word.

Huldah promises Josiah that he will die in peace. It did not work out that way (1 Kgs 23:29). Does he forfeit the right to claim this promise from his co-worker?

Finally, there are Vashti, Esther, and Mordecai. Mordecai is Esther's cousin, stepfather, and mentor, but she has the position of influence at court because the king fancies her and makes her queen in place of the radical feminist Vashti, who is too feisty for the king. Traditional roles are reversed as Mordecai passes on the gossip that Esther is in a position to do something about (Esth 2:22). He later urges her to take her life into her hands to do what in her position she can do, as he cannot, to save her people. This involves being involved in the politics of the court. Mordecai does the backroom work, fasting. She both fasts and does the frontline work.

At the close of the story, Esther and Mordecai proclaim that Jewish people should henceforth observe the feast of Purim, as they still do. Only Moses and Aaron have previously exercised such power. But it is Mordecai who ends up as second-in-command in the empire. Esther dominates the center of the story but is missing at its beginning and end.

3. Women and Men in the New Testament

The significance of sexuality is qualified in distinctive ways by the New Testament. At Cana, Jesus affirms marriage but refuses to allow it to interfere with considerations of whether his time is yet come. He apparently remained celibate, as did Paul. The time being short, Paul rather wished that all believers could do so, though he recognizes this is unrealistic (1 Cor 7).

Given this position, it is striking to find Paul affirming the position of women here and elsewhere in 1 Corinthians. His views need to be understood against the background of the way the average pagan Corinthian saw women and the way the Corinthian Christian women saw themselves.[17] In Greek cities generally, girls were mostly confined to the home, except for occasions such as festivals and funerals. Women were not expected to be educated. They might learn to read and write and to cook and sew, but they were not expected to be able to appreciate intellectual matters or serious conversation. Married women were regarded as inferior to their husbands; their place was in the home looking after the house and raising the family. They could go to the theater but took no part in intellectual, political, or civil life. A man's serious personal relationships would be with other men, not with his wife. Intellectual writers addressed their teaching to other men. A woman had no legal status separate from her husband's; she was part of his property. He had no obligation to be faithful to her, though indiscretion on her part could lead to divorce, whereas it was much harder for her to get a divorce from him.

The women believers at Corinth were released from the conventions, standards, and values of this age and called to witness to those of the age to come. Many of the activities Paul condemns among the Corinthians likely reflect their understanding of their Christian freedom. Sexuality was one area this affected. Man and woman are one by creation (Gen 1–2) and one in Christ Jesus (Gal 3:28). As the Corinthians apparently put it, "everyone has Christ for his [or her] head" (1 Cor 11:13); Paul seems to be quoting the Corinthians' own catchphrase, both to affirm and to qualify it. In light of this, why keep distinctions such as the way you wear your hair? Why not let your hair down? Why should a man not be free to have a perm or a woman to have a crew cut if each person feels like it? Why keep to arbitrary conventions? (It is likely that neither hats nor veils are the issue in 1 Cor 11; more likely the whole chapter is about coiffure. But the main point is not affected by this question.)

In responding to the Corinthians' excesses, Paul does not go back on "all are one in Christ Jesus." He shows himself as interested in teaching wives as husbands (see 1 Cor 7). Both are morally responsible. They are on equal footing regarding sexual gratification. The wife has authority over her husband, as well as vice versa (1 Cor 7:4). Ephesians 5 works in a parallel way. Wives are to defer to their husbands; but this exhortation comes in the context of a command to all believers to defer to one another, a command that does not imply the one to be deferred to has

---

[17] What follows is largely dependent on R. J. Banks, "Paul and Women's Liberation," *Interchange* 18 (Sydney: AFES, 1976): 81–105; cf. Banks, *Paul's Idea of Community* (Exeter: Paternoster, 1980), 113–31.

the right or responsibility to give the orders. The implications of the command are rather exemplified in what follows in the exhortation. Their implication for husbands is more demanding than it is for wives: their headship implies not that they make the decisions but that they make the sacrifices. It is husbands who have to walk the self-denying way of the cross. And the submission of their wives lies in their letting them do so.

In 1 Cor 16, Paul speaks of Aquila and Priscilla together having a congregation meeting in their house (it was hardly their house legally); both are Paul's colleagues in Acts, Priscilla often being named first. In 1 Cor 11, Paul assumes that in church it is normal for women to take part in prayer and prophecy, which would likely be seen as the two most important activities that happened there. There is thus apparently no difference in the roles women and men play in worship. Yet outward differences between them are to be preserved. All are one and all are equal, but all are not identical. Paul takes up the point fundamental to Gen 2 itself, that men and women were created different. The talk about "headship" underlines this point; "head of" in Greek as much suggests "origin of" as "master of." Man and woman are of different origin, and that is a parable of their different nature, to be preserved by differences of appearance. Paul's view contrasts with the one that asserts that men and women are really the same, apart from certain superficial physical differences. He does not pronounce on what these differences are; he simply invites us not to lose sight of them. They are one aspect of the diversity of humanity that is part of the way God has made it.

First Timothy 2 takes a contrary view of the involvement of men and women in leading worship and compares with the fact that all Jesus' twelve disciples were men. The difference is often taken to imply that 1 Timothy is by someone other than Paul, though this does not solve the question of the theological relationship between the passages. First Timothy embodies an alternative way of responding to a tricky situation similar to that at Corinth, though perhaps more severe. The Pastoral Epistles indicate in various ways a need in the churches addressed to cope with difficult pastoral problems by firm leadership and affirmation of the church's tradition, and the attitude to the position of women belongs in this context. The way Genesis is used to support the positions taken, like much other use of scripture in the New Testament, follows conventional contemporary forms of argument rather than reflecting the meaning of Genesis itself, but this does not make 1 Timothy unfaithful to the First Testament, for a similar stance to the one taken in 1 Timothy sometimes appears in the First Testament (even if it is not in Gen 1–3). Both Testaments offer creation and redemption visions of what it means to be a man and a woman; both also implicitly recognize the difficulty of living by those visions. Both offer paradigms of believers trying to live in the light of these visions, yet to live realistically in a wayward world.

24

WHAT MIGHT THE SONG OF SONGS DO FOR PEOPLE?

Only perhaps in communities that are both essentially patriarchal and committed to the authority of the Bible may the Song still have a liberating effect and be able to suggest a vision of an alternative style of being. (David Clines)[1]

Keep this book away from your girlfriend—it contains too many of your secrets to let it fall into the wrong hands.[2]

Soon after I moved to California, someone commented (perhaps quoting from someone else) that in Britain one does theology looking over one's shoulder at the Germans but in the United States one does theology looking over one's shoulder at fundamentalism. Most of my students come from communities that are "essentially patriarchal and committed to the authority of the Bible," indeed fundamentalist. They themselves mostly repudiate patriarchalism and fundamentalism (or keep quiet about the matter), though they may have a hard time ministering in such communities when they return to them—as they will have a hard time ministering in the light of other aspects of the different understanding of the Bible into which the seminary has sought to invite them. But then, surely most readers of the Bible belong to patriarchal communities that are committed to the Bible's authority? It would therefore be no trivial achievement if the Song of Songs were to have a liberating effect and suggest an alternative style of being for such average Bible readers.[3]

So what would this look like? I begin from stories about such communities on three continents.

---

[1] David J. A. Clines, *Interested Parties* (JSOTSup 205; Sheffield: Sheffield Academic Press, 1995), 117.

[2] From a review of Nick Hornby's novel *High Fidelity*, as quoted in the blurb of his novel *About a Boy*.

[3] First published as "So What Might the Song of Songs Do to Them?" in *Reading From Right to Left* (ed. J. C. Exum and H. G. M. Williamson; Festschrift for David J. A. Clines; London / New York: Sheffield Academic Press, 2003), 173–83.

1. The Context

The southern part of the United States is the most Christian part of this quintessentially Christian nation. At a Dixie Chicks' concert in Los Angeles, no song received a more enthusiastic response than Dennis Linde's "Goodbye Earl." According to the story it tells, Earl started abusing Wanda soon after they married. After Wanda initiated divorce proceedings and Earl responded by putting her into intensive care, she and her friend Mary Anne formed a plan. They cooked Earl a nice southern meal with black-eyed peas and something more sinister, and when it had done its work they wrapped his body in a tarpaulin and dropped it in the lake. At the end of the story Mary Anne and Wanda are running a roadside stand on Highway 109, selling Tennessee ham and strawberry jam. The disclaimer "The Dixie Chicks do not advocate premeditated murder, but love getting even" was not enough to stop their song getting banned on the radio, presumably by men.

This past quarter, a student of mine from southern Africa wrote a paper on gender violence in Judges and Isaiah, interweaving biblical study with accounts of her life at home. She began with an account of homestead life in her grandparents' day. Her grandfather had eleven wives, each of whom had six to ten children. His wives' huts stood in a half-moon, his in the center so that he could monitor and control his family. If another man angered him and he could not fight the man, he would beat one of his wives. When one wife got pregnant and he thought another man was the father, before the other wives he beat her till she aborted. The wives fled but returned in fear of wild animals, and as the ringleader the student's grandmother was beaten, her collarbone being broken. Her parents were among the first people who came to believe in Christ when Christian missionaries followed on the coattails of British colonists and soldiers, but one should not assume that Christianization totally transforms a culture in this respect. The woman had just heard about the death of a friend after being beaten by her husband. The story of the Levite's concubine in Judg 19 reminded her of a woman who used to run away to her brother's house because her husband beat her. The husband would always come to get his wife back, and the brother would always surrender her because the husband had the right to do what he liked with her, as his property. If she had run back to her parents' home, this would be to invite a lecture from her mother on submission to her husband. Eventually he hit her on the head with an iron bar, and she died. The same property understanding of marriage means that women have no right to withhold themselves sexually from their husbands when the latter have contracted AIDS or HIV through their promiscuity, so that many of the countless women who have died from AIDS were infected by their husbands.

Another student spoke of the place of women in society and church in his experience of growing up in Korea. He thinks Korean culture was once more egalitarian, but under Confucian influence the family came to be thought of in patrilineal terms, and the church now strongly supports the patriarchal tradition. So if a woman's first child is a girl, Christians may wonder whether she must have committed a sin. Marriages are arranged by the couple's parents and their pastor. It is then assumed that a woman leaves her parents' family when she marries and joins her husband's parents' family. The married couple is expected to live in his parents' house and under their authority, especially if he is the eldest son. This tradition is seen as an ethical principle, and a couple who resisted the expectation would cause a scandal in society worthy of reporting in the newspaper. The church accepts this tradition as part of its emphasis on the duty of respect to parents, though it does not emphasize any correlative obligation of parents to children. On marriage a woman is expected to resign her job to stay at home in the shared ménage, and the situation is a frequent cause of conflict between the parents and the married couple, especially between mother-in-law and daughter-in-law. The church's teaching is that one should be thankful in the context of such difficulties and believe that an attitude of thankfulness is the key to resolving difficulties. The situation is also a cause of conflict between the couple themselves, and a cause of a kind of formalization of the relationship rather than the development of a personal relationship. It is a major reason for divorce and for Korean emigration to North America.

What might the Song of Songs do for such Christian cultures?

2. Allegory and Displacement

Let us first dispose of one possible misapprehension. It is traditional to understand the Song of Songs as an allegory of Christ's relationship with us. Now sometimes allegorical interpretation derives from unease about a text's literal meaning, and the origin of allegorical interpretation of the Song could then lie in unease about sex. But the background of allegorical interpretation in general is more complex, and so is its function with regard to the Song. The problem about the Bible which generates allegorical interpretation is not so much what it says about the issues it talks about. It is that it does not always talk about the issues that interpreters think it should talk about. For instance, many Christians are inclined to assume that the Bible is supposed to be a manual about how to relate to God, and allegorical interpretation can focus on making texts speak to that agenda. While applying allegorical interpretation to the Song will help people who are uneasy about sex, its background need not lie in that unease but rather in that broader assumption about what the Song must be about. I doubt whether Christians in general are in great need of liberation from sexual repression into the joy of sex. I recently heard a conservative pastor say that to satisfy the interests of his congregation, he really needed only three Sunday school classes—one on sex, one on the end times, and one on whether there will be sex in the end times. Conservative Christians are as keen on sex as anyone else. But their presuppositions about God and the Bible do not encourage them to bring Bible and sex into relationship, except in certain moralistic ways. Their traditional Christian morality may indeed have some effect on the way they give expression to their enthusiasm for sex. The divorce rate among conservative Christians in the United States is apparently even higher than among other groups, because people still feel obliged to get married in order to have sex, but the marriages then do not last. In this connection the liberating effect of the Song of Songs might lie in encouraging conservative Christians to rework the way they think about sex and marriage and their relationship, given that the Song does not link these two.

I do not mean the Song would not presuppose a link, which in its own culture is unlikely. If heuristically we may reify the lovers in the Song as if the poems all concern the same couple, whether or not this was originally so, the Song does point to their being a man and a woman whose sexual involvement belongs in the context of an exclusive one-to-one relationship so all-consuming that one would expect them to reckon it would be lifelong—in other words, a quasi-marital relationship. (The wisdom of the poems may be Solomonic, but it is difficult to imagine the historical Solomon in a relationship like this one.) Certainly the process whereby the Judean community came to treat the Song as scripture would have involved the presupposition that the sexual relationship belongs in the context of marriage. "Certainly" means I have no evidence of this, but the circumstantial evidence is strong. Indirect testimony to the fact that readers knew how to read the Song appears in the rabbinic warning about singing it in the banquet hall as if it were an ordinary piece of music (e.g., *b. Sanhedrin* 101a). In contrast, there is neither direct nor circumstantial evidence for the often-stated view that the Song was accepted into the canon only on the basis of first having been understood as a treatise on the relationship between Yahweh and Israel.

Yet some people who listened to the Song presumably noticed that either the couple were not married or that theirs was a very odd kind of relationship involving an inversion of the practice of living together without being married. The Song may take for granted that this couple were on their way to marriage, at least, or had an odd kind of marriage, but it is not very interested in that aspect of the relationship. Indeed, it is not interested in it at all, except in the picture of a wedding procession in 3:6–11 and the epithet "bride" in 4:8–5:1. It assumes that marriage is not the only framework within which sex needs to be considered, because marriage is about many things other than sex. There is food for thought in the joke about marriage being when two people stop having sex. Marriage is, for instance, a way of imaging God in the world as two people who are markedly different from each other make a lifelong commitment to each other that creates something bigger than the sum of their parts and persists no matter what pressures drive them apart. Marriage is an institutionalized, legal, community structure for such a lifelong one-on-one relationship. Marriage is an arrangement in whose context people can have sex so that within it children may be born, brought up, educated, and looked after. Marriage is a device whereby a woman moves from the ownership and protection of one man (her father) to those of another man (her husband).

We could have most of those things without having marriage, but marriage provides a way of having them. The Song is concerned with none of them but with the happiness and the fear, the anxiety and the fulfillment of sexual love. In some cultures there has been little link between those and marriage, as is so now in Western culture. There is little direct indication that First Testament or New Testament scriptures link the happiness and the fear, the anxiety and the fulfillment of sexual love, with marriage. Even if the Genesis accounts of the origin of man and woman are much less patriarchal than they have been read, they do not emphasize the personal relationship of marriage in the way we might wish.[4] Indeed, outside the Song the scriptures show little interest in the happiness and the fear, the anxiety and the fulfillment of sexual love. This is food for thought regarding either the scriptures or Western culture or both. But the importance of this topic in Western culture shows how important the Song is. Not its least significance is to require Christians to bring the topic of sex into Christian discussion in connections other than the moral ones that often preoccupy us.

Roland E. Murphy observes that an interpretation of the Song as portraying the relationship between God and the people of God "held sway from late antiquity until relatively modern times and continues even today to find some support."[5] These words could give the impression that such an understanding has now been generally abandoned. This is only the case in the rarified groves of the academe. It is still the way most readers understand the song. Perhaps paradoxically (or perhaps not), even in some Christian circles that are enthusiastic about sex, an interpretation of the Song as referring to the love relationship of God and the believer remains alive and well. It is important to continue to urge that this is a meaning imposed on the Song. It offers no hint that the poems have anything to do with our love relationship with God or God's with us. The allegorical understanding has been provided with partial justification on the grounds that elsewhere scripture portrays the relationship between God and people by analogy with marriage, but this justification does not work. We have noted that the Song is not concerned with marriage. Conversely, there is no hint elsewhere in scripture (for instance, in the Psalms) that we have a relationship with God that on our side has the dynamics of sexual love.

The kind of love that our love for God resembles is rather that of adult children and parents, or subjects and rulers, or students and teachers. The relationship is characterized by warmth, affection, mutual self-sacrifice, and commitment, but the disparity of status and power make the dynamics of the love portrayed in the Song inappropriate to it. Perhaps it would be odd if we thought we had a relationship like this with the Holy One, and the scriptures do not suggest we do. As the Song does not speak of a love that involves self-sacrifice and commitment, so the scriptures never speak of our emotional relationship with God in terms of passionate love. Love for God is a matter of commitment. Indeed, in scripture, people never declare that they love God. In the English Bible the exception that proves the rule is the opening of Psalm 18, where the verb is *rakham*—the only use of the qal of this verb and surely one of the strangest and most enigmatic readings in the Hebrew Bible (it perhaps follows Aramaic usage, where the word refers to commitment). The converse may be less true; scripture is less reticent in attributing emotion to God's relationship with us, which may also be suggestive about being a parent or a leader or a teacher. But the Song's particular portrayal of relationship is misleading when applied to God. The allegorical interpretation of the Song thus fails a standard traditional test for such interpretation, that it should fit the way other parts of scripture

---

[4] See, e.g., David J. A. Clines, *What Does Eve Do to Help?* (JSOTSup 94; Sheffield: Sheffield Academic Press, 1990), 25–48.

[5] *The Song of Songs* (Minneapolis: Fortress, 1990), 11.

speak more directly. Love's shafts are fiery, flames of Yahweh (8:6). If human love reflects God's love in this respect,[6] this is a frightening fact. Other parts of scripture imply that God is always reaching out for us and wanting to be in relationship with us, like a parent in relation to children. It is not a normal part of this relationship for God to be like a beloved whom you are not sure you will be able to find.

Perhaps looking for an emotional love relationship with God is a form of displacement; we look to God for something that is designed to appear in our human relationships. As with many other aspects of life, no doubt God is prepared to live with this displacement on the part of people who do not have other human beings with whom to enjoy this love relationship. But there are dangers in the displacement. We may be avoiding the human relationships that are designed to be the context in which these human capacities are realized, perhaps because these are more fraught with risk and vulnerability. Getting it off on God provides us with a cheap form of intimacy. In the Song, there are at least two sorts of reasons for the pain of the relationship, reasons that come from other people's attitudes and reasons that come from inside the individuals. In our own relationships, at least, even the first kind may be externalizations of the latter, of the hesitations that lie inside the individuals: the tension between seeking intimacy and fearing intimacy. Further, we may be avoiding the form of love appropriate to a relationship with God: the acceptance and the making of sacrifice. Our love for God is more about letting God make a sacrifice for us and committing ourselves to trusting God and living for God than about woozy feelings. The allegorical understanding of the Song might (or might not) have been an edifying way for medieval celibates to use it, but it is important for people, especially men, in the cultures to which I have referred not to evade the implications of its literal meaning. Whereas Helmut Gollwitzer suggested that sexual love is here celebrated as "its own legitimation,"[7] Murphy declared that on the contrary it is to be treasured because it is a vital part of God's gracious design for human life.[8] While Murphy is right theologically, as far as the Song itself is concerned Gollwitzer seems to me to have the better of the argument.

3. The Nature of the Relationship

So what does the Song tell us about the sexual relationship? It opens with shocking directness: "May he kiss me with the kisses of his mouth" (1:2). The poems draw—or rather yank—readers straight inside the physical relationship between two people. Like many movies in their portrayal of such relationships, the Song is not saying human beings should be like this, but just that we are, and that readers had better own the fact—in the way that much of Proverbs does not say that life should be a certain way, simply that it is. Secular poetry, music, films, and novels presuppose this, even though religious literature usually does not.

---

[6] So Murphy, *The Song of Songs*, 104.
[7] *A Song of Love* (Philadelphia: Fortress, 1979), 30.
[8] *The Song of Songs*, 101.

The poems open with the woman's words, notwithstanding this being "the Song of Songs which is *lishelomoh*." Whatever the meaning of that expression,[9] it is striking that the phrase introduces poems in which a woman speaks first and longest and often takes the initiative in the relationship. Whereas NIV's headings describe the man and the woman as "lover" and "beloved," the poems point readers to a more egalitarian understanding of the relationship, questioning any assumption that the man has to make the approaches or set the pace (TNIV has "he" and "she"). A woman is free to take the initiative and a man is free to expect that. Both express appreciation and longing for the other.

The poems do not prioritize the physical over the relational or the relational over the physical. They assume that the two belong together, like body and spirit. They do reflect the fact that physical appearance may be more important to a man than to a woman; the man spends more time talking about this than the woman does. They invite a woman to be aware of that. She may make the most of it if she wishes, but she might also be wary of it. If David Clines is right that the Song is a male fantasy,[10] then one of its values to women will be its revelations regarding what men are like. Women could of course discover this by watching movies or sitcoms, but these are not in the Bible and therefore have less formal authority than the Song of Songs, even if they have more effect in shaping behavior than the average book of the Bible does. Or, the Song's angle may suggest it was written by a woman; whether or not this is so, it does (sometimes) represent a woman's perspective.

The presence of the Song in scripture implies that the kind of relationship it celebrates might be significant for people in general, not just for young people on their way to marriage. One reason is that "Everybody's searching for intimacy. . . . Everybody's hurting for intimacy."[11] The Song is significant, for instance, for married people with their lives focused on their children and their work, and middle-aged people whose children now have children of their own, and people whose spouse is handicapped or has died, and in Western culture, for people who have stayed single or have divorced. In Western culture, the attractiveness of romantic comedies for people in all these situations parallels this. So does the capacity of middle-aged or old people to fall in love again when their marriage has gone stale or they have divorced. There is nothing time-limited about falling in love.

---

[9] EVV imply that *l* suggests authorship, but BDB notes that this is a rare usage and other meanings of the preposition seem more likely. It might mean "to"; were these poems offered or dedicated to Solomon? It might mean "belonging to" (cf. "Belonging to the Korahites," Ps. 42); in other words, they count as Wisdom. It might mean "for"; for Solomon to use or learn from? Since he was especially inclined to use sexual relationships as a political device, this would be a telling hope. It might mean "on behalf of," with similar implications. It might mean "about," with some irony. The succeeding references to Solomon (1:5; 3:6–11; 8:11–12) suggest "about" or some similar meaning rather than "by." My guess is that (as BDB implies in connection with *l* in the Psalms) the meaning of the expression changed over the centuries. If it originally suggested "to" it may have come to mean "belonging to" and then "by," when people wanted to associate the authorship of works within scripture with someone famous.

[10] See "Why Is There a Song of Songs, and What Does It Do to You If You Read It?" *Interested Parties*, 94–121.

[11] From a song by Billy Steinberg and others.

In the good old days, people often had marriages arranged for them by their parents or by the community, or had to get their family's involvement even if first they did get drawn to one another. If they were lucky or the job was well done, they could then fall in love with each other (cf. Gen 24). Western cultures do not have the benefit of that arrangement, and many people stay single not out of choice but because their numbers never come up in the lottery. But because people are still single in their thirties or forties or fifties, that does not mean they stop longing for such a relationship. Of course there are also people who stay single by choice and are happy that way, so we must not assume that every single person wishes he or she were married. And there are many married people who wish they were single. But in traditional cultures, no doubt many arranged marriages never led to love, and the way we organize relationships in our culture means that many people are not going to get married.

In California, where "Everybody's Searching for Intimacy" was written,[12] everybody is avoiding intimacy. This is not to deny that at some level they are longing for it, but the problem is that they are also hurting for it. A therapist friend pointed out to me, when I was dismissive about their avoiding intimacy, that half of them have been brought up in broken homes and are disabled for intimacy. As another country song puts it, "Nobody love, nobody gets hurt,"[13] but people are in no position to take the risk. The Song invites readers to summon up the strength to take the risk. Sitting under the surface of their lives, if not on the surface, most have the kind of feelings described in the Song. These poems, like the romantic comedies, bring them to the surface in some way. One might have thought that was a risky thing, but maybe the existence of the poems in scripture suggests it is a good thing, or perhaps just a thing that happens. One reason is that if readers do not own these feelings, the feelings may catch them out as they find expression in inappropriate ways. They may, for instance, fall in love when they are not in a position to do so. The Song gives expression to intrinsic human needs. It presupposes the human need for loving recognition and acceptance, for the sense of being special, which makes self-acceptance more possible. The girl describes herself as dark-complexioned or darkened by the sun, but pretty (1:5–6); she is okay about herself because she is loved. She is only a common wildflower, but to him she is a lovely flower against the background of weeds (2:1–2). He is not an impressive tree compared with the giant redwoods; but as far as she is concerned, he provides shade and produces lovely fruit (2:3). They are just an ordinary couple, but their love turns them into a prince and a princess (3:6–11).

The Song invites its readers to recognize that relationships are always on the way and continue to involve risk. They cannot be taken for granted. The couple spend much time in ecstatic enjoyment of each other's presence but also spend much time in pained grief at separation from each other. This separation makes them feel ill (2:5; 5:8). They long for meeting and seek each other anxiously. She

---

[12] It was sung in its hit version by The Corrs, who are Irish, but Steinberg is a Californian.
[13] A song by Bobbie Cryner, known to me in the version by Suzy Bogguss. They are allegedly words written out by the orthographically challenged would-be robber of a twenty-four-hour supermarket who meant to write "Nobody move, nobody gets hurt."

does not know where she may find him (1:7–8). She can only dream of their being able to live together (3:1–5). She dreams of missing him or losing him and of her dreams turning to nightmares, as happens in a romantic comedy (5:2–8). He seems to have disappeared: is he off with someone else (6:1–3)? There is an "if only" about the relationship, caused by the need to observe society's constraints (8:1–3). She still wants him to make her the most valuable thing in the world to him. Her passionate, jealous love for him (*'ahabah* is explained by *qin'ah*) is fierce as death, as strong as Sheol. He will not be able to resist it. Vast floods could not quench those fiery flames it flashes (8:6–7). Experience suggests this is not true of every passionate love; people do fall out of love. In the Song the point is that when you are the subject or the object of such love, you cannot do anything to make yourself stop loving the other person or to make the other person stop loving you. And as you cannot decide when it goes, so you cannot decide when it comes, and therefore, for instance, try to buy it (8:7b).

"I am my beloved's and his desire is for me" (7:10). There are a number of ways of reading the statement, all of which may be instructive. The word "desire" comes only twice elsewhere. In Gen 4:7 it is unequivocally negative, referring to sin's desire for Cain. Does the Song realistically acknowledge the way our selfish instincts spoil even the idyll of love? There is no Hollywood ending here, then. But in Gen 3:16 "desire" could be neutral or positive: the woman will have a natural sexual desire for her husband, but he will dominate her sexually and in other ways. Or, the negative connotations of the man's domination and of the word "desire" in Gen 4 could imply that in Gen 3 it refers to lust. Song 7:10 could then be implying that sexual desire (here the man's) is okay, or could be accepting the fact that love and lust are mixed and not be fretting at it (cf. 7:12: "There I will give you my love"?).

Notwithstanding the impossibility of controlling whether another person falls in love with one, or of making oneself fall out of love, the poems talk about not arousing love till the right moment (e.g., 2:7). To some extent, then, at least, we can control whether love gets aroused. This implication contrasts with the mythology of Western culture, which takes love as an irresistible force. Yet the Song also talks about having one's heart captured (4:9); that is, it recognizes that one person may overwhelm another whether the latter wants this or not. The poems keep asking for love not to be aroused before its time, but they themselves arouse love in a way that for many readers may be before its time.

They also raise the question whether people can rekindle love when the flame seems to have gone, in a way that also fits the exhortation in Prov 5:15–19. People do find security in a love relationship that leads to marriage, but once they take that for granted, they may imperil it, in several senses. Part of the thrill of the not-yet-married relationship is its not-yet-ness. It has the excitement of being on a journey. This is also one of the attractions of having an affair. So there is a sense in which couples need not to take each other for granted and need to see themselves as still on the way. One image in the poems is that of wanting to get away from everyone else (2:10–13), and couples need that.

The first time I gave a nascent version of this chapter in a lecture, a man in his thirties rather scornfully suggested that I was taking these expressions of teenage feelings too seriously, but he then told his discussion group (I later heard) that he said this because he was uncomfortably aware that his marriage no longer had the spark of the Song. He knew I was raising the question whether he might have a vision for rekindling love. In papers they wrote, three middle-aged women in the class also described their interaction with the Song. For one, getting attracted to another man was making her try to rekindle love in her relationship with her husband; she was succeeding, and getting a response. The second as a single person had been caused to revisit the great love of her life and do some more coming to terms with the fact that that relationship came to an end, and yet somehow find hope for this part of her. The third had been abused as a teenager and had never been at ease about sex, but the Song had been giving her a new vision or hope for her sexual relationship with her husband. The Song thus came to her, too, as a gospel text, a promise about God's vision for us that may only be fully realized at the resurrection, but in some sense will be realized. She reminded me of an aspect of my experience with my handicapped wife. When Ann was first diagnosed with multiple sclerosis, a pastor invited us to live with the comment once made to Jesus at a wedding, "You have kept the good wine till last" (John 2:10). Our experience over the years has been that Ann has lost more and more of her mobility and mental abilities, and I do not know what that pastor's words might mean. Yet I know they are somehow true, and not just in the slightly trivial sense that everything will be okay in heaven. Indeed, thinking about the Song makes me reflect on the way over the past year or two I have been trying to let myself feel the warmth of feelings for Ann that I used to have, which is a painful business because it reminds me of happier times and because I can never know whether there is any response from her; but it still feels also a good thing.

If the Bible-believing patriarchal communities of southern Africa or of the U.S. south or of the flourishing Korean church were to read the Song of Songs, it could surely be a liberating text that suggested a vision of an alternative style of being. No doubt it would cause some trouble, too, as liberation does.

25

How Should We Think about Same-Sex Relationships?

It is easy to speak or write on this subject in a way that comes across as offensive or as condescending to some people.[1] I am sorry if anything I say has that effect.

1. Resources and Norms

Christian life and theology are traditionally committed to shaping themselves by what they find in scripture, the Christian tradition, and human insight. Scripture means the Torah, the Prophets, and the Writings, plus the New Testament, with some churches adding the further books in the Greek and other canons as works they read and utilize but do not reckon to treat as inherently authoritative theological resources. Christian tradition means the stream of informally recognized key figures such as Athanasius, Augustine, Thomas Aquinas, Luther, Calvin, and (for Anglicans/Episcopalians like me) Hooker, plus the agreements that many Christian churches came to make that are expressed in the historic creeds, plus convictions expressed in different denominations' confessions (for Anglicans/Episcopalians, the Thirty-Nine Articles). I then use the term "human insight" as a catch-all expression covering reason, experience (religious and other), and scientific discovery. Scripture and tradition are also repositories of human insight, but I will use this last expression simply to denote insight that comes from elsewhere.

These potential sources of wisdom, truth, and guidance constitute both resources and norms. They include resources that we can utilize freely, by our own discretion, sources of wisdom and obligation whose inherent authority we respond to. They also include norms that we recognize and to which we surrender our discretion. Traditionally, scripture is "the primary norm for Christian faith and life."[2] It is our supreme resource and norm because of its distinctive and crucial link with the story of God's activity in Israel that came to a climax in Jesus. Christian tradition and human insight are also significant resources, but they cannot trump scripture.

---

[1] Not previously published.
[2] So the "Virginia Report," *The Report of the Inter-Anglican Theological and Doctrinal Commission* (London: Anglican Consultative Council, 1997), §3.6.

Further, the collocation of faith and life in that phrase is significant: questions such as same-sex relationships concern not merely ethics or human rights but theology, and theology needs to shape ethics. How we live is to be based on the way things are and the way God designed them to be. At least, that is the traditional Christian position; in terms of the relationship between theology and ethics, liberation theology has drawn attention to an opposite possibility: praxis makes us ask new questions about theology and maybe come to different answers. But in doing so, it already rests on some implicit theological assumptions.

There are Christians who would put the resources of scripture, tradition, and insight into a more dynamic relationship and reckon there is no fixed differential in status between them. They simply offer us a range of resources, and we engage in a continual process of reflection on issues in light of them. I make two negative comments on this. First, if we see ourselves as making our own decisions between these resources, in reality we are not declining to locate normative status anywhere. We are making our human insight the norm; we condemn ourselves to believing only things that make sense to us. There is thus a pragmatic reason for resisting this view; it makes us forever the prisoners of our own perspective and culture. Second, there is a more explicitly theological reason for resisting this more open view. The assumption that the three sources stand in undifferentiated relationship is not the historic Christian position, and theologically that is so because the normative nature of the scriptures is tied up with a central feature of Christian faith. Christian faith came into being in essential relationship to certain events in the past. It is not historical in merely the same sense as any set of convictions is historical, in that it came into being in history. It is a set of convictions about the significance of some historical events. It reckons that in Israel and in Jesus God did something decisive to restore the world and take it to its destiny. The normative status of the human insights expressed in scripture issues from the fact that this act of God took place back then. God continues to act now, but anything God is doing now issues from that decisive act of God which is not taking place now. And it is scripture that tells us what God did back then.

What Christian tradition and human insight can do is drive us back to ask fresh questions of scripture and see new insights there. An instance in recent history is the raising of questions concerning the position of women in church ministry. Human insight made the church question the dominant Christian tradition about women in ministry and made it go back to scripture and ask whether scripture really implied that there were forms of ministry that were open only to men. The conclusion of many denominations was that this was not so. They then felt free to let human insight have its way concerning this question in the conviction that it opened the church up to implications within scripture and it could thus disagree with the dominant Christian *tradition* and with its interpretation of scripture in this connection. Not all denominations agree that this is so; and one way of formulating our dilemma over same-sex relationships is to see it as a discussion over whether the same conclusion here applies. The universal Christian tradition and its interpretation of scripture see scripture as viewing same-sex relationships as irregular and morally inappropriate. The question is whether human insight, particularly in the Western world, is opening our eyes to other possibilities within scripture.

2. First Testament

I begin with specific scriptural references. First, it is possible that the story of Noah and Ham (Gen 9:20–27) refers to a homosexual act, though if so, it was at least as significantly an act of incest. The story of Sodom (Gen 19) certainly refers to a proposed homosexual act, though it was at least as significantly a proposed act of homosexual rape. It has been suggested that the relationships between Ruth and Naomi and between David and Jonathan were homosexual, though here the converse applies. Whereas those two stories in Genesis may well refer to homosexual acts, they are not the kind of homosexual acts that would be seen by anyone advocating the blessing or ordination of people in same-sex relationships or the recognition of same-sex marriage as expressive of the kind of relationships they would like to see recognized and blessed. Conversely, whereas the two stories in Ruth and 1 Samuel describe deep and committed same-sex relationships, the stories do not portray them as physically expressed.

In between these four stories come the two verses in the Torah that ban homosexual acts, Lev 18:22 and 20:13. Both describe such an act as a *to'ebah*, conventionally an "abomination." In Leviticus this term is otherwise applied only to forbidden sexual relationships, though Deuteronomy applies it to religious practices such as the making of images, to forbidden foods, and to dishonesty in business. The term does not directly suggest a feeling of disgust but a conviction that these practices are to be absolutely repudiated as incompatible with membership of Yahweh's people; their repudiation is part of its purity as a people. It is difficult to see any other principle that is common to all the practices to which the term *to'ebah* applies. The value judgment it makes on homosexual acts is confirmed and underlined by the declaration that two people who engage in a homosexual act should be executed. Generally in the Torah, such declarations are not declarations of the penalty that a court should impose; at least, it is the rule rather than the exception that Israel does not exact the death penalty from people who are guilty of offenses to which this declaration is applied, such as murder, adultery, and idolatry. To say "such a person should be executed" is a way of underscoring the seriousness of the offense, not a way of prescribing the sanction attaching to it.

We do not know when Leviticus was written. Plausible theories locate its origin in priestly circles in Jerusalem before the exile, or in Babylon during the exile, or in Jerusalem after the exile, but we do not have enough information to know which of these theories (or some other) is correct. We do not therefore have the kind of background information that would help us understand the historical significance of the prohibition on homosexual acts. Leviticus itself perhaps implies two rationales for its negative attitude. Both its passages appear in the context of prohibitions concerning certain other sexual relationships, particularly sexual relationships within the family; the book is concerned to avoid imperiling the family, and it implies that homosexual acts do this. The first passage also emphasizes the need for Israel to adopt different practices from the cultures around (same-sex relationships do not seem to have been disapproved in Mesopotamia or Egypt or later in Greece and Rome; we lack evidence for Canaan). In the broader context, the teaching in Leviticus shows a

concern for living in light of the way God created the world. In a slightly paradoxical sense, this applies to its teaching about animals that may not be eaten; Israelites
may eat animals that fit into proper creation categories (the regulation is paradoxical
because God of course created the animals that do not fit into creation categories).
It applies to not having different species of cattle mate, not sowing fields with two
kind of seed, and not putting on cloth made from two kinds of material (Lev 19:19).
Humanity should fit into creation. Homosexual acts do not do that.

But there is something odd about trying to discern the First Testament's significance for our understanding of same-sex relationships from these individual passages that are open to varying interpretations. At least as important is the broader
question concerning the significance of sexual relationships and of marriage. A
church I drive past on the way to our own church every Sunday has a poster, "Love
makes a family; we support marriage equality." Our culture's assumption is that
the heart and bedrock of marriage is romantic love and our personal choice to get
married on the basis of this love, but it is becoming a commonplace to note that
this is simply our culture's recent assumption. While the First Testament believes
in romantic love (see the Song of Songs), it does not see that as the heart and bedrock of marriage. In Genesis, God instituted the sexual relationship as a means of
implementing the divine purpose to subdue the earth and serve the garden. To that
end this relationship involves a mutual commitment to forming a new context in
which children may be born, nurtured, and taught the faith and may share in the
work of the extended family business, in making the farm work; it is also a context
in which the vulnerable and needy may be protected and looked after. The First
Testament's view that heterosexual relationships are the norm forms part of a set
of convictions about family and about humanity's vocation in the world. Although
the First Testament recognizes that in practice family works in patriarchal fashion
and recognizes polygamy and divorce, Gen 1–2 undermines rather than supports
the idea that patriarchy, polygamy, or divorce are natural.

3. New Testament

Both Testaments assume that in general the Torah's regulations about purity do
not apply to Gentiles, and the offer of the gospel to Gentiles does not include the
assumption that they must take on these regulations. But most regulations in the
Torah are not simply expressive of one principle, such as purity. Thomas Aquinas
gave systematic formulation to a distinction between moral, religious, and social
regulations,[3] and it is a useful categorization, but not one that enables us to allo-
cate individual regulations to one of these categories. Regulations for society, for
instance, are not morally and religiously neutral; they reflect moral and religious
values. Some New Testament documents imply that the First Testament's regulations about sacrifice not only impose no obligations on Gentiles who come to
believe in Jesus but are passing away in significance even for Jews, yet they see them

---

[3] *Summa theologica* II/1, questions 99–103.

as of continuing theological and behavioral significance as they seek to expound the nature of the Christian gospel and of Christian commitment.

Whereas L. William Countryman argued that the annulment of the rules on purity would extend to rules about same-sex relationships,[4] the implications of annulling purity rules would have to be considered on a case-by-case basis in light of the way the religious, the theological, the social, and the ethical come together in different regulations. The fact that the gospel annuls the regulation about textile mixtures, for instance, need not mean it annuls other regulations in which purity concerns are expressed. And the way the New Testament speaks about same-sex relationships in particular confirms that this regulation in the Torah indeed concerns a matter that relates to more than purity. In 1 Cor 6:9–11, Paul declares that among the people who will not inherit the kingdom of God are the greedy, which seems to include everybody in the Western world. But along with them are the _malakoi_; while NRSV and TNIV have "male prostitutes," it has been argued that these are the passive partners in same-sex relationships. More certainly the _arsenokoitai_, etymologically the "male-liers," are people involved in homosexual acts; the word takes up the language of the two passages in Leviticus as it appears in the Septuagint. In other words, Paul did not assume that the Levitical teaching at this point was irrelevant to his Gentile readers. The word recurs in a similar list in 1 Tim 1:10.

I think Countryman is right in seeing same-sex relationships as morally analogous to polygamy and some other sexual relationships that do not involve monogamous lifelong heterosexual marriage (his list is different from mine, but the principle is similar). I do not follow him in seeing them all as morally neutral.

The third passage in the Epistles relating directly to same-sex relationships is Rom 1:24–27, which includes the only scriptural reference to lesbian acts. Here Paul declares that as a result of their rejection of real worship of God for idolatry, God gave humanity over to further impurity in the form of male and female same-sex acts that are "against nature," and thus to "shamefulness," another word that recurs in Lev 18. Richard B. Hays suggests that one significance of Paul's argument in Romans is that same-sex relationships are not something that causes God's wrath to fall on the people involved in them but something that reflects the fall of God's wrath on humanity in general.[5] It is because humanity is sinful that God surrenders it to the further outworking of that sinfulness, and this is one result. The implication is that people who find same-sex relationships natural are paying the price for the way humanity in general has turned away from God. It would not be surprising, then, that a culture so perverted as that of the West in its greed, militarism, and self-centeredness has had God give it up to forms of sexual expression that do not correspond to nature. "You are therefore without excuse, anyone who judges, because when you judge another person, you pass judgment on yourself" (Rom 2:1).

In what sense do same-sex relationships go against nature? The expression could have varying meanings in Paul, from a reference to the way people were created, to the link between sex and procreation, to the attitudes that prevail in a

---

[4] See _Dirt, Greed, and Sex_ (Philadelphia: Fortress, 1988).
[5] See _The Moral Vision of the New Testament_ (San Francisco: Harper, 1996), 379–406.

culture. The first two of these are really two aspects of one. Heterosexual relations correspond to the way the human body is made in a way that same-sex relationships do not. Linked to that, the way Gen 1 and Gen 2 describe the creation of humanity and the purpose of that creation suggests that sex was designed for expression within a monogamous lifelong heterosexual relationship in order to fill and subdue the world and serve the garden. Much of the sexual activity of heterosexual people falls short of that vision and intent for sexual relationships; that might be reckoned to be true in different ways of adultery, polygamy, incest, prostitution, divorce, remarriage, masturbation, living together before or without marriage, and the deliberate lifelong avoidance of conception (I do not suggest that all these are equally problematic morally, and there is room for debate on whether some are problematic at all). It is also true of same-sex relationships.

The question whether same-sex relations go against nature has further resonances in our own culture; for a person drawn to people of the same sex, same-sex relationships are natural. But then, for a heterosexual person, heterosexual relations are natural, but we do not reckon that this means we can simply do what comes naturally irrespective of moral considerations. Neither single people nor married people can do that. In this respect, the same applies to sex as applies to eating. Something can be natural yet wrong. There are few signs that the scientific debate about the naturalness of homosexuality is coming to a conclusion, but even if it did so, this would not establish that what is natural is right.[6]

4. Living by Creation and Living in Context

Jesus' aim was to reassert God's creation vision and make possible a mending of the world that is spoiled by the way humanity has fallen short of God's vision and intent. The call of the church is then to live by creation. Whereas it has been argued that the ban on same-sex relationships is an aspect of the teaching in the Torah that is abrogated when Jesus comes or is binding only on Israel, the argument that the Torah has been abrogated also works in the opposite direction. Whereas the Torah allows for divorce, Jesus takes a more rigorous stance in connection with it, appealing precisely to God's creation intent. Jesus' approach to divorce could likewise be applied to slavery. The Torah allows for slavery (or rather for servitude; its servitude is very different from Roman slavery or the slavery imposed on the forebears of African Americans), as does the New Testament, but that is an allowance made "for your hardness of hearts," like the divorce regulation. It does not match the way Genesis speaks of humanity's creation. Christian recognition that slavery is wrong does not provide a model for recognition that same-sex relationships can be accepted; the former involves recognizing the implications of how God made things at the beginning according to Genesis, the latter does not.

---

[6] For an illuminating survey, see David de Pomerai and Glynn Harrison, "The Witness of Science," in *The Anglican Communion and Homosexuality* (ed. Philip Groves; London: SPCK, 2008), 267–332.

Yet the church has not universally taken the view that practices such as polygamy and divorce/remarriage debar someone from membership of the church or
(in the latter case) from ordination. The stance of the church has differed among
different denominations, among different nations, and among different societies.
Fifty years ago, hardly any churches would solemnize marriage after divorce if the
first partner was still alive, nor would they ordain a person who had divorced and
married again if the first partner was still alive. Many churches now do so. This
change was not stimulated by renewed study of scripture but by social change,
though in principle the change is in keeping with scripture. The First Testament
explicitly and the New Testament implicitly recognize that human sinfulness within
the people of God means it is not realistic for God simply to affirm the ultimate
creation standards and then leave a culture on its own when it cannot live up to
those standards. So Jesus notes how Deut 24 assumes the occurrence of divorce,
even though divorce and a second marriage stand in some tension with Gen 1–2.
And Paul accepts an institution such as slavery (a much more inhuman institution
than the temporary debt servitude accepted in the Torah) even though it stands in
some tension with that same creation vision.

We cannot take this simply and unequivocally as a model for the way we might
approach same-sex relationships, because of differences between scripture's way of
handling same-sex relationships over against its way of handling divorce/remar-
riage, slavery, or polygamy. While scripture may imply that the dysfunctionality of
many First Testament marriages is related to their polygamous nature, it accepts
polygamy as a practice, as it accepts divorce and second marriage. There is thus a
contrast with its explicit criticism of same-sex relationships, along with its declining to make any allowances for them. Yet the bishops of the Church of England, at
least, have explicitly allowed for the acceptance into the church of people in committed same-sex relationships, even while officially not allowing for their ordination.[7] Archbishop Rowan Williams more recently opposed any "double standard,"[8]
though the New Testament declaration that an *episkopos* or *diakonos* must be "the
husband of one wife" (1 Tim 3:2, 12) looks like a precedent for a double standard.
It is not clear whether that requirement is designed to exclude polygamy or second
marriage after divorce or asceticism. What it does suggest is that it is possible to
have stronger expectations of leaders in the church than those applying to ordinary
members. (The Church of England for some time had such a double standard over
divorce and second marriage; you could be married in church while your first
spouse was still alive, and a divorced person could be ordained, but a person who
had remarried could not be ordained.)

There is another double standard that does need examining. I have suggested
that in falling short of God's intention for sexual relationships, same-sex relationships belong with other practices such as polygamy and divorce/second marriage,

---

[7] See the report of the Church of England House of Bishops, *Issues in Human Sexuality*
(London: Church House / Harrisburg, Pa.: Morehouse, 1991).

[8] See, e.g., J. S. Siker, "The Church of England," in *Homosexuality and Religion* (ed. J. S.
Siker; Westport, Conn.: Greenwood, 2006), 89.

though these fall short in varying ways. Yet churches take different stances to each of these. In particular, in the West it has eased its stance on divorce/remarriage and toughened its stance on same-sex relationships. There do not seem to be theological or ethical reasons for this. With regard to each, we are called to a stance and a practice that seeks somehow to hold together a witness to God's creation vision and intent and a pastoral love for people for whom it is costly to live by the rigor and demands of that vision. We are not very good at doing this in any of these areas. But I do not think we can justify, for instance, a tough stance in connection with same-sex relationships or polygamy and a libertarian one with regard to divorce/remarriage.

The energy in the current debate over same-sex relationships, like that over divorce and second marriage and over the ordination of women, derives from our current social context, at least in the West. There are many aspects to that context. The committed, covenanted same-sex relationships that might give reason for services of blessing and for same-sex marriage in church, and that might not seem a disqualification for the ordination of a person in such a relationship, are not what the scriptures refer to when they speak of particular sexual acts. We are aware that being attracted to members of the same sex is not a matter of choice; in this sense, same-sex relationships are natural, at least for some people. We have great confidence in our own insight and convictions and are inclined to reckon that when we differ from other generations, we must be right. We are a highly sexualized culture. And we believe in free choice.

Our culture also places an emphasis on justice, and this consideration is commonly introduced into the church's debate on same-sex relationships, though the way this happens requires further reflection. Does everyone have the right to be considered for ordination? Do the notions of rights and ordination belong together? In what sense is same-sex marriage a justice issue? The freedom of people of different races to marry is a justice issue on the basis of a certain understanding of humanity. Same-sex marriage is a justice issue only if one first presupposes that marriage does not integrally involve two people of the opposite sex. (There might be other justice questions that do affect same-sex relationships, such as employment and participation in the military.)

Our notion of justice, which is commonly taken to imply the conviction that everyone should be treated the same way, is Western rather than scriptural. God does not treat everyone the same way. God gives different nations and individuals different assets, abilities, callings, and so on, and gives more to some than to others. Biblical words commonly translated "justice" and "righteousness" such as *mishpat* and *tsedaqah* refer more to something like the exercise of power and authority in a way that does right by the people to whom one has commitments, and in particular that implements a concern for the needy.[9] "Justice" and "righteousness" are not about treating everyone the same. But one implication of them would indeed be that in relating to its members who are attracted to the same sex, and to people outside it who are so attracted, the church would be committed to seeking

---

[9] See chapter 16, § 2, above.

to counterbalance the disadvantageous way they are often treated in society and committed to relating to them in the pastoral love referred to above. Linked to this is the fact that the notion of rights is also Western rather than scriptural. The Bible is more concerned with the responsibility of the powerful toward the powerless than with equal rights for everyone.

One of our current problems is that the question of same-sex relationships has gained significance out of all proportion to its inherent importance. The Jewish lesbian comedian Lynne Lavner comments on her album *Butch Fatale*, "There are six admonitions in the Bible concerning homosexual activity and . . . there are three hundred and sixty-two admonitions in the Bible concerning heterosexual activity. I don't mean to imply by this that God doesn't love straight people, only that they seem to require a great deal more supervision." In scripture, immorality in heterosexual relationships is a much bigger issue than same-sex relationships, and among ordinary Christian people and among pastors, irregular heterosexual relationships are much more of a problem than same-sex relationships. We have same-sex relationships out of all proportion. At the beginning of the seminary year on one occasion, I was part of a faculty panel discussing with new students issues about coming to seminary. Near the end a student asked what is most likely to make a train wreck of one's time at seminary. In my response I included "getting in a mess over sex." One of the students then asked whether I was referring to same-sex relationships. I did not have that in mind at all, but rather the fact that anecdotal evidence suggests that our seminary students can get into as much of a mess over heterosexual relationships as people in the rest of the culture. But this student assumed that the problem for Christians was same-sex relationships. Not so much. It is problematic heterosexual relations that are the elephant in the room.

Related to that is the fact that in our current discussion at least as much importance attaches to ecclesiology as to ethics. I disagree with the stance that the Episcopal Church takes over same-sex relationships, but that does not make me reckon I must therefore leave the Episcopal Church (for another denomination that I would disagree with over other matters?). I am given more food for thought by Episcopalians who think about seceding on the basis of more central issues such as the fact that Jesus is the only way to salvation. Christians need to discuss further how we can live together when we disagree and how we can continue to relate together in Christ when some of us decide that we cannot live together.

Also related is the question of our place in our culture. Fifty years ago it was perhaps possible to reckon that there was not too much tension between being a Christian and being a U.S. citizen. There is now much more tension. In addition to our militarism and the gun culture, we are in a terrible mess over consumerism, debt, workaholism, heterosexual relationships, and the family. The assertion of gay rights and the acceptance of same-sex relationships as just as valid as heterosexual ones are part of the way the culture stands in tension with scripture and the church's tradition. Perhaps there was much more tension between being a Christian and being a U.S. citizen fifty years ago. Certainly in the third millennium the vocation of the church is to be an alternative community that embodies God's creation vision. That will mean revisiting what it might mean to be family, local community, and nation, and revisiting attitudes to sex, work, and possessions. It will mean treating brothers and sisters who are attracted to people of the same sex with the same love, faithfulness, and commitment as the ones we show to brothers and sisters who are attracted to people of the opposite sex, and persisting in those attitudes to our brothers and sisters when they do find it costly to live with the moral demands that life places on them. It will not mean just accepting same-sex relationships as simply an equally-valid lifestyle choice.

INDEX OF MODERN AUTHORS

INDEX OF ANCIENT SOURCES